EBENEZER'S
GRANDSON

Other books by Leonard Holder:

Selina of Sussex 1818–1886
Selina's Legacy

EBENEZER'S GRANDSON

PROVING GOD'S FAITHFULNESS ON THE ROAD TO HAUS BARNABAS

LEONARD AND PHYLLIS HOLDER

To order additional copies of this book, contact:
Xlibris
UK TFN: 0800 0148620 (Toll Free inside the UK)
UK Local: 02036 956328 (+44 20 3695 6328 from outside the UK)
www.Xlibrispublishing.co.uk
Orders@Xlibrispublishing.co.uk
829710

CONTENTS

Family Tree ix
Acknowledgments with Thanks xi
Foreword xiii
Prologue xv

PART 1 EARLY LIFE IN BRIGHTON
1946–1957

Chapter 1   War Years 1
Chapter 2   A Happy, Loving Home 5
Chapter 3   Childhood Activities 11
Chapter 4   Sundays 14
Chapter 5   Hospital 18
Chapter 6   Holidays 21

PART 2 SWANWICK SHORE
1957–1965

Chapter 1   'Aenon' 27
Chapter 2   Price's Grammar School 31
Chapter 3   Ducks, Dog and Rabbits 33
Chapter 4   Swanwick Shore Chapel 38
Chapter 5   Birds, Badgers and Squirrels 42
Chapter 6   A Summer in Malta 47
Chapter 7   'Trust and Obey' 51
Chapter 8   Duncan Road Brethren Assembly 56
Chapter 9   Theological Issues 60
Chapter 10 Climping Camp 64
Chapter 11 Motor Bike and Three-Wheeler 69
Chapter 12 Illness 75
Chapter 13 A Change of Direction 79

PART 3 HORLEY
1965–1976

Chapter 1   Early Days in Horley 85
Chapter 2   A Call to Preach. 88
Chapter 3   Engagement. 92
Chapter 4   Wedding Plans. 96
Chapter 5   The Passing of Ebenezer Dan 101
Chapter 6   Wedding and Honeymoon 106
Chapter 7   Early Preaching Experiences. 110
Chapter 8   The Arrival of Children 115
Chapter 9   Home as 'Open House' 121
Chapter 10 Is This God's Call?. 130
Chapter 11 A Way Forward 134
Chapter 12 Spying Out the Land 139
Chapter 13 The Time is Not Ripe 142

PART 4 YORKSHIRE
1976–1983

Chapter 1   Moving in a Pig Truck. 149
Chapter 2   Wycliffe Lodge 155
Chapter 3   The Job 158
Chapter 4   Serving God in Yorkshire. 161
Chapter 5   Kirkbymoorside. 165
Chapter 6   63 Kirkby Road. 168
Chapter 7   Pig Breeding 171
Chapter 8   Scottish Holidays 175
Chapter 9   Ripon Grammar School. 179
Chapter 10 Visitors in Yorkshire. 182
Chapter 11 Church Incidents 186
Chapter 12 The Renewed Call to German-Speaking Europe . 189
Chapter 13 An Unsettling Time. 193
Chapter 14 Preparing for Europe 195
Chapter 15 Language Preparation. 198

PART 5 BASEL
1983-1989

Chapter 1   Awayday Ticket? 207
Chapter 2   Settling into Life in Basel 214
Chapter 3   First Year at the FETA 220
Chapter 4   Home Difficulties but also Encouragements 223
Chapter 5   Basel Christian Fellowship 227
Chapter 6   A Local Swiss Home Group 233
Chapter 7   A Family Crisis and God's Wonderful Solution . . . 236
Chapter 8   New Friends 242
Chapter 9   Exams and a New Flat 248
Chapter 10 An Italian Adventure 253
Chapter 11 Visits from Family and Friends 260
Chapter 12 Changes. 264
Chapter 13 Pastures New. 266
Chapter 14 Summers Whilst in Basel 271
Chapter 15 Studies in Zürich 274
Chapter 16 Last Year in Basel. 279
Chapter 17 The Boys on Their Own 285

PART 6 GERMANY ESTABLISHING
A MISSION WORK
1989-2002

Chapter 1   On the Move. 291
Chapter 2   The Black Forest 299
Chapter 3   The Basis for a Residence Permit 303
Chapter 4   Christmases in Britain 308
Chapter 5   Black Forest Holiday Services. 311
Chapter 6   Early English Teaching. 316
Chapter 7   British Holiday Guests 319
Chapter 8   German Believers. 326
Chapter 9   Sunday Fellowship 329
Chapter 10 An Enormous Step of Faith 333
Chapter 11 Furnishing an Empty Guesthouse 339
Chapter 12 Early Haus Barnabas Guests 344
Chapter 13 Bible Meetings in Haus Barnabas 352

Chapter 14 Interesting Contacts through English Teaching . . . 359
Chapter 15 Support in Haus Barnabas. 364
Chapter 16 Eric. 366
Chapter 17 Tourist Trips to Britain. 372
Chapter 18 British Students 376
Chapter 19 Other Interesting Guests. 379
Chapter 20 A Remarkable Experience 384
Chapter 21 'Enlarge the Place of Your Tent' 387

PART 7 'HAUS BARNABAS IM ENGEL'
2002 Onwards

Chapter 1 Language School 395
Chapter 2 'For Such a Time as This'. 399
Chapter 3 'In My Dreams, I Can See!' 403
Chapter 4 More Polish Experiences 408
Chapter 5 A Bridge Too Far? 412
Chapter 6 A Home for The Homeless. 416
Chapter 7 Café Engel. 421
Chapter 8 Groups and Theme Weeks 427
Chapter 9 Family Holiday Weeks 433
Chapter 10 God's Provision for House Maintenance 440
Chapter 11 Testimonies of God's Amazing Love and Grace. . . 445
Chapter 12 Voluntary Helpers in Haus Barnabas 452
Chapter 13 Haus Barnabas Animals 459
Chapter 14 Into All The World 465
Chapter 15 Providing Support and Fellowship 472
Chapter 16 Anniversaries. 476
Chapter 17 Blessings a Hundredfold 480

Appendix 1 485
Index. 487

FAMILY TREE

(Simplified)

Eli Page   -   Selina Westgate
b. 11.Oct 1817   *b. 17 Aug 1818*

Married 12 Feb 1838

I

Ruth Page   -   Dan Holder
b. 2 July 1841   *b. 9 Jan 1844*

Married ..13 April 1868

I

Ebenezer Dan Holder – Mary Gertrude White
b. 3 April 1877   *b. 31 Dec 1883*

Married 13 Sept 1908

I

Edgar Ebenezer Holder   -   Ellen Rachel Wilkins
b.15 July 1909   *b 28 July 1908*

Married 16 Jan 1937

I

Leonard Edgar   **- Phyllis Mary Pittwell**
Holder
b 3 April 1946   *22 Nov 1946*

Married 3 June 1967

I

Geoffrey Leonard Holder
b. 5 April 1968
and Ruth Anne Leyshon
Married 30 Dec 1995
I
Barnaby John Holder
b. 31ˢᵗ Oct 1997
Timothy Dafydd Leonard Holder
b. 12 Feb 1999
Beatrice Ellen Holder
b. 13 July 2000

Daniel Francis Holder
b. 5 May 1970
and Martina Franz
Married 12 Sept 1993
I
Sophia Evangeline Holder
b. 23 Jan 1998
David Gregory Holder
b. 28 Jan 2000
Benedict Francis Holder
b. 16 Oct 2001
John Michael Holder
b. 2 Feb 2008

ACKNOWLEDGMENTS
WITH THANKS

Cherrie Irwin for her detailed editorial work.

A range of friends for their memories and comments. These were originally contributed on the request of Leonard and Phyllis' sons as they gathered material for a celebratory folder on the occasion of their parents' twenty-fifth wedding anniversary.

FOREWORD

This book comes as the third in a series of biographies tracing God's dealings in one ordinary English family over several generations. In telling his grandchildren the stories of their own family, the author is passing on the legacy of their forebears and encouraging them to take the baton of faith into their own lives. The books capture the realities of life with its joys and pains, human successes and failures, and God's goodness in all this. Over the two hundred years from the childhood of the first story's protagonist, Selina, to the present day, life has changed in so many ways, from work and play to travel and technology. However, people have remained essentially the same, and God remains the same, actively calling individuals to His family, the church, forgiving and transforming them for eternity in Jesus Christ and enabling them to live fruitful lives by the power of the Holy Spirit. It's these changes and these constants both that make the story of these people gripping and relevant for all of us.

My interest in the story is very personal too because I am in it. The authors of this volume are my parents and that makes me Ebenezer's great-grandson and Selina's great-great-great-grandson (one of many). As Leonard tells the story of his own life in this volume – joined by his wife, Phyllis, and then by his two sons and eventually their own families – I recognise events and characters. I even contributed some details from my own diaries. I can attest to the truthfulness of his message: God is faithful to His people; God is faithful to us. You can risk everything for Him, proving the promises He made in His Word and reiterated to men and women of generations since. My parents have trusted God and put their lives, though weak and wrong at times, into the service of our Lord, who is strong and right, patient and loving. They risked family, friends, and finance as they followed God's call from England to Switzerland and Germany, finally founding Haus Barnabas as the embodiment of their work and proving that God is good. This is an inspiration and example to me, and I hope that it might be that to you too – not just a read of personal and historical interest but also an encouragement to turn in trust to the same Lord. Life can be difficult and painful. It would please Leonard and Phyllis to know that they have been able to comfort those in affliction with the comfort with which they themselves have been comforted by God (2 Corinthians 1:4).

Geoffrey Holder

PROLOGUE

Extracts from Ruth Holder's Thoughts and Prayers in Selina's Legacy *by Leonard Holder*

1850

That night in bed, I thought over these amazing facts and talked to God about them.

'Lord Jesus,' I prayed, 'I believe you've shown me that you are going to give me a husband and children like you did for Ruth of old. I do pray that my children and their families will know your special blessing and, like Ruth's family, will be part of your purpose to extend your kingdom and bring blessing to this world.'

Page 32

1875

I felt strongly then one day God would give me another Ebenezer who would have his special blessing.

'That's lovely, Ruth,' responded my husband. 'Why not call our next little boy Ebenezer Dan and pray he will grow up to be a blessing to many?'

Page 168

1920

During my latter years, I often reminisced about the idea I once had that Ebenezer, the son I believe God gave me to replace the little brother taken from us when I was only nine, would be used by God to further His kingdom. I've said nothing of this directly to Eb himself but pray regularly for him and his children and have watched with great interest the development of his life.

God's Providence

Grant Colfax Tullar (1869–1950)

My life is but a weaving
Between my God and me.
I cannot choose the colours
He weaveth steadily.
Oft' times He weaveth sorrow;
And I in foolish pride
Forget He sees the upper
And I the underside.
Not 'til the loom is silent
And the shuttles cease to fly
Will God unroll the canvas
And reveal the reason why.
The dark threads are as needful
In the weaver's skilful hand
As the threads of gold and silver
In the pattern He has planned.
He knows, He loves, He cares;
Nothing this truth can dim.
He gives the very best to those
Who leave the choice to Him.

PART 1

EARLY LIFE IN BRIGHTON
1946–1957

Train up a child in the way he should go, and
when he is old, he will not depart from it.
— Proverbs 22:6

CHAPTER

1

War Years

Before I formed you in the womb, I knew
you; before you were born, I sanctified you.
— Jeremiah 1:5

The year was 1946. The whole world had just experienced a second major war, and although there was great relief in Britain that this was now over and Nazism had been defeated, every family had been affected, and it would take years for things to become stable again.

Ebenezer Dan Holder (son of Dan and Ruth Holder and grandson of Eli and Selina Page), having been born in 1877, was nearing the end of his working life when the war began in 1939. The London insurance firm where he had worked all his life moved out of the city during these years, and it had been necessary for Eb, as one of the few employees not called up for war service, to move with them down to Minehead in the west country and spend time away from his wife, Gertie, and daughter, Ruth, and their home in Highdown Road, Hove.

Edgar, Eb and Gertie's eldest child and only son, had married Ellen Rachael Wilkins in January 1937. Ellen had served as housemaid in the home of Pastor J. K. Popham of Galeed Chapel, Brighton, for a good number of years, and both she and Edgar were baptised members of Galeed when they married. They had been seeing each other for about seven years before Ebenezer had helped his son to buy a house in the Hollingbury area of Brighton, 79 Hertford Road, and encouraged him to take the plunge into matrimony.

Ellen was an ideal wife for Edgar. She had a quiet disposition and was well experienced in the practical aspects of running a home. Their first child, whom they named John Ebenezer, was born before the end of their marriage year on 13 November 1937. A daughter, Evelyn Rosemary, arrived sixteen months later on 9 March 1939, just six months before the start of the war.

Edgar worked for Bennett's, an ironmongery business in North Street, Brighton. One aspect of his training was learning the skill of cutting replica keys. Back then, this was done completely by hand using a vice, a hacksaw and a file. It was work he enjoyed, and he would sometimes bring key-cutting jobs home to work in the evenings.

Edgar and Ellen with their firstborn son, John
1937

Once the war started, Edgar, being a fit young man of 30 years, very quickly received his call-up papers.

'Oh dear, Edgar,' said his wife one lunchtime as she placed a plate of cold lamb, boiled potatoes, cabbage, and carrots in front of her husband. 'There's an official-looking envelope for you here. It came in the post this morning.'

Bennett's closed for a two-hour lunch break, giving Edgar enough time to cycle home and have a quick lunch before returning to work.

Edgar tore open the envelope without a word and then looking at his wife – who, sitting opposite him, had begun to spoon a mashed-up version of the same dinner into young John's open mouth – said with a sigh, 'It had to come, my dear! Our life is going to have to change.'

There was silence for a few moments, and then he added, 'We mustn't forget that our times are in God's hands, and we have the many promises of His Word to reassure us of His abiding presence with us both, whatever happens and wherever we are when separate from each other.'

Ellen nodded. She believed and knew this comforting fact, but nevertheless, there remained this rather indescribable, tight feeling of anxiety in her chest.

For several months after his compulsory recruitment, Edgar was under army training and had days of leave when he could return home to his family. However, on 16 January 1941 – which, rather ironically, was his and Ellen's fourth wedding anniversary – he was enlisted into the Twenty-second Medical and Heavy Transport Regiment of the Royal Artillery and, shortly after, was sent out to India. It was four years later before he returned to Sussex and his beloved wife and two children.

Edgar never talked much about his war experiences, but there was one incident during his journey out to India which he often referred to as a remarkable illustration of God's blessing. The troop ship taking him out to India along with hundreds of other soldiers called in at Cape Town in South Africa. They were allowed to disembark, and as Edgar was walking along the dock, he heard a loud shout from another troop ship moored further along the dock side. Looking up, he saw a khaki-clad

Ben Wilkins

soldier waving from a porthole. It turned out to be Ben Wilkins, one of his wife's brothers. They were able to spend several hours together and to encourage each other in their faith. Ben's ship was heading for North Africa, and both men agreed that to meet like that amongst the thousands of troops travelling – and the fact that Ben happened to be looking out of a porthole just as Edgar walked by – was God's providential blessing for them both. That time they had together in Cape Town, although brief, sealed a friendship for the rest of their lives.

Ellen initially struggled with the absence of her husband but was aware it was wartime, and everyone needed to pull their weight. It helped to have her parents-in-law near at hand, and they were extremely supportive. One of the worst moments during the four years of Edgar's absence was when Evelyn Rosemary – or simply Rosemary, as she was known – caught pneumonia. Her life was hanging on a thread, and she was rushed away for hospital care. Ellen wrote to her husband, many miles away, expressing the fear that they were about to lose their only daughter. Then – praise the Lord – Rosemary passed the danger point and began to improve. As soon as this was confirmed, Ellen wrote again to Edgar, giving him the good news. What she wasn't to know until sometime later was that because of army postal difficulties, Edgar received the letter saying his infant daughter was improving before he got the letter informing him of her dangerous illness.

Edgar was back in Britain in 1945 and able to have some home leave. He was finally discharged from the army in 1946 and could return to his old job at Bennett's.

On Wednesday, 3 April 1946, Ebenezer Dan had his 67th birthday, and on this same day, his fifth grandchild, Leonard Edgar, the third child of Edgar and Ellen, came into the world.

CHAPTER

2

A Happy, Loving Home

John was 9, and Rosemary had recently had her 7th birthday when Leonard, the latest addition to the family, arrived. A further child, Frank Benjamin, was born in June 1948.

Family life was well-structured, following a regular routine. Conditions at that time made this rather easier than in later years. For one thing, there were very few outside influences or distractions. The home had no radio – or wireless, as it was then called – no television, and no telephone. News of the outside world arrived with the *Daily Sketch* delivered each morning, except Sunday, by the newspaper boy.

Rosemary with her two brothers

Edgar had regular working hours. He needed to leave by 8:00 a.m., so the children were woken up at 7:00 a.m. with a biscuit whilst still in their beds, and it was a

5

strict rule that everyone had to be downstairs and dressed by 7:30 a.m. This was prayer time sitting around the breakfast table. All who could read had their own Bible, and a chapter or so of the Holy Scriptures was read together, each person reading a verse in turn. Chairs were then turned around, and the whole family would kneel in front of their own chair as Edgar talked to their Father in heaven.

What this meant for Leonard was that a belief in an invisible God, who was his Creator and the One who ultimately cared for him, was as natural to him as his own existence. It also meant that the Bible was one of the first books he had ever read. While Leonard was sitting on his mother's knee as the Bible was read each morning, Ellen would indicate the words as they were read, and very soon, his father encouraged him to read a verse himself, helping him with the bigger words.

The parents breakfasted before prayers, so immediately after family devotions were over, Edgar cycled off to work, and the children had their breakfast before going off to school.

Edgar's faith in God was real and practical. The gospel of God's love in Jesus Christ was very precious to him. He had found assurance through the Scriptures and the witness of the Holy Spirit that through his faith in Christ, he was an adopted child of God. He rejoiced that he was redeemed from all his sin through Jesus's death on his behalf. However, as Edgar was a member of Galeed Chapel, Brighton, his level of assurance was surprising. The preaching at the chapel at that time encouraged personal soul-searching, giving the impression that assurance comes through experiences and feelings rather than looking away from ourselves and trusting Christ and the promises of His Word. When Christian believers keep looking at their feelings, any assurance of salvation they might find is likely to come and go as these feelings change. Also, it opens the way for fear that their spiritual feelings are simply of themselves and not of God, and thus, it keeps them from speaking of any hope in Christ lest it should prove to be presumption. It seems likely that Edgar found his assurance of God's love to him in Christ whilst away from Britain during his years in India and Burma. Rosemary remembers hearing about the correspondence her mother received from Edgar which spoke of the Christian fellowship God had given him whilst a long way from home.

The Holder family lived up Hertford Road, a steep hill with the infant and junior school at the bottom and their home, number seventy-nine, at the top. There were very few cars about in those early years after the war and little or no fear of children being abducted or abused, so it was not considered dangerous for John and Rosemary, subsequently Leonard and eventually Frank, to make their way to and from school without their mother's company. Leonard remembers being very upset that his sister had been sent to meet him after his first day at school when he was just 4 years old. Rosemary was herself about to begin her secondary school education at Varndean Girls' Grammar School at that point, and her school started a week later.

Leonard,
aged 5 or 6

Their home had no central heating. In fact, central heating in homes was very rare in those days. The evangelist Billy Graham came to Britain in the 1950s and, in his autobiography, comments how cold British homes were. In addition to the kitchen, the house had two downstairs rooms: the dining room and the sitting room. The former was the room for everyday use and, in winter, was heated by a coal fire. Another coal fire could be lit in the sitting room when required for special occasions. Leonard well remembers watching the coalman coming through the back gate with great filthy black sacks of coal. He brought them in one by one on his shoulder and tipped their contents into the coal bunker. The living room opened through French windows on to a fairly narrow concrete terrace, and the coal bunker was at one end of this. In cold winters, Edgar supplemented the warmth from these fires with paraffin heaters. His firm sold paraffin, so there was a ready source of supply.

To ensure the family kept warm in bed in winter in their unheated bedrooms, as the weather got colder, the summer horsehair mattresses were supplemented with what was referred to as feather beds. These were feather-filled duvet-like items of bedding which were placed on top of the mattress to lie on. A sheet and blankets tucked one in, and as necessary, there could be an eiderdown quilt on top. During frosty nights, Jack Frost would often 'paint' beautiful fernlike patterns on the inside of the bedroom windows. To be able to see through the frosted glass, the secret Leonard learned was to heat a penny in his hand and push it onto the frost on the glass, creating a spyhole to look through.

At the end of January 1954, Brighton had a heavy fall of snow which lay around a full week. Leonard remembers watching the snow build up outside the French windows until the step down from the terrace to the garden path was no longer visible. This amount of snow is unusual in the south of England, and the experiences of sledging down Hertford Road were never to be repeated during his childhood. The children built a snowman in the centre of the garden, and when, after about a week, they awoke one morning to the sound of torrential rain, a very forlorn and much shrunken skeleton of a snowman, with his carrot nose lying beside him on the ground, was all that was left of the white blanket God had spread over His created world.

The local shops were at the bottom of Hertford Road in an area known as the 'Dip', into which four roads converged from different directions. It was, however, a steep climb back up to their home, and Ellen was happy to avail herself of a grocery store who delivered orders to the door. Their representative was a Christian man known to the family, and he would call on a Monday afternoon to talk over the family's requirement and pick up the order. The groceries were then delivered on Tuesday. The younger children looked forward to this, not so much for the groceries but for the big cardboard box in which everything arrived, which gave them a 'boat' to play in. Meat was bought from the butcher in the Dip, and as a teenager, Leonard's big brother

John had a Saturday job delivering meat around the neighbourhood. The butcher equipped him with a black bicycle for the purpose. It had a large metal frame in front of the handlebars in which rested a basket containing the meat, all wrapped up in newspaper. The most economical meat in those days was a shoulder of New Zealand lamb. Roast pork with crackling and roast beef with Yorkshire pudding were reserved for special occasions. The family also regularly had dinners of liver and bacon, toad in the hole, or macaroni cheese. Boiled potatoes came with virtually every dinner.

An additional member of the family arrived when Leonard was 7. He and his younger brother, Frank, were then sharing a bedroom. Their elder brother, John, had left home to begin his experience and training in horticulture, and this meant Leonard and Frank could have a bed each in the boys' bedroom. Then suddenly, one morning, they woke up to find themselves together in the larger of the two beds and another little boy asleep in the second bed.

When the strange boy woke up, he looked across at the other bed and said, 'Hello, I'm John. They brought me here last night. Who are you?'

Leonard looked at the new John in amazement and, recognising him to be more senior than themselves, quite nervously told him their names.

Later, the story slowly came out as to who John was and how he had arrived in their bedroom.

John was 11 years old and had a twin sister,

Holder family
together with Jack

Joyce. Their mother had been a sister of friends of Edgar and Ellen from Galeed Chapel, and she had sadly died some time earlier. The father was in the merchant navy, and although he wanted to keep his two children, their aunt feared that because of his lifestyle, the twins were at risk. They were left alone a lot and shared the same bed, which, their aunt felt, was unsuitable for a boy and a girl approaching puberty. Going round one evening to check on them, she found them alone and decided enough was enough and something had to be done.

She and her husband were willing to take Joyce to live with them but didn't feel able to have John as well. She approached Edgar about this, and he and Ellen decided they needed to be willing to give a home to John. It all happened very suddenly without any dialogue with the twins' father. As Leonard understood the situation, finding the children again alone in the house, the aunt, together with Edgar, simply asked the children to pack a few clothes and took them away.

The Holder family were not relatives of John in any way, and John's father took Edgar to court for kidnapping his son. Leonard was too young at the time to understand all that was happening, but the outcome was that the court gave Edgar and Ellen custody of John. He never remembers John's father ever coming to their house or of any talk of John ever having contact with him. Because the family already had a John, the new John agreed they could call him Jack. He lived with the Holders until he left school at 16 and went to a naval training college. They had good contact also with Jack's sister, Joyce, and the twins would refer to Leonard's parents as Ma and Pop.

Leonard is not aware of Edgar and Ellen ever receiving any financial provision from Jack's father for providing a home for his son.

CHAPTER

3

Childhood Activities

Without the means of entertainment typically enjoyed by children nowadays, Leonard grew up nurturing an avid interest in the natural world around him. He would occasionally wake early and sit by his bedroom window, watching for birds in the garden. There was not a wide selection, but he took a real interest in a pair of dunnocks – or hedge sparrows, as he then called them – feeding at the base of the privet hedge which ran down the length of their small garden. Later, he was to discover their nest in the hedge, and one of their bright blue eggs set in motion his own bird egg collection. The latter was never large, but Leonard took great delight in looking at his grandfather's collection, made years before (it became illegal to take wild birds' eggs from nests in 1954). For instance, his grandfather Ebenezer had a rook's

Blackbird's nest

egg in his collection on which a date in the 1880s had been inscribed.

That same privet hedge, at different times, also became a nesting place for both blackbirds and song thrushes. Song thrushes are less common now, but they used to be regularly seen cracking open the shell of a snail to reach the juicy body inside. Leonard discovered that a thrush lines its nest with mud, which no doubt acts as an insulating material, and the female then lays bright sky-blue, black-spotted eggs. He found that the blackbird also uses mud in its nest but then adds grass to give a softer base for its eggs.

Books on birds and other aspects of nature were his favourite library books, and he remembers once borrowing a book about the black woodpecker with many photos all taken in the Black Forest of Germany. Leonard had no real idea where the Black Forest was. To him, it was simply somewhere abroad, and it would have amazed him enormously if he had known one day he would spend thirty years of his life living there.

At that time, before further housing development, the Holders' home was less than five minutes from the open countryside. Here, the children could wander and play at leisure. Leonard had a friend, Kenneth, who lived close by and who had started school the same time as him. Together with a few other local children, including another classmate whom everyone called Clumsy, they would roam the countryside. Within easy reach was an old Roman camp. The children had no regard for its history, but with its humps and ditches, it was a wonderful place to play cowboys and Indians. Interestingly, Wikipedia refers to it as an iron-age hillfort, now known as Hollingbury Castle or Hollingbury Camp.

This access to acres of open countryside enabled Leonard to pursue another of his hobbies, collecting butterflies. He would chase the meadow butterflies (such as marbled whites, chalkhill blues, and small skippers) with his net as

Red admiral butterfly

they flitted from bloom to bloom across the Downs. Patiently, he would wait by a butterfly bush (the buddleia shrub, as it is commonly known) to catch the range of species that were attracted to this particular source of nectar. Peacocks, red admirals, small tortoiseshells, commas, as well as common cabbage whites were often there in profusion. The books he read told him how best to kill these extremely pretty creatures without damaging them and how to pin them out with their wings displayed. Since he seemed to be following in the footsteps of famous lepidopterists (although he would never have known this name), he had no qualms about it; however, he never kept more than one or two of each species.

One afternoon he caught a painted lady butterfly for the first time. These beautiful insects migrate all over the world, and because they aren't normally able to survive British winters, most of the painted lady butterflies found in Britain have flown across from North Africa.

It really excited Leonard to catch his first painted lady, and coming home into his gateway and seeing his mother talking to an unknown woman visitor at the door, he called out loudly, 'Mum, a painted lady!'

Ellen had little or no knowledge of butterflies and, to Leonard's consternation, seemed rather embarrassed and, looking at him accusingly, said in an unusually strict tone, 'Go indoors at once, Leonard. I'll talk to you later.'

Confused and very deflated after the thrill of achieving this prize catch, Leonard went quietly into the house.

Thankfully, it didn't take long to convince his mother that his remark referred to the butterfly in his jam jar and not the lady on the doorstep, who, unlike most of the family's circle of friends, *had* been wearing bright red lipstick!

CHAPTER

4

Sundays

In twentieth-century Britain, the following was a verse often quoted in Christian circles. Whether one was religious or not, in general, only essential services ran on Sundays, and as much as possible, it was a day to rest from work and spend time with the wife and family.

A Sabbath well spent brings a week of content
And strength for the toils of the morrow,
But a Sabbath profaned, what'er may be gained,
Is a certain forerunner of sorrow.

Galeed Chapel
Brighton

Certainly, in the Holder household, Sunday was a different day. The whole family would dress in their best clothes and walk down Hertford Road to the Dip and then up the hill westward to the Five Ways. There, they would catch a trolley bus taking them down to St Peters Church and the Old Steine, in the centre of Brighton. They followed a walk through a variety of small streets into Gloucester Road, where

Galeed Chapel was situated. The whole journey took about thirty to forty minutes.

Galeed was a Strict Baptist chapel aligned to the *Gospel Standard* branch of this denomination. It had been founded in 1868, and in its early days, Leonard's great-great-grandfather, Eli Page, had sometimes preached here. Ebenezer's mother, Ruth, had been a baptised member,[1] as was his wife, Gertie.[2] Ebenezer himself attended the services regularly but had never joined as a church member.

The young Leonard remembers that the usual Holder family seat in the chapel was about three rows back in the gallery, looking down into the main seating area below with the deacon's desk and pulpit at the front. The chapel had two aisles with three sections of rows of pews, and the minister would appear through a door behind the pulpit to take his place, leading the whole service apart from the announcement of hymns. This was the duty, or perhaps privilege, of the chief deacon, Mr Paul. In this period after the war, the church depended on itinerant preachers. Mr Popham had passed to glory, and it was only later that the church called Mr Frank Gosden to be pastor. Among the regular ministers were the well-known Strict Baptist preachers Mr Jesse Delves, Mr John Gosden, and his brother, Frank Gosden.

The service was very simple: a hymn from the Gadsby hymn book, a Bible reading and prayer by the minister, and then a second hymn followed by a forty-five-minute sermon. The hymns were sung without accompaniment. A deacon sitting in the so-called singing seat announced the name of the tune and, after setting the first note with his tuning whistle, led the congregation in the singing of the hymn. During the singing of the second hymn in the service, Edgar would regularly take his younger two boys out to the men's toilet round the back of the chapel. Leonard sometimes wondered whether this was more for their father's benefit than for theirs, but it did give a welcome break before the long sermon.

---

1 *Selina's Legacy*, Leonard Holder.
2 Received into the church in April 1919.

Leonard was taken to the chapel each Sunday morning from a few weeks old. It was part of his weekly life and simply supplemented the faith that was practised in his daily life at home. There was a real sense of reverence in the services. God was honoured and worshipped, and although, for several years, Leonard never really understood much of what was said in the sermons, he could follow some of the Bible readings, particularly when these were stories he had also heard at home. There were also a few of the hymns that he enjoyed for different reasons. For instance, he remembers as a 9-year-old lad thinking that the following somehow qualified him to be a follower of Jesus:

When Jesus would his grace proclaim,
He called the simple, blind, and lame
To come and be his guests.
Such simple folk, the world despise,
Yet simple folk have sharpest eyes
And learn to walk the best.

After the service, the family would meet up with Grandfather Ebenezer. His regular pew in the chapel was downstairs, but after the service, he would wait for Edgar and his family on the pavement opposite the chapel, always having sweets for the children. In Leonard's memory, his grandmother never attended the morning worship but remained at home to prepare a roast Sunday lunch to which her two married children, with their families, were often invited. Her turn for chapel came with the evening service.

Leonard well remembers his grandma's Sunday dinners: roast beef with Yorkshire pudding and a range of vegetables fit for royalty. Dessert followed – jelly and 'fluffy duck', which was red jelly whipped up with carnation milk, creating numerous bubbles and then allowed to set in a mould. One such mould produced

Grandma Holder
Gertrude Mary White
1883–1971

a pink bunny rabbit, so it seemed strange to call it fluffy duck. If anyone claimed to be full up with the first course, Grandma's comment invariably was 'Come now. A little jelly will just squeeze down the gaps'.

Sunday afternoon was Sunday school time. Galeed Chapel had no Sunday school, and the Holder children were therefore sent to Sunday afternoon school at Providence Chapel, Church Street. Providence Chapel was Independent rather than Baptist and, in the first half of the nineteenth century, had come under the pastoral care of John Vinall of Jireh Chapel, Lewes. It was here that John Grace, who had been such a blessing to the Page family, had first preached before being called to the Tabernacle Chapel in West Street, Brighton. Church Street was at least fifteen minutes' walk from their grandparents' house down Dyke Road, so this ensured dinner was well settled in one's tummy before sitting in Sunday school. During Leonard's Sunday school days, Mr Peckham was the superintendent. The teacher of the Bible class which his elder brother and sister attended was a Mr Fred Wilderspin, who, interestingly, was a member at Galeed.

Leonard and Frank, as the younger children in the family, were rarely taken to the Sunday evening service, and Leonard remembers evenings when his father looked after them at home and read to them before they were sent to bed. One book he dipped into was William Huntington's *The Bank of Faith*, which gave interesting examples of how God provided for Huntington's daily needs in miraculous ways when living as a vagrant having removed himself from society to a degree. The fact that the God of the Bible continued to provide for those who trusted Him impressed Leonard.

CHAPTER

5

Hospital

There are many factors from our childhood which have an effect on the type of person we become. Certainly, the most influential factor in Leonard's life was the faith and Christian lifestyle of his parents, but in God's providence, there was a dramatic period of six weeks which almost certainly had an impact on the independent streak developing in Leonard.

When he was just 4 years old, Leonard caught scarlet fever. He was rushed away from his parents and siblings in an ambulance to Foredown Isolation Hospital, which, as the name implies, had been built on the edge of the Downs behind Brighton and Hove.

In the earlier part of the twentieth century, scarlet fever was the leading cause of death in children. There was no vaccine for it, but antibiotics could usually prevent further complications. It is most common among children between 5 and 15 years. The bacteria spreads through coughing and sneezing and also via things touched, so the isolation of scarlet fever victims was recommended at that time.

It was obviously a dramatic incident for the young boy and indeed the whole family. It is interesting to learn what Leonard himself remembers of that traumatic experience.

'I was just 4 years old at the time, and I'm sure the experience of being isolated, taken away from my family at that tender age, had a profound effect on me.

'I was in a fairly big room with lots of other children, and as we were being kept in complete isolation, no visitors, including our parents, were allowed into the ward to see us. The windows were quite high up – at least, they seemed so to me – and occasionally, parents came and looked through them, but I never recognised a familiar face. My sister, Rosemary, told me recently that she remembers coming with Mum or our Aunt Ruth on the number 14 bus to bring things to me. They probably brought picture books, but I don't really remember, and of course, they couldn't give them to me personally. Also, nothing I had in the hospital could come home with me because of infection. Rosemary says she remembers that my absence from home was very difficult, particularly for my mother, and that it sometimes brought her to tears as she was so concerned for me.

'I don't remember any pain or discomfort from the illness itself, and I don't remember crying, so I reckon I was pretty stoic about my predicament. I'm sure my parents were praying for me, and I guess the measure of acceptance I had about the situation was the result of their prayers. God was looking after me.

'I led a very sheltered, secure, and happy home life, and it seems that the things that stand out most in my mind were new experiences which I had never encountered before, taking me out of my personal comfort zone. For instance, I found it very difficult to achieve anything in my bed pan when it seemed so public. There were no bed curtains, and everyone saw what everyone else was doing. For several days, I deliberately stopped myself when the pot was put under me until laxative medicine caused me to dirty the bed sheets one night. Strange to say, after that, I didn't care who was watching me and would have sat on the pot before the whole world if necessary.

'I think most of the nurses must have been kind, but at least one I remember was less so. One dinner time she brought me my meal, which I think must have been a beef stew, and the meat was so tough that I found it impossible to swallow. I chewed and chewed, but no way would it go down. I was frightened of this nurse's possible reaction if she saw I hadn't eaten my dinner up, and this fear caused me to hide the chewed bits of meat under my pillow. Thankfully, it must have been a kind nurse who next made the bed as I heard no more about it.

'When I could eventually go home, I remember being collected in the car of a family friend and being very shy when meeting people again. I remember Mum commenting I was so very polite for several days. However, within a very short time of being home, I developed chickenpox, which Mum was quite angry about as it was clear I must have caught it in hospital.'

Every circumstance in our lives is part of God's plan and, when controlled by Him, can be the means of moulding our characters. No doubt, being separated from his parents and family for that time, at such a young age, made Leonard (a pretty shy boy by nature) more independent, and it was doubtless preparation for the future God had planned.

There was one other consequence for Leonard after his many weeks away from school. On the first day back, he saw sums written on the blackboard, which frightened him as he had no idea how to work them out. The next morning, he cried and refused to go down the road to school. His mother didn't know what to do but suddenly had the idea of simply going down to the school herself and talking to the headmistress about Leonard's fear. The school had a solution. The headmistress sent two attractive student teachers back with Ellen, and very soon, Leonard was running down Hertford Road to school with an attractive young lady holding each hand. He never looked back and, a few years later, passed his eleven-plus exam to go to grammar school.

CHAPTER

6

Holidays

Without a car and with limited income, family holidays had to be fairly simple. On several occasions during those years in Brighton, Leonard went with his parents and younger brother to stay with his Uncle Ben, his Auntie Evelyn and cousins Rhoda and Veronica in the village of Normandy near Aldershot in Surrey. Ben Wilkins was one of his mother's younger brothers. She had had eight brothers and three sisters. Ben was also the brother-in-law who had called to Edgar from a troop ship's porthole as he walked along the dockside in Cape Town. Ben was a jobbing gardener and also a Strict Baptist minister. His income was minimal, and the family of four lived in a small four-roomed cottage in the village. The cottage had an outside toilet and no bathroom. With only two bedrooms, Leonard has since wondered how they were accommodated. No doubt Ben and Evelyn had slept in the sitting room downstairs and given up their bedroom to Leonard and Frank with their parents. Leonard remembers being bathed in a galvanised tub in the kitchen.

However, these holidays were times to be remembered. There was a sizable garden and lots of countryside around to play in. Veronica was just a year older than Leonard, and they got on well together. Rhoda and Veronica introduced their cousins to their play haunts: a 'Faraway Tree' in the woods opposite the cottage, named after the magic tree in a series of books by Enid Blyton, and the bracken, as tall as themselves, where they played hide and seek. Then there was a bus ride to the open-air swimming pool in Guildford. Leonard, less than 8 at the time, was still to learn to swim but remembers the thrill of coming down a water slide and finding himself sitting on the bottom of the pool, completely underwater, and watching bubbles arise in front of his eyes. Thankfully, there was someone on hand to save him from any real danger.

Another memorable holiday was a week with his Auntie Mary and Uncle Albert, another of his mother's brothers, at the Dicker in Sussex. Albert was a farm worker, the single employee of Miss Gander, who had a small farm with a few cows. The farm cottage where they stayed was at the bottom of one of Miss Gander's fields and situated on Camberlot Road. What Leonard hadn't known at the time was that his grandfather's grandfather, Eli Page, had grown up on a farm on the same Camberlot Road and had himself later – with Selina, his wife – farmed Clifton Farm, which is almost opposite his uncle's cottage home, also on Camberlot Road.

Leonard's Uncle Albert and Auntie Mary Wilkins

Leonard spent as much time as he could with his uncle and was fascinated with the concept of farming. Albert did everything on the farm; he not only milked the cows by hand but also, after the milk had been cooled, bottled it and delivered it around the neighbourhood. He showed Leonard how the returned milk bottles needed to be scorched in boiling water before being refilled. Leonard determined he would one day be a farmer himself.

Interestingly, later at school, when asked to give examples of collective nouns, Leonard put his hand up and gave the answer: breeds of cows such as Friesian, Sussex, Shorthorn, Jersey, and Guernsey.

He remembers his teacher commenting with a smile, 'Here's our budding farmer.'

However, there was another holiday, made in May 1956, which had dramatic significance for the whole family. Edgar had been suffering from stress, which was severely affecting his health. Leonard believes that although the major cause of this arose from greater responsibility at work, there were also things at Galeed Chapel which he found difficult to cope with. Anyway, Edgar had applied for a job with a firm in Southampton with which he had come into contact whilst working at Bennett's. The object of this holiday, therefore, was to find a suitable location for the family to move to.

About five miles out of Southampton on the Portsmouth side is the village of Lower Swanwick, situated on the estuary of the River Hamble. Very close to the shore but lying on the main Southampton Road is a small Strict Baptist chapel known in the denomination as Swanwick Shore Chapel. The chapel had no pastor but was run by two deacons, the brothers Fred and Leslie Bevis. Fred was the senior of the two but was extremely deaf, his hearing having been damaged by the roar of cannon fire in the First World War. Leslie Bevis and his wife, Edith, advertised in the *Gospel Standard* the possibility of holiday accommodation in their home. Inspired, Edgar decided this would give a wonderful opportunity to spy out the area, including the chapel, as a possible new location for the family, within easy reach of Southampton.

The holiday was a great success in every way. Leslie and Edith Bevis were a lovely Christian couple, and Edith was a wonderful hostess. Leonard remembers how thrilled he was on waking up the first morning. Looking out of the window into the garden, he saw a jay in the fruit trees. This was a bird he'd only seen in his bird books. With its reddish-brown body colouring, black and white markings on its wings, and additional striking blue feathers, he was enthralled.

At breakfast, he proudly announced his sighting of this pretty bird but was rather deflated when his host commented, 'Yes, we get too many of them. They are a great nuisance in the garden, and I try and shoot them if I can. You'll probably see bullfinches as well,

Leonard, and actually, they do more damage this time of year as they peck at the fruit buds.'

Leonard brightened again at the thought that he might also see a bullfinch. He knew from pictures in his book just how pretty the male bullfinch is, with its bright red breast, slate grey back, and black head. He determined this time that if he spotted a bullfinch in the garden, he would not tell Leslie Bevis.

The congregation in the chapel was small. Fred Bevis (a retired postman) and his wife, Margaret, had had no children. Leslie and Edith had a daughter, Mary, but their son, John, had been killed tragically in a motorcycle accident. The largest family in the chapel were the Edwards. Mary Edwards diligently brought her five children to the services, even though her husband, Arthur, no longer attended. Arthur Edward's father, Richard, had recently died, and Arthur was now responsible for selling the house that his father had owned. This proved to be God's wonderful provision for the Holder family.

The house was situated up a rough, untarmacked lane opposite the chapel. It was a detached three-bedroomed house with two additional bedrooms on a second floor under the sloping roof. There was a long garden which included an orchard of apple trees. The garden descended into a small valley where its far boundary was a narrow stream running through a bed of reeds. Richard had made as much use as he could of the different areas of his garden and, in its lower reaches, had dug out a small pond into which he had directed the stream. When the Holder family took over the property, the pond was very silted up, but there were still signs of the water cress Richard had cultivated there. Remarkably, in light of today's prices for houses, Edgar was able to purchase the house and land for £1,500.

PART 2

SWANWICK SHORE
1957–1965

*Then you will call upon Me and go and
pray to Me, and I will listen to you. And
you will seek Me and find Me when you
search for Me with all your heart. I will
be found by you, says the LORD.*
— Jeremiah 29:13–14

CHAPTER

⚜

1

'Aenon'

This part of the story begins with a man named James Edwards. James was born in 1814 and lived in Fleet End, Hook, on the Hamble estuary in Hampshire. The River Hamble runs into Southampton Water, on which one of Britain's main ports, Southampton, is situated. James Edwards began his working life as a gardener, and when he was able to build himself a boat, he left gardening and began to earn his living from fishing. Southampton Water runs inland from the Solent, which is a twenty-mile stretch of sea between the mainland and the Isle of Wight and has a maximum width of five miles. It is comparatively shallow but deep enough to allow large vessels to sail up into Southampton Port and is ideal fishing ground for small vessels.

A short distance further inland up the River Hamble is the little town of Warsash and then just before the Bursledon Bridge the small village of Lower Swanwick. On the opposite bank is the village of Hamble, after which the river is named. Up to Bursledon Bridge, the river is wide and prone to flooding at extremely high tides; also, its shoreline is an expanse of mud at low tide. James was very familiar with all this water and the communities which bordered it. When he heard that a preacher was leading Sunday services in a converted boathouse on the shore at Lower Swanwick, he began to attend. Mr George Harding was the preacher. He was a local man, born in the area's district town of Fareham. He moved to Swanwick as a 5-year-old when his father was appointed foreman at Oslands, a brick tile yard owned by the Eckless family. Through Mr George Harding's ministry, James Edwards came to faith in Christ and was baptised in 1847. He then continued to attend the services at Swanwick until shortly before his death in 1896. In the earlier days, he boated up the Hamble to the chapel, but later, it was his custom to walk the four miles twice each Sunday for many years.

The boathouse was far from ideal, and extreme high tides would flood the room they met in. George Harding remembers an occasion when, after a flooded chapel one Sunday morning, the church members worked hard as the tide retreated to ensure that they had acceptable conditions for the evening service.

In 1846, they were able to build a new, simple but adequate chapel a short distance from the shore on the main road. They constructed a baptistery under the floor, just in front of the pulpit, and James Edwards was one of the first to be baptised in 1849.

James and his wife, Mary Ann, had twelve children, but it's their son, Richard Cobden Edwards, who is relevant to our story.

Another member of the chapel at Swanwick Shore was Asher Bevis. Asher was born in 1818. He, like James Edwards, was a fisherman. He lived with his wife, Mary Ann, in Swanwick Lane, and together, they had eleven children, although one son, Hiram, died in infancy. Mary Ann ran a grocery store which later included the local post office. Asher

Asher Bevis with daughter Isabella

died in 1877, and Mary Ann continued to run the grocery and post office with the help of her daughters. In 1878, James Edwards's son Richard married Isabella Bevis, one of Asher and Mary Ann's elder daughters, thus bringing the two families together. Richard and

Isabella spent most of their married life in Hook, Warsash. They had just one child, a son named Richard Cobden Edwards, after his father.

This history is significant to Leonard's story from several points of view. The wife he eventually married was a great-granddaughter of Alice Ann Bevis (another daughter of Asher and Mary Ann), and his sister, Rosemary, married a great-grandson of Richard and Isabella, David Edwards, but all this was still well in the future. For the immediate, we continue the story as the house Edgar bought was in Oslands Lane, opposite Swanwick Shore Chapel and purchased from the Edwards family. Richard Edwards Jr had died in 1956, and the family were looking for a buyer for his

Mary Ann Bevis
1823–1907

house just as Edgar and his family were looking to move into the area.

The move to Lower Swanwick in Hampshire was at the exact point when Leonard was due to change schools, and thus commenced a wonderful new era in his life.

Oslands Lane was classified as unadopted, which meant the council had no responsibility to tarmac or maintain it. Accordingly, it was a stony rough track which, after fronting a row of three detached houses and a bungalow, led past two small market gardens (growing mainly strawberries), culminating in a simple footpath.

Their new house was constructed of red bricks manufactured locally at the Bursledon Brick Works. It appeared tall and rather narrow with front windows revealing its three stories. The upper, single smaller window was framed by the V shape of the sharply sloping roof.

The Holder family moved into their new home in August 1957. It was a depleted family as Rosemary was just starting her nursing training and had moved into the nurses' home at Southlands Hospital, Shoreham, near Brighton. Jack had also left the Holder home that summer to start training at a naval school, and as has already been recorded, the eldest son, John, had left home a number of years earlier. For Leonard, it was an ideal time to move locations as he had finished primary school after passing the eleven-plus exam at the end of that summer term. He could now start the autumn term at Price's Grammar School, Fareham, a half-hour bus journey from the family's new home.

Edgar named their new home 'Aenon'. This is a Greek word with Hebrew origins found in John's Gospel. We read that 'John was baptising at Aenon, near Salim, because there was much water there'.[3] The word means 'springs of water'. The Holders' new home had a running stream at the bottom of its longish garden, and a small spring bubbled out of the ground into the ditch by the front gate.

---

3 John 3:23.

CHAPTER

2

Price's Grammar School

Leonard started at Price's School in September 1957. The school had a history. William Price was a timber merchant in Fareham in the eighteenth century and left funds in his will to start a school. One of William Price's greatest aims was to enable children to learn to read the Bible. Price's school started in a small way in 1721 in West Street, Fareham. It later became a state school for boys, and its site up Trinity Street with a large playing field and a schoolhouse with dormitories for boarders was opened on 18 January 1908. The school badge bore these two dates: 1721 and 1908.

By 1957, several additional buildings had been added, and the school provided a grammar school education for about 350 boys. There was a particularly striking school uniform which essentially consisted of grey trousers, a dark blue blazer with distinctive light blue and white braid and the school badge, and finally, a school cap which was compulsory even outside of school, when wearing the school uniform. It was usual for boys in the first two school years to wear grey shorts. In fact, Leonard was 13 before he wore long trousers at any time.

Each day began with a school assembly at 9:00 a.m. The sound of the school bell echoed around the neighbourhood at 8:50 a.m., and all 350 boys crowded into the school hall, standing in rows, with the lower forms at the front and sixth-formers at the back. Sixth-formers who had been appointed school prefects were responsible to keep order, and boys they spotted misbehaving or talking too loudly were ordered to line up at the front of the hall. Each new pupil was given a small pocket-sized copy of the Anglican *Ancient and Modern Hymnal* on joining the school, and it was compulsory to keep this in the blazer pocket for daily use in assembly. At 9:00 a.m., the headmaster appeared on the podium at the front of the hall in his scholastic gown. The masters would stand along one side of the hall and along the back. A passage of the Bible was read, usually either by a master or one of the prefects. The whole school would then sing one of the hymns from the *Ancient and Modern Hymnal*, and the headmaster would read a prayer. After any school announcements, the head made his descent from the podium and, unless it was a lucky day for those concerned, would order any boys sent to the front by prefects to follow him to his study. The normal procedure under the headship of Mr G. A. Ashton was, as Leonard heard from those who had suffered under it, 'six of the best' on their backsides with a cane and no questions asked or excuses heard. In 1959, Mr George Ashton retired after twenty-five years as head, and the younger Mr Eric Poyner took his place. Thankfully, he, as a committed Anglican Christian, was more merciful.

Continuing, no doubt, from the days when many of the boys were boarders, the school timetable stretched over six days, with Wednesday and Saturday afternoons allocated to games. There was football in the autumn term, hockey in the spring term, and cricket in the summer term. Leonard was thankful when, with the arrival of the new headmaster, the school conformed with the more normal practice of a five-day week.

Leonard continued at Price's until 1965. He gained ten O-level passes and three A-levels. Subjects for the latter were biology, chemistry, and physics as these would prepare him for medical studies at university. He, in fact, took the A-level subjects two years running to try and improve the grades but, as you will subsequently discover, felt guided by God into another direction entirely.

CHAPTER

3

Ducks, Dog and Rabbits

The move to Swanwick changed daily life for all of the Holder family. Edgar soon got into the swing of his new job, but because the trip to Southampton was rather too long to cycle, one evening he arrived home on a motor scooter.

'Cor, Dad! Will I be allowed to use it?' asked Leonard enthusiastically.

'I can certainly take people on the back,' answered Edgar, 'and when you are old enough, we'll see about getting you a licence.'

The motor scooter became quite a feature of the Holder household for a number of years, and eventually, both Leonard and Frank were able to ride it, at least on provisional driving licences.

Eventually, Edgar bought a Ford Anglia car, passed his driving test, and became a well-known sight in the neighbourhood, driving around, not always so carefully, with the text 'Salvation is of the Lord' displayed on the back window.

Edgar also found relaxation in cultivating and growing vegetables in the garden and then came up with the idea of keeping ducks to provide the family with a ready supply of eggs. There was a tin shed at the bottom of the garden in good enough condition to be fairly easily adapted into a night-time shelter for the ducks. The small pond had got silted up, but this was dug out to allow more of the stream to flow into it. The result was that very soon, the Holders were the proud owners of twelve Khaki Campbell ducks and a small pond for them to swim in. This breed has the reputation of being good layers, and very quickly, the Holder family were eating duck eggs for breakfast every day. Indeed, Ellen even had sufficient eggs for all the baking she needed to do.

Khaki Campbell ducks

Leonard's farming urge was also brought into play. It quickly became his responsibility for ensuring the ducks were safely in their shed at night, and he also took it on himself to care for them generally, changing their bedding straw as necessary. The birds would generally lay eggs early morning in their nesting straw, and only spasmodically did an egg appear in the grass outside or even very occasionally in the mud at the bottom of the pond.

Ducks, unlike chickens, do not have the sense to make their own way into their night shelter, and since there were often foxes roaming around at night, their lives would be in danger if they were not securely shut in. There was one night-time experience that Leonard never forgot. Through his neglect that particular evening, darkness had fallen, and the ducks were not in their hut. When Leonard eventually went down the garden to correct this, it was pitch dark, and he found the ducks huddled together in their pond. The pond was roughly circular, about three or four metres across, and certainly didn't provide the birds any security from hungry foxes. Normally, the ducks would cooperate and be easily driven up the path into their hut, but that night, probably as a consequence of the darkness and maybe even because a fox had already been roaming around, they refused to leave the water. Leonard tried everything he could think of to drive them out of the pond into their home but to no avail. Eventually, he even waded into the water to try and force them onto the bank. This, they did but only to scatter, making it impossible to drive them together into their hut. He was tempted to simply leave them to their possible fate in the teeth of Brer Fox but then decided to pray to God about the situation. Having explained his fear for their safety to his heavenly Father, he asked the Creator of heaven and earth for His help. To his amazement, almost immediately, the ducks obediently clambered out of the pond, where they had regathered and trotted, with virtually no persuasion, up the narrow path and into their hut.

Leonard often thought back to this answer to his prayer. Later experience showed him that he couldn't use God simply like a machine to answer requests within his own human time frame. He decided that God's quick answer to his prayer on that occasion, when he was a young teenager, was to demonstrate His existence, power, and personal interest and care to nurture a young lad's faith.

On another occasion when getting the ducks in at night, Leonard realised there was one missing. He knew that sometimes they wandered upstream into the reed beds, but they had always returned for their food. It seems, however, that this time, one had failed to return. It was still light enough to search for the stray, and very quickly, he saw it. It was lying dead amongst the reeds in about six inches of water. This was the first duck they had lost in this way, and inspecting the body, Leonard realised the head was missing. What animal would catch a duck and bite off its head? Somehow it didn't seem the typical tactics of a fox. Leonard left the body where it was and, the next morning, came to see if the predator had returned for its prey. He saw at once that a creature he didn't recognise was gorging itself on the dead body of the duck. It looked something like a ferret but bigger. The neighbour solved the problem for them. He had been informed that another neighbour bred mink and that one had recently escaped. Thankfully, the owner of the mink was able to set a trap and catch the creature; also, he was happy to pay the Holders for the duck they had lost.

The ducks and the presence of the mash fed to them attracted rats. The ducks' domain was far enough from the house for these rodents not to be a household nuisance, but Edgar bought a couple of large nipper-type rat traps. When the first victim caught was an innocent robin, found by Leonard one morning completely decapitated by the strong spring of the nipper trap, it was decided that it would be good to have a dog. Edgar had heard that fox terriers are good ratters, so one evening he appeared home with a young female puppy of this breed. After a family discussion, it was agreed that her name should be Jesse. Leonard can't remember who suggested this and why, but Jesse she was.

Jesse became an important part of Leonard's life for most of his teenage years.

A neighbour and friend who had previously bred rabbits as a source of meat had ceased breeding and now had a row of six rabbit hutches unused. Leonard, now about 14, recognised breeding rabbits as an aspect of farming possible for him to develop in his back garden. He approached the neighbour and agreed to pay five shillings for the six hutches. They were a bit worse for wear but still usable and adequate. After visiting the animal market in Fareham – which, at that time, met each Monday morning – he acquired a big black buck rabbit and two does. So in addition to the ducks for eggs, the budding farmer had the means to begin meat production.

There was much to learn, but books gave him the basic instructions. Usually, the buck need only be introduced into the doe's hutch for a very short period before coupling takes place. The female is then left alone, ensuring she has sufficient nesting material, and babies arrive after around thirty days. Interestingly, the mother rabbit will pluck fur from her breast to line the nest before giving birth to her naked and blind babies. Later, Leonard also bred guinea pigs, and their offspring are very much more developed at birth – being sighted, having fur, and ready to immediately run around. The mother guinea pig, however, only produces one or two offspring at a time, whilst rabbits give birth to an average of six and often more babies.

Leonard also read up on how to kill and gut the animals, and although he never looked forward to this aspect of producing meat, he became quite skilful at it. One interesting development from this came later when, studying biology in the sixth form, he suggested to his teacher that he could bring a young rabbit or two for the class to dissect. The biology master took up this offer enthusiastically and paid Leonard for a couple of animals. He took the animals to school alive, and the teacher asked him to stand at the front of the class and to demonstrate to his classmates how to kill them. It's unlikely this would be allowed in the twenty-first century.

To supplement the food pellets, during months when vegetation was growing, Leonard would cut grass from the orchard and from the hedgerows up the lane for his rabbits. He also dug an area of ground lower down the garden and grew kale for rabbit food.

This was an age devoid of computers or smart phones, and the Holder household had no television; indeed, they rarely listened to a radio. This meant that although the young Leonard had detailed knowledge of subjects that interested him, his general knowledge of the wider world was extremely limited. However, on the positive side, he spent many hours a day outdoors, either pursuing his 'farming' activities or walking Jesse around the fields and woodlands surrounding his home. There were no long pull-out leashes in those days, so Jesse would mostly run free and, unless very engrossed in pursuing smells, would respond to a whistle to come to heel.

CHAPTER

4

Swanwick Shore Chapel

The Holder family soon became very involved in chapel life, and their presence was greatly appreciated by the small congregation meeting there week by week. Edgar had some musical ability, teaching each of his four children to play the piano. He himself concentrated on playing simple hymn tunes, never seeing the need

Swanwick Shore Chapel

to develop his gifts any further; nevertheless, the chapel deacons appreciated the ability he had and were very pleased for him to lead the hymn singing on the small harmonium in the chapel.

Being part of a small church fellowship was very different from church life at Galeed, Brighton. There was one other family with children, two boys older than Leonard and three girls younger. A year or two after their move to the area, an additional young lady named Sheila also began to attend. There was nothing organised specifically for the young people, and Edgar decided it would be helpful for them to meet together on a Sunday evening. Leonard's elder brother, John, would also come home to the family for weekends from time to time and probably had some involvement in initiating this Sunday evening meeting. Edgar bought in a dozen copies of the Golden Bells hymn book to sing from, and apart from a short Bible reading and a prayer, most of the hour was spent singing. They each chose hymns they liked from the new hymn book.

Heating in winter for the congregation was from a large tortoise stove in the middle of the chapel. It burnt coke and, in cold weather, needed to be lit several hours before the morning service. The vicinity immediate to the stove tended to be too hot, and equally, one got cold feet sitting farther away.

It was customary to have an evening service on a Tuesday, and Leonard regularly attended this. In his younger days, he did this largely because he knew it pleased his parents and because something inside him wanted to please God; he thought God would bless him if he made this effort. In the winter months, they met in the home of the older deacon, Mr Fred Bevis. Fred and his wife, Margaret, lived in an old cottage without electricity or water. There was an extremely cosy atmosphere in their small lounge on a Tuesday evening as the small group sat together around a paraffin lamp. Once a month on a Tuesday, Pastor Leonard Broome from Southampton preached at the chapel, but otherwise, the weekly meeting was devoted to prayer, often with part of a sermon read (mostly from the *Gospel Standard* magazine) by one of the deacons.

Leonard grew up believing he was, in some ways, different from most of his contemporaries. The Christian teaching, he imbibed, and the faith which he thought he had in God made him proud. He remembers looking around the assembly hall at school and wondering whether there were any other Christians there. His attitude was rather like the Pharisee in Jesus's parable who, in his prayer, said, 'God, I thank You that I am not like other men.' God had a lot to teach him.

When Leonard was 15, he slowly became aware of evil in some of his thoughts and feelings, and he began to realise he had no grounds for assuming he was a child of God. His understanding of the Bible made him aware that a person must be born again by

God's Spirit before he could be a true Christian. This disturbed him greatly. The awareness of his sinful nature and the uncertainty as to whether he was one of the elect and so could be sure that Christ had died for him personally began to torment him. Each Sunday, he prayed earnestly that God would speak to him through His Word or the sermon preached, but Sunday by Sunday, nothing came to relieve his anguish. Finally, on Sunday, 1 April 1962, two days before Leonard's 16th birthday, when God had been silent to him through two services at the chapel, Leonard pleaded with God on his knees beside his bed.

'Lord, I can't go through another week in this state of mind. Please speak to reassure me of your love and that I am one of your chosen children, unworthy as I am.'

Leonard's prayer was continuing in a similar vein when suddenly, a verse he knew by heart from John's Gospel flashed into his mind: 'God so loved the world that He gave His only begotten Son, that whosoever believes in Him should not perish but have everlasting life.'[4]

This Scripture text came quite unexpectedly. It not only came into his mind but simultaneously enlightened his whole being. Later, he would identify it as his own experience of the Apostle Paul's words to the Corinthian believers: 'For it is God who commanded light to shine out of darkness, who has shone in our hearts to give the light of knowledge of the glory of God in the face of Jesus Christ.'[5]

Leonard was alone in his little bedroom under the eaves at the top of the house, and this Word from God overwhelmed him with a deep sense of peace and thrilled him with joy. God had spoken to him. This was the way to know Him and to have eternal life. It was simply by believing and trusting in the Son of God, Jesus Christ. After years of reading the Bible and hearing sermons, Leonard now understood the simple message of the Gospel for the first time. This was clarified to him even further through reading the words of Jesus, as recorded by John, which preceded those that had so

---

4 John 3:16.
5 2 Corinthians 4:6.

powerfully enlightened him: 'As Moses lifted up the serpent in the wilderness, even so must the Son of Man be lifted up, that whoever believes in Him should not perish but have eternal life.'[6]

As Leonard got into bed, he felt happier than he had ever felt before, and in fact, it was to be the most thrilling moment of his life! He was suddenly fully convinced in his mind, from deep within, that he, Leonard Holder, was a child of God, chosen from before the foundation of the world to know God and live with Him forever. The Bible refers to this as follows: 'The Spirit Himself bears witness with our spirit that we are children of God.'[7] The thought came to him: *I can die now.* In fact, at that moment, to go to be with his Saviour seemed preferable to continuing life here on earth.

---

6 John 3:14–15.
7 Romans 8:16.

CHAPTER

5

Birds, Badgers and Squirrels

The experience recounted in the previous chapter became a turning point in Leonard's life, and the development of his new life in Jesus will be enlarged upon in more detail later. However, to get a better overall picture of his teenage years, we need to look at his other main interest – nature.

Perhaps it's important first to state that for Leonard, nature was God's world and has sometimes been described as God's second book, complimenting the revelation of Himself in the Bible. King David describes it in this way in Psalm 19, for example, in verses 2 and 3: 'Day unto day utters speech, and night unto night reveals knowledge. There is no speech nor language where their voice is not heard.' The seraphim around God's throne, as Isaiah saw them in his vision, were crying, 'Holy, holy, holy is the LORD of hosts; the whole earth is full of His glory.'[8]

The countryside surrounding his new home immediately introduced Leonard to a variety of habitats where he had the opportunity to study more bird species, increasing his ornithological knowledge.

---

8 Isaiah 6:3.

At the bottom of his garden were a stream, quite an extensive reed bed, and a few substantial willow trees. Leonard made a habit of heading down the garden to where he'd stand perfectly still and quiet on a particular tree stump. From the latter, he had a superb view of the surrounding area, and patiently, he would wait and watch. As a result, for the first time, he was seeing water rail, snipe, reed warblers, and reed buntings, and one day he was thrilled to see a very colourful orange and blue-grey bird fly onto the willow tree near him, which he couldn't immediately identify. It clambered up the bark of the tree and then surprisingly turned and clambered down again. Searching his bird book back at the house, he discovered it was a nuthatch. The snipe were interesting. When disturbed, they would fly up, zigzagging from side to side as they rose into the air. This flight pattern makes it difficult for wild fowlers to shoot them.

Green woodpeckers used to feed on ants at the edge of the path leading from the house into the garden. Also, great spotted woodpeckers would occasionally visit the bird table.

House martins nested under the eaves of the house, both at the front and the back. One nest was immediately above Leonard's bedroom window, and he found the birds a joy to watch, swooping around in front of him as he sat at his desk under the window, doing schoolwork. One year a nest must have dried out because it fell down with four fledglings in it. The parent birds stopped feeding their young, unwilling, it seemed, to bring flies down to the ground for them. Leonard, not wanting to let the young birds die, began putting the ducks' food mash into their open mouths. This was obviously a very different diet from the flies they normally got from their parents, but they seemed to thrive on it. The next question was how to encourage them to fly when they were ready. During the day, Leonard put them on the garden lawn in their box, and one day his mother informed him when he came home from school that they had suddenly taken to the wing and flown off! He just trusted that they had the instinct to open their mouths and catch flies on the wing without guidance from their parents.

Birds of prey were only rarely seen in Southern England at that time, and Leonard remembers seeing with delight his first buzzard when in Shropshire at a Christian camp.

He had a friend at school who was as enthusiastic about birds and wildlife as he was, and he remembers an excursion one Saturday morning when the two set off on their bikes to visit as many different habitats as they could, to count as many different species of birds as they could. The tour included the marshland and coast of the Meon Estuary, a sand quarry where vegetation was beginning to grow again, pastureland, and also gardens. He seems to remember they counted about seventy different species, but he has difficulty in justifying this number as he thinks back now.

A book Leonard borrowed from the library provided a wealth of information on badgers and a most interesting account of visiting a badger's sett at twilight, along with photographs of the animals emerging from their burrow. Having located a badger's sett in the woodland near his home, Leonard was able to persuade his school friend Richard to come with him one evening when they hid themselves outside the sett to watch for these intriguing animals. It was an interesting outing but not very successful. There was no moon, and within the wood, it was really too dark to see anything. They heard an animal moving around and saw a shape but sadly little more.

Richard's grandparents lived in a farmhouse further inland in the Hampshire countryside near Droxford. When Richard visited them, he had permission to roam the surrounding farmland and copses. Leonard remembers several eventful occasions when he and Richard cycled to the grandparents together. The farmers considered wood pigeons to be pests as they could do a lot of damage to growing crops. Richard's grandfather possessed both a powerful air rifle and a twelve-bore shotgun; he entrusted these to the two boys, allowing them to shoot any pigeons and grey squirrels they could locate. Leonard's love of nature didn't prohibit him from shooting pests, and the thrill of the hunt can become quite addictive. Their success in this was minimal, but Leonard remembers taking at least one pigeon home for his mother to cook. However, one Saturday visit to Droxford was particularly significant. The boys spotted a large nest in a small tree which was possible to climb up to. Out of curiosity, they decided to clamber up and see if there was anything in the nest. They imagined it could belong to magpies.

Richard climbed up and, peering into the nest, called down, 'Guess what's here, Len! Two young squirrels. What do you think? We could each take one home as a pet.'

Although he was a little dubious, Leonard was quite excited about the idea, and after a brief conversation, Richard clambered back down to the ground with the two squirrel babies – or kittens, as they are called. Squirrels are born naked and blind; these two already had a good amount of fur, although their eyes were still closed.

Grey squirrel

Feeding the youngster was the challenge, but Leonard found the way to get warm milk into its hungry mouth. He kept it in his bedroom, and it thrived. When it was old enough, he constructed a cage of chicken wire around a small apple tree in his garden which kept it enclosed for a couple of weeks. Eventually, however, it would find its way out. The first time it did this, Leonard was at school, and his mother tried to catch it. Unfortunately, it bit her, and she vowed to have nothing more to do with the creature. Leonard then decided it was time to allow it its freedom. It lived in the garden freely for a while, coming when called and either dropping down from a tree or running up Leonard's leg to sit on his shoulder. There was one unfortunate incident when it tried to climb up Leonard's sister, Rosemary's, leg in the same way. It learned that day that a woman's dress doesn't give the same access to the shoulder as a pair of trousers do. During the summer holiday, Leonard was away helping at a camp, and there was no sign of the squirrel when he returned. Hopefully, it had happily established itself in the wild.

Leonard had another experience when out with Richard which he has never forgotten. They had taken their bikes into the New Forest beyond Southampton, having caught the Hythe ferry across the Southampton Water. It had been a good day as the New Forest is full of interest to those who love exploring nature.

It was, by then, late afternoon, and they had eaten their sandwiches and had just begun the journey back when suddenly, Richard exclaimed, 'Len, I feel awful!'

They stopped in a bus shelter miles, it seemed, from civilisation. As they were sitting down in the shelter, Leonard remembers the sound of a New Forest pony foal suckling its mother behind the small building.

Richard put his head in his hands and groaned. 'I've got such a pain in my stomach, Len, and a headache too. I can't go on anymore.'

This obviously worried Leonard considerably. They were about twenty miles from home. It was the days before mobile phones, and in fact, at that time, Leonard's home didn't have a landline either. What could he do? He did what any believing Christian would have done in this situation: he prayed.

After about a quarter of an hour of silence, apart from the gurgling sound of the foal suckling, Richard stood up and, after a minute or two, suddenly said, 'That's strange, Len. As I stood up, it was as though my pains dropped down through my feet. I feel as good as new. Let's go!'

There was no doubt to Leonard that God had heard his prayer and that a miracle had happened. However, he acknowledges, to his shame, that he didn't have the courage to mention to Richard that he had prayed and that he believed it was God who had healed him. When, a few days later at school, Richard made reference to the incident again, mentioning how he'd been wondering about the suddenness with which his pains had disappeared, once again, Leonard said nothing. His only excuse (if it is an excuse) is that all this happened before he had the assurance of his salvation and the inner strength of the Holy Spirit.

CHAPTER
6

A Summer in Malta

Wow! said Leonard to himself, looking down several thousand feet from the window of a BEA Comet 4B. *That's the most fantastic view I've ever seen.*

The plane was approaching the island of Malta, and the dark shape of the little island against the beautiful blue of the Mediterranean Sea, bordered by a white rim of little waves, was enchanting. Perhaps this scene excited Leonard particularly as it was his first trip outside of Britain and he had certainly never seen such a blue sea before. That first glimpse of his destination with those little white waves added greatly to his anticipation of a great adventure to come.

It was the summer of 1960. Leonard was just 14 and was travelling by himself. Edgar had run him up to London on the motor scooter; they had stayed overnight with Ellen's sister Ruth and family in Feltham and, early that morning, had driven the short distance to Heathrow Airport.

Waiting for Leonard at Luqa Airport was his brother John. Compared with Heathrow, this was, of course, a very small airport, and as Leonard walked across the tarmac to the arrivals terminal, there was John – head and shoulders, it seemed, above everyone else, waving wildly.

John had a qualification in horticulture from the famous Writtle College, and the Sussex firm he was now employed by had set up a nursery in Malta for the production of chrysanthemum cuttings. The strong sunlight brought the little plants on quickly, and they were then airfreighted to nurseries in Europe. John was there to manage the concern whilst a Maltese national was being trained. He had generously invited his younger brother to come and expand his life experience.

New experiences, there certainly were! The first of these was to race pillion, helmetless, through the Maltese countryside on the back of his brother's motor bike. Yes, this was not just a scooter; it was a real motor bike. Leonard has no memory of its make, but with his limited knowledge, it seemed large. John's lodgings were up a narrow street in the village of Attard, in the home of a Maltese widow. Leonard's bedroom was large and airy, and he shared it with a gecko, who lived on the wall near the ceiling. There was also a ginger cat in the household who would occasionally appear; it had the habit of jumping onto one's shoulder.

John's job was full-time, but he did very well at making his brother's stay a memorable one. Occasionally, he was able to come back to the flat during the morning and take Leonard with him to the nursery, giving him some simple jobs to do. He introduced Leonard to the public transport on the island. The buses were antiquated and rattled terribly as they rumbled round the Maltese roads, but it enabled Leonard to visit different areas that John recommended.

One thing that was almost immediately obvious was the power and influence of the Roman Catholic Church and the superstition which accompanied this. The priests were almost worshipped to such an extent that if one got on a

Valletta, Malta

bus, ladies far older than he would jump up to give him a seat, which he would take as if it were his right. During those summer months, there seemed to be almost constant firework displays, apparently in celebration of various saint's days. The priests would go around collecting money for fireworks from families who could ill afford it, and it all went up in smoke. An interesting feature was the fact that many churches had two clock towers, each reading a different time. John informed Leonard that this was intended to deceive the devil so he didn't know what time mass was being said.

John was a member of the Brethren Assembly on the island and also was actively involved with a Sunday school for the children of British naval and air force families. The power of the Catholic Church was such that it was illegal to evangelise the Maltese people themselves. This link with the Brethren Assembly meant that Leonard was introduced to several different families, which added to the interest of his stay. He spent many happy hours with the daughter of a naval officer. They chased butterflies together in the parks, and Julie showed Leonard the best places to swim, encouraging him to dive off higher rocks than he would have dared to on his own.

One evening John took Leonard to an open-air presentation of Shakespeare's *Midsummer Night's Dream* in one of the parks, in the company of a British doctor and his wife. This was a new cultural experience for the lad brought up without radio or television and from a home which considered cinemas and theatres as worldly and to be avoided like the plague.

This introduction to Malta was significant for another reason. Later, Leonard worked on the publication side of the Trinitarian Bible Society (TBS), and whilst there, the society was supporting the work of a certain Mr Z, who was translating the New Testament into Maltese. It is difficult to believe that in the twentieth century, this needed to be done in secret, but as in the case of William Tyndale in the sixteenth century, this was so, and very few people knew what Mr Z was doing. Apparently, not even his own wife was aware of his secret. A few selected Christians from the assembly were in the know and gave him what support they could. When the translation was completed, it was printed in Britain, and the first boxes of printed copies were flown out to the island secretly in the cockpit of a Christian air force pilot. In the early 1970s, Leonard and his family had afternoon tea with this pilot and his wife in Lincolnshire and heard more of the story first-hand.

One further link with Malta came whilst Leonard was managing many aspects of the production of Scriptures for the TBS. At that time, there were grants available for firms to set up factories in Malta, and a British printer established St Paul's Press on the island. The society used this press for the printing and binding of a Portuguese New Testament, and Leonard flew out by invitation from the firm to see their establishment. He had some free time and, whilst out walking, saw his first hoopoe, an interesting Mediterranean bird which, in recent years, has also been seen in Britain.

Still, our story is somewhat running ahead of itself.

CHAPTER

7

'Trust and Obey'

The Scriptures state, 'With the heart, one believes unto righteousness, and with the mouth, confession is made unto salvation.'[9] Leonard knew this, and very soon after that Sunday evening bedroom experience which gave him the assurance of his salvation, he was convicted of the need to own his faith publicly by being baptised. This was the practice of the Baptist denomination he was brought up in and also the practice that he believed to be biblical.

However, Leonard hesitated. He knew he ought to be baptised, and he wanted to be because he knew it would honour his Lord and Master to make a stand for Him, but as he considered the future, he feared his immaturity, and he doubted his spiritual ability to live up to what would be required of him as a baptised member of the church. For one thing, he realised he would be expected to pray publicly at the prayer meetings as it was the practice at the chapel for the deacon to ask baptised church members by name to pray! The Lord graciously answered these fears for him as He showed Leonard through Scripture that He doesn't expect His children to serve Him

---

9 Romans 10:10.

in their own strength. 'Without Me, you can do nothing,'[10] He tells us, and to compliment this, we have the bold statement by the Apostle Paul: 'I can do all things through Christ who strengthens me.'[11]

Also, Leonard was in the habit of spending up to an hour or so most days playing on the piano and singing to himself hymns from the Golden Bells hymnal, and one verse that challenged him powerfully was from 'Trust and Obey':

We never can prove the delights of His love
Until all on the altar we lay.
For the favour He shows and the love He bestows
Are for those who will trust and obey.[12]

Leonard now really wanted to be baptised, but there was a further problem. He couldn't bring himself to request it. He decided he would talk to his father first and tried to do this, even going downstairs from his bedroom with the express purpose of telling his parents of the assurance of salvation he had found in Jesus. He had no doubt they would welcome this, but his timidity overcame him, and on each of several attempts at this, he turned back at the last moment. This situation tortured

Leonard as a teenager

Leonard. He found a spot of comfort when reading in the New Testament about a man with a dumb spirit which Jesus could heal.

The release came one Sunday evening. The preacher was Mr Reg Payne, who later became pastor of Wivelsfield Chapel in Sussex. His Bible reading was from Acts 8, and his sermon was based on the account of the Ethiopian who found faith in Jesus as the Son of God through reading Isaiah 53 and being instructed by

---

10 John 15:5.
11 Philippians 4:13.
12 'Trust and Obey' by J. H. Sammi, 1887.

Philip as to its meaning. He requested baptism, and on the basis of his acknowledged faith, Philip baptised him there and then. In a wonderful way, through that sermon, God freed Leonard from whatever it was that was binding him. He now had the confidence and courage to go forward, speaking about it to his father as they walked up Oslands Lane home. The next evening, he called in to see Mr Leslie Bevis and requested baptism.

That Sunday evening's sermon had also spoken to someone else in the congregation. Mary, the mother of the larger family who worshipped regularly in the chapel, also requested baptism. She and Leonard were asked to give their testimony to the other church members, and an evening was arranged for the baptism. Mr Reg Payne came back to preach and baptise the two candidates, and it was a significant occasion for Leonard – one could even say the beginning of a new era. One hymn sung moved Leonard particularly as he felt able to identify fully with the sentiments it expressed.

Jesus! and shall it ever be!
A mortal man ashamed of Thee?
Ashamed of Thee, who angels praise,
Whose glories shine through endless days?

Ashamed of Jesus! that dear friend
On whom my hopes of heaven depend!
No; when I blush, be this my shame,
That I no more revere His name.

Ashamed of Jesus! yes, I may,
When I've no guilt to wash away;
No tear to wipe, no joy to crave,
No fears to quell, no soul to save.

Till then nor is my boasting vain,
Till then I'll boast a Saviour slain!
And, oh, may this my portion be,
That Christ is not ashamed of me![13]

---

13 Joseph Grigg (1720–1768).

Charles Spurgeon commented that baptism loosened his tongue, and looking back now, Leonard can see it did so for him too. Although his shy, rather reticent character was not fundamentally changed, after his baptism, Leonard found he wanted to share his faith with others. Swanwick Shore Chapel had no programme of evangelism. Anyone was warmly welcomed to the services, but apart from praying to God to extend His kingdom, no attempt was made to contact homes in the area to invite people in. Leonard wanted to do this. He spoke to the deacons about it, and they had no objection. Consequently, he began to knock on doors of homes in the immediate area of the chapel with a tract and an invitation to come to a Sunday service. In most cases, he was received courteously but without any noticeable results. He remembers one gentleman who commented that he might well come to the service one day probably after his death. When Leonard looked puzzled by this, he added that he was a spiritualist.

Later, in the sixth form at Price's School, Leonard also took a leading role in the school's Christian Union. This was run completely by the scholars but with some support from the Inter-School Christian Fellowship (ISCF), and in his final school year, he took over as secretary. He remembers organising and showing 'Fact and Faith' films such as *The City of Bees* and arranging for speakers to lead meetings.

On an aside, with reference to the sixth form at Price's, a rather interesting incident is worthy of mention. The sixth form scholars decided, for fun, to organise a competitive race to Land's End in Cornwall and back, which is 386 miles in each direction from the school. Pupils were to travel in pairs and not use paid transport; hence, they should hitchhike and walk. To ensure the pairs didn't cheat, they needed to send a postcard back to Price's School from the letterbox at Land's End.

Leonard set off with a friend named Gerald, and remarkably, they completed the race many hours quicker than any other pair. What gave them the advantage was a factor that many would call luck but which Leonard recognised as God showing his young follower that He cared for him and, when looking back later, could draw courage from. It was evidence that his God was quite capable of drawing on every possible means to provide for those who trust Him.

On the last stretch of road to Penzance, a young man who was heading to a scuba diving club meeting picked them up. He expressed interest in the race they were competing in and dropped them off at Penzance to go to his meeting. As Leonard and Gerald found the road they needed out of the town to get them nearer to their destination, their hearts sank when they noticed a signboard stating there was still ten miles to go. It was already evening, and there was little hope of any traffic heading down that lonely route to provide them with a lift. Suddenly, a car pulled up beside them. It was their scuba diver friend. He explained he'd got the wrong week and there was no club meeting that particular night. If they liked, he would happily run them to Land's End to post their postcard and then bring them back again. Amazing!

Leonard and Gerald were then later picked up by a lorry driver travelling back to London and then by a milk tanker. The lorry driver needed them to keep him awake. His firm expected him to stay in Penzance overnight, but he explained he had jobs to do at home, and by travelling back through the night, this would give him time to do these. Whenever his foot relaxed off the accelerator, Leonard or Gerald started another conversation. Thankfully, they got safely to Andover, although by then, it was about 2:00 a.m. They had to walk for a bit, but then an early morning milk tanker took them almost to Fareham. They had completed the return trip in about twenty-two hours, many hours quicker than any of the others. It is unlikely that any school would allow such a competition today, but at the time, it was a challenge and a real adventure.

CHAPTER

8

Duncan Road Brethren Assembly

Duncan Road Assembly outside
Old Gospel Hall
28 June 1964

Shortly before his baptism, Leonard and the few other young people at the Baptist chapel were introduced to a regular Monday evening youth meeting run by the Brethren Assembly. This was a mile or two from Lower Swanwick, near the Swanwick railway station. Leonard's brother John had initiated the contact. He was concerned about the lack of fellowship for young people at the chapel, and because of his experience with the Brethren Assembly in Malta, he sought out the local Brethren and found out the details of the Monday youth meeting.

Several events which would have a lasting impact on Leonard's whole life came out of this contact.

First, he made a new friendship which later developed into marriage! Second, it forced him to think more critically about his theological position as a Christian, and third, through a speaker at the Monday youth meeting, he volunteered to help in a boys' summer camp.

Each of the aforementioned requires a chapter in its own right, so the account of Leonard's new friendship is related here first.

Phyllis Pittwell
1960

Phyllis Pittwell was the daughter of one of the leading elders of the assembly, as the Brethren call their churches. Phyllis's mother, Mina May, was the granddaughter of Alice Bevis, a daughter of Asher Bevis, who has been already mentioned in a previous chapter. Of course, Leonard knew nothing of this when he first met Phyllis at Monday evening – Teenagers.

Their friendship started slowly. It was fairly normal for the boys to accompany the girls home after the meeting, and after a few weeks, Leonard began to walk home with Phyllis. She took this more earnestly than he did as Leonard was not seriously thinking about having a girlfriend. They both travelled into Fareham to school, Leonard to the boys' grammar school and Phyllis to the girls' grammar school at the other end of the town. This, however, meant they often found themselves on the same bus. At first, in the company of their peers, it was just a question of smiling and nodding to each other, but eventually, they got bolder and would, as the opportunity arose, sit and chat together. Phyllis played the violin at school, and when there was a school concert planned, she invited Leonard to attend. After some thought, he did. It was good to see his girlfriend, as he now considered her, skilfully playing her part in the orchestra. When the concert was over, Phyllis quickly found Leonard, grabbed him by the hand, and dragged him across to where her parents were waiting for her.

'This is Len,' she said breathlessly. 'Can he come home with us?'

Leonard had, up to that point, not met Phyllis's parents, but to his credit, without demur, Mr Pittwell agreed with a smile, and the two climbed into the back of the car together.

This took place during 1962, the same year that Leonard was baptised and also the same year that he took his O-level exams. During that summer, Leonard was 16 years old and Phyllis 15 as her birthday is in November. Their relationship developed slowly.

Memories from Others

David

I have a vague memory as a schoolboy on the top deck of the bus with Len, pinging paper pellets at Phyl and other girls from her school. It was the boys' grammar school versus the girls'. I can't really remember how involved Len was. Was this the start of true love?

Joan

I had Phyl in my Sunday school class and Young Sowers League and no doubt both Len and Phyl in the Monday night young people's group. The only memory of their courtship which stands out was Phyl's concern, lest she should be late home from one of the outings. Obviously, there must have been some parental deadline.

Jennifer

I knew Phyl very well when we were at junior school, and we were still close to the age of 16 when I moved to the Coventry area to work. I do remember, when we were young and used to play together, she wasn't interested in the things that other girls usually like but preferred marbles, climbing trees, and making dens.

I remember being very surprised when she said she was getting married – before me, even.

Maureen

I was one of the girls that used to catch the bus home with Phyl in the evenings from school in Fareham. Len used to be on the bus – and his brother Frank too.

One incident that springs to mind was when Phyl, Rosie, my sister Sandra, and I used to play a lot together. One time we decided to make a den in the garage attic at Phyl's house. We furnished it with what we could and used to play Monopoly day in and day out. It was somewhere we could leave the game out all the time and always come back to it. We had a great time until the day a mouse was spotted! No one could be seen for dust. Then about thirty years later, when Phyl's family decided to move, our son James was helping Mr P clear things out, and he discovered the den with everything in it – exactly as we had left it!

Mum Pittwell

I remember Phyllis telling Grandma and me she had met a nice boy – we should like him. Len was a prefect at his school and had a very smart cap with a gold tassel; he seemed to carry this in his pocket until he felt he must put it on in case he might be spotted without it.

C H A P T E R

9

Theological Issues

As he was now a member of the Strict Baptist chapel at Lower Swanwick, it would have been wrong for Leonard to begin to forsake the services to attend the Brethren Assembly with his new girlfriend. Very occasionally, however, he did attend a Sunday evening gospel service, as the Brethren used to call this weekly meeting. On the first occasion he was there, Phyllis was playing the piano to accompany the singing, and the first hymn he heard her play was the following:

Jesus, Saviour, pilot me
Over life's tempestuous sea;
Unknown waves before me roll,
Hiding rock and treach'rous shoal.
Chart and compass come from Thee.
Jesus, Saviour, pilot me.[14]

Still contemplating whether it was right for him to seriously pursue this friendship, he felt this prayer most significant. He respected very much the faith, godliness, and enthusiasm of the

---

14 Edward Hopper (1816–1888).

believers at the Gospel Hall but was immediately aware of theological differences. The chapel teaching warned of the error of 'free will', and clearly, these dear Brethren folk were 'free-willers', to use a Strict Baptist phrase. Still, clearly, they loved the Lord and had an earnest desire for the salvation of others. As the months went by, Leonard attended an increasing number of meetings with his girlfriend other than those on Sunday. There were after-service 'squashes' in different homes, and Leonard and the other young people from the chapel could usually manage to get to these after their own service on a Sunday evening. Some years, Leonard remembers, there were programmes of monthly 'rallies' arranged for young people in Fareham on Saturday evenings. On bank holidays, there was the occasional open-air rally with games followed by a preaching meeting in a large marquee. Phyllis's Bible class leader would take his car with a loudspeaker installed on top around the Hampshire villages. He would give a simple gospel message on a Saturday afternoon and liked Phyllis and one or two of her friends to go with him to sing gospel hymns. Phyllis had been baptised at the hall a few years earlier.

Leonard and Phyllis with sister Rosie at Owlesbury Bank Holiday rally 1963

All that Leonard had participated in at the Gospel Hall gave him a different perspective on Christian life and witness, which he appreciated as no such activities were happening at the chapel. However, his allegiance was still to the chapel. He found blessing from at least some of the preaching there, and in the depth of his being, his theological persuasion was Calvinistic and reformed.

It disturbed him, for instance, to hear a speaker at one of the youth meetings, in challenging the young people to believe in Jesus, say, 'I received Jesus into my heart when I was a young man. It was the best thing I did. I have no regrets and can recommend the Christian life.'

He saw that this way of expressing conversion, whether intended or not, puts the credit for conversion on the person concerned, whereas the Bible always gives the credit to God and His grace.

However, Leonard also felt sure that to confine preaching to Sunday services within closed walls and to frown on offering the Gospel of our Lord Jesus to unregenerate people in case it gave them the impression that they had the 'free will' and the ability to accept salvation at any time they wanted was not biblical. It didn't appear to tie in with the preaching of Jesus and later the apostles as recorded in the New Testament.

As Leonard battled in his mind with this conflict between the thinking and practice of the two denominations, he picked up a book that must have been on the bookshelf in his home entitled *Revival Year Sermons 1859* by C. H. Spurgeon. This was the first time he had come across this London preacher of the previous century, and reading the book revealed to him a possible middle road through the two extremes he was facing. Spurgeon was a firm believer in the indispensable power of the Holy Spirit to bring a person to saving faith in Christ, and yet as Peter did on the day of Pentecost, he had no hesitation in calling his hearers to repentance and faith.

Leonard also later came to the conclusion that all true born-again believers know in their hearts that the Holy Spirit is the agent of conversion. The minds of some, however, have not caught up with the truth placed in their hearts by the Holy Spirit that it is actually God's amazing grace which has opened their eyes and drawn them to Christ. They agree with the power of prayer and will pray earnestly for the salvation of those they love but will argue forcefully against the thought that we are all so totally spiritually dead that we have no wish and no power to give ourselves spiritual life until God's Spirit breathes His life into us. Paul expressed this truth in Chapter 2 of his letter to the Ephesian Church: 'For by grace you have been saved through faith and that not of yourselves; it is the gift of God.'[15]

This encounter with the works of Charles Spurgeon led Leonard to hold the man as a preacher in high regard; indeed, throughout Leonard's life, he has continued to benefit from this much-esteemed preacher's sermons and writings.

---

15 Ephesians 2:8.

CHAPTER

10

Climping Camp

'Young people, boys and girls, the Kingdom of God needs you!' Mr
Jack Nickless was the invited speaker at a Monday evening teenager
meeting in the early summer of 1963.

He and his wife, Joy, ran a children's holiday home by the sea in
Belgrave House in Littlehampton, Sussex. The house belonged to the
Brethren Assemblies and was used with the object of bringing the
Gospel and biblical teaching to young people. During much of the
year, boys and girls needing breaks away for various reasons were
sent to Belgrave House by
different councils, many from
London. However, in the summer
months, the house ran holiday
camps for girls and simultaneously
ran a camp for boys in a field they
owned just outside Littlehampton.
At that Monday evening meeting,
Jack Nickless was calling for older
Christian teenagers to help in the
running of these camps as room or
tent leaders and in other vital ways.

Leonard and Phyllis
1970

As Leonard walked his girlfriend home that evening, he commented to her in a thoughtful tone, 'Phyl, I felt challenged by that call to help in Littlehampton and wonder whether I should apply.'

'It's interesting you should say that, Len,' answered Phyllis, smiling, 'because helping in a girls' camp like that is something I would love to do.'

She went on to tell him how a year or two earlier, she had spent a few days in a Müller Home in Bristol over Christmas. Joan, who lived next door to the Pittwell family, had an elder sister, Hilda, who was a housemother in one of these children's homes, and Joan had taken Phyllis on a visit.

'I have kept in touch with some of the girls,' said Phyllis. 'Auntie Hilda said they really appreciate any interest taken in them, so I'm corresponding with several of them.'

Both Leonard and Phyllis contacted Jack Nickless and offered their help at the summer camps.

The position that Jack Nickless offered Leonard was to be cook's assistant in the kitchen at Climping Camp. Over the summer months, there were several camps planned, lasting a week or ten days each. An older Christian woman who had cooked for the camps before had volunteered again for that year, but with camps of fifty to sixty boys, she valued some practical help in food preparation. Leonard was willing to do whatever was required and agreed readily, little knowing how this was preparation for the future.

The camp was in a field at the end of a lane in the village of Climping, and from the field, there was a footpath straight down to sand dunes, a stretch of sandy beach, and the sea. In a semi-circle around the edge of part of the field were individual concrete tent bases designed for bell tents to be erected over them. There was a building with a few toilets and also an open-sided, roofed area for washing hands and faces and dirty dishes. In addition, there was a larger building providing an adequately sized hall where the boys could both eat and gather for meetings. At one end of this building was a kitchen and a small bedroom and toilet facilities for the cook. The cook's assistant was allocated a place to sleep in one of the tents.

Each boy was required to bring a sleeping bag and, on arrival, was provided with a palliasse. This was a large canvas bag which the boys stuffed with straw as a mattress to sleep on. This was Leonard's first experience of camping.

During the first week, all went smoothly. Leonard got on well with Mrs Hall, the cook, and they worked efficiently together. Then tragedy struck. Mrs Hall was unexpectedly required to return home urgently to care for a family member who was ill.

'Len, there's no one I can call on to take Mrs Hall's place at this short notice,' said Jack Nickless apologetically. 'Do you think you will be able to manage on your own? I'll be able to bring all the supplies in, and if you need advice, I know Miss Mogford, the cook in Belgrave House, will willingly do all she can.'

Leonard was given a menu of meals planned for each week and provided with a book of recipes, and thus equipped, with some trepidation, he stepped up to the challenge.

The advantage of this promotion was that he now had the use of the only bedroom on the camp, a proper bed and mattress, and warm water facilities for washing. It seems there was leg pulling, probably out of jealousy from other helpers. One evening he came to bed and found the mattress missing. After searching, he discovered it hidden in the main hall. On another occasion, his alarm clock was reset to 3:00 a.m. The strange thing was that Leonard got so tired from his duties that he had begun to do certain things automatically, and getting up was one of them. On hearing the alarm, he had jumped out of bed and got his clothes on before it occurred to him that it was still very dark outside.

'Drat!' he exclaimed, looking at his clock. 'What wretch has been changing my alarm?'

Actually, they were a good group of leaders, and Leonard got on well with them, but they each had their own area of responsibility, and it was Leonard alone who was expected to have food ready for them when they needed it. Mr Nickless came in every day and talked with him about the menu for that day.

There was really only one disaster. The dessert for one evening meal was spotted dick pudding. The recipe book gave all the details and clearly read sixteen pounds of dried fruit. Having never made it before, Leonard never questioned this, and weighing out the amount stated – which was, in fact, the whole quantity in the pantry cupboard for the entire season – he mixed in the flour and other ingredients and put the mixture in the oven to cook. Alas, when it was time to dish it up and fifty-plus boys were waiting expectantly, the pudding looked exactly the same as it had before going into the oven – all soft and gooey. Leonard had no idea why it hadn't cooked, and after a discussion with the leader, it was decided to open some tins of peaches to have with the custard already prepared.

Jack Nickless very easily solved the mystery the next morning. Sixteen pounds of fruit is far, far too much, he said, but he agreed on looking at the book that this was indeed what was clearly stated. Of course, the fruit couldn't be wasted, so for several days, Leonard mixed the gooey mess with generous amounts of flour and sugar and baked it as cakes. The boys ate it all greedily around the campfire in the evenings. It became known as 'dog's body'!

Several other memories remain for Leonard from that first Climping Camp, one being that it was there, at an evening meeting, that he gave his first evangelistic public talk. It wouldn't have been called a sermon and wasn't intended to be, but it initiated Leonard in speaking publicly and gave him the exercise of prayerfully seeking from the Lord the right message to give to his hearers, in this case a room full of boys. Another memory is the chorus which staff and boys sang together before every meal:

Christ is the answer to my every need.
Christ is the answer; He is my friend indeed.
Problems of life, my spirit may assail.
With Christ, my Saviour, I need never fail,
For Christ is the answer to my need.

There were a few free hours each day, and on an occasional afternoon, Leonard walked into Littlehampton to see Phyllis. That summer was a significant time for her too, and the couple are still in touch with some of the friends she made at Belgrave House.

Both teenagers returned to Climping and Belgrave the following summer, and it was on one of these summer camps that

Leonard had a memorable prayer time, talking to the Lord whilst walking by himself one afternoon; it had a powerful effect on his life. His prayer involved a chorus they had been singing. He felt led, in deep sincerity, to make the words his plea to the Lord.

Spirit of the living God, fall afresh on me.
Spirit of the living God, fall afresh on me.
Melt me, mould me, fill me, use me.
Spirit of the living God, fall afresh on me.

If one is looking for an easy, comfortable life, it is rather dangerous to pray a prayer like this.

At the end of that summer season, Leonard stayed on one more night to help pack the tents and equipment away. The next morning was Sunday, and another helper who had also stayed over offered to run Leonard to the railway station to catch a train back to his nearest home station, Burseldon. At the last moment, the friend suggested it would be just as easy to take him all the way home. Leonard remembers the experience of riding pillion (before the legal requirement of a crash helmet) along an almost empty, Sunday morning A27 up to speeds of ninety miles per hour back to Lower Swanwick.

CHAPTER

11

Motor Bike and Three-Wheeler

When Leonard was 16, he acquired a motor bike. For those with an interest in such machines, it was a Royal Enfield 250cc, and he bought it for £10 from a schoolmate. He had to wheel it five miles home as it wouldn't start, but what can one expect for £10? It turned out that the previous owner had replaced the piston, and this had proved too much for the big end bearing. With no money to make it possible to take it to a garage, Leonard acquired a handbook, and working in his father's garden shed, he replaced the bearing. It served the young teenager well.

Phyllis's father refused permission for his daughter to travel on the back of the bike, so he had to wheel it when walking her home after 'Teenagers' on Monday evenings. Occasionally, they rebelled against this parental injunction. After all, they reasoned, it was only about half a mile, with so little traffic about. Leonard did, however, ensure he turned the engine off before gliding into the Pittwell family driveway.

The bike wasn't too reliable, and after a Saturday evening Christian rally in the village of North Boarhunt, Leonard has memories of pushing the heavy bike home in the rain, and that wasn't the only time. On another occasion, when he was coming back from a weekend visit with a friend to his sister, who was district nursing in South West London, the bike's clutch failed. They were south of Guildford on the Hog's Back, and clearly, this was too far to push the bike home. So not having membership of the AA or a similar organisation, what could Leonard do?

Motorbikes were more basic in those days, and having a good idea already of how the machine functioned through the work he had done on it, Leonard knew that the essential part of the clutch was a plate with corks set into it, and he suspected that the corks had worn down, causing the clutch to slip. Accordingly, he was able to dismantle the clutch and extract the faulty part needing replaced. He and the friend with him then committed the bike to God's care, pushed it behind a hedge out of sight from the road, and hitch-hiked home. Within a day or two, he was able to get replacement corks in the clutch plate and hitch-hike back to where he had left the bike. Thankfully, it was exactly where he had left it, and he could install the reconditioned part. Lo and behold, all was well, and he could ride home. That would have been about 1963, when there was far less traffic motoring across the Hog's Back.

There's one further incident to mention in regard to Leonard's Royal Enfield 250cc. He had applied to study medicine at Bristol University and was offered an interview. He decided, perhaps foolishly, to go on his bike. By that stage, he had not had much road experience with the bike, and sadly, this led to his downfall. He chose to take the route around Southampton through Swaythling; the road crossing the River Itchen involved, at that time, a tight U-bend over a very narrow bridge. Although not travelling fast, Leonard remained in too high a gear and consequently could not slow down quickly enough as he attempted to negotiate such a tight bend. The bike ran into the stone wall of the bridge; he came off and, at one stage, found himself hanging across the bridge with his face looking down at the water beneath him. There was thankfully no one else about, and he was not aware of being injured in any way. Also, the bike was not damaged, but the incident convinced him it was not the best plan to travel on by motorbike. Thankfully, he had allowed himself plenty of time. He therefore readjusted his thinking and rode into the Southampton railway station, where he was able to get a train to Bristol. It was not until he was sitting quietly on the train that he had time to assess the situation. He discovered that he had torn the trousers of his new suit, bought for his brother's wedding, being worn for the first time, and that his leg was bleeding rather badly. A visit to the toilet on the train, where there was a wash basin, enabled him to clean himself and tie his handkerchief around the cut on his leg under his trousers.

When he reached Bristol, Leonard was very conscious of the tear in his trouser leg and decided to try and buy a safety pin to pin up the triangular piece of trouser material that hung down. What would they think of him when he went into his interview? Finding a corner shop which looked hopeful, he explained his problem to a very sympathetic young lady. Although not selling the commodity he needed, she very kindly went out the back of shop, came back with a safety pin, and, I believe, helped to pin up his trouser tear. Bristol hadn't been his first choice of university anyway!

After his 17th birthday, Leonard was old enough to have a driving licence for a car, but whilst he was still at school, there was no way that was going to be possible. However, he had, by then, passed his test for a motorcycle licence and discovered that this also entitled him to drive a three-wheeler Reliant vehicle on the condition it didn't have a reverse gear. Somehow he heard that his uncle Bob in Feltham, London, had a Reliant he wanted to sell, and when £25 was agreed for the purchase, Leonard went up to Feltham to collect it.

The greatest problem was that Leonard had never driven a car in his life, although his motorcycle licence entitled him to drive this one. In addition to the driving complications, the car had a crash gearbox. His uncle showed him the essentials and accompanied him as he tried his skills around a few streets in Feltham, but he then had to drive it back to Lower Swanwick, a distance of more than sixty miles. Anne, a friend of his cousin, came back with him as a passenger. It was an eventful journey, but thankfully, there was far less traffic than nowadays. An initial hurdle for Leonard was to be confined *within* a vehicle and not to have the same freedom of vision there was on his motor bike. Then he needed to be able to judge the width of the vehicle to position himself rightly in relation to the kerb. Poor Anne's spine was jarred more than once when they hit the side of the road. Naturally, there was also the problem of gear change as sadly, Leonard never really learned the skill of changing down gears with the crash gearbox. He would sometimes have to glide around corners on the clutch and then stop and start off again in first gear.

One difficulty he remembers clearly on that journey was coming past Guildford on the A3 and wanting to turn right across oncoming traffic on to the Hog's Back road towards Farnham and Alton. Today you pull off left and cross the A3 by a bridge, but back then, one needed to stop on the hill to wait for a gap in the traffic and make a hill start to turn right. This was a real headache for Leonard. It took nearly a dozen attempts over about ten minutes before he managed it!

There were various interesting incidents and experiences with the Reliant. It had a plywood floor, and a previous owner, on replacing the exhaust system, had set it too high, so it touched the wooden floor at one point. As the exhaust pipe got hot, it scorched the wood, slowly burning a hole through it. Leonard's uncle kept a bottle of water under the driver's seat to pour on the floor when it began smoking. Thankfully, by the time Leonard possessed the vehicle, there was a big enough hole to avoid any more smoking problems.

The vehicle had a spare wheel but no jack. Leonard was out with Phyllis one afternoon when one of the back tyres deflated. The car swerved badly, but thankfully, Leonard controlled it and got it to the side of the road. He detached the spare wheel in readiness for replacing the punctured one and was just wondering how to do this without a jack when a motor cyclist kindly stopped and asked whether he could help.

'Yes, please,' said Leonard thankfully. 'Could you please hold the car up while I take the punctured wheel off and put the spare on?'

The fibreglass Renault was light enough for the helpful cyclist to do this, and soon, they were on their way again.

Because of its lack of power, Leonard decided the car needed new piston rings. He managed to replace the rings, but he had a real problem getting the timing right to get the best power from the vehicle.

Phyllis liked to tell people later with a smile, 'We were so slow going up Sarisbury Hill that people walking overtook us! Also, when following a bus, Leonard didn't dare overtake when it stopped at a bus stop, so we would wait behind it until it set off again. Going around corners was also interesting. If he needed to slow down, he had to do this on the clutch and brake. Then the only way my boyfriend driver could accelerate off again, because of his helplessness with the crash gearbox, was to stop completely to get into a low gear.'

With Leonard having no money to take it to a garage, the Reliant proved itself to be a teenage adventure but thankfully, with God's protection, never involved Leonard and his girlfriend in an accident.

Incidentally, when Leonard eventually took driving lessons to get his car licence, one of his driving instructor's first comments when he witnessed how Leonard used the foot pedals was 'What have you been driving? A tank?'

Just an aside for anyone paying for driving lessons today – in 1966, Leonard got his driving lessons at a special offer of £10 for ten lessons!

Memories from Others

Norman

Len and I met when Len's father bought my grandfather's house in Lower Swanwick and the family started coming to the Strict Baptist chapel where I went. As we were the only two families with teenagers in the chapel, we soon got to know each other.

All the boys were at the bottom of the hill in the Baptist church, and the girls were in the Brethren church at the top of the hill, so as boys will be boys, we climbed the hill and won the hearts of the girls.

Two things stick in my mind. First was the boat we built that had a small leak the first trip out, and we put chewing gum in the hole. We went out fishing in that boat many times but never caught any fish. I think the boat was finally stolen from its mooring. The other item was the motor bike, which gave fun and heartache, especially when it broke down and was pushed home a distance of four miles. I remember Len going for an interview but, going too fast, hit the parapet of a bridge. Thankfully, he survived apart from torn trousers and an odd cut and bruise. I'm not sure how the interview went!

CHAPTER

12

Illness

The two years 1963 and 1964 were very difficult years in the Pittwell household. For most of Phyllis's early life, the home had been stressful, and the reason for this is very understandable. The home belonged to Phyllis's maternal grandmother. The grandparents had been market gardeners with a good number of

Marriage of Phyllis's grandparents
Mina May and Thomas Biddle
April 1908

acres of strawberries until in 1943, her grandfather, Thomas Biddle died from TB, aged 62. Phyllis's mother, Mina May Biddle, as the only child, had been given a good education and had become a primary school teacher. At the time of her father's tragic death, she was still living at home and was engaged to be married to Francis Ronald Pittwell. Shortly before his death, Thomas had spoken with his son-in-law-to-be.

'Ron,' he said in a very serious tone, 'we all know I haven't long to live. I'm not afraid to die as I know the Lord Jesus has died for me and is preparing a place for me in glory, but I'm concerned about leaving the two people I love most. You are engaged to marry my daughter. Can I please request of you that you marry her as soon as possible and care for both her and my beloved wife?'

Phyllis's parents' wedding
Ron Pittwell and May Biddle
27 December 1943

Thus, on his marriage, Ron Pittwell entered his wife's home, which was being run by his mother-in-law, Mina Mabel. Mina had a strong personality and would have found it very difficult to take a back seat in the home. Ron had an equally strong personality and, by nature, was a proud man, lacking somewhat in patience. He took over management of the household finances but found the situation of a new wife and mother-in-law difficult to cope with. For May, of course, it was constantly a dilemma as to whose side she should take when clashes occurred. What made the matter worse was the fact that legally at that time, Mina May, now as a married woman, could no longer be a primary school teacher. She had little domestic experience or skills and was happy for her mother to continue doing all the cooking and household duties. Phyllis remembers that it was her grandmother who effectively brought her up when a young girl, not her mother. One can imagine the pleasure the little granddaughter gave Mina, who was still mourning the loss of her beloved husband. Under these circumstances, it is not surprising that in her early days, Phyllis's view of her father was that he was the one who often made her beloved grandmother cry. It was only in later years that she realised how equally difficult the situation must have been for her father.

It must be added that Phyllis loved both of her parents dearly, and Ron Pittwell was greatly respected, both in Duncan Road

Assembly, where he was an elder and, for many years, the Sunday school superintendent, and in the community, where many local small businesses found him to be a highly competent and trustworthy accountant.

In June 1962, Mina Mabel Clara Biddle died aged 81. She had had a heart condition for some years. For Phyllis, then in her 16th year and studying for her O-level examinations, her grandmother's death was traumatic. She had loved her dearly. For some weeks, she would cycle regularly to the grave in the Sarisbury churchyard and talk to her grandma. Eventually, the Lord revealed to her that her beloved grandma was, in fact, now in heaven and not in the ground, and the visits to the graveyard stopped abruptly.

Phyllis's gran
Mina Mabel Clara Biddle
1881–1962

Phyllis's mother developed severe depression after the death of her mother, and this affected the whole family. Ron was under pressure on several fronts. The ever-increasing volume of traffic on the A27 into Southampton meant that often the daily journey in both directions was a crawl in nose-to-tail traffic. Such a stressful commute, together with the attempt to have patience with a depressed wife when he was home, finally led to a nervous breakdown. In 1964, it became necessary for him to have some time right away from the whole complicated situation. The doctors decided that his wife should go into a psychiatric hospital for a while, and Phyllis, who was also suffering from depression and anxiety, was sent to spend time in Belgrave House convalescing. With the whole family split up, Ron's parents came to look after the house and to care for Phyllis's younger sister, for whom this must also have been a very stressful time.

Leonard tried to support Phyllis as much as he could during this period. It tested their relationship and brought them closer together. The following year, Phyllis developed severe mucus colitis and spent a couple of weeks in hospital. Leonard remembers walking up and down his garden, pleading with the Lord for her healing.

With the circumstances at home and the condition of Phyllis's own health, which was clearly brought on by home pressures, there was no way for her to immediately pursue further education. When her health had improved sufficiently, she was able to get a job in a dentist surgery as a receptionist. This, however, was suddenly brought to an abrupt end when her mother took a turn for the worse. Her father decided, without ever discussing it with his daughter, to terminate her employment so that she could care for her mother and give her company at home. This action by her father typified much of Phyllis's upbringing. There seemed to be no discussion about anything or any attempt to understand Phyllis's point of view. Her mother bought her clothes for her and gave her no real choice in this regard, and her father made his own decisions unilaterally about most other things that affected her.

It should, of course, be said that Ron had been brought up in the days when etiquette considered the husband very much head of the household, and he sincerely believed that he was doing his best for his wife and family.

Interestingly, there was no opposition in regard to Phyllis's friendship with Leonard. He was welcomed into the home as her boyfriend, and it was expected that he would join her on any family and church outings. When Leonard requested permission for them to become engaged at Christmas 1965, this was granted on the condition that they would not plan to marry for at least a year.

Phyllis's mother made an interesting comment a few years later when she said, 'I don't know what would have happened to you, Phyllis, if Len hadn't married you.'

CHAPTER

13

A Change of Direction

A major decision for all the boys at Price's Grammar School as they progressed towards the sixth form was whether they wanted to concentrate on science or the art subjects. Leonard was drawn more towards science. Latin was a compulsory subject for the first two years, but the then well-known schoolboy rhyme was often quoted:

Latin is a language as dead as dead could be.
It killed the ancient Romans, and now it's killing me.

Having had great sympathy with that concept, Leonard now realises he learned more about the structure of language through his Latin lessons than he ever did through English.

The main foreign language taught was French. Leonard struggled with French. He had never had the opportunity to visit the continent of Europe and so didn't see the subject as something living. He learned it in a scientific way and found it extremely difficult to get his mouth around the sounds when forced to speak it. However, at that time, entry to any university required at least one foreign language pass at O-level, so Leonard persevered. After failing it once, he then took it again twice a year in the sixth form and passed on the fifth attempt!

Being drawn to biology and with his interest in people and their needs, Leonard decided he would like to study medicine. Accordingly, he opted to take biology, chemistry, and physics at A-level, which he enjoyed. Physics was the most difficult for him. Many students taking physics also study mathematics, giving them an advantage in tackling many aspects of this subject.

Leonard applied to study medicine at three universities: Bristol, Newcastle, and one of the London hospitals. There was the disastrous trip to Bristol, but his journey up to Newcastle also had its points of interest. He went by coach overnight and remembers that the young lady in the seat beside him went to sleep with her head on his shoulder. Coming home, they went through fog so thick that the second driver got out of the coach and walked in front of the vehicle to lead the way and ensure the road was clear. Having never been farther north than Oxfordshire and Shropshire, for Leonard, it was a new experience to wander around the northern city of Newcastle by foot in the early morning, biding time before his appointment at the university.

There was obviously a keen demand for university places to study medicine, and very high grades in A-level exams were required. Newcastle said there would be no problem offering him a place to study dentistry, and then when his A-level grades didn't give him access into a medical course, Manchester University offered him the chance of studying chemistry.

Leonard decided to persevere with his wish to be a doctor and went back to the sixth form for an additional year, aiming to retake the exams with the hope of improving his grades.

During that final year at school, Leonard's priorities were slowly changing. He had his 19th birthday during that year and was experiencing a closeness to the Lord Jesus. Some of the moments when he experienced the closest fellowship with his Lord was while walking home at night after spending time with his girlfriend. It seemed that finding human love drew his heart out towards the God of love in a new way.

Leonard was praying regularly at the weekly prayer meetings at the chapel. The practice at these meetings was for the deacon who chaired the meeting to call on specific members to pray.

This gave Leonard no choice, and it had the advantage of forcing him to speak publicly, which he might not otherwise have done. He remembers that often he would begin his prayers by asking for God's help and would often then find his heart pouring out its praise and thankfulness, which he attributed to the Holy Spirit inspiring him. Emerging from these experiences was the conviction that God wanted him to devote his life to serve the spiritual lives of people rather than simply their physical needs. Hence, when his second sitting of A-levels still didn't give him access into a medical school, he was not at all disappointed but rather saw this as God's guidance for his life.

Leonard's assumption was that the next step should be Bible College, but realising it was rather too late to begin to apply at that point in late August, he decided he would have a gap year.

He had no plan as to what he would do, but God did.

One Sunday that summer, Pastor David Ellis of Providence Chapel, Horley, came to preach at the chapel. During a conversation over tea in the Holders' home, Edgar asked him how things were going in his church. David Ellis was very happy to talk about his work and responded to this question with a smile.

'We are very encouraged with the way God is bringing children and youngsters to us,' he said. 'We have an afternoon Sunday school which is growing fast and have recently started a youth club on a Friday evening. We do crafts with the youngsters and then give them a Bible talk. In the main, it's simply myself and my wife, Eunice, running things, although we do have a young lady, a member of the church, who is also a great help. Ideally, we would love to have an enthusiastic young man to work with us in this.'

Leonard's not sure whether David Ellis actually looked across the table at him or not as he said this, but he sensed this was a call from God.

PART 3

HORLEY
1965–1976

You did not choose Me, but I chose you and appointed you that you should go and bear fruit and that your fruit should remain.
— John 15:16

CHAPTER

1

—

Early Days in Horley

Before that summer of 1965 was over, Leonard was established in Horley. The chapel funds didn't allow him to be paid for the help he had come to give with the work amongst the young people, but David and Eunice Ellis were both appreciative and generous, providing him with lodgings in their own home. They had four children in a three-bedroom house, so initially, Leonard had a bed in the living room. Eunice had also kept an eye on job adverts in the local papers and had found him work with the National Sunday School Union, a short distance from Horley in Nutfield. This enabled Leonard to pay for his accommodation and food and gave him some independence. He also enjoyed the ride to Nutfield each day through country lanes on his motor bike.

God was blessing the ministry of David Ellis at Horley. He and his wife related well to the young people who came to their youth club in the hall behind the chapel, and any who wanted to spend more time with them were welcomed into their home.

Leonard helped in the Friday club and also started a Sunday afternoon Bible class for teenagers who were too old for the Sunday school. He remembers one Sunday afternoon vividly. A notorious lad from one of the council estate areas of the town came into the class wearing a studded leather jacket, blue jeans, and ankle-length heavy leather boots. Roy continued to come to Bible class regularly. Also, experiencing a warm, caring welcome in the Ellises' home, he was soon attending the chapel services. Within a short while, he came to faith in Christ, eventually married a girl from a neighbouring chapel, and later became a deacon in a chapel in Kent. God was working.

In the summer of 1966, Leonard decided it would be beneficial to attend the Keswick convention meetings in the Lake District. This was quite an adventure. After discussion, he was able to recruit three other lads to join him: his brother Frank; Ray, who was the eldest Ellis boy, and Roy from his Bible class. They hitch-hiked north, taking sleeping bags and two tents. David Ellis had a friend who was a leading member of Wycliffe Hall, Sheffield, and he arranged for them to spend the weekend there, sleeping in the chapel hall. They got up to Sheffield in one day, but the next stage of the journey was slower. As darkness had fallen before they reached Keswick, they pitched one of their tents in a field just off the road.

Leonard remembers two incidents from that night. First, to give themselves a hot drink, they had scooped water from a stream, boiled it on their small camping gas stove, and made mugs of coffee. They had no torch with them to see what they were doing, and in the light of morning, they realised there was a very significant layer of silt from the stream at the bottom of the saucepan.

'It's a good job we boiled the water before making the coffee,' said Leonard, looking at the dirty silt. 'I guess that explains the interesting flavour. Was it you, Frank, that said it was particularly good coffee?'

The other thing Leonard remembers from that night was lying in close quarters, four in a two-man tent, and hearing in the quietness of the night a shuffling sound as someone or something moved around their night shelter. He remembers lying very still, expecting to be woken up at any moment by an enraged landowner. Nothing happened, and later, he rather assumed it could have been a hedgehog.

God was very kind to them that summer at Keswick. The weather was dry and sunny; they had a secure camping spot in a recognised site and could walk easily down to the big tent in which the meetings were held.

The memory and blessing of that Keswick holiday must have remained with at least one member of that foursome as about forty years later, on answering the phone, Leonard heard a voice he didn't recognise. On him asking who it was, the retort came back.

'Think of a holiday in Keswick in 1966!'

'Roy! How are you doing?' answered Leonard excitedly.

For some years, Leonard had only heard about Roy indirectly. His wife had sadly died of cancer, and he had moved up to Scotland to be near his married son.

Before that Keswick holiday, there had been another significant development in Leonard's life. Living at Reigate near Horley was the chairman of the committee running the TBS. Hearing that Leonard was packing books at the National Sunday School Union, he approached him through Mr Ellis, suggesting the possibility of him transferring his energies and talents to the work of the TBS. He indicated that although the employment would start in the packing room, the general secretary was looking for someone to train up on the publishing side of the work. The TBS published Bibles, New Testaments, and portions of Scripture in different languages and shipped them all over the world. Leonard was attracted to this, and after an interview with Mr Terence Brown, the general secretary, he found himself catching a train each morning up to London Bridge at about seven thirty and walking across Central London to Bury Place, Holborn.

CHAPTER

✸✸✸

2

A Call to Preach

Those early months in Horley were bringing many new experiences into Leonard's life. In a short period, so much seemed to happen. It was a time of spiritual blessing as Leonard was devouring good Christian books and being challenged into an increasing commitment to Jesus Christ. He believes, thinking back now, it was a book by Alan Redpath on studies in Joshua which was one of the means God used to draw him into a closer dependence on Him and take a major step of faith.

The call to preach and share the Gospel, which had become so precious to him, began to become a repeating theme on his mind and in his heart. Day after day, his Bible readings all seemed to be urging him in this direction. God's message, as he read it in the Book of Joshua, made it so clear that obedience brings blessing and disobedience disaster. Leonard wanted to please God because he sincerely believed that God's way for his life was the best way. Some modern versions of the Bible translate 'blessing' as 'happiness', and Leonard understood that the happiness that God gives is a deep inner joy and peace which, in an amazing way, is not dependent on the circumstances of life. The hymn verse that challenged him to be baptised continued to speak to him:

But you never can prove
the delights of His love
until all on the altar you lay.
For the favour He shows
and the joy He bestows
are for those who will
trust and obey.

He now felt convicted that the trust and obedience God was demanding of him was that he should make himself available to preach the Gospel – but how could he? He felt himself bringing the same excuses that Moses and Jeremiah did centuries earlier.

Moses's response to God's call had been 'Who am I that I should go?'[16] and Jeremiah had said, 'Ah, Lord God! Behold, I cannot speak: for I am a youth.'[17]

The answers God gave to these His servants of old were both comforting and challenging. 'Do not say, "I am a youth," for you shall go to all to whom I send you, and whatever I command you, you shall speak. Do not be afraid of their faces, for I am with you to deliver you,'[18] said the Lord to Jeremiah. To Moses, He said, 'I will certainly be with you.'[19]

Despite all the promises of God in the Scriptures, Leonard still hesitated to talk to Pastor Ellis about what he was increasingly sensing was God's call. Within the denomination he was part of, the requirement for their ministers was a personal call from God, which then had to be recognised by the man's home church, through what his fellow church members knew of his character and the natural and spiritual gifts he exercised amongst them. Any formal theological training was considered to be of less importance.

Without doubting God's power through the Holy Spirit to help him, Leonard struggled with the fear that it was all in his imagination. One evening, on reading his Bible, he felt such a blessing and the reassurance that truly, this was God calling him,

---

16 Exodus 3:11.

17 Jeremiah 1:6.

18 Jeremiah 1:6–7.

19 Exodus 3:12.

that he felt prepared to approach his pastor. Then came the fear: *Tomorrow morning this blessing will be forgotten, and I'll be back with my old doubts.*

This compelled him to pray, 'Lord, please give me something tangible to hold on to that will still be there tomorrow.'

He looked at the text calendar on the wall beside his bed and pulled off the sheet to reveal tomorrow's text. The verse he read was from Acts 18:9–10. 'Do not be afraid, but speak, and do not keep silent, for I am with you.'

'Oh! Thank you, Lord Jesus,' Leonard cried, tears in his eyes. 'What more do I need? That text will be in front of my eyes again when I wake in the morning. If I doubt further, I'd be a coward and a rebel, defying my Master's instructions.'

Pastor David Ellis's first reaction was to advise Leonard not to be hasty and to look for further confirmation from God. Leonard continued to sense God urging him forward, and eventually, his pastor agreed to talk to the church members about the matter. A date was arranged for Leonard to preach before a congregation of just the church members. What followed was a unanimous agreement that Providence Chapel, Horley, would make it known that they could recommend Leonard as an acceptable preacher of the Gospel.[20]

With close connections to Providence Chapel, Horley, was a small chapel in the neighbouring village of Charlwood.[21] The chapel building itself was an unusual wooden construction dating back several centuries. There

Providence Chapel, Charlwood, Surrey

---

20 In the author's first book, *Selina of Sussex 1818–1886*, the sermon outline attributed to Eli Page, when he preached before the church at the Dicker, is, in fact, the outline of the sermon Leonard preached before the church members at Horley in 1966!

21 Charlwood Chapel has been renovated in recent years. See https://www.providencechapelcharlwood.org.

was strong evidence for the claim that the wood for the structure had come from an old stable for Oliver Cromwell's army's horses.

The main village store in Charlwood was run by the Eade family. Mr Eade was one of the deacons of Horley Chapel, but he and his wife and daughters were also committed to ensuring that services continued at their village chapel. Accordingly, it's not surprising that Leonard's first public preaching engagement was at the invitation of Mr Roy Eade at Charlwood Chapel. It was due to take place very shortly after his return from the Keswick convention, and Leonard remembers sitting at the front of his tent, perhaps not unlike Abraham, preparing his sermon. The text he felt drawn to was from Proverbs 29:25: 'The fear of man brings a snare, but whoever trusts in the LORD shall be safe.' Leonard has no memory now of how he dealt with this text, but it would seem to have been as much for his own comfort as for his congregation's.

Very soon, Strict Baptist chapels in the area around were inviting Leonard to preach for them, and within a year, he found that unless he deliberately kept Sundays free, he would have been engaged to preach every Sunday the whole year through. He was working at the TBS at the same time and, during the working week, would be praying and searching his Bible for the text God wanted him to preach from the following Sunday. By meditating on this text, reading commentaries, and seeking to get the message of the text as a burden on his soul, he could, with brief notes, preach it from his heart. He got into the habit of getting into the TBS office early enough to give himself a good thirty minutes a day to begin a course of study on New Testament Greek supplied by the London Bible College. Life was busy but very satisfying.

CHAPTER

3

Engagement

When Leonard left home in September 1965, Phyllis was caring for her mother at home, her father having taken her out of her employment with a local dentist. Leonard had committed himself to her as her boyfriend and would ride down to see her on a Saturday, at least once a month. They also wrote regularly to each other and occasionally spoke on the phone, but obviously, these were days before mobile networks or computers.

Mrs Eunice Ellis took a real interest in Leonard's romantic attachment, and he felt able to talk to her about his concern for Phyllis. Clearly, to care for her mother was something highly commendable, but Leonard's fear was that she would become indispensable to her parents in the family home.

'Look, Leonard,' said Mrs Ellis thoughtfully, 'if you are fully convinced of your love for Phyllis and that you want to spend the rest of your life with her, why not tell her this and propose an engagement? If her father agrees to this, it will put you both in a far better position to suggest a change in the way things are. Maybe Phyllis could get a job up here. We could find lodgings for her, and you could make plans to get married.'

Leonard liked the suggestion. He thought and prayed about it for several days. Then finding an inner peace, it appealed to him even more, and he decided it was right to go ahead.

With the advantage of greater maturity and a better understanding of the opposite sex, perhaps Leonard would have gone about things differently. He was not a reader of romantic novels, and only sometime later did he realise that a decision to become engaged with a view to marriage is totally different from a decision in business, and girls love a romantic proposal.

Having decided the matter in his own mind and taking for granted that their courtship was leading in this direction anyway, he felt it enough to chat with Phyllis on the phone, tell her the way he was thinking, and then write to her father. The first slip in carrying out this plan was when he picked up the phone to ring his beloved but couldn't remember her number. This was completely ridiculous because he knew it by heart, using it regularly. Perhaps it was the excitement of what he was doing and a subconscious awareness of the enormity of the step he was taking that robbed him of his memory at that moment. In any case, he had no note of the number, and since his brain refused to cooperate, he couldn't speak to her. He decided to write the letter to her father anyway, not for one moment imagining that Phyllis would be anything other than delighted with this development.

He believes now that he was able to talk to Phyllis before her father got the letter and that at the time, she *was* delighted at the prospect of starting a whole new way of life, and he hoped also of being engaged to him, but later in their marriage, this matter kept cropping up.

'You know,' Phyllis would say with a sigh, 'Len never proposed to me. He assumed I would want to marry him.'

Soon after this, Leonard rode down to Swanwick again for a Saturday on his motorbike and had an interview with Mr P, as the young people of the assembly would call him. He agreed to an engagement on the understanding, he said, that they didn't think about marriage for at least twelve months. The couple went out together to search for a suitable engagement ring. Phyllis chose one with a small central diamond and a small red ruby on each side of it, and Leonard emptied his post office account to pay for it. He believes it cost £15. They made the announcement of their engagement that Christmas, and Leonard had wrapped up the ring and put it with other presents under the Christmas tree. It was Christmas 1965, and they were both 19 years old.

During the following year, Phyllis's parents agreed for her to move up to Horley. A young couple who had begun to come regularly to the chapel had a spare bedroom which they kindly offered to her, and as Pastor David Ellis was looking for additional help in the office of the Sovereign Grace Union (SGU) at Redhill, where he was the general secretary, he was able to provide her employment. The health of May Pittwell had, by then, already improved, and although Phyllis had some concern as to how leaving home would affect her mother, she continued to improve. She didn't actually voice it, but the couple sensed that May Pittwell was actually pleased and relieved that her daughter could now begin to have a life of her own.

Memories from Others

Rita

You and I go a long way back, Phyl. One thing I can remember as very young girls were those church outings to the seaside and your and my knitted swimsuits. I hated mine because it was a horrible yellow colour, and it also stretched when it got wet!

I always remember calling for Phyl on Sunday mornings to go to early morning Sunday school. Phyl was never ready when I called, and I was always ushered into 'Grandma's room' by Mrs Pittwell to play the piano because she liked to hear how I was progressing. Once a month on a Sunday morning, Mr Pittwell and family went to Bishops Waltham Gospel Hall to help Mr Madgewick. I always went with them for some reason but enjoyed these outings, which have stayed in my memory. Phyl, Valerie, and I would often sing at various meetings.

During our mid-teens, Duncan Road Gospel Hall was invaded by boys from Lower Swanwick Strict Baptist Chapel. Need I mention who these lads were? After a while, Phyl paired up with Len and I with Norman.

One Christmas, I remember sitting in the morning meeting and noticed Phyl had kept her gloves on. I had also kept my gloves on. We both looked at each other and burst out laughing. Yes, you've guessed it – we had both got engaged and had kept it a secret from each other! We both married the same year, and although Len and Phyl moved away, I have felt a closeness with Phyl and always kept in touch. I have valued your friendship over the years, Phyl. We had many good times together.

CHAPTER

❧❧❧

4

—

Wedding Plans

Somehow, when one was young, each year seemed much longer with many more significant developments than in the later stages of life. The year 1966 was such for Leonard.

At the end of the previous year, he had become engaged to marry Phyllis. Then in January, he began a daily commute from Horley to Central London for his new employment with the TBS. During the spring months, he had felt God's call to preach and, by July, had been approved by Providence Chapel to begin an itinerant ministry. Also, by early summer, his parents had bought a house in Balcombe Road, Horley, and moved up there to enable his father to start a new job in Crawley. This meant Leonard could move in with his parents and younger brother once again, thus relieving the pressure of bedroom space in the Ellises' home. It had been a good time there, and he had appreciated their kindness and the welcome he had experienced within the family.

He tried to see Phyllis as much as possible, but that summer, because of his growing commitments, he was unable to accompany her down to Littlehampton, where she went for the third and final year to Belgrave House as a dormitory leader. Friendships made at Belgrave have stood the test of time, and after more than fifty years, there continues to be meaningful contact with a number of girls Phyllis first met there in the early 1960s.

After the time in Littlehampton, Phyllis had moved up to Horley, and thus, another phase of life started for her. This was a time of blossoming into a more independent young adult, away from the constraints of living with her parents, and she thrived. She and Leonard could spend several evenings together each week, and they were both involved in the youth club at the chapel. Her work at the SGU brought her into a rather different doctrinal environment from the Brethren way of thinking in which she had been brought up. She worked closely at the SGU with another lady, Valerie, from Horley Chapel, and they had many hours of discussion over reformed doctrine and the five points of Calvinism promoted by the union before Phyllis was convinced that this was biblical truth.

By the end of the year, the couple were thinking and talking about a wedding. After a discussion with Phyllis's parents, they settled on 14 October 1967 and began to think, pray, and search for somewhere to live. They were still young and had no capital to put down on the purchase of a house, and also, Leonard's wages from the TBS were extremely basic. Initially, there was no great urgency, and they took comfort from their faith in their heavenly Father's promises to care and provide for those who trust Him. Phyllis's parents had a couple of small semi-detached houses in the locality of their home in Hampshire which had been in the family since Phyllis's grandfather's time. One of these had been promised to Phyllis, but it was small and with no inside bathroom; in any case, it would not be available until the sitting tenant chose to move out or died.

The couple looked at various possibilities, including a mobile home, but everything was out of their reach financially. Then suddenly, when all their own efforts seemed hopeless, God stepped in. Leonard had begun to become quite well-known amongst the Strict Baptist congregations around Sussex through his preaching, and one evening his parents answered a phone call for him from a Christian lady in Brighton.

'It was Mrs Payne,' his father reported to him happily. 'She's the wife of James Payne, the pastor of Ebenezer Chapel, Brighton. She owns a small three-bedroomed house in Queens Road here in Horley, which belonged to an aunt of hers. Anyway, she says an old lady who has been renting it has recently died. It's, at present, empty, being redecorated, and she's offering it to you.'

7 Queens Road, Horley
(in more recent years)

'Wow! That's amazing,' said Leonard. 'But what does she want for it? Can we afford it?'

'I think you should be able to pay for it without difficulty,' said Edgar. 'I asked her for some details, and she mentioned a rent of £5 a week.'

'A three-bedroomed house for £5 a week! That's amazing!'

'There is one difficulty,' continued Edgar. 'She says if you are interested, she would need you to start paying the rent as soon as possible and certainly by 1 May.'

There was no doubt to the couple that this was God's wonderful provision and a tangible confirmation of His blessing on their marriage and future life together.

'Do you think we should get married a little sooner?' suggested Leonard the next day as he talked to Phyllis about this wonderful offer. 'It'll be silly to pay rent for the house for weeks and weeks without living there. Although we shall need to furnish and equip the place to make it comfortable.'

'Dad's offered to pay for the wedding,' answered Phyllis, 'so we shall need to talk about another date with him.'

Leonard reported back to Mrs Payne, and they arranged a time to be shown over the house. It was a semi-detached dwelling with a small front garden. A path down the side of the house was shared by the neighbour, and a back gate opened onto a very narrow backyard, giving access to the back door of the house opening into a reasonable-sized kitchen. Downstairs were two further small living rooms, and out from the back of the kitchen, a bathroom had been added, leading into a small separate toilet. Upstairs were two good-sized bedrooms and a third which Leonard imagined he could use as a study. There was also a long narrow back garden.

'This will suit us just fine,' whispered Phyllis to her fiancé as Mrs Payne finished showing them around.

They agreed there and then to accept the house and to begin paying rent from 1 May, which was about four weeks off.

Opportunities for a new date for the wedding were limited by Leonard's preaching engagements and also those of his prospective father-in-law. Leonard felt able to free up the first Sunday in June, and since this weekend also suited Phyllis's father, they settled on Saturday, 3 June.

Later, when Phyllis thought back to the way her early life had been dictated to her, she would comment somewhat rebelliously, 'Even my wedding day was determined by the preaching engagements of my men-folk.'

However, at the time, they were both thrilled to have not only a house to move into but also now a firm wedding date in the not-too-distant future.

Another factor was the wedding venue. Duncan Road Assembly was in the process of constructing a substantial new brick building to replace the tin-covered structure built in the war years when the assembly was founded. Interestingly, Phyllis's grandfather had been one of the founding elders of the assembly, and this added weight to her wish to be married in that venue. There seemed every reason to believe the new building would be ready by 3 June, but one of Phyllis's close friends had also planned to be married there in March. This had not proved possible, and the disappointment of this had rankled somewhat with the bride's parents.

It was accepted practice at that time for the bride's father to pay the wedding expenses, and with far less elaborate occasions than couples often expect today, these costs were more manageable. Phyllis's father arranged for the reception to be held in a local village hall, with caterers supplying a sit-down meal for about fifty guests.

The couple had invited Pastor David Ellis to marry them, but when he declined for health reasons, they asked Mr Jack Nickless of Belgrave House, Littlehampton, to take the ceremony, which he was delighted to do.

CHAPTER

5

—

The Passing of Ebenezer Dan

Although it was not until many years later that Leonard explored his Christian heritage and came to appreciate the place that Eli and Selina Page played in this, in 1967, the direct living link he had with this past was taken away.

As readers of Leonard's earlier books will know, his grandfather, Ebenezer Dan Holder, was the grandson of Eli and Selina and the son of their eldest daughter, Ruth. He was born in 1877 and, from his home in Patcham, would have spent many happy hours at Perching Manor Farm, Edburton, before his grandmother Selina was called home to glory in 1886 and his grandfather Eli in 1896.

Ebenezer Dan Holder
Leonard's grandfather
1877–1967

As a child in Brighton, Leonard had spent many happy hours in his grandparents' home in Highdown Road, Hove. Rarely had a week gone by without a visit, either for afternoon tea on a Thursday or for Sunday lunch, often both.

Hanging on the wall in his grandparents' living room was the same portrait of Eli Page that still hangs in the vestry in Mayfield Chapel, where he was pastor. It was clear that grandfather Ebenezer had a great respect for his grandfather Eli.

Ebenezer Dan died on 13 February 1967, about six weeks before his 90th birthday. It would appear that the final factor resulting in his death was kidney failure. His body was sufficiently embalmed for it to lie at home in his own bedroom until the funeral, and friends and family were able to come and pay their last respects. For Leonard, it was the first time he had seen a dead human body. He later said he would not have missed this experience. The body was the grandfather he had known, but it was clear Grandfather himself was no longer there. The body was lifeless. Although this is an obvious thing to say, the sight of his grandfather's body came back to him vividly when, shortly afterwards, he read in the book of James, 'For as the body without the spirit is dead, so faith without works is dead also.'[22]

We can see a spiritual lesson here. However much a person may talk about having received Christ and of having faith, if the life of the Spirit is not being lived out through that person, they are as dead as Leonard's grandfather's corpse. The life or fruit of the Spirit is described as 'love, joy, peace, longsuffering, kindness, goodness, faithfulness, gentleness, self-control'.[23]

Ebenezer Dan had demonstrated through his life that God's Spirit lived within him. Many have spoken of his kind, generous nature. Leonard remembers one Sunday lunchtime when his grandfather had not returned home from the chapel service at the usual time. Dinner had begun without him, and the family was worried. When he did return, he confessed he had gone home with a man who had begged him for money. To give more than simply a coin out of his pocket and perhaps also to verify the man's story, he had called to visit and encourage the man's sick wife.

Another instance of his kindness and goodness came a few years after his death. Leonard had given up paid employment for a year

---

22 James 2:26.
23 Galatians 5:22–23.

of theological study, trusting God for his family's financial support. One morning an envelope appeared through the letterbox of 7 Queens Road, Horley, containing a cheque for £50.

The sender was unknown to Leonard, but the enclosed note stated, 'Your grandfather was so generous to me, and I wanted to repay something of this to his grandson.'

It appears, however, that Eb lived much of his life without any clear assurance of his salvation. As has already been said, Galeed Chapel, which he attended regularly, preached a searching, self-examining Gospel message, which directed the hearers to look more within themselves for signs of the new birth, with less emphasis on the need to look away from themselves to Christ. Although this may have robbed Eb of a joyful Christian life, we can praise God that in his dying moments, Jesus Christ must have clearly revealed Himself to him. Those with him at the time could testify that he died with a smile and with a final cry: 'Victory!'

In the author's account of Ruth Holder's life, she is seen to have had a prayerful hope that her son Ebenezer would be the means of honouring her beloved Saviour in the world and extending His kingdom. The role that Ebenezer himself played in promoting the kingdom of God was quiet and self-effacing; indeed, it is only in recent years that this has become more widely known.

Leonard had been aware that his grandfather had been proficient at writing shorthand, a skill required for secretarial work in the last century, but he has only very recently known of the extent his grandfather used this for God's kingdom. The present pastor of Galeed Chapel, Brighton, Matthew Hyde, has informed Leonard that the chapel has three trunks full of notebooks containing about 1,200 sermons by James C. Popham, pastor of Galeed (1883–1937), all taken down in shorthand by his grandfather Ebenezer. A member of the church has been transcribing these over the years, and an eleventh final volume of these sermons is shortly to be published. This will include a photo of Grandfather Ebenezer Dan Holder with an acknowledgement of the debt owed to him for sitting in his pew in Galeed Chapel with his notebook and pencil, recording these sermons as they were preached over many years.

Ebenezer had six grandchildren, and each were to serve God in different ways. The two granddaughters each had Christian husbands and witnessed both in their daily lives and within evangelical churches. Each of his four grandsons served God for a part of their lives in Britain and then also in other countries. There are many things that the present author has no knowledge of, but

Ebenezer and Gertie Holder
with their first grandchildren

grandson David spent the latter part of his life in Cyprus, where he was a member of the Anglican Church, playing the church organ.

John Holder
Ebenezer's oldest grandson
with his two sons

His eldest grandson, John, spent most of his working life in Shepperton, Australia, where he ran a nursery and garden centre. For some years, he was a member of the Full Gospel Business Men's Fellowship International. He once told his brother an incident when he had a number of Muslim customers coming into his shop. Wanting to be a Christian witness, he found the way of printing the Bible verse John 3:16 in Arabic, which he hung up in the shop: 'God so loved the world that He gave His only begotten Son, that whoever believes in Him should not perish but have everlasting life.'

John's next comment was extremely interesting.

'I was prepared for them to be offended,' he said, 'and hoped for the opportunity to explain the meaning of the verse, but the opposite happened. Seeing the text in Arabic, several of the Muslim men came up to me, smiling, shook me by the hand, and called me brother. I finally realised what this was all about. Seeing an obvious religious text in Arabic, they assumed it came from the Koran and that I had become a Muslim. I decided it was wisest to take the text down.'

His youngest grandson, Frank, also moved out to Australia and had an insurance brokers' business in Melbourne. He became a member of the Presbyterian Church, serving on the denomination's finance committee. For some years, he and his family worshipped in a small Presbyterian church at Kangaroo Ground.

His widow once said, 'Some Sundays, Frank did nearly everything in the service, including announcing the hymns and then moving across to the organ to lead the singing.' She then added with a smile, 'I had to put my foot down to stop him offering to preach as well!'

You are, of course, now reading the story of his third grandson, Leonard, in far greater detail!

Frank Holder
Ebenezer's youngest grandson

CHAPTER

6

Wedding and Honeymoon

Leonard's marriage to Phyllis took place on Saturday, 3 June 1967, in the newly built Duncan Road Church, Park Gate, in Hampshire. It was one of the earliest public meetings in the building and certainly the first wedding. Mr Jack Nickless of Belgrave House married the couple, and Leonard's younger brother, Frank, was the best man. Phyllis had two bridesmaids, her younger sister, Rosie, and a close friend, Beryl, whom she had met at Belgrave House.

Leonard and Phyllis's
wedding day
3 June 1967

Just a brief introduction to Beryl: as her parents were spiritualists, when she became a Christian as a young teenager and wouldn't give up her faith, they refused to have her living in their home. The Lord provided for her after her conversion in a wonderful way. A Christian benefactor financed her through her education, and Jack and Joy Nickless took her in, giving her a home until she left to go to a teacher's training college. Interestingly enough, Phyllis realised later that, although at different times, Beryl had attended the same grammar school as herself for a few years.

Phyllis's mother's best friend, who was a very precious auntie to Phyllis, had a small plot of land for strawberries and flowers and ran a small florist stall. She kindly offered to supply the flowers for the wedding and made a beautiful bouquet of red roses for the bride. Unfortunately, in the haste of leaving for the church with her father, Phyllis forgot to pick up her flowers. Arriving at the entrance of the church without them, she refused to go in until the flowers could

Phyllis with bridesmaids Beryl and Rosie

be fetched. Her father motored back home to retrieve them, which took about a quarter of an hour. Joan, who had run a branch of the Young Sowers' League in her home and had helped Phyllis a lot in her younger days, was the organist. Not knowing the reason for the delay of the bride's entrance, particularly as the usher had indicated her arrival outside, she nobly kept on playing well-known hymn tunes whilst everybody waited. Leonard, sitting at the front of the church with his best man, had no idea why his bride was so delayed and became increasingly flushed as the sudden fear took over his mind that his wife-to-be had got cold feet and was forsaking him!

Thankfully, all eventually was well. Jack Nickless led the couple as they expressed their vows to each other, and he finally pronounced them man and wife, to remain true to each other until death did them part. The congregation of family and friends joined with them in singing, 'All the way, my Saviour leads me. What have

I to want beside?' and then the majority accompanied them to the Catisfield village hall for the reception.

There had to be some restriction on the number invited for the meal, so when several of the teenage girls from their youth club in Horley very much wanted to be at the wedding, Dorothy from TBS, with whom Leonard worked, very kindly agreed to run them to the church in her little grey Austin A35 just to witness the ceremony.

Leonard's father kindly loaned the couple the use of his Hillman Imp for their honeymoon, and later that day, they drove down to Exmouth to a Christian guesthouse for a week's holiday together. They were wonderfully surprised when registering in at the reception desk to hear that their bill had already been paid by Phyllis's father! This was rather typical of Ron Pittwell. He chose to express his love for his family by doing practical things for them.

The newlyweds had chosen Exmouth for their honeymoon because Phyllis had enjoyed the Devon coast on holidays with her parents and little sister in past years. The family had Christian friends at Budleigh Salterton, and when the couple attended the Sunday morning breaking of bread service at the Brethren Assembly there, they were invited to call in for afternoon tea one day.

The happy couple

The week went far too quickly, and what the couple didn't know, being too absorbed in themselves to be concerned about the outside world, was that during that same week, Israel had been at war with its neighbours in what became known as the Six-Day War.

Leonard hadn't cancelled his preaching engagement for the following Sunday, so after they returned to their new home in Horley on the Saturday, the following day, Phyllis accompanied him down to the little chapel in Henfield, where he preached at the morning and afternoon services.

At the time, Leonard had no idea of the significance of Henfield Chapel for the Holder family or of the Pickett family, who entertained them for lunch between the services. First, Leonard's grandfather's grandfather, Eli Page, had nurtured the early believers in Henfield through leading a weekly preaching service for them in one or other of their cottage homes prior to them forming a church membership and having a building in 1897.

Second, fifty years or so after Leonard and Phyllis's visit to Henfield in 1967, the granddaughter of their host and hostess at that time (with her husband and children) is providing a home base for them in Kent, where they can live in their motorhome.

Memories from Others

Joan

My most vivid memory of their wedding is of poor Len wondering if his bride would arrive. She got to the church without her bouquet, hence the delay. I was playing the organ and had to replay a few pieces to fill the time, with a few reassuring glances at the groom.

Beryl

All I remember about the wedding is that it was very hot, and I had to sacrifice having some delicious food on my holiday the previous week to lose weight and fit neatly into my lemon bridesmaid's dress. I had red arms against the lemon colour. But you were appreciative of my efforts, Phyl.

CHAPTER

༒

7

—

Early Preaching Experiences

In the early years of their marriage, Phyllis would often accompany Leonard on Sunday preaching engagements and occasionally even after the children arrived, if specifically invited.

The experience Leonard had shortly before his 16th birthday, when the Lord graciously opened his eyes to the Gospel, had given him the assurance of his salvation through faith in Jesus and continued to be the motivation behind his preaching. Leonard, through his own experience of much of the preaching in Strict Baptist chapels, was concerned to be faithful to the Scriptures and to lift up the Lord Jesus as the Saviour of sinners. It concerned him to see young people sitting sedately in their seats, week after week in their best suits, showing no animation in their singing or change of expression during the preaching. He remembers one small village chapel where there was a lovely godly family he had got to know quite well, where the parents, a little older than himself, had never been baptised or progressed in any active way as Christians within the church. Leonard felt directed to preach from the account of the lame man by the pool of Bethesda and particularly on Jesus' question to him: 'Do you want to be made well?'[24] In God's purpose, this so challenged them that they were able to take the step of faith in owning their Lord in baptism and to become active in serving Him in various ways.

Some months after their marriage, Leonard was invited to preach at a chapel in Bedfordshire. He had never been there before and, not having a car, was uncertain of the best way of travelling to the chapel. Phyllis had a friend she had met at Belgrave House whose father ran a butcher's shop in Cambridge. Since there had been an invitation to visit for a weekend any time, it was agreed that the couple would visit on the Saturday, and the friend's father would kindly loan them the use of his butcher's van to travel to the chapel in Bedfordshire on the Sunday morning. It was a journey never to be forgotten through country lanes in a rattling vehicle with a makeshift wooden passenger seat for Phyllis. They got a bit lost and arrived late at the chapel. The deacon had already started the service by the time Leonard walked through the door but graciously smiled, stepped aside thankfully, and ushered the expected preacher into the pulpit.

That weekend was memorable for another reason. Leonard was due in the TBS office in Central London by 9:00 a.m. on the Monday, and the couple had planned to catch an appropriate train from Cambridge so Leonard could go to work and Phyllis proceed on further to Horley. However, that morning, Phyllis was feeling very sick, so it was agreed that she would catch a later train. Further events proved that her sickness that morning was the first indication of her pregnancy with their first child.

After their firstborn, Geoffrey, was born, Leonard was preaching at Rehoboth Chapel, Tunbridge Wells, and the whole family went across there from Horley for the weekend. Geoffrey was in a rather flimsy carrycot, and during the service, Phyllis had him beside her on the pew. During the so-called long prayer in the service, Geoffrey must have moved suddenly as he managed to upset the carrycot and tip it off the pew. He landed headfirst in the small space between the heating pipes and the outside wall.

---

24 John 5:6.

Recounting this event later, Phyllis commented with a glance towards her husband, 'With the help of Joy Mortimer, who was sitting with me, I grabbed Geoff by his legs and, with some difficulty, yanked my distressed son back up and onto my lap. I glanced at my husband in the pulpit. He had opened his eyes, seen what was causing the commotion, but then hurriedly closed his eyes tight again and continued praying as though nothing was happening.'

On another Sunday, Leonard was preaching at the chapel in Dorking. The custom there, as in many chapels, was for one or more of the deacons to pray with the preacher in the vestry before the start of the service. One of the deacons would then start the service and announce the first hymn, after which the minister would begin his contribution to the service by reading his chosen passage of Scripture. On this Sunday morning, there were a few minutes after the vestry prayer before the service was due to start, and Leonard decided it would be wise for him to visit the minister's toilet, which was through a door leading out of the vestry. Probably unnecessarily, as he closed the door behind him, he slipped a catch across to lock it. When he was ready to leave, he found he couldn't withdraw the catch to unlock the door. It was completely jammed, and he then realised there was a more recent lock fitted, and he had used an ancient, rather rusty one. He struggled for some time to force it open, but it was hopeless. Hearing the congregation beginning to sing the first hymn of the service, he felt his heart beating a little faster and had a brief cry for help to his Lord and Master. Then he realised it wouldn't be impossible for him to get through the small window by clambering onto the toilet seat. Knowing it would disturb the service considerably if he hadn't arrived in the pulpit in time to read the Scriptures, even more so if they needed to send out a search party for him, he wriggled through the small aperture. This brought him outside of the building completely, so he needed to run around the chapel as quick as he could to be able to access the vestry again through the back entrance. Brushing himself down hurriedly with his hand and smoothing down his hair, he walked calmly into the chapel and climbed the pulpit steps just before the congregation finished singing the opening hymn. *Thank you, Lord* was his silent prayer.

A few years later, when the couple's second son was about 3, the whole family had been invited to Streatham for the Sunday when Leonard was preaching. The children knew the family depended on the Lord for their daily needs, having no doubt heard their parents talking at times about finances and also knowing how they brought these needs to their heavenly Father in family prayers.

Suddenly, as Daniel was tucking into his bread and jam and looking at the cream cakes in the middle of the table, he said loudly for all to hear, 'One of the lovely things about coming out to tea is we don't have to pay for it!'

Travelling around chapels in different villages and meeting with Christians in their homes was, as Leonard really only appreciated later, a great privilege. He remembers admiring the obvious tenacity and patience of an older widow in Leicestershire who entertained him for afternoon tea one Sunday. She lived in a small cottage with two rooms downstairs, two upstairs, and a basic toilet outside the house. She described how she had brought up seven children in this home without electricity or running water.

On another occasion, Leonard had been invited to preach at Stamford, Lincolnshire. He had done this journey by train before and knew the necessary connections. However, on this Saturday evening, he realised when he got to Peterborough that on previous occasions, he'd been an hour earlier, and now there was no further train to Stamford until the next morning. Oh dear! What would he do? These were days before mobile phones, and it was unlikely that the older couple with whom he was to stay the night had a house phone anyway. He didn't even consider the possibility of a taxi. Such a means of travelling had never been a financial possibility for him. He decided the only way was to walk and hitch-hike. So dressed in his best suit, as befits a Strict Baptist minister, he set off on foot from the station to find the main route to Stamford. Road signs told him it was fourteen miles. He had walked for a good half an hour when a police car stopped. A friendly policeman asked whether he could help him, and when Leonard mentioned he had missed the last train and needed to get to Stamford, he kindly invited Leonard to jump in as he also was going to Stamford, where he lived. During the journey, Leonard had the opportunity to talk about his faith and how, through his foolishness, he had missed the last train. He then invited him to the service at the Baptist chapel in North Street, where he was to be the preacher.

Being an itinerant minister can provide the opportunity for the most unusual and often unexpected circumstances. One such elderly minister who occasionally took meetings in very rural settings loved to regale his experiences. One of the most amusing was about a weekend visit to a small village in Suffolk. On Saturday evening, with everyone having all talked happily together, the elderly deacon suggested to his wife that she could go off to bed. The two men chatted a bit longer, and then at his host's invitation, the two men went upstairs. Being shown into a bedroom, the minister realised to his alarm that the wife was already in there. The old deacon gently asked his wife to move over a bit more, and then it became clear to the elderly minister that there was only the one bed for all three of them for the night.

CHAPTER

8

The Arrival of Children

Phyllis had not yet reached her 21st birthday when she informed Leonard that the morning sickness whilst visiting Cambridge was indicating they could soon expect the arrival of a baby.

As the infant developed – hidden from view and, in those days, of unidentifiable gender – he became known as Charlie. Little Charlie's birth wasn't the easiest. The parents were young and inexperienced, and certainly, Leonard, the most laid back of the two, treated the whole experience more casually than he should have.

'After all,' he reasoned, 'this was surely a very natural thing to happen, and our heavenly Father was in control.'

When Phyllis's waters broke, they spoke to the midwife, who indicated there was no desperate hurry, so they walked together up to the nearby library so the mother-to-be could borrow a book or two to read in the hospital. They then motored down to the hospital in Crawley in Leonard's father's car.

After the nursing staff at the hospital had sent Leonard home, saying it would be unlikely that anything would happen before the morning and suggesting he ring back at about 6:00 a.m., Phyllis began labour in earnest.

Ultrasound scans were not a normal procedure in those days, so only as the baby began to arrive did the hospital realise baby Charlie was lying in an 'occiput posterior position', which is quite a high risk for delivery and usually necessitates forceps or a caesarean section. The midwife immediately contacted the doctor on night duty, and because it was an unusual situation, he called in a team of student doctors to witness the birth.

It was a long and painful night for poor Phyllis, but with the help of the medical staff, she eventually managed to give birth to baby Charlie herself without the doctor needing to use forceps.

Through all this, not knowing what was happening, Leonard slept peacefully at home, getting up early to go out to the telephone box to ring the hospital for information.

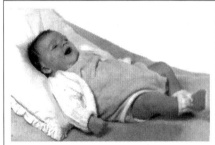

Leonard and Phyllis's firstborn Geoffrey Leonard Holder (born 5 April 1968)

'Congratulations – you have a healthy little son born at five fifty and weighing eight pounds, twelve ounces' was the news he got from the ward sister.

This reminds me of another first-time father who, on getting the message from the hospital – 'You have a lovely little boy, and it's seven pounds ten' – answered, 'Will it be all right if I bring a cheque when I come?'

Leonard hurried back to the Crawley hospital, thrilled at the news and with no idea of the traumatic experience poor Phyllis had been through.

To his shame, Leonard now confesses that his old–fashioned attitude, with a lack of understanding of the trauma of giving birth and his responsibility as a father, meant he never considered cancelling his Sunday preaching engagements at the time of little Charlie's birth. Phyllis, bless her, at the time, accepted this situation without argument. Charlie was born on Friday, 5 April, and as she was still in hospital the following Sunday, Leonard wrote her a 'love letter' to open during visiting time.

The couple decided to call baby Charlie, Geoffrey Leonard. The little lad was a very slow feeder. This caused a problem with the nursing staff who brought the babies in to their mothers for feeding and expected to take them away again after a short period. Geoffrey would go to sleep at his mother's breast, and very soon, the hospital very strongly recommended he be bottle fed. At that time, their practice was to give babies watered-down carnation milk, and unfortunately, Geoffrey didn't take to this at all.

It all came to a head the following weekend, when Phyllis and baby were back home. It was Easter, and Leonard had a preaching engagement farther away and needed to be away between Saturday and Monday. This was certainly not well planned as Phyllis had only just come home from hospital the day before he went off. Baby Geoffrey couldn't take the carnation milk supplied by the hospital, and he cried and cried uncontrollably. The house had no telephone, so Phyllis couldn't call anyone, and Leonard couldn't contact her. After a very disturbed night, there was still a crying baby on Easter Sunday morning. The next-door neighbour, on hearing the persistent crying, called in to see if she could help. She very quickly assessed the situation and poured scorn on the hospital's choice of baby milk.

'I've found my babies did well on Cow and Gate powdered milk, which you can get at all chemists,' said Daphne.

'But it's Easter Sunday, and no chemists are open,' responded Phyllis in despair.

'I'll have a word with my husband,' answered the kind neighbour. 'He knows the chemist up at Salfords, and I'm sure he will be able to get you some milk as the chemist lives above the shop.'

Daphne's husband soon came back with the Cow and Gate milk, suitable for new-born babies, and baby Geoffrey took this happily and was soon peacefully asleep.

When, two years later, Phyllis realised that she was once again pregnant, she was extremely distressed. The memory of all that had been involved in giving birth to her first child came flooding back, and she dreaded the thought of having to go through it all again. Thankfully, Phyllis now so enjoyed her little son that the joyful thought of providing Geoffrey with an infant brother or sister soon overcame her fear, at least most of the time. The truth of Jesus's words has been borne out again and again by mothers all over the world: 'A woman, when she is in labour, has sorrow because her hour has come; but as soon as she has given birth to the child, she no longer remembers the anguish for joy that a human being has been born into the world.'[25]

When quoting the above, it's also good to remember the point that Jesus was, in fact, making to His disciples as He was about to be separated from them in death: 'Therefore, you now have sorrow; but I will see you again, and your heart will rejoice, and your joy, no one will take from you.'[26]

As is usual, no two births are the same, and after two years, arrangements had changed at the Crawley hospital. They now provided single-bed wards for midwives to use solely for the mothers they had under their care. The hospital staff only then became involved if the midwife needed help. The Horley midwife at that time was a very jolly Welsh lady who seemed to have brought a large proportion of Horley children into the world.

When Phyllis's contractions started – which, wonderfully, was before Leonard had left for work – they phoned the midwife from the neighbour's house across the road, and Phyllis, together with husband Leonard, went down to Crawley.

Phyllis later often commented, 'On arriving at the hospital, I ordered my midday dinner and then had my baby in time to eat my food.'

The atmosphere in the birth room was very relaxed. The midwife chatted happily with Leonard, and at one point, a little voice came from the bed.

'Hi, you two. Don't forget I'm having a baby here!'

One thing Leonard remembers about the birth of his second child was the baby's length. It – or, should we say, he, as was immediately obvious – seemed to keep arriving. The midwife complemented Leonard.

---

25 John 16:21.
26 John 16:22.

'I've had a number of fathers present who go as white as a sheet and even faint,' she commented.

The couple took a few days to decide on a name for their second child. Interestingly, the Scripture text on the calendar the day before the birth was from Psalm 30:5 – 'Joy cometh in the morning' – and Phyllis had responded happily to this:

Leonard and Phyllis
with Geoffrey and Daniel
(Daniel born 5 May 1970)

'What do you think, Len? Joy would be a great name for our baby if it's a girl.'

They discussed a number of boys' names and then got their list down to two: Nathaniel or Daniel. They settled on Daniel but then had some hesitation as they didn't know any Daniels amongst their circle of friends. Strange to say they didn't think (or even know) at the time that Leonard's grandfather was Ebenezer Dan and that his father was Dan Holder. It seems certain that God influenced them in the choice of both of their sons' names. They've understood more recently that the name Geoffrey is probably a derivation of Godfrey with a Germanic root combining the German words *Gott* and *Friede*, hence having the meaning of 'peace with God'. The parents are so thankful that their Geoffrey has found his peace with God and is passing it on to others in making known the good news of Jesus Christ, God's Son, who came into the world to reconcile sinful man to his holy Creator.

Then the name Daniel is straight from the biblical character of that name in the Hebrew Scriptures and means 'God is my judge'. Of the biblical Daniel, when those who hated him tried to find reasons to discredit him before the king of Babylon, the following was said:

'They could find no charge or fault because he was faithful; nor was there any error or fault found in him. Then these men said,

"We shall not find any charge against this Daniel unless we find it against him concerning the law of his God."[27]

When we are trusting Jesus Christ as our Saviour and advocate, we can stand before God, our judge, guiltless.

John Wesley's translation of some of the lines of Count Zinzendorf's wonderful hymn describes it in this way:

Jesus, thy blood and righteousness,
My beauty are, my glorious dress.
Bold shall I stand in thy great day;
For who aught to my charge shall lay?
Fully absolved through these, I am
From sin and fear, from guilt and shame.

Now, fifty years after his son's birth, Leonard is proud to testify that his Daniel is preaching this same Gospel.

---

27 Daniel 6:4–5.

CHAPTER

9

Home as 'Open House'

Both Leonard and Phyllis had a heart for people. The mini message given by Jack Nickless at their wedding had exhorted them to invite the Lord Jesus into their marriage and home; therefore, having a home for Him had always been their intention and hope. Words of Jesus recorded in John's Gospel had both inspired this thought and also confirmed its possibility: 'If anyone loves Me, he will keep My word; and My Father will love him, and We will come to him and make Our home with him.'[28]

They therefore wanted to use their little house in Queens Road, Horley, as a home into which others would be welcome to come to find love, acceptance, and prayer.

Leonard had been brought up to see the home as much a place of worship and prayer as the church, and perhaps for a child, the former would be even more significant. The phrase 'the family altar' was one often used when he was a teenager. He remembers hearing one Christian gentleman arguing against this phraseology, saying the altar is an Old Testament term signifying a place where blood sacrifices were made. However, the counterargument is

---

28 John 14:23.

that Scripture also refers to the 'sacrifice of praise', and Leonard and Phyllis both wanted there to be a place in their home for praise and prayer and would gather their sons around the kitchen table after breakfasting together to read the Scriptures, to pray, and occasionally to sing. He remembers reading a comment by Spurgeon that to pray is good, and to read the Bible and pray is better, but to read the Bible, sing, and pray is better still.

One amusing incident: one morning, after Leonard had finished the family prayer and Phyllis was still concluding her prayerful thoughts with her eyes closed, Daniel, as a 2-year-old, looked across the table and said, 'Time to wake up now, Mummy.'

When Phyllis had been a girl, her neighbour Joan had run a children's club in her home, which, under the direction of the Scripture Gift Mission, was known as the Young Sowers League. Its object was to familiarise children with the Bible. There were books of Bible verses supplied by the Scripture Gift Mission, and the children must locate the verse of a given Bible chapter where each occurred. By completing a certain number of these verses, which had to be verified by the leader, children earned for themselves first a Gospel and then a New Testament and then, as they proceeded further, a complete Bible and, finally, a Bible concordance. Phyllis, having benefitted herself from 'YSL', as she called it, decided she would like to run such a group in her own home. She soon had a group up and running with some children from the chapel as a nucleus, who consequently brought a few other children along. Knowing there was nearly always a welcome at 7 Queens Road, several of the young teenagers would wander in at different times, particularly during their school lunch hour. They were encouraged to come along to a Sunday service at the chapel, and any who did knew there was a welcome back at 'Len and Phyl's' after the evening service whether either of the couple were at chapel that evening or not. Leonard was often away preaching and Phyllis at home with the young children.

In the summer of 1973, Leonard and Phyllis decided it would be good to take several of the girls away for a week's camp. They were able to borrow two boys' brigade–type bell tents and set up a camp in the grounds of Phyllis's parents' home. Their two young boys slept in the house, Leonard and Phyllis in one tent, and the five girls in the second. They were able to give the girls some biblical input, but there were a few unanticipated problems. To have a group of attractive young girls camping in Brook Lane quite naturally attracted some of the local lads, who had to be strongly dissuaded from intruding into Mr Pittwell's garden. Also, having only basic washing facilities of cold water for the young ladies and providing enticing food for them was more of a challenge than Leonard and Phyllis were used to with their two young sons!

Several interesting developments came out of this contact with these young people. Lesley, one of the girls, who didn't come from a Christian home, was baptised and, after wandering away from the Lord for several years (during which she got married), is now a very enthusiastic Christian and working closely with her local Baptist church.

Phyllis with Lesley
in more recent years

They were thrilled when they heard that a young lady, Sue, who had earlier come to the youth club when Leonard had first come to Horley, had become a Christian. She had been one of the girls whom Dorothy had brought to their wedding. She attached herself to other young Christians from the Horley Methodist church, and when Leonard suggested a Bible study evening, she brought a small group along to 7 Queens Road for this. One evening Sue came by to request earnest prayer for a young man she was trying to help who was on drugs. When, despite fervent prayer for him, the lad died, Sue was devastated. The incident shattered her faith, and sadly, she drifted away from the Lord. The last the couple heard of her was that she had married and was living in Devon or Cornwall. Leonard and Phyllis sometimes still think and pray for Sue, and it would be wonderful to know that she had come back to faith and a relationship with the Lord. They often sense that they are simply links in the chain of God's gracious dealings in peoples' lives but also pray that their failures may never be a hindrance to anyone's salvation.

Early in their married life, the couple also became involved with a few young people in the neighbouring village of Charlwood. Leonard was invited quite frequently to preach at Sunday services at the quaint little chapel there, and when Mrs Eade from the village store encouraged a few young people to come into her home for some craft work and Bible teaching, Leonard, Phyllis, and the two small boys would regularly go across to support her and give a Bible message.

There was a young couple living in Chapel Lane who had married about the same year as Leonard and Phyllis and came along fairly regularly to Sunday services at the chapel. Mrs Eade became quite a mother figure to Ruby, the wife, and after Ruby had her first baby, Mrs Eade was most concerned about the postnatal depression which the young mother experienced, landing her in the psychiatric department of the Crawley hospital. Mrs Eade understood Ruby's temperament and was convinced that all she needed was a bit of love and care. The problem seemed to have arisen because Ruby's husband had felt out of his depth and referred her to the hospital.

Leonard and Phyllis did something which, with hindsight, they probably should have hesitated to do. After talking to Rob, Ruby's husband, he went with them to the hospital, and they persuaded Ruby to discharge herself. They offered to have Ruby and her baby girl in their home for a few days, which satisfied the hospital staff to some degree. Thankfully, Ruby went on well and could soon return home to her husband.

On another occasion, a friend Phyllis had made at Belgrave House arrived unexpectedly on the Holders' doorstep with three small children. She informed Phyllis that she had left her husband and could think of nowhere else to go. Having come down to Horley from her home, a good fifty miles north of London, this was not a simple journey, and clearly, she needed to be taken in and helped. Leonard insisted she contact her husband, and after a few days, she was persuaded to return to him. The same friend

124

approached the Holders some years later. asking whether they would look after her youngest daughter because it was likely she herself would have to go to prison. She had apparently attacked her husband with an implement during a domestic quarrel. Thankfully, the sentence she received from the court was a certain number of hours of community service rather than time in prison, which solved the need of care for her daughter. We praise God that this same friend is now going on well with the Lord in a church fellowship and is with a believing husband.

Another incident happened during the early 1970s which had a profound effect on the future for Leonard and Phyllis. One Sunday evening two Swiss young ladies came into the Sunday service. The bus stop was immediately outside Providence Chapel, and on looking for a church service, this was the one immediately at hand. Neither Leonard nor Phyllis could be at that evening service. Leonard was preaching away, and Phyllis was at home, looking after their two small boys. This could have been a one-off visit to the chapel by the girls with no further consequences for Leonard and Phyllis; however, this was not to be. The daughter of one of the church members, Melita, chatted with the girls after the service and invited them round to Leonard and Phyllis's home.

When the girls hesitated, saying that they didn't know Leonard and Phyllis, Melita's response was 'That doesn't matter. Everyone goes round to Len and Phyl's.'

It had not been a good evening for Phyllis. She had only just got the boys settled and was looking forward to sitting down quietly. Thankfully, in her customary way, she oozed enthusiasm when opening the door, and the two Swiss girls and Melita felt welcomed. Phyllis learned that they were over in Britain as au pairs

The

RECOGNITION SERVICE

of Mr. Leonard E. Holder

AS PASTOR OF

**PROVIDENCE STRICT BAPTIST CHAPEL
VICTORIA ROAD, HORLEY**

will be held, God willing, on

SATURDAY, JANUARY 20th, 1973

at 3.30 p.m.

Chairman: Pastor F. MORTIMER (Horsham)

Charge to Church: Pastor D. OLDHAM (Stamford)

Charge to Pastor: Pastor JAMES PAYNE (Brighton)

Refreshments after the Service

A warm welcome to all

Advertising recognition service for Leonard as pastor of Providence Chapel, Horley to improve their English and were working in different homes in two villages outside Horley. They were both named Erika and had been friends since childhood, living in small neighbouring villages in Canton Zürich. After getting home himself, Leonard was also pleased to make their acquaintance, and the couple invited them to come to afternoon tea on any Sunday they were free and to come to the evening service at the chapel. Leonard then ran them back to the families with whom they were living.

Providence Chapel, just prior to this, invited Leonard to be their pastor. David Ellis had to resign because of ill health a few years earlier, and Leonard gained the honour of being appreciated and trusted by the church fellowship which had known him for several years and sent him into the ministry. Consequently, most Sundays, he was preaching at the chapel, making it more natural for the two Erikas to come along to the service after Sunday tea. Sunday was a free day for the two girls, and soon, they were coming regularly to 7 Queens Road for tea and staying on for the chapel service. They would also come back afterward, sometimes with others too, and the evening would conclude with a Bible reading and prayer. The girls were accustomed to more formal services in the Swiss Reformed Church, of which they were nominally members, and later commented on the surprise they initially had at the ease with which Leonard prayed at the end of the evening and how his and Phyllis's faith in Jesus shone through in all they did. They commented that in Switzerland, they had listened to Billy Graham on Transworld Radio and had decided, when in Britain, to find a church that preached that same Gospel.

There was the opportunity to talk to them in very direct ways about their thoughts and about the Gospel, and before they had to return to Switzerland after six months in Britain, they both professed a real personal faith in the Lord Jesus as their Saviour and friend. Their return to Switzerland was not the end of this story.

Memories from Others

Lesley

When I think back to the 'Horley Days', it's your 'open house', Len and Phyl, which always comes to the forefront of my thoughts. You yourselves were very warm, open people and always had an open door for many. When I was a teenager, it was somewhere I loved to go, because your home always seemed full of other young people. It was almost like a meeting place for many of us. Then of course, there were many visitors to the chapel – some short term, some long; whatever their length of stay or the reason, they were always very welcome at No. 7 Queens Road. I have many a happy memory of Sunday evenings after the service, several of us going to your house for coffee. Sometimes we had a good singsong around the piano too.

Melita

There were the times Len and I worked together at TBS and the times the car broke down. For instance, once, the gear stick broke off, and we had to drive home changing gear with pliers! When I was baptised – Mr Ellis came back to Horley – he preached, and you, Len, baptised me. I was the first person you baptised. I remember my Sunday school teaching days and when Geoff and Dan were in my class. I remember you as a very loving couple, always ready to share your lives, children, and home with others – an example to us. I remember having Bible studies in the front room and fun in the kitchen. I remember the problem of peer pressure having to be sorted out by you, Phyl, between all of us who came round to see you.

Erika: Samstagern, Switzerland

I enjoy thinking back to the time I met you both, Phyl and Len, as many good memories of my time in England as an au pair reappear. At the time, I was living in Ifield, not far away from my friend Erika Moser, who was staying with a family in

Charlwood. At one point, Erika and I felt the need to find a church somewhere. I don't know why, really, because at that time, I was fairly indifferent about things to do with church. We discovered a small chapel with a board outside saying, 'Strict Baptist Chapel', so we decided to go in, much to the surprise of the mainly older people already inside. As all the ladies wore hats, we must have looked a little strange in trousers and without hats. After the service, a young lady named Melita – who seemed different from the rest, first because she was younger and second because she had a very wide-brimmed hat on her head – invited us to go with her for coffee to the young pastor's family.

Yes, and that family was you, Phyl and Len. Geoff and Dan were 4 and 2 at the time. You took us in so warmly that we felt at home straight away. Then when you, Phyl, invited us to come round any time, we felt we wanted to, and so it happened that we came to Horley every Sunday for tea with you and then went to the chapel. With time, we began to be more and more interested in the sermons which you, Len, were preaching. You also took our questions seriously and were very understanding. Before you would take us home in the evenings, you, Len, would pray with us. During those prayers, I realised for the first time that they were not just going out into thin air. Somehow I felt there was someone out there who you both trusted and who was giving you strength. It was new for me to experience the Gospel as good news and not as a threat! Up to that point, I had thought of Christianity as just a list of moral commands which I didn't have any chance of keeping anyway. There – with you, Phyl and Len, in your home – I got to know another type of Christianity which gives freedom, courage, strength, peace, and trust. This has changed my life in a decisive way.

(Translated from German)

Erika: Glarus, Switzerland

I just felt so attracted to your home in Horley. Usually, we came to the Sunday evening service; sometimes you, Len, preached, and what you said made me think. Slowly, I realised it wasn't enough just to go to church every now and then and try to be nice. It became clear to me that I needed a personal relationship with Jesus.

One evening, as you took me home, Len, I asked you how one could become a Christian. Soon after that, I was able to give my life to Jesus. I shall always be grateful to you, Phyl and Len, that you showed me the way to Christ.

Before Christmas, you took us to a carol service in London. You didn't know the way very well, and I remember going around a roundabout several times. At that time, there weren't any roundabouts in Switzerland, so that stayed in my memory. On the Christmas card you gave me was written 'May Christ make Christmas wonderful to you'.

Erika with Geoffrey and Daniel 1973

I also remember an evening with the young people around a bonfire. You, Len, gave a little talk on heaven and hell. I was very impressed. On my last evening before I came back to Switzerland, we played Scrabble. My only comfort was the thought that you might come for a visit to Switzerland sometime . . .

(Translated from German)

CHAPTER

10

Is This God's Call?

Our Swiss friends returned to their homes with a glowing report of their time in England and the kindness they had experienced. As a result of this, an enthusiastic invitation arrived from the parents of one of the girls for Leonard, Phyllis, and their boys to come and spend a holiday with them. This seemed a wonderful opportunity to experience the world beyond the south of England, providing the ideal time to encourage the faith of their new friends, so the arrangements were made to go.

It was 1973. Geoffrey was 5 and Daniel 3 when the family set off on their first overseas trip. They were treated like royalty by Erika, her parents, and her brother. They had two weeks, and Erika had taken most of this time off work to show them her beloved country. Her parents' home, where they all stayed, was a detached house in a tiny village surrounded by fields, many of which were full of growing crops of maize. It was an unusual sight for them to see deer leaping through the crops.

There were various memorable, very Swiss experiences: roasting 'cervelat' sausages on sticks over a campfire on the shore of a lake; eating wonderfully cooked meals under a vine canopy in the family garden; being offered an ice cream and discovering this was not merely a vanilla ice cream in a wafer cornet but a sit-down experience with a large ice cream sundae in a beautifully shaped glass. However, the ultimate experience was a car trip of a few hours into the Bernese Alps, a narrow-gauge train up to the car-free village of Mürren, followed by a cable car to the revolving restaurant on Mount Schilthorn (2,970 metres). Erika's brother joined the party, and the second Erika, on the back of her boyfriend's motorbike, added two more to the group. Although the first of many further experiences of the Swiss Alps, this initial visit, like a precious gem, abides in the memory of the English travellers from the flat lands of Horley.

On both Sunday mornings of their visit, the family experienced church services in the Erikas' local *Evangelisch-reformierte Kirche*, but with them knowing no German, it was an experience without much meaning. The simplicity of the church building was very noticeable, as was the centrality of the pulpit and the obvious priority of the sermon in the service. However, the Erikas told Leonard and Phyllis that they didn't feel they were being taught Bible truths in a way that would feed their new faith and enable them to grow as Christians. There were opportunities for times of Bible reading, discussions, and prayer together in Erika's home. When Erika commented that she didn't feel their pastor believed the Bible to be God's Word, Leonard asked if there were other denominations. Erika's response was very negative.

'There's a family in our village who we know belong to a different Christian group, but they are rather strange in the way they dress and the way they live and are not particularly friendly,' she answered with a sigh.

On another occasion during the visit, in what Leonard took to be a light-hearted suggestion, the thought was voiced that he and Phyllis should consider coming out to Switzerland to pastor one of their churches.

Later, as they drove through a particular village, Erika said, 'The church here is needing a pastor.' Then, on passing an impressive-looking house, she commented: 'And that's the manse you would have.'

In no way did Leonard consider this seriously, but later, back in Horley, believing that the link with the Erikas was of God, he decided it would be a helpful thing to learn German. After making enquiries, he enrolled in an adult evening course in Crawley which would lead to an O-level in the German language. He encouraged Phyllis to join him, but after a few weeks, with the added problem of needing to get a babysitter, she decided it was too much for her.

Leonard continued with the course for three years, fitting it in around his other responsibilities. He had reduced his work at TBS to four days a week as the pastorate at Providence Chapel, Horley, required him to prepare three sermons a week: morning and evening on Sunday as well as Tuesday evening, when he needed to give an address before a time of prayer.

During those three years, there was a deepening conviction that God was calling him to German-speaking Europe. His mind battled with this thought as he had no idea how it could come about or in what capacity he could be of any use outside of the country and denomination he knew so well.

Phyllis's Memories and Comments

I guess most families have a saying or sayings that crop up in their lives at significant intervals. In our family, it was 'Boys, what would you say if . . .' Then in later years, we would often say, 'Is that a "now" or a "now now"?' to distinguish between whether a decided course of action should be undertaken after sitting a bit longer and perhaps having a cup of tea or immediately.

In 1976, we asked our boys the question 'What would you say if we moved to Switzerland?' many years before we actually *did* that. Though our boys' response was excitedly favourable, there were many, many things we had to go through and hopefully learn from before the move could come. When it did come, it was not at all easy and involved many unexpected experiences which really tested our confidence that God was guiding and controlling everything. Len had been part-time pastor of a small congregation in Surrey for a few years during which Swiss au pair girls had come into the church services and to our home. Two had been drawn to the Lord and given us an interest in Switzerland and the spiritual state of

German-speaking Europe. We visited Switzerland for the first time when our two boys, Geoffrey and Daniel, were 5 and 3 years old, respectively. The fact that we did not get to go out to Switzerland with Len's call until the boys were 13 and 15 years old shows that God had many things for us to go through and learn before the move could come.

CHAPTER

11

A Way Forward

Leonard realised that if the thought of serving God in some way in German-speaking Europe was of God, then God Himself must open up the way. However, he also knew that he would have to begin looking for the way forward and make some hard decisions. He had a wife and two young children for which he was responsible, so how could he even consider uprooting them from the life they shared together in the south of England? The answer to this came when he felt convinced with all his heart that the only place of real blessing for him and his family was to be in God's will. Also, he felt challenged once again from the verse of the hymn that had spoken to him before his baptism:

For we never can prove the delights of His love
Until all on the altar we lay.
For the favour He shows
And the joy He bestows
Are for those who will trust and obey.

The greatest fear in Leonard's mind was a fear of missing God's blessing both for himself and also for Phyllis and his boys through rejecting God's guidance.

Leonard is not sure now of the order of the steps he took and of things that happened, but one very significant development was a Bible passage that God spoke very clearly to Phyllis. He had shared his inner thoughts with his wife before starting the German language course which she had initially joined with him. Phyllis was very dubious about such a move into another language and culture, but one weekend she had been unwell with flu and had stayed in bed. She had been reading her Bible when a verse spoke so powerfully to her that she has made reference to this constantly over the years as God's Word to her. It was God's promise to Jacob: 'Behold, I am with you and will keep you wherever you go and will bring you back to this land; for I will not leave you until I have done what I have spoken to you.'[29]

Then Jacob's response was as follows: 'If God will be with me and keep me in this way that I am going and give me bread to eat and clothing to put on so that I come back to my father's house in peace, then the LORD shall be my God.'[30]

A Scripture that spoke equally powerfully to Leonard during this period of uncertainty was the 107th psalm. The psalm describes how God led the children of Israel and provided for them in every way they needed. It mentions their many failures but also the deliverances they experienced when they turned back to Him. It repeatedly exhorts men to 'praise the Lord for His goodness and His wonderful works to the children of men'. The verses that impressed themselves on Leonard at that time were 7 and 16: 'He led them forth by the right way that they might go to a city for a dwelling place . . . He has broken the gates of bronze and cut the bars of iron in two.'

What the psalm teaches us is that God can be trusted, that He guides His children in right ways and can break through apparently impossible situations to do this. Then came the wonderfully confirming verses in Isaiah 45:

'I will go before you and make the crooked places straight; I will break in pieces the gates of bronze and cut the bars of iron. I

---

29 Genesis 28:15.
30 Genesis 28:20–21.

will give you the treasures of darkness and hidden riches of secret places, that you may know that I, the LORD, Who call you by your name, am the God of Israel.'[31]

Leonard had no idea where God was leading, simply that he felt convinced that there was a purpose in the Erikas' conversion through his ministry and the witness of their home and that this unexpected introduction to the German-speaking world was, in some way, calling to them.

To enquire further into the spiritual needs of Switzerland and Germany, he wrote to Frances Schaffer, who was running the shelter L'Abri in Switzerland and who had many contacts throughout both this country and Germany. Leonard hardly expected an answer but was thrilled to get a letter back giving Frances Schaffer's analysis of the spiritual scene in the German-speaking world. In essence, his view was that the German-speaking Christian Church was in a desperate state. On the one hand, a liberal, critical view of the Bible had so overtaken the theological training establishments and had so influenced the majority of churches that very few Christians now believed there was any basis for accepting the complete Bible as the inspired Word of God. Then on the other hand, there was the pietistic movement, which, although aiming to be true to the Bible, had a strong mystical element and a tendency towards a legalistic rigidity in their teaching.

After much thought and prayer, Leonard approached a missionary society which already had workers in Europe. He expressed his interest in the German-speaking world and the reasons he had for thinking God was calling him to work for Him in some capacity in Switzerland. The mission took this enquiry seriously. They saw their involvement in mission work as a cooperation with a sending church by way of advising, gathering financial support, and encouraging those working from UK churches overseas.

When the mission adopted potential missionaries, they advised stages of preparation: first, to link them with an appropriate sending

---

31 Isaiah 45:2.

church (ideally, this should be the candidate's own church, but sometimes this wasn't possible); second, to ensure the candidates had sufficient Bible and theological training; and then third, to help to arrange any appropriate language training before, finally, finding the right situation for them to work in, preferably in conjunction with a local church in that country. They advised Leonard, if he was serious about this call, to relinquish his work at TBS and also his pastoral duties to devote himself full-time to preparation for future work on the continent of Europe. They advised that he and his family should attach themselves to a larger church which would be prepared to consider him as a possible missionary candidate and support him. They suggested a church about thirty minutes by car from Horley, and the pastor there kindly agreed to provide Leonard with a structured course of theological reading under his guidance. It would be necessary for Leonard and Phyllis to become members of this church and to attend the services regularly so the other members could get to know them.

If Leonard were to leave his employment with the TBS and his pastorate, the family would need to depend on God for their financial support, but the mission could recommend them to a specific charity for a possible grant during this period of study.

Although this involved a tremendous step of faith, after prayer, Leonard and Phyllis agreed to follow this recommended path. The years were 1975 into 1976, and their sons were 5 and 7 years old, and Leonard and Phyllis were in their 30th year.

The Horley church was not happy about Leonard's resignation from the pastorate and could not understand why, if he was called to work in Europe, they couldn't send him out and be behind him. The mission, however, was adamant that there needed to be a bigger sending church with a strong pastoral ministry and the possibility of providing some financial support for him.

Leonard talked to Terence Brown, the general secretary of TBS, about his convictions and the mission's suggested way forward. The agreement was that he would give the society a month's notice and introduce a successor to the work he had been doing. However, before the month's notice had hardly begun in 1974, his life at the TBS came to a sudden, unexpected end. Phyllis had had a streaming cold whilst fulfilling the role of bridesmaid at her sister's wedding, and this developed into pneumonia. Her mother came to help with the boys, but as Phyllis was beginning to recuperate after several weeks in bed, she lost the baby she was carrying. The doctor they had in Horley at that time was Dr Brown. He came to the house promptly when called, assessed the situation, and called for an ambulance. It was Tuesday evening, and Leonard was due to lead a service at the chapel.

'I can't possibly go into hospital yet,' Phyllis informed the doctor anxiously. 'My husband needs to be at the chapel, and there's no one else to look after the boys.'

After a brief discussion, Phyllis was told in no uncertain terms that at that moment, her need was greater. Dr Brown stated he would call in at the chapel on his way back to the surgery and inform the waiting congregation that unfortunately, their pastor couldn't be with them that evening.

This was not the most encouraging way to begin a new phase of their life, but Leonard never really doubted that God was guiding.

CHAPTER

12

Spying Out the Land

'I think I should lend you another ground sheet if you are going to sleep here in a tent tonight.'

It was now June 1976, and Leonard and his family had arrived at a campsite in the northern part of Germany's Black Forest and had been told it had been raining hard for several days. The campsite manager was very helpful and soon returned with a substantial ground sheet.

The next morning, the sun was shining, and this was the beginning of probably the warmest and driest summer of the century both in England and in Continental Europe.

Leonard's year of theological study and fellowship with a new church had been a challenging but enriching experience in many ways. Not least was to have experienced the variety of ways God had provided for them without any settled income. One amazing providence had been the provision of good-quality clothes and footwear for the boys. The children's health visitor was a Methodist Christian and had admired the step of faith Leonard and Phyllis had taken, and since she had nephews slightly older than Geoffrey and Daniel, more than once, she brought round different items of clothing her nephews had grown out of. 'If God so clothes the grass of the field, which today is and tomorrow is thrown into the oven, will He not much more clothe you, O you of little faith?'[32]

Leonard had contacted a number of different churches and Christian organisations working in Switzerland and Southern Germany to investigate possible opportunities for ministry. He had organised an extensive itinerary for that June, following up these links. His father had kindly loaned them the use of his Ford Cortina, and they had camping equipment with them.

After that first night near Freudenstadt, they motored into Switzerland and camped beside Lake Walensee, before revisiting their friend Erika, spending a few nights as guests once again in her parent's home at Bisikon.

Prayerfully seeking for an indication from God of where He would have them work for Him, they visited and talked with a range of different Christians working in different fields of ministry. A British family entertained them for a night or two in Rapperswil, at the top end of Lake Zurich, where they were introduced to a Christian bookshop run by the evangelical church there; they spent a weekend in the Alps, camping above L'Abri and attending a Sunday morning service and one of Frances Schaffer's evening sessions; they camped in a cherry orchard in the grounds of a Bible college outside Geneva; they visited Bodenseehof Bible School on Lake Constance, which has links with Capernwray in the Lake District; and they called in at Kilchzimmer, the European Centre for Child Evangelism Fellowship (CEF). Finally, before returning to Horley, they spent a few days in a small flat just outside Basel, in the home of an English lady married to a Swiss man named Leonhard.

They had an interesting experience on the way home. As they were motoring on a nearly empty Belgium motorway, their car radiator suddenly boiled, and they realised one of the hoses had sprung a leak. They were in danger of missing their ferry, and Leonard was uncertain of what to do. Little Geoffrey was particularly worried, and so they had a brief prayer together, asking God to help them and show them what to do.

---

32 Matthew 6:30.

Almost before they had finished praying, a VW camper pulled up behind them, and a voice with a very Australian accent shouted to them, 'What's up, mate? Can we help?'

In no time, the thoughtful rescuer had cut off the split bit of hose and repositioned the good bit to get over the difficulty.

They were an Australian family who, having toured Europe, were now on their way to Britain to sell their right-hand–drive van before flying back home. Their arrival at that very moment was so clearly God's provision, and it was a dramatic demonstration to the whole family, including the boys, of how God can answer the prayers of His children.

There was a lot to digest from the trip but no obvious indication of where God was leading.

CHAPTER

13

The Time is Not Ripe

With hindsight, it is easy to understand why Leonard and Phyllis were not ready in 1976 for the move that would, in due course, readjust the whole tenure of their lives, put them both under tremendous pressure, and dramatically affect the destiny of their two sons. However, when there didn't appear to be a way forward, Leonard decided, also having listened to the advice of others, that whatever the longer-term future held, for the time being, it would be wrong to try to force open a door that seemed firmly closed. This was a pretty shattering experience. They had been working towards this for many, many months, and now was he to understand his conviction of God's call was imagination?

Slowly, Leonard realised that he had been too satisfied that his life was pretty much in order. His preaching ministry had been appreciated, he loved and valued his wife, and God had given them two healthy sons who had brought him and Phyllis much joy. God had been good to them. Although Leonard had never earned a substantial income, God had met all their needs, and they were living without debt. His denominational experience and involvement with the TBS had left him rather prejudiced towards the wider evangelical Christian Church, and he would later see that

God wanted to give him a wider experience before sending him into a very different Christian world in German-speaking Europe. He would also realise that his faith needed strengthening and that this can only happen through facing difficulties and seemingly impossible situations.

Two different personal temperaments along with baggage that each had from past experiences, personal failures, and sins are all things that two people bring with them into a marriage. Leonard and Phyllis began going out together whilst still teenagers and then married early, so in many ways, they grew and developed together. However, their temperaments are very different, and perhaps it was this that attracted them to each other. Leonard is, to a large degree, self-sufficient, is optimistic, is not in the habit of analysing his thoughts and feelings, and certainly was never in the habit of sharing these with anyone or even feeling he needed to. His childhood home life was a happy one; he respected and conformed contentedly with the wishes of his parents but rarely saw the need to ask them for advice or to expect them to understand him. They, on the other hand, gave him complete freedom to develop his own interests and rarely, if ever, enquired into what he was learning at school or the books he was reading. This, of course, might well have been different if he had showed any indication of straying from the standards which they expected of him.

Phyllis's background and temperament were very different. She grew up with little self-confidence as she wasn't encouraged to make decisions for herself. Through the particular slant on biblical teaching that her father had imbibed or perhaps the way he expressed it, she grew up thinking any personal inclinations or abilities she had which others might call natural gifts were to be subdued as they were sinful. She has, for instance, a lovely singing voice, but apart from using this for singing Gospel songs, there was no encouragement to develop it further. Her home life was stressful, with constant tension between her father and her grandmother. As a young girl, she developed OCD symptoms. Initially, these were manifested in a felt need to keep washing her hands but then developed into a range of other issues, such as the need to keep checking anything personal to her to ensure it was still safely there.

Before getting to know Phyllis, Leonard had virtually no experience of girls. His sister was seven years older than him, and he had attended a boys-only grammar school. He was attracted to girls but saw them as somewhat mystical beings. If Phyllis hadn't pursued the friendship, he no doubt would have taken far longer to have established a relationship with the opposite sex.

He remembers, for instance, in the early days, how, in a frustrated mood, his girlfriend thumped him several times on his chest, saying, 'Girls need to be told they are loved!'

Leonard remembers a friend complaining about her husband, feeling that he seemed to treat her more or less like a housemate. Leonard fears that perhaps that was true of him too and that he had taken Phyllis too much for granted without trying to understand her. He had no thought that there was anything wrong in their relationship, but Phyllis told him later that she realised she was subconsciously thinking of him in the same light that she saw her father. She hadn't felt able to share her deeper self with him as she feared rejection.

Phyllis loved people and had a God-given gift in understanding and relating to those she befriended. This has been a major part of the ministry she and Leonard have had together which led them to set up Haus Barnabas as a house of encouragement. However, Phyllis has always known that her role in life was to encourage people and help them to see that they are important as she herself had often longed for such encouragement in her own life.

It had taken Leonard some years to realise he and Phyllis needed to find ways of getting closer to each other and that he needed to understand and support his wife better. He remembered how a year or so earlier, a friend whom Phyllis had obviously shared her thoughts with had written him a letter pointing out that his wife was depressed and needed more of his support. Leonard's problem was that his TBS work and his preaching took so much of his time and thought that although he wanted to be all his wife needed, nothing had really changed.

So Europe, for the moment, was off, and Leonard needed to find another job, earn some income, and settle down with his family. God was arranging for them what Phyllis later described as a more normal life. Later, he appreciated very clearly that God was in all that had happened, and they both had a lot to learn if they were to serve their heavenly Master in an effective way together in the future.

What God had planned for them was a period with a more normal life, including a settled income.

PART 4

YORKSHIRE
1976–1983

'For My thoughts are not your thoughts.
Nor are your ways My ways,' says the LORD.
'For as the heavens are higher than the earth,
So are My ways higher than your ways
And My thoughts than your thoughts.'
— Isaiah 55:8–9

CHAPTER

1

Moving in a Pig Truck

Christian farmer with extensive acreage in Yorkshire is looking for reliable company secretary. Telephone . . . for more details.

'Darling, do you think I dare apply for this one?'

It had taken Leonard and Phyllis a week or so to come to a change in their thinking, but they knew they could only go forward as God enabled them, and for the immediate, it seemed clear the door for them to work in German-speaking Europe was closed. Accordingly, it was imperative that Leonard find paid employment. He had toyed with the idea of applying to the TBS again, but he knew they had already replaced him, so he concluded that phase of his life was past, and he needed to look for pastures new.

'Why not look in the *Evangelical Times*?' Phyllis had suggested, so Leonard agreed this was worth a try.

They were praying God would open the opportunity of His choice, and so with a brief silent prayer, Leonard hunted out a copy of the *ET*. The copies they read had been passed on to them by his parents, and so the edition he found was already several months old.

'Can you imagine me working for a farmer in Yorkshire?' said Leonard with a smile. 'It's an old advert, but it's the sort of job that appeals to me, so there's no harm in giving the number a ring.'

The farmer wasn't at home when Leonard rang, but his wife promised that her husband would ring back, probably that evening. The outcome was that Leonard was offered an interview for the job. The farmer offered him and the whole family accommodation for a couple of nights in the little flat he had in his home, which he referred to as the 'prophet's chamber'.[33]

So amazingly, within a few weeks of their plans for a move to Europe collapsing, God demonstrated to them that He was still guiding and providing for them.

The drive up to Ripon in Yorkshire took a full day, but as the family approached their destination and turned off the A1, they found themselves driving through open agricultural land with many acres of cornfields. Some had already been harvested, and moving trains of dust on the horizon showed where combine harvesters were still at work.

Leonard's prospective boss drove him out in his car the next day, showing him the surrounding area, and they ended up in the grounds of Fountains Abbey, where the main part of the interview took place.

Fountains Abbey with Studley Park

Two brothers had been left farms by their father which, for a time, they had farmed together. However, after they had both married and begun to have families of their own, it seemed most prudent to divide up. As things had prospered, each brother had been able to buy additional farmland. They had a secretary who looked after most of the paperwork for both brothers, but they now felt the time had come to divide this aspect of the work also, hence the need for a new secretary.

Leonard explained he had no training as a secretary or experience in farming but had run the publishing department of the TBS under the general secretary, Rev. Terence Brown.

33 A reference to the room allocated to Elisha the prophet in 2 Kings 4:10.

At the TBS, relations among the members of staff had been very formal. They were discouraged from calling each other by their Christian names, so Leonard had always been Mr Holder, and even the youngest female staff member was Miss Mercer.

So it came as a bit of a surprise to Leonard to be informed by the farmer who was interviewing him, 'I'm happy for all my workers to call me Willis. I don't believe respect comes through merely addressing someone in a formal way. We all get on happily on Christian name terms.'

Willis explained that he was currently farming approximately one thousand acres on three farms. There was a further holding that he and his brother farmed together, although he allowed his brother to take the lead in managing that particular one. Finally, he owned one further farm which had been purchased with a sitting tenant. Willis was content to let him continue to farm the land there until he was ready to retire.

He explained that he had recently set up a charitable trust and that all the income from one of the farms was covenanted into this. This income was then used to support Christian work. What he was looking for in his secretary was a capable person who was sympathetic to this Christian work. He himself had no agricultural qualifications, having learned farming from his father, and so was not necessarily looking for paper qualifications from his secretary.

Willis explained that his farming activities were confined almost exclusively to intensive pig fattening and cereal and potato growing. In addition to his farms, he also had a feed mill where cereal grain was ground and mixed with other necessary ingredients to manufacture the animal food required for the pigs on each of the farms. Each farm had a pig fattening unit providing the facilities to house a maximum of about a thousand animals at any one time. There was a farm manager on each farm, but Willis did all the buying and selling. There was a small farm office in the farmyard nearest his house which his secretary would use. He himself worked at home. His secretary would be required to keep up all the records which were written by hand in ledgers (there were no computers in those days). He would need to check all invoices coming in and write out cheques ready for Willis to sign, calculate and pay monthly VAT, and deal with a variety of correspondence.

Willis asked Leonard how he reacted to this and if he was interested. He mentioned a salary that was considerably more than his previous one at TBS and said he would pay for moving costs, even initially providing rent-free accommodation. In the longer term, he would expect his secretary to buy a house suitable to his status as his company secretary.

Maybe if Leonard had been of a pessimistic nature, he might have felt the demands of this job were beyond him. However, farming had appealed to him since childhood, and everything that was explained to him seemed rather like a dream, with the beauty of the Yorkshire countryside thrown in as a bonus, so he rose to the challenge.

That evening, Leonard explained the job to Phyllis with everything that was on offer with it. They thanked the Lord together for His goodness as they believed most certainly that God had provided this opportunity for them. A Bible verse from Genesis came to their minds. Abraham's servant made this comment when God blessed his mission on behalf of his master: 'I being in the way, the Lord led me.'[34]

The next morning, Leonard confirmed to Willis that he would be happy to accept the job and do his best for him. The family then motored back to Horley.

There was a lot to do by way of preparation for the move to Yorkshire, but suddenly, on 5 September, Willis rang them.

'I have a driver bringing a load of pigs down to Leicestershire, and it's suddenly occurred to me – he could continue down to Horley, load your furniture and goods in the truck, and bring everything up to Ripon. You could follow in your car and come to us for the night.'

The boss had spoken, and who would dare disobey?

Willis added, 'If this is all right with you, I'll contact the driver and request he give the truck a thorough clean and give him directions to 7 Queens Road.'

---

34 Genesis 24:27.

The truck turned out to be a thirty-two-tonne vehicle. The trailer for carrying the animals had an aluminium body and was two tiered, carrying up to eighty pigs. When it arrived in Queens Road, it covered the frontage of at least three houses.

Richard, the driver, was a charming Yorkshire lad with a wife and two small children of his own. He had indeed thoroughly cleaned the vehicle as in any case, this was a legal requirement after moving animals; nevertheless, one couldn't help noticing a certain odour pervading the air. Leonard and Phyllis gave Richard a bed for the night. As this extra trip was an afterthought from his boss, he wasn't prepared for an overnight stay and remarked that he had no toothbrush.

It took the whole of the next day to empty the house and load everything into the articulated animal trailer. Phyllis particularly remembers trundling their piano along the narrow front path to the trailer. When everything was packed in, Richard jumped into the cab, but when he tried to start the engine, the battery was flat, and the vehicle had no life whatsoever. Oh dear, oh dear!

Leonard rang two different garages, but as soon as they heard the size of vehicle, they regretfully said they couldn't help. He spoke to his father, and he recommended another garage who might have the means to give the heavy lorry a pull. Thankfully, this firm was prepared to send a mechanic with a four-wheel-drive vehicle. A very slight movement enabled the larger vehicle to start, and Richard was off with all their possessions, but it was already six o'clock in the evening.

Leonard's father had generously given them his blue Ford Cortina car to start their new life, and the family set off as soon as they could after Richard. They motored through the centre of London as the M25 had not then been built, pausing briefly at the Watford Gap motorway stop on the M1. On continuing northward, they eventually arrived in Ripon at exactly midnight, and Leonard's new boss came downstairs in his pyjamas to welcome them.

After a breakfast kindly supplied by Willis's wife, they were introduced to their new home in Ripon, Wycliffe Lodge. This had been Willis's parents' home where, no doubt, he had been brought up himself, but it was now divided up into four dwellings. Willis's sister had a good proportion of the house, including a walled garden, and the other part was divided into three flats. The accommodation provided for the Holder family included the original main front door at the top of stone steps as well as a large hallway which led to a rather grand stairway up to two bedrooms and a bathroom. Downstairs, there was a large dining room/ lounge and a small kitchen. The house was fronted by a high stone wall and ornate metal gates, with a small lawn adjacent to the front door. The other two flats had entrances around the

Wycliffe Lodge, Ripon

back of the building. Richard, with the help of another farm worker, had already unloaded much of their furniture and most of the boxes by the time they arrived.

Just at that point, it began to rain. It was 7 September 1976, and the arrival of rain was significant as the summer had been exceptionally warm and dry, with not a drop of rain since the beginning of June – a very unusual year for Britain. It was almost as if even the weather had been holding its breath until God had led the Holder family to the new home He had planned for them.

CHAPTER

2

Wycliffe Lodge

The apartment which had been provided for the Holders in Ripon was essentially unfurnished except for a couple of largish, antique-looking pieces of furniture in the entrance hall. The kitchen was small, rather narrow, and windowless, and it was soon obvious it had originally been the space allocated for the ground floor entrance to a lift. Surprisingly, at the top of the ornate staircase was a stained-glass window. Later, Phyllis realised that behind the latter was the apartment for a caretaker/gardener of Willis's sister. Phyllis soon got to know the gardener's wife and would have brief chats through the stained glass, with the two using this means of communication to invite each other to coffee.

A major consideration once they had time to get themselves settled was to find a school for the boys. Geoffrey was then 8 and Daniel 6 years old. They were informed that the primary school allocated for that area of Ripon was Greystones. This was a new school built on an estate on the outskirts of the city. Ripon, with its ancient cathedral, is indeed a British 'city', albeit one of its smallest in the country, with a population of a little more than sixteen thousand. Unlike the primary school in Horley, which was just minutes away, Greystones was a good mile to walk, and it was necessary for Phyllis to accompany the boys each end of the school day. Coming from the south of England and mixing with lads and lasses from a northern estate had its difficulties. The boys' ears needed to get attuned to the broad Yorkshire accent, and it would take time for them to relate to these northern children. Another difficulty to get accustomed to was the school's open plan design, with several classes gathering in different areas of the same large room. However, Leonard and Phyllis were extremely satisfied with the teachers at Greystones. They took a real interest in these two lads from Surrey, and the boys, in turn, made good progress.

Soon after the family arrived in Ripon, Leonard decided it would be great to have a dog. He had so enjoyed the animal he had as a teenager and felt the environment of their new home lent itself to having such a pet again. One weekend, on searching a local newspaper, they discovered an advertisement offering free puppies to good homes. This was worth investigating. So they set off to Harrogate to find out what was on offer.

The animals in question were border collies with, they were told, some part Samoyed, which are white furry, husky-type dogs. There was very little evidence of the latter breed in the puppy they chose, which was an attractive little black-and-white bitch. The family named her Shep, although she soon became affectionately known as Looney. Shep soon became an important family member and a very significant part of the Holders' family life in Yorkshire. She forced Leonard out for a brisk walk before breakfast, and Phyllis still talks, more than forty years later, of the joy of walking alongside the swift-flowing Skell River, with the scent of wild garlic wafting in the still air. Shep could run free, and these were days before anyone thought of gathering dog poo in little bags.

Leonard was very soon into the daily routine of work. His farm office was about a six-minute drive from Wycliffe Lodge, and he needed to be there by 8:00 a.m. The centre of Ripon, with its market square, was within walking distance for Phyllis to do shopping. However, when they were first in their new habitat, there were no supermarkets in the city, and Phyllis found it strange, having to wander from the butcher's shop to the baker's and the greengrocer's and then to a general grocer's.

She commented to Leonard one evening, 'It takes so long. In each shop, the assistant is chatting about the weather and the customer's mother-in-law and so forth, and other customers simply have to wait their turn.'

Once a week, stalls appeared in the market square, and customers flocked into the city to buy from the wide range of produce displayed. On the morning of another day, there was an animal market, and Leonard well remembers seeing the city butcher herding one or more cows, sheep, and pigs up the alley way into the back of his shop. His trade would have included the skill of slaughtering and cutting up the animals he then displayed for sale in his shopfront. He no doubt also purchased at the same market many of the fowl, rabbits, and game birds whose limp bodies added to the colourful but somewhat bloody scene behind the plate glass of his store. All this was very different from the supermarkets in the southern suburbia, where Phyllis was more used to shopping.

CHAPTER

3

The Job

A man named Geoff had been secretary to both the farming brothers. With Willis having now acquired his own secretary, Geoff made his office available for Leonard's use and set about moving to a newly equipped office on the brother's home farm. He stayed on for a day or two to introduce Leonard to the way he worked and promised to be at the end of a phone if needed.

Leonard very soon learned that he was expected to use his own initiative and, as much as possible, think things through himself rather than ask questions of his boss. Soon after starting his new job, he rang Willis to ask him something or other and got a rather abrupt answer.

'Listen, Len. I ask you that kind of question, not you me!'

Unless notified otherwise, the daily routine included a short walk across the road from the farm office to his boss's house for a meeting at nine thirty each morning. He would then sit with Willis at his breakfast table, partake of a cup of coffee with a biscuit or two provided by Willis's wife, and talk business. Anything appropriate for Leonard to deal with in the post was passed over, and in return, Leonard would get his boss's signature on cheques for the payment of bills and for the cash he needed to withdraw to meet the men's wages on the three farms. Leonard banked all business cheques at the Ripon branch of Barclays Bank and, once a week, got the bank balances for the various bank accounts he was concerned with. Interestingly, Willis wasn't happy if his bank accounts were in credit. He preferred them to be in the red, maintaining that money sitting in the bank was wasted as he could make better use of it by investing it in one of his farming enterprises.

Opposite Leonard's office was a weighbridge which was also used by Willis's brother's wagons, so most days, heavy lorries were driving in out of the yard at least once or twice a day and far more often during harvest time. The feed mill, manufacturing feed for the pigs on each farm, was also accessed past his office; a thousand pigs consume a lot of food, so there was plenty of daily activity.

One night the office was broken into, but since there was nothing of value kept there and those were days before computers, the potential thief contented himself in scratching a swear word across the desk.

The three farms for which Leonard had the responsibility of keeping the accounts were well spread out across North Yorkshire, one nearer York and another further east near Pickering. Each had a farm manager, but Willis kept everything under tight control and visited each farm at least once a week. Leonard needed to get to know each of the managers and have some idea of the workings of each farm, so occasionally, he needed to visit them too.

There was a swift turnaround with the pigs, and often when Leonard joined his boss in the mornings, he would be ringing around getting the best price he could for the animals that were ready for slaughter. He bought in young pigs, weaners, at a weight of about thirty-two kilograms and usually sold them for bacon at a weight of eighty to a hundred kilograms. Pigs for pork were sold at a weight of about sixty kilograms. With his own transporter and driver, he could send animals to all parts of the country at a moment's notice, and when an abattoir needed animals to meet contracts, he could be a tough negotiator. In earlier days, pigs from different sources were bought at local animal markets, but since pigs are very susceptible to disease, particularly in intensive fattening units, during most of Leonard's time as farm secretary, his boss was buying weaners from a particular source of genetically improved animals. Shortly before Leonard came up to Yorkshire, swine vesicular disease had been rampant in the country, and Willis's whole stock had to be destroyed, the premises thoroughly disinfected and kept empty for a specific period. It was probably after this that Willis stopped buying pigs from public animal markets.

His boss would occasionally pass ideas for other business projects over to Leonard for him to get information about or make calculations to bring back to him to talk through. One of the farms had some old barns on the edge of the village for which Willis was able to get permission for a building development. There was additional planning permission granted for a couple of building plots on an adjacent field. He took Leonard across to look these over with a view to getting some ideas as to how best to convert the barns. Of course, an architect had to do the main design work, but overseeing the construction work himself, Willis employed a local builder before negotiating the sale of the finished dwellings. Leonard was involved in some aspects of the administrative work for this.

Christian ministry in German-speaking Europe was pushed to the back of Leonard's mind after the move up to Yorkshire. Was the call that he had felt so strongly to be from the Lord merely a figment of his imagination? What he didn't realise was that this new experience was all preparation for God's future plans.

CHAPTER

4

Serving God in Yorkshire

Shortly before the Holders moved up to Ripon, the evangelical church there had experienced a split amongst its membership, but of course, Leonard and Phyllis knew nothing of the background leading to this. Willis had explained that he was the elder of Zion Evangelical Church, and it seemed that the natural thing for the newcomers was to attend this church on the first Sunday after their arrival. Numbers were small, and Willis and his wife and four children, together with the four Holders, made up nearly half of the total congregation. Willis led the two services and preached, while a man named Roger, who had a South African background, played the piano. Roger and his wife, Brenda, had two children of similar age to Geoffrey and Daniel, and the two families became good friends.

One afternoon, during the following week, Willis asked Leonard to join him at his house. As they were relaxing in the comfortable sitting room together, he attempted to explain to Leonard the background to the church and what had recently happened. He himself had been a Methodist lay preacher for a number of years. Historically, since the days of John Wesley in the eighteenth century, Methodism had been strong in the villages of Yorkshire. However, a good number of Christians within the Methodist tradition had become very dissatisfied with the more liberal theology that had infiltrated the denomination, resulting in evangelical fellowships springing up, free from the control of a denominational committee, in several places.

Willis had initiated such a group in Ripon, purchasing a Methodist church building which the denomination no longer used. He had assumed the role of elder, and from what Leonard understood, over time, dissatisfaction had crept in concerning his leadership. One Sunday morning, when Willis and family arrived for the service, most of the congregation weren't there; they had agreed to meet by themselves at another venue, Willis discovered later. Fairly quickly, the new situation stabilised, with one or two coming back to the original group, whilst a few others left.

The building Willis had bought included a good-sized hall behind the original main church auditorium. The hall had been converted into the assembly room for the new evangelical church, and the original church was being used as a warehouse and offices for the Evangelical Press, of which Willis was the managing director. The previously mentioned pianist, Roger, was employed by Evangelical Press as manager.

Willis assured Leonard that his employment as his secretary was, in no way, dependent on him attending the church where he was elder and that if he chose to attend the breakaway fellowship, he would accept this without question. Having had no contact with other Christians in Ripon at that point, there seemed no reason not to continue attending Zion, and everything else being equal, this clearly would be the most comfortable relationship with the man who had employed him.

After a few weeks, Willis invited Leonard to lead one of the services and to preach, so before very long, they had come to an arrangement whereby Leonard preached Sunday mornings and Willis Sunday evenings. Some months later, a church membership was formed with an initial eight members covenanting together. The arrangement with Leonard and Willis sharing the Sunday preaching, with an occasional guest preacher, continued for several years until the church called a pastor.

Leonard preferred to have responsibility for the morning service as he could get up early on a Sunday and finalise his thoughts and his notes for the sermon. Then after the service was over, he could relax. However, for several years, he also taught a Sunday school class in the afternoons.

Willis was an active member of the Gideon organisation, which exists to further God's kingdom through the distribution of copies of the Bible and the New Testament. Having got to know Leonard somewhat, he suggested to him that he might also like to become a member and recommended him to the local Harrogate branch.

Gideon branches are expected to finance the purchase of the Scriptures, which they then circulate without charge, so the members tend to be businessmen who have the means to do this. When Leonard joined the branch, he found that at the monthly meetings, he was associating with influential Christian men from a range of professions. In addition to several prosperous businessmen farmers, other members included Neville Knox, the then chief executive of Harrogate District Council, and Verna Wright, professor of rheumatology at the University of Leeds. Leonard appreciated the privilege of knowing Verna. He was extremely active in Christian work as well as being internationally known in his field of rheumatology. After Leonard spent a few months as a Gideon, the Harrogate branch appointed Leonard as their padre. What this meant was that he was expected to open each meeting with a Bible reading and a short devotion and lead them in prayer.

The monthly Gideon meetings tended to go on quite late and ended with a more-than-adequate supper, inevitably including the Yorkshire treat of fruitcake eaten with chunks of cheese. Leonard generally had a disturbed night after this unaccustomed culinary delight, and it has to be acknowledged that Phyllis showed him no sympathy. However, fruitcake with cheese was just a minor perk of becoming a Gideon. Their main purpose was to distribute copies of the Scriptures, and Willis was happy for Leonard to take time away from the office to accompany him into a range of schools, hotels, and army barracks in pursuit of this end. Whenever possible, the practice was to hand over the Scriptures personally with a shake of the hand. In school assemblies, with up to perhaps a hundred pupils receiving New Testaments, this obviously needed to be carried out at speed, and personal identification of the recipient when all looked much the same in their school blazers and ties was difficult.

One evening Geoffrey commented to his father, 'Thanks for the New Testament you gave me this morning, Dad.'

'Yes, I was at your school today, son, but I didn't see you,' responded his father with a smile.

'But, Dad!' answered Geoff, bewildered. 'You gave me my copy and shook hands with me.'

Leonard also had hands-on involvement with Willis's charitable trust fund. He was sometimes invited to meetings of the trustees when it was decided to whom money should be sent. Also, under Willis's guidance, he looked after the investment of the funds.

Leonard had responded to the initial advert he had seen for the job of farming company secretary in Yorkshire with no idea of what would be involved. Looking back, it's so encouraging to see how, when one commits their life to God and is looking to Him for guidance, God does indeed guide and provides in wonderful ways.

Memories from Others

Willis

Len gave the impression of being serious but was always ready with dry humour and laughter, having the ability of seeing the funny side of things. For instance, our David was being ticked off by his mother for leaving ten-pound notes in his overalls. He had given them to her for going through the washer; the notes were found by his mother quite intact. Your immediate comment, Len, was 'Well, that, at least, shouldn't be filthy lucre'.

CHAPTER

5

Kirkbymoorside

Before leaving Horley in 1976, during the period of great uncertainty after the door into German-speaking Europe seemed to have closed, Leonard and Phyllis and their small boys spent a few days with a family Leonard had met through his preaching. He had discovered that the wife was related to him through his grandfather, and it had been good to make this contact. The family had recently returned from a blissful camping holiday in Cornwall. As you may remember hearing, the summer that year had been particularly dry and warm and so ideal camping weather, but an added blessing during the holiday was finding another young family on the campsite who were Christians. The parents were both from non-Christian families but had very recently been converted and were ready to talk about their new-found faith in Jesus whenever and wherever there was opportunity. They were from Kirkbymoorside in Yorkshire, and when it was known that Leonard and Phyllis were moving up to Ripon, their friends in Surrey were very keen that they should be introduced to their new campsite friends.

The result of this was that the Mosley family from Kirkbymoorside were the first Yorkshire Christians the Holders got to know other than the friends they met in the Ripon church.

It was so encouraging to learn how God had been working in Kirkbymoorside. The Holders' new friends had been converted first and then, in their enthusiasm, had witnessed to their neighbour who had also come to faith, and soon, others, relatives and neighbours alike, were infected by this living spiritual fervour. Eventually, the evangelical church in Whitby, about twenty-five miles away, took the small group under their wing, with their pastor, Peter Brumby, providing valuable teaching and support. After a few years, when it was clear that Pastor Peter Brumby was not able to provide Bible ministry every week, Leonard expressed a willingness to lead a Bible study on a Thursday evening. So very soon, Leonard, Phyllis, and their boys were motoring the nearly forty miles across to Kirkbymoorside and Pickering most Thursday evenings, where the Bible study took place in different homes.

Whenever possible, Leonard found it helpful for Phyllis and him to work together as a team. Phyllis had a God-given gift in relating to people. This stemmed from a genuine interest in others as well as an ability to recognise unspoken needs and to converse in a natural way, all of which enabled people to feel she was a genuine friend whom they could feel free to relate to in a more intimate way than they would with a casual enquirer. Phyllis also felt very strongly about the place of loyalty where her friends were concerned and could be trusted to keep personal disclosures to herself. One of the members of the Kirkbymoorside fellowship was a young hairdresser whom the Holders came to an extremely helpful arrangement with in that she came across to Ripon for a weekend about every four or five weeks and, in exchange for the hospitality, cut all the family's hair.

There are two interesting memories that Geoffrey and Daniel have of those journeys over the Sutton Bank towards the Yorkshire Moors and Kirkbymoorside and Pickering. First, their parents would listen to the Archers during the journey, and this usually ended as they neared the top of the climb up the Sutton Bank. At that point, Phyllis's conscience would inevitably trouble her as she realised she hadn't had a single thought about her sons in the back seat for at least fifteen minutes.

'Are you still there, boys?' would come the question.

After a few weeks of this regular enquiry at the top of Sutton Bank, the retort would come back: 'No, Mum. We fell out ten minutes ago.'

Second, since it would often be as late as 11:00 p.m. before the family got home, the boys would fall asleep on the journey back and would then need to be helped upstairs to bed.

Some years later, when talking about this, Daniel, with a little sly grin, made the following comment: 'You know, we weren't always asleep. Often we just pretended because we knew that we wouldn't need to have a wash and clean our teeth!'

After a few years, the Kirkbymoorside friends were provided with a pastor through the financial help of some neighbouring Yorkshire churches. It's interesting that the main spiritual growth, when others were converted, was, in those early days, after the first family came to the Lord and were full of enthusiasm to share their new-found faith. Sadly, a few individuals have drifted away; however, Leonard and Phyllis maintain contact with a few of that original number (some are already in glory) after more than forty years.

CHAPTER

6

63 Kirkby Road

The Holders' accommodation in Wycliffe Lodge was intended to be temporary. Leonard's boss had indicated he would like his secretary to have a house of his own which reflected his position. Clearly, however, this couldn't happen at once as the family had no savings. Still, Leonard was now earning a reasonable income, and since his employer was known and respected in the city, his position as Willis's personal secretary would add weight to any application for a mortgage.

In the spring of 1978, Leonard and Phyllis began to look for a suitable house. They weren't impressed by the new modern houses and decided they wanted to be more on the edge of the town than in the centre. Eventually, they found a semi-detached three-bedroomed dwelling with good-sized rooms. The kitchen had been extended by a couple of metres and

63 Kirkby Road, Ripon

had a large picture window looking out on an expanse of lawn bordered on two sides by neat flower beds and ending in a shrub garden with a small Japanese maple as its main feature. Beyond the garden were a few acres of market garden, and beyond this, one could see the Ripon Grammar School buildings and clock tower. Separated from the house by a covered passageway was a substantial garage. Built on the end of the garage, with access from the passageway and from outside the backdoor of the house, was an extremely useful utility room. In the front, the house looked out on open fields, with a wooden stile leading onto a footpath which ran along the hedge, separating two of the fields. To have a footpath immediately opposite the house is, of course, ideal for dog walking. Also, opposite and slightly to the right were ornate iron gates giving access to a cemetery.

As a kind friend commented, 'Not far to go for the next move!' Little did he or anyone else know what God had planned for the Holders' future.

Leonard and Phyllis were able to buy the house for £17,500, securing a mortgage that was manageable with Leonard's monthly income. Kirkby Road led straight out of Blossom Gate, where Zion Church was situated, leading on towards the village of Kirkby Malzeard, famous as a centre for the manufacture of Wensleydale cheese. Included in the purchase of the house were fitted carpets and most of the curtains. The house was heated, with a few night storage heaters and electric fires in the two living rooms to give additional heat as required.

After a few years in the house, Leonard decided to make a few improvements. This started with the replacement of the bath in the upstairs bathroom. Only the sudden appearance of a Christian friend to lend a hand saved a disaster whilst Leonard was getting the old bath down the stairs. Leonard later read that a hefty hit with a sledgehammer will usually break a cast-iron bath in two, making it easier to move. Then over a period of about two years, Leonard installed central heating, which was fired by a gas boiler in the utility room. Before completing this, he decided it would be useful to add a downstairs toilet in the utility room also. All this work needed to be fitted in on evenings and Saturdays; Leonard was learning as he went along with the help of DIY guidebooks. Thankfully, there were no major catastrophes. It was a great advantage that through his contact with local firms, because of his work with Willis, he was able to obtain a discount on the majority of his purchases.

Phyllis later would often refer to this time in Yorkshire as their 'normal' life. Leonard had fairly regular work hours and was earning a reasonable income, their two boys were happily attending a regular school, they had a house of their own, they were involved in a local church, and to crown it all, a delightful border collie added another dimension to their family life.

Memories from Others

Joanna

I came to know Phyl from going to the 'Pitter Patter Club' held in the Christian Alliance Centre in Ripon. This was run by Hazel Bancroft and Phyl on Friday afternoons, where you could leave your tiny tots for an hour or two whilst you went shopping.

I was expecting my second child; my husband was in the army and due to go away down to the south of England as soon as the child was born. Phyl said she would like to help, and every week after Colin was born, she cycled on her old bike to the army quarters for a chat.

Soon after, we moved from Ripon to Beaconsfield in Bucks, to our next army posting. I was suffering from depression and had been suicidal. I wrote to Phyl regularly at her request. She must have received some weird letters from me.

Although I didn't realise at the time, Phyl, Len, and other Christians I met in Ripon prayed for me. My husband, Barry, and I eventually became Christians and later our children too.

When I think of you, Phyl and Len, I see you as dependable, strong in faith, showing genuine concern and understanding of people. I can see Jesus shining through your lives.

CHAPTER

7

Pig Breeding

Leonard had felt a draw towards farming since childhood, and now God had given him a position on a Yorkshire farm. He and Phyllis very much enjoyed the countryside around them, and the fact of needing to walk Looney each day ensured they both, mostly at different times, got to know the fields and walks around them. However, Leonard felt he would like a farming project of his own in addition to the secretarial work for Willis. He's not sure now how it started, but he must, at some convenient point, have mentioned to Willis that he would like to try his hand at breeding pigs. Willis had learned a lot of his farming and business skills from his father and considered that an important part of fatherhood was to teach sons practical lessons of life by example, and Leonard believes this was one reason why he offered his secretary an unused stable opposite the farm office for him to use for breeding pigs. He also made a very practical suggestion.

'Look, Len,' he said as they were talking about it, 'the easiest way to start would be to buy a sow already in pig.'

In layman's terms, this meant a pregnant female pig.

'Why not talk to the pig breeder from whom we buy many of our weaners? They will have a policy of allowing sows to have a certain number of litters before sending them for slaughter. I would imagine they'd be prepared to sell you a pregnant sow at the end of her working life. You could get her piglets and then send her to market yourself. This would avoid the need of having a boar.'

Leonard had already learned through breeding rabbits that to farm, one needs to hold sentiment in check.

The family were pleased to take an interest in this farming project, and Leonard was able to buy a second-hand farrowing crate and timber to construct a low-level pen. When the sow was nearing time to farrow, she was enticed into the farrowing crate, which was a sort of metal cage. Pigs are heavy and have a habit of simply collapsing down when they need to lie. This can be fatal for any piglet which happens to be under her at that time. The object of the farrowing crate is to confine the animal when she is giving birth to her piglets and immediately afterwards when the offspring are young. It ensures that when the sow wants to lie down, she will first lean against the bars of the crate and slide down. This gives piglets time to move away. Leonard, with some help from his sons, constructed a pen for the piglets about eighteen inches high around the farrow crate, with an area at one end where an infrared lamp was hung. When the piglets are very young, they gravitate to the warmth of the lamp when they are not suckling from their mother.

Having bought the first pregnant sow, Leonard read up all he could about breeding pigs and decided he needed to be present at the birth to ensure all went well. It's not difficult to pick up signs when a mother pig is ready to produce, so at this stage, he looked in on her every few hours, also motoring up to the farmyard a couple of times during the night. The highest number of piglets that Leonard's sows produced was fifteen, but on his first experience as midwife, his sow produced ten healthy offspring. Being comparatively small, the piglets are usually born easily, but if there is too long a gap in the births, it's recommended that the 'midwife' farmer feel up the animal to ensure there's no extra- large or even a dead piglet blocking the passageway and needs easing along. Leonard got quite proficient with this procedure.

The books recommended that the sharp tips of piglets' teeth be snipped to make it more comfortable for the mother sow when they are suckling and that the ends of their tails are snipped off at the same time. Pigs kept in close contact during the fattening stage of their lives are tempted to nibble one another's tails, and with them having shorter tails, this can be avoided. Leonard got used to performing these operations on the piglets when they were a day or two old, and neither procedure appeared to give them much discomfort.

The books advised to watch for signs of mastitis in the sows when they are producing milk to suckle their piglets, and with more experience, Leonard would have noticed this problem developing in his first sow. The vet was able to give medication which dealt with the problem, but since milk dried up in several of the mother pig's teats (incidentally, a sow has twelve or more teats), the piglets needed feeding by hand. Phyllis managed this very well, but it was a commitment because her squealing foster babies needed feeding from a bottle every few hours, including a couple of times through the night. She found she needed to spray some colour on each piglet's back after it had its turn at the bottle as each insisted on coming back for more. Geoffrey and Daniel laughingly suggested that the piglets were imagining Phyllis was their mother. The vet was extremely impressed that all the piglets had been kept alive and congratulated Phyllis on her diligence and care.

The young pigs were soon weaned onto solid pellet food, but there was one further operation to be performed to ensure the best price before they could be sold on. The male piglets needed to be castrated. Boar meat is apparently not popular as it has a stronger flavour, so pig farmers buying weaners to fatten won't pay as much for male pigs, and the answer is to castrate them. Leonard read up how to do this, acquired a suitable scalpel, and, before the piglets got too big, gritted his teeth, told himself he was a farmer, and did the deed.

Sow with piglets

The ten piglets all survived, and Willis bought them, paying by weight at the going market price when they were approximately thirty-two kilograms. The unfortunate mother sow had been sold for slaughter by this time, and Leonard had bought another pregnant pig, and so the cycle continued. The biggest litter produced by one of the incoming pregnant mums was fifteen piglets, but one of these was very tiny, the runt of the litter. The boys named him Archie Gemmill after the five-foot, five-inch footballer, famous at the time. Unfortunately, little Archie, the runt, didn't survive.

After a year or so, the piggery declined for some reason or other to sell Leonard any further in-pig sows, so he bought three gilts, which were sows less than 1 year old. Watching for the right time, these were artificially inseminated to 'bring them into pig', and so the breeding cycle continued until there was a threat of swine disease in the country, and Willis decided it was too risky to have Leonard's pigs located so close to his feed mill in case they caught the disease.

It was a fascinating side-line while it lasted, and because of Willis's on-hand facility for disposing of the manure produced as well as his willingness to purchase the young weaners and provide free use of the buildings with electricity, the project did produce some financial profit.

Memories from Others

Willis

I remember your pig breeding days chiefly through the mental picture of this obviously town-bred person in office-type clothing complete with a tie, mucking out pigs. Quite sufficient to make anybody stop and say, 'What on earth am I seeing?'

Barbara

After the move to Ripon, they had to start all over again. But them, being them, it didn't take long. And who could help but fall in love with that beautiful countryside? And as for the pigs and being able to be there when farrowing etc., it was great. I loved it as much as they did.

CHAPTER

8

Scottish Holidays

Coming from the far south of England, when Leonard and Phyllis moved up to Yorkshire, they imagined in their ignorance that they were close to Scotland. They were certainly closer than when in the counties of their birth, but when planning a holiday in the most northern part of the UK, they realised Scotland was still quite a drive further upwards towards the Arctic Circle.

Holiday in Scotland:
Phyllis with boys and
dog Sheppie

One holiday in particular was impacted significantly by their pig breeding activities. Leonard had, for some time, been aware that the male contingent of the latest litter of piglets needed castrating. It was not a task that he particularly enjoyed, but this farming side of his life was calling, and the job needed doing before the holiday. Phyllis and son Daniel would often hold the 'patient' for him while he performed the operation, but on the evening in question,

Daniel was at a children's club run by the Christian Alliance, so Phyllis volunteered to be Leonard's sole accomplice. The procedure necessitated the assistant holding the animal firmly upside down between his or her legs to expose the animal part to be treated. Unlike sheep, pigs squeal at the slightest provocation and, of course, wriggle. These piglets were bigger than was usually the case when this operation was performed, and when the pig Phyllis was holding did an extra violent wriggle, the scalpel in Leonard's hand sank into his wife's thigh. Because the implement was very sharp, she didn't immediately notice what had happened, and neither did the assailant. When the half dozen animals had been successfully treated, Phyllis suddenly realised her Wellington boot was filling with blood, which hadn't stemmed from the patients she had been holding. Thankfully, Ripon still had an active cottage hospital at that time, so treatment could be quickly administered. The doctor on duty insisted on a tetanus injection in addition to penicillin and four stitches.

Leonard left Phyllis to have the treatment while he picked up Geoffrey and Daniel from their club. He ran their friend Dave back to his home and then headed back to the hospital.

'Where are we going, Dad?' exclaimed Leonard's elder son, surprised at the direction his father was driving.

'We are going to the hospital to pick up your mum,' answered his father. 'I stabbed her!'

A few days later, the family had planned to motor up to Scotland for a camping holiday. Although Phyllis was now suffering from a very stiff leg with restricted movement, being a long-suffering wife and mother, she, at no time, suggested a change of plan, so they set off at the appointed hour. They found a campsite near a lake not far from Fort William with a good view of Ben Nevis, Britain's highest mountain, and pitched their family tent.

Apart from the difficulty of making any movement that required bending her leg (obviously, living in a tent with this restriction is not easy), there were two specific occasions when Phyllis remembers being particularly hindered by her injury during the holiday. One was when Leonard suggested climbing Ben

Nevis, and the other was when they attended a service at a Free Presbyterian church.

The boys were keen to climb Britain's highest mountain, which they could see from the door of their canvas holiday home. After discussion, it was agreed that Leonard would set off with Geoffrey and Looney the dog at first light, which was about 5:00 a.m. or even earlier, and Daniel would keep his mother company. The adventurers would then return as soon as possible so the whole day would not be lost to the two forced to stay back at camp.

It wasn't possible to plan the outing as Leonard didn't have an appropriate map. He quite expected to find a carpark and a signpost indicating the footpath that would take them up the mountain. They set off as intended and toured around what they believed to be the foot of Ben Nevis, but there was no obvious path to take. At last, seeing a farmer with his milking cows, Leonard asked him where to find the correct footpath. Thankfully, it was nearby, and very soon, they were, all three, climbing upwards, two walking steadily and the third running round in circles, finding exciting smells. The sun was giving warmth but not too much, and there was no one else in sight. As they got near the top, the grassland turned to shale and rocks, and a light mist engulfed them. There was no reason to linger, so they retraced their steps, trusting they were on the path which would lead them back to the car. Thinking back, Leonard is certain God was looking after them as they were not very well prepared and hadn't realised the possibility of danger. The following morning, looking up to the mountain from their campsite, they were surprised to see a sprinkling of snow covering the peak. It was the Whitsun school holiday in 1980.

On the Sunday, the family found a Free Presbyterian church to attend. It was their first experience of this Scottish denomination, and they were in for a few surprises. First, everyone sat for the singing – which suited Phyllis, with her gammy leg, very well – but when they discovered everyone stood up for the prayer, this was less comfortable. The preacher appeared to be fairly old and, although mainly speaking in English, would occasionally lapse into Gaelic. The prayer was long or seemed so when one was standing for it, and the young people in front of the Holders' pew obviously knew by the phraseology when the end was drawing near as their bottoms were getting ever closer to their seats as the amen approached.

The next surprise was the speed with which the congregation left the church building. By the time Phyllis had got herself together and stood up, the place was empty. Also, as they left the building, there was no one to be seen outside. Thinking this so strange, as they walked around the corner, there was a family waiting for them, and they were invited home for Sunday lunch. Thinking back, Leonard believes their host's family name was Ross, and they were certainly very kind. They insisted their guests stayed all day and fetched Looney into the house as well. The animal was delighted to have a very unaccustomed treat of fried egg and bacon placed in a dish on the floor for her. After supper at the end of the day, they were invited to share in family prayers. They left the supper table and went into the sitting room for this. After the Bible reading, the host and hostess and family set the example by all kneeling and burying their heads in cushions on their seats. This, of course, wasn't so easy for Phyllis, with her sore and stiff leg, and of course, the story of how her loving husband had stabbed her had to be recounted. The whole visit was a wonderful illustration of Scottish hospitality, and it became clear that the quick departure from church was not intended to show a lack of friendliness but rather was the traditional way of showing respect and reverence towards God whilst in His house.

CHAPTER

9

Ripon Grammar School

The move to Kirkby Road brought the family into another junior school catchment area, and so the boys changed to Trinity, which was a Church of England school within easy walking distance of the family's new home. Both Geoffrey and Daniel did well at Trinity, and there was no question about their suitability for a grammar school education.

It can surely be recognised as a further blessing of God's gracious leading and provision for the Holder family that at the point where Geoffrey and Daniel needed to progress to senior education, they were living in such close proximity to a grammar school, described by the *Sunday Times* as 'the top state school in the north'. Ripon Grammar School's webpage informs us that the school had evolved from an Anglo-Saxon grammar school attached to the collegiate church of St Wilfrid in Ripon, with its history well documented since the Middle Ages.

'The current foundation dates from 1555. when Queen Mary and King Philip signed its charter. The school was required to provide a free education for the boys of Ripon, although the master also took in paying boarders. By the 19th century, the school had outgrown its town centre buildings and so moved to its current location, on the west side of Ripon. In the late nineteenth century, the school was taken under local authority control and, in the nineteen sixties, amalgamated with Ripon Girls' High School.'

The school continues to take boarders in addition to day students.

One morning at breakfast in the kitchen at Kirkby Road, Phyllis noticed whiffs of smoke arising from one of the grammar school roofs, which were visible across the field beyond the garden. Because of their vantage point, she was

Ripon Grammar School

probably one of the first to recognise that there was a fire at the school. Soon, there was the sound of fire engines, and the boys were chuffed about, having a morning without lessons. It turned out that one of the boarders had crept up to an attic room in the roof of his dormitory block for a quiet smoke and that an unextinguished cigarette end had started the fire.

The school has had some notable pupils over the years, one being William Hague, who was a boarder there for a few years and later became a leader of the British Conservative Party.

Geoffrey began at Ripon Grammar in 1979, and Daniel followed in 1981. The school was very rigid about school uniform, and school blazers and ties were to be worn at all times. Rugby was an important game for the school, and Geoffrey was a member of the school rugby team for his age group until he broke the tip of his middle finger. Unfortunately, during his first time back into the game after the finger healed, it broke again in the same place. Rugby matches can be very rough, and since they take place in winter, they are often played on a waterlogged, muddy pitch, with the players often bracing the elements, namely, sleet and snow.

Geoffrey loved to use and play with words and assured his parents that this was the only reason prompting him to write a short essay in which he described the feelings of a poor destitute beggar, feelings which had led the wretch to throw himself off a bridge in utter despair. This was the only essay chosen to grace the school magazine that year, and it did cause the bewildered Phyllis to wonder how her son could possibly have known the feelings he had so eloquently expressed.

Memories from Others

Cynthia

It was in the late seventies, when Len and Phyl came to live in Ripon, that my husband and I got to know them through the friendship of Geoff and Dan with our sons, Mark and David, who attended the same schools. The boys would play in each other's houses and go on cycle rides together. The friendliness and good natures of Geoff and Dan made a favourable impression.

Walking home together from Tuesday evenings at the Christian Alliance open house meetings, Phyl and I got to know each other better, and Len's occasional ministry at Bethel Evangelical Church was appreciated.

On a lighter note: we have tangible reminders of you in particular, Len, in the form of pieces of furniture, fashioned by my innovative husband, from what we call 'pig wood' – obtained from you when you dismantled your pig pens before leaving Ripon.

CHAPTER

10

Visitors in Yorkshire

The Holders' move to Yorkshire aroused much interest amongst their southern friends and family. Within a few years and on the retirement of Leonard's father, Leonard's parents sold their home in Horley and bought a bungalow in Ripon. Phyllis's parents very much enjoyed coming up to Yorkshire and soon were regularly having at least two holidays a year with their daughter and family. Leonard's sister and family of three children came several times and used the house in Kirkby Road for a holiday when Leonard and Phyllis and boys were themselves on holiday.

There are several interesting incidents relating to visits from family and friends. The proximity of the Yorkshire Dales was a real attraction, and guests were always pleased to have someone to guide and introduce them to some of the delightful villages and places of interest. Friends from Horley days were visiting during one of the earlier months of the year, and there had been heavy falls of snow in the Dales. With the main roads clear and the sun shining, the views when motoring through Pateley Bridge and on to Grassington and other little towns take on a wonderful fairy tale–like appearance, with the landscape of hills, valleys, and occasional farms all bedecked with a glistening white covering. Phyllis decided it was an ideal day to take her guests from Surrey to see the Dales in all its snow-covered beauty. The guests were entranced. It was a wonderful drive. Phyllis was in front with the driver to direct the way, and the friend from Horley youth club days was in the back with her mother. To make an interesting detour on the way home, they decided to take a narrower road which should have led down a valley and up to the other side onto another main road. There was a road sign fallen over, so they decided it must be no longer relevant as the road had been cleared of snow.

'We'll take this lane,' said Phyllis, looking at the map on her lap. 'It'll bring us out onto another interesting route home.'

Famous last words. As they descended into the valley, a black cloud appeared, and a hefty snow shower ensued. There was snow from previous days heaped up on either side of them, and Phyllis began to pray that they wouldn't meet a

Snow experience in the Yorkshire Dales

vehicle coming the other way as there was certainly not enough space to pass even a small car. Then as they almost reached the lowest part of the valley, in front of them, filling the whole road, was a snowplough. Beyond the snowplough was a mountain of snow several feet high. It was obvious that the local council was in the process of making access through the valley and no doubt freeing up a way out for a snowed-up farm at the bottom.

The Horley friend driving the car looked at Phyllis despairingly. 'We can't turn. We can't go on, and I'm not sure I can reverse up the gradient we've just come down.' There was a hint of accusation in his tone.

In the back of the car, the mother and daughter began to panic. Taking the bull by the horns, the driver immediately calmed himself and took control of the situation.

'It's all right!' he exclaimed. 'We'll get out of this. I've just got to back as far as I need to before we have enough road width to turn.'

Putting words into action, he engaged the reverse gear and let out the clutch. Very soon, it was clear there was another problem. They had come down the hill easily enough, but in reversing against the gradient, it became obvious that the compressed snow on the road surface was icy, and the wheels began to spin. Rising to the occasion, Phyllis indicated to him that she would get out and push. From the back seat came sounds of hysterical crying. This was a completely new situation for folk from the southern counties. To have banks of snow on either side, a wall of snow in front, and an icy uphill gradient which seemed impossible to negotiate behind, this was the worst situation imaginable. It was a nightmare.

It was decided that it was best for the backseat passengers to stay put as their weight helped the reversing process. There were several places where Phyllis and the driver needed to ease snow away from the back wheels, but eventually – with Phyllis pushing, wheels spinning, and the clutch smoking – they eventually got to a place where the car could be turned, even if it had to be about a twenty point one.

That trip up to the Holders in Yorkshire was not quickly forgotten by those good Surrey friends.

The Holders also had several guests from overseas. At different times, both of his brothers who lived in Australia visited with their families, also the Swiss Erikas from Horley days who, at this stage, were both married. The latter, on separate occasions, came to Britain for a touring holiday, making a stop with Leonard, Phyllis, and the boys in Yorkshire – the icing on the cake. Leonard remembers standing on the seafront at Whitby with one of the Erikas, watching the wild waves washing over the groyne whilst eating fish and chips out of newspaper.

For a few weeks, the Holder family also gave a home to an Austrian young lady who wanted to improve her English. Elizabeth was an evangelical Christian (perhaps a comparative rarity in a strongly Roman Catholic country), and she exuberated a love of life and of God's creation around her. She was an early riser and would often go for a walk before breakfast, coming back full of enthusiasm for the Yorkshire countryside. On several occasions, she came back expressing wonder at British cloud formations. It would appear from her comments that clouds in Austria were much more boring than the constantly changing formations in Yorkshire. Her English was already impressive, but the Holders were very amused at some of her faux pas. Often on a Sunday evening Willis would invite several of the evening congregation back to supper at his house.

Elizabeth endeavoured to be on her best behaviour for this privilege; however, on being offered another piece of delicious fruitcake, she responded, 'No, thank you. I'm fed up.'

This produced a smile, and as soon as they got home, Phyllis put her right on this wrong use of words.

On another occasion, as she was trying exceedingly hard to be correct, she looked longingly at the cake being offered and uttered, 'I'd love to, but I'm afraid my womb is full.'

One of Willis's daughters was offering round the refreshments that evening, and this comment provoked a slight colouration of her cheeks, followed by complete silence.

Willis's two daughters kindly suggested they could show Elizabeth some of the Yorkshire countryside and one day took her into the Dales for a walk across the hills. They were shocked when, in walking across the heather-covered hillside, Elizabeth took off her footwear, tied the laces together, and hung them around her neck, walking barefoot.

Another friend from Belgrave days had joined the army as a driver and, when based in Yorkshire, frequently spent her leave days at Kirkby Road. She took a great interest in the Holders' pigs and liked to help with them as much as possible. On one occasion, one of the weaners had a ruptured bowel. Leonard decided they should

Barbara with newly born piglet

fatten this pig themselves as its value for selling was severely reduced. Rupture, as the creature was named, became quite a pet, but when it reached a suitable weight, with the help of one of Willis's farm managers, Leonard took it to a small local abattoir to be slaughtered.

Therefore, one day, when the army friend was visiting and enjoying a delicious pork roast, to her consternation, Daniel remarked to her, 'Are you enjoying the meat? It's actually Rupture!'

185

CHAPTER

11

Church Incidents

Leonard and Willis shared the main preaching at Zion Evangelical Church during the early years the Holders were in Ripon. The members, having covenanted together in a formal church membership, began prayerfully to seek for a full-time pastor, but there were several years before God provided this.

Willis was quite unique as a preacher. He would often stand in the pulpit, displaying red braces and frequently flexing them with his thumbs as he preached.

On one memorable occasion, he began preaching by announcing his sermon had four points and then added, 'I'm fearful I may not have time for my fourth point, so to ensure it doesn't get lost, I'm beginning with it.'

Leonard's morning sermons were more biblically consecutive. He remembers working with great personal spiritual profit through the Epistle to the Hebrews. A. W. Pink's commentary on this letter was helpful and inspiring, and he also delved occasionally into John Owen's classic work on this epistle. Those were days, however, before the internet, and he was dependent on printed books and only had access to one of the several volumes which made up this Puritan's massive contribution to an understanding of this wonderful New Testament book. In Hebrews, we have a powerful demonstration of Jesus Christ as the Eternal Son of God who fulfils all the ceremonial religious rituals of the Old Testament.

One regular member of the congregation was a Second World War veteran named Jimmy. Jimmy was well known in Ripon. He wandered round the city each day with his white stick, and several charities recruited him to collect funds for them. He was very persuasive in requesting donations and had even been known to hinder passers-by with his white stick if they ignored him. Jimmy was also an almost daily visitor to the Evangelical Press office and warehouse, where, if he wasn't too busy, Roger would give him a cup of tea. One day, when the tea wasn't forthcoming, Jimmy took it on himself to put the kettle on. When Roger returned, he noticed something strange when he tried to pour the boiling water.

'What's this, Jimmy?' Roger exclaimed.

'I'm just boiling my handkerchief,' answered Jimmy. 'It was getting dirty.'

Jimmy was never again permitted to make the tea.

As well as Jimmy having failing eyesight, his hearing was deteriorating, but in the church service, he loved to listen to Phyllis singing and always wanted to sit immediately in front of her so she effectively was singing right into his ear. Someone would pick Jimmy up from the care home where he was living and, on arriving at church, would know they needed to steer him to a seat in front of the Holders' row.

When occasionally, he was left to find his own way to a seat, he was known to call out in a loud voice, 'Where is she then?'

Being simply a hall in a Methodist chapel, the church had no baptistery, and this a was a deficiency they felt they needed to rectify – but how best, from a practical point of view, to install a baptistery large enough for the full immersion of adults? This was the question. After much thought, discussion, and investigation into possibilities, the best way forward suddenly seemed obvious to this farming community. They would install a fibreglass sheep dip within the raised platform at the front of the hall. There seemed something so theologically correct for believers to be baptised in a sheep dip!

The next question was how to bring such a large rigid fibreglass object into the hall. Measurements indicated it would be possible if the window frame was taken out. So eventually, all this happened, and Zion Evangelical Church was equipped for adult baptisms.

Following this, one day Jimmy asked for baptism. Willis didn't know how seriously to take this as it wasn't clear how much Jimmy understood of the Gospel and of the meaning of baptism. Leonard was invited to go with Willis to visit Jimmy in his room in the home. They would try and explain the church's practice of believer's baptism and that rather than being merely a religious ritual, it was a serious expression of personal faith and commitment to Jesus Christ.

Leonard can't now remember much about that meeting. Jimmy's speech was always somewhat slurred and his understanding limited, but as the two men were leaving, Jimmy's final word, clear to understand, was 'And I haven't been circumcised either'.

Willis allowed the matter of Jimmy's baptism, for the time being, to fall by default until the church had the pastor for which they were praying.

In the event, after a pastor had accepted the church's call, one of the first believers to be immersed in the church's sheep dip was Leonard and Phyllis's younger son, Daniel. It was the summer of 1980, and Daniel was 10 years old, but the pastor was impressed by the sincerity of his confession of faith and desire to follow Jesus.

It seems likely that God gives his children people like Jimmy to test and nurture their patience and grace. One lasting image Leonard and Phyllis have of Jimmy was by the sea on a church outing. Jimmy had wanted to paddle, and one of the men of the fellowship had helped him roll up his trouser legs and then led him into the shallow water. Following a refreshing paddle, Leslie had then helped Jimmy to sit on a deck chair whilst he dried Jimmy's feet with his own towel. An incident recorded in John's Gospel would give us to understand that this was something Jesus himself would have done.

12

The Renewed Call to German-Speaking Europe

When Erika and her husband and daughter, Sarah, visited the Holders in Ripon, they invited them back to Switzerland for a holiday in their home in Glarus, and this became possible in the summer of 1982. This was the first time Leonard and Phyllis had returned to the country since their extended tour six years earlier. This time, it was for a simple holiday. They would travel by car and spend most of the time with Erika and her family in Glarus but intended to travel back to England slowly, with various stops camping on the way.

Erika and her husband, Ruedi, entertained them well. A couple of outings remain in their minds for various reasons. Phyllis was very uncertain and rather nervous about chairlifts and cable cars, particularly when these were open and you felt as if you were hanging in mid-air. Their Swiss friends couldn't understand or fully appreciate this fear as they had been brought up amongst mountains, and this mode of transport was part of everyday life. So they planned a day out walking high up in the Alps, built up as a mystery tour, and not until they had brought their guests to the foot of a steeply rising mountainside was any mention made of the dreaded transport hanging from a cable. Their hosts had their very large family dog with them, and the way he ascended the mountain, sitting on his master's knee on an open chairlift, was a sight to behold. Realising that to funk the situation would upset all the carefully laid plans for the day, Phyllis grasped hold of her fears and boldly clambered onto a swinging chair.

It was a most interesting walk high up in the hills and included wandering around a small mountain lake. Although it was now midsummer, Leonard was surprised to see tadpoles swimming around in the shallower water. The answer was simple. At the lake's altitude, it would probably have been frozen over until May or even June, and as the frogs wouldn't have the opportunity to spawn before then, the whole breeding cycle is later than at lower levels.

After a few hours, Erika knew she would have to leave to meet her daughter from school, so it was arranged that the rest of the group would walk on and meet at an arranged point. Phyllis decided she would accompany Erika, and this led to another incident. When Erika and Phyllis reached the cable car to descend, they discovered it to be simply an open carriage, with sides about waist high, hanging on the edge of a precipice. There was no one to operate it but a telephone to ring down to the station below when passengers were ready to descend. Phyllis boarded the 'box' with very great care, and Erika went to the telephone to ring down to controls. Before she could ring, a group of school children arrived with their teacher. The teacher had a conversation with Erika; everything was, of course, in Swiss German, and Erika agreed to look after about half of the group while the other half would come down with the teacher on a second journey. As they descended, several of the children began to hang over the side to get a better view of the ground beneath. Both of the older, more responsible passengers felt obliged to hold onto shirt tails as Erika realised that she was responsible for these children's safety. The half carriage swung across a gaping void as it descended to the valley beneath, and the children were chatting excitedly.

Once safely down at a lower level, Erika turned to Phyllis, saying with a smile, 'I'm so glad you couldn't understand what those youngsters were saying. They were trying to imagine and describe what they would look like if they fell over the edge. The descriptions were getting more and more gruesome.'

None of this, of course, enticed Phyllis to look forward to further such adventures in the mountains.

Another outing was memorable for quite a different reason. Having given a sightseeing tour around various places of interest, Erika asked her guests whether they would like to eat in Switzerland or Italy. Having adjusted their minds to even the possibility of such a question and never having visited Italy before, they opted for the latter. Although they were not expected to meet the cost of the meals themselves, when their generous host showed them the menu, the prices looked unbelievable. The figures were in thousands. This was, of course, when Italy was still using lire before the days of the euro.

Erika's husband, Ruedi, was a Swiss policeman, and one evening, returning home in uniform, he allowed two intrigued boys to inspect his pistol. This was one of the things that had interested the boys when first entering Germany and then Switzerland, to observe that all the border guards carried pistols very visibly in holsters around their waists. We later realised that not only the border guards but also all the police were armed.

It was extremely encouraging for Leonard and Phyllis to see that Erika's faith in the Lord Jesus seemed as strong as ever, and they couldn't help thinking back to that Sunday evening in Horley ten years earlier when Melita had brought the two Swiss au pair girls to their home. On that holiday Sunday in Glarus, their hosts introduced them to the Methodist church they were active in at that time. Ruedi was also a believer, and this may have been through Erika's influence. Later, they joined a Free Evangelical church in Glarus.

After a very satisfactory visit to their kind and generous Swiss friends, the Holder family began their journey home. They intended to camp just outside Basel and attend the English-speaking Basel Christian Fellowship (BCF) on the Sunday morning. However, finding the Swiss camping sites full to overflowing, they crossed the border into Germany, and motoring up the Wiesental

Valley, they found a campsite just off the main road at Mambach. Little did they realise how familiar the Wiesental would become.

Leonard remembers that night at Mambach for a very negative reason. He was suffering painfully from what was later diagnosed as an anal fissure which, once back to Ripon, required a simple operation.

That Sunday morning, they motored back into Basel for the English service, and this proved extremely significant. In conversation after the service, Leonard mentioned his thought of serving the Lord in some capacity in Switzerland, and this resulted in being introduced to a Swiss gentleman who lectured at a Bible college in Basel. Dr Henry von Siebenthal taught Greek and Hebrew at the Freie Evangelische-Theologische Akademie, and he suggested to Leonard that he should seriously consider applying to study there if he wanted to work in Switzerland. He went on to say that the secretary to the leader of the academy had a flat at the back of the church where they were meeting, and if Leonard would like, he could take him there and then to meet Reinhard Müller.

Leonard really felt that this apparent coincidence was clearly of the Lord, and the outcome was that he had an appointment to see over the college and meet the founder and active principal of the Bible college, Samuel Külling, before the family returned to England. Leonard was encouraged to apply to study there, and various practical considerations were discussed. It was clear that the college would help in any way they could to enable this to happen.

As the family returned to Yorkshire, Leonard was sensing that after seven years from that first attempt to move out to the continent of Europe, God was, at last, confirming His call and opening up a way to move forward. The blessing that Leonard had felt years earlier from Psalm 107 came back to his mind: 'He led them forth by the right way, that they might go to a city for a dwelling place' and 'He has broken the gates of bronze and cut the bars of iron in two'.[35]

However, there were still further barriers to be broken down.

---

35 Psalm 107:7, 16.

CHAPTER

13

An Unsettling Time

After about four years during which Leonard shared the Sunday ministry with his employer at Zion Evangelical Church, the church called a full-time pastor. For a couple of years, the church experienced blessing. Slowly over the weeks, a few more people began to attend. Some came from other churches, and there was at least one family who had not had any other serious church connection before.

By not involving the previous elder in any active way, the new pastor hoped the breakaway group might be encouraged to re-join the original church, of which he was now pastor. Sadly, this never happened. He involved Leonard and Roger as acting deacons and, for a time, also a warrant officer based at the Ripon army camp. Occasional special meetings of evangelistic preaching were held in the town hall, and there were other attempts to reach out to the local community. When several couples were coming across to the services from Harrogate and Knaresborough, the pastor felt there was a sufficient reason to attempt to plant a new church in Harrogate. With the Ripon church behind him in this, Jennyfields Evangelical Church was established. Zion Evangelical Church, on the recommendation of the pastor, also engaged a trainee pastor straight from Bible college who, under the pastor's guidance, shared the preaching ministry. During this time, Leonard and Phyllis were thrilled when their younger son, Daniel, was baptised on the confession of his personal faith in the Lord Jesus.

One of the families who began to attend the church and had had little or no previous church connections consisted of a married couple, both employed on the estate of a landowner just outside Ripon, and their teenage daughter. The pastor asked Leonard and Phyllis if they would try and nurture friendship with the family. On the Holders' befriending them, the whole family were given an open invitation to call by to chat and play snooker. This proved so mutually popular that for a period, it became almost a weekly event.

Then things began to go wrong. This was shortly after the Holders' return from their Swiss holiday and the renewing to Leonard of the Lord's call to serve Him in German-speaking Europe. Leonard had said nothing of this to anyone, but what became clear was that after the resignation of the pastor and wholescale desertion of the church by most of the members, there was no way he could approach Zion Evangelical Church to be a supporting church if they moved out to Switzerland.

Several of the congregation also left, and for different reasons, several church members moved away until the church was back to simply Willis's family, Roger's family, and the Holders. At this, when Roger told Leonard he really didn't feel he could continue to support the church any longer, Leonard felt he should make one last attempt to bring the two evangelical churches in Ripon together. He got an appointment to speak with an influential minister, Herbert Carson, whom he knew both sides respected. Herbert was very sympathetic but, knowing something about the people involved, regretfully declined to get involved.

At this point, Leonard and Phyllis and family began to attend Bethel Church in Ripon.

CHAPTER

14

Preparing for Europe

Whilst these problems were happening in Ripon, Leonard had been very exercised about a move to Switzerland which, following their holiday, had suddenly become a possibility. Ripon had become a less comfortable place to be, but that in itself could not be considered a good enough reason to undertake the move contemplated. He thought back to the Horley days, six years earlier, and to what he had firmly believed had been God's call to German-speaking Europe at that time. The family's time in Ripon and Leonard's work with Willis had certainly added considerably to his experience. It had clearly been of God, and if it was now God's time for them to make the move to Continental Europe, Leonard didn't want to hesitate in obeying. Although not enthusiastic, Phyllis was supportive of this move, and for the boys, it was an exciting adventure, but if this was not of God and didn't have His blessing, it could be disastrous.

Geoffrey was 15 and coming up to his O-level exams at Ripon Grammar School. He had been studying German at school, but Daniel, at 13, had never, as yet, had the opportunity for German language lessons. To uproot them and take them into a situation where they would need to continue their studies in German could be a frightening mistake and destroy their chances of a successful education. Also, financially, this move would be a complete and utter step of faith in God. There was no financial support on offer. Switzerland was not generally considered a country needing missionaries, and Leonard didn't feel able to approach a missionary organisation for support. The recent circumstances in Ripon also made it extremely unlikely that either of the evangelical churches there would consider offering any financial support. Still, despite all these negative points, after agonising thought and prayer, Leonard felt an inner assurance that God was leading and they must tentatively follow, step by step.

He applied formally to enrol as a student at the Freie Evangelische-Theologische Akademie Basel for the year commencing October 1983 and, subject to producing evidence of qualifications at A-level (sufficient for acceptance to university level in England), was accepted. The course was no walk in the park, but a few years of study would lead to the equivalent of a master's degree in theology. Being completely in German with the requirement to pass exams in Greek, Hebrew, and Latin prior to more intense theological studies, it would take a minimum of five years and, for an English person with very basic German, was, naturally speaking, a foolhardy venture. However, Scripture, such as Moses's call and Joshua's call, encouraged courageous steps of faith, also warnings, as seen when the children of Israel doubted God and refused to enter Canaan because of the giants there – all challenged Leonard. God's Word assures us that in following God, we must not look to ourselves but to our sovereign God through whom we 'can do all things'.[36]

The college had suggested that the Holders spend the summer before the course working on the German language, and they promised to make some suggestions as to where and how. Eventually, after looking at a few very expensive German language courses in Germany, Leonard's idea of the family working on a self-study Linguaphone course with cassettes, whilst living in Germany for three months, materialised with an arrangement negotiated for them by the college. They were offered the use of a

---

36 Philippians 4:13; 2 Samuel 22:30.

house in the village of Lemgo in North Germany near the Brake Bible School. During the summer, the Bible college was used for group and family holidays with meetings every evening. The plan was that the Holders could study German together as a family in their accommodation, attend the evening meetings and Sunday morning service at the college, and get the feel of living in Germany. Hopefully, over two or three months, this would enable each of the family to make some real progress in learning the German language.

Having this plan before them, Leonard, with a certain amount of fear and trepidation but also a degree of excitement, gave in his notice to Willis and finished at the end of May. There were quite a lot of arrangements to make during June. They decided to travel by ferry and train and consequently sold their car, buying two substantial suitcases on wheels. They also put their house on the market with the intention of using income from this, after paying back their mortgage, as a financial starting point to live on in Switzerland.

It was decided that Geoffrey should remain in Ripon for a further year to enable him to take his O-level exams during the summer of 1984. Marcus, the pastor of Bethel Evangelical Church in Ripon, and his wife, May, also had two boys approximately the same age as Geoffrey and Daniel, and they kindly agreed to give Geoffrey a home for the year. They lived on a farm just outside Ripon, and Geoffrey was happy about the situation. The idea of being able to travel alone out to Switzerland in his holidays added to the adventure that the arrangement offered. In the meantime, the whole family would have most of July, the whole of August, and a part of September together in Northern Germany.

Memories from Others

Dad Pittwell

It seemed to all onlookers that their situation in Ripon was ideal, the job was good, and as a family, they were at last putting down roots. Then in 1983, Len and Phyllis broke the news to us that they were putting their house on the market, selling up, and going out to Switzerland as missionaries.

CHAPTER

15

Language Preparation

In early July 1983, the Holder family set off for Germany, and life could never be quite the same again.

They had packed all they had expected to need for the summer in two suitcases and a couple of smaller bags, but at the last minute, Daniel suddenly raced upstairs and grabbed his money box full of small English coins, saying, 'I can't leave this behind!' That money box was to have great significance for the family on their return journey eight weeks or so later.

Details of the journey are rather vague, but Leonard remembers that when they finally alighted from the German train at the station of Brake, which should have been their destination, it was the wrong place. The name appeared to be the same, but on enquiry, there was no *Bibelschule* nearby. Eventually, after another train journey, they arrived at the correct Brake, and a short walk brought them to the Bible College. Thankfully, they were expected, and a kind groundsman at the college ran them to the house which had been allocated for them. It was down the end of a lonely lane with just two houses, one allocated for them and the other where the college groundsman and his family lived. For them to get around, the college loaned them four bicycles. Presumably, this was possible because most of the students were away.

The house was very sparsely furnished, but being used to camping holidays, the family found it was sufficient for their needs. It was a very rural setting, and it was soon discovered that at least one family of mice was in residence. Leonard acquired a little nipper mouse trap and one evening caught seven young mice! Very shortly after one was caught and the trap reset, a brother or sister was also attracted to the bait.

The family next door spoke no English, and one evening, inviting the Holders over for supper, the kind lady of the house asked in German, 'Do you like mice on toast?'

This alarmed Phyllis a little until she realised that 'mice' was not mice but *Mais*, the German word for maize or sweetcorn.

On another occasion, the husband called Leonard – 'Come and see this eagle.'

With great interest, Leonard followed him into his orchard, and there, under a cherry tree, was a bloated, sleeping hedgehog, an *Igel*. It had gorged itself on cherries and was lying on its back, snoring contentedly.

Each morning, the family worked on the German language Linguaphone course. Most of this was revision for Leonard, and Geoffrey also had a couple of years of German at school under his belt. They had a German Bible, which they used for family devotions, but it was extremely difficult for them to converse with one another in this foreign language apart from when they did exercises related to their course.

The weather was warm and sunny almost the whole time, and as part of their language learning, they cycled off in the afternoons to walk around the shops or visit the local open-air swimming pool. They soon discovered it was compulsory for everyone, men and women, to wear plastic head caps to cover their hair in the pool, so these had to be bought. There were other German customs they had to learn. On their first Saturday afternoon, they got ready with their shopping bags to set off on their bikes to buy in their grocery needs. Their neighbour, spotting them from her garden, called out, asking whether they knew the German shops all closed on Saturday afternoons and didn't open again until Monday morning. Oh dear! It was a weekend of making do with what meagre resources they had in the cupboard. They later learned that until a more recent change in German law, shops were obliged to close midday Saturday except for one so-called *lange Samstag* (long Saturday) a month, when they were allowed to stay open until 4:00 p.m.

The Bible college buildings and facilities were used as a centre for Christian holidays, and several of these holidays took place whilst the Holders were staying in Brake. Some of the students would give up weeks of their summer break to serve the holiday guests. Each evening, the college provided a spiritual time of ministry and fellowship for the guests, and Leonard and Phyllis and boys cycled over to the college to share in this. It was more a question of listening and trying to understand the German spoken than participating in any meaningful way, but this was all part of the learning process and no doubt was beneficial. On Sunday mornings, they attended the Brethren Assembly meeting, of which the leader of the college was an elder. Hanging in the house where they were living was a poster which read, 'Aller Anfang ist schwer.' Once the Holders understood this, they acknowledged the truth of it. In English, it means 'Every beginning is hard.'

A few families invited the Holders for a meal, and it was interesting to experience German culture and cuisine. One family had two boys who were allocated to amuse Geoffrey and Daniel.

The name of one was Burkhardt, and on the way home, Daniel commented, 'That lad had a funny name. I hardly liked to use it. He said he was "Workhard"!'

During this time, Leonard was also trying to make arrangements for their move to Basel. The college had said they would find them a cheap flat to rent, and they also had to arrange to get their essential belongings there. The idea was to sell their house, so to use an old phrase attributed to the ancient Romans, they were going to burn their bridges behind them, meaning there was no turning back. Leonard was very conscious of their dependence on God and that without His provision and blessing, the whole venture would be a disaster. Each day in their prayer time, Leonard and Phyllis prayed for God to direct them in all arrangements and provide what they needed. Suddenly, one morning, a letter arrived in the post with an offer to transport their belongings out to Basel, but it did stipulate a certain limited capacity. The letter was from a young man in Bethel Church, Ripon. He explained that he had volunteered to hire a van and drive some personal items across to Spain for a missionary couple who were going out there for the first time. He realised if he hired a slightly bigger van, he would have extra space and was prepared to motor to Spain via Basel to take their belongings too. This seemed so remarkable that Leonard could not but recognise God's hand in it, seeing this as a further confirmation that He was calling the family to take this gigantic step.

Then a sudden hiccup! There was another letter in the post, this time from the principal of the college in Basel. The letter requested Leonard to attend the college for an interview prior to the start of the course. Thinking his application had already been accepted, Leonard found that this was completely unexpected. It would be no simple journey to make as Brake is in North Germany and Basel in Switzerland. A map revealed that the distance was 390 miles, but if an interview was necessary, the journey had to be made. A visit to the train station showed that an overnight train journey would be the way to do it, so Leonard arranged a date to see Professor Külling and booked a train.

Before doing this, however, another little miracle happened. Their friend Erika in Glarus had been in touch, and when Leonard mentioned the need to attend the FETA in Basel for an interview, she wrote back and said she and her husband would like to drive up to Brake to see Leonard, Phyllis, and the boys for a couple of days and suggested they could meet Leonard in Basel, bringing him those 390 miles back to his family. It's through such acts of interest, love, and care from fellow believers that God encourages His children. As they had been separated for several weeks from friends with which they could more easily converse, this offer from Erika to come all that way to visit Leonard and Phyllis was a real encouragement to them. It was a blessing from God.

The journey back to Ripon in early September was another adventure with evidence of God's providential blessing.

They had booked and paid in advance for train tickets to Ostend, with a ferry across to Dover and a train north to Yorkshire, but when their German train got to the Belgium border at Aachan, they were informed it could go no further as there was a railway strike in Belgium. Along with everyone else in the train, they descended onto the platform and waited for further instructions. Eventually, they realised the Belgium authorities were running buses to replace the strike-bound trains, but as they queued to get tickets, they realised they would need to pay for the bus journey as their train tickets weren't acceptable to the bus company. Leonard just hoped that the meagre amount of cash he had left would be enough, but to their dismay, having got to the ticket desk and being told the cost for a family ticket to Ostend, he realised he was quite a bit short.

'We'll accept any currency, including English pounds,' said the ticket clerk, trying to be helpful.

However, putting together every penny he and Phyllis had, Leonard found that they were still short.

Then a little voice said, 'I've got some money, Dad.'

Daniel extracted his piggy bank from his personal hand luggage and handed it to his father with a smile. They tipped out all the small loose change, and on counting it up, there was just enough to cover the cost of the necessary ticket. Praise the Lord!

Leonard quite expects his son, if he reads this, to ask, 'Did you ever pay me back, Dad?'

Interestingly, a good number of weeks later, an official with a money purse came to the Holders' flat in Basel and paid back in cash, in Swiss francs, the value of the train ticket they had been unable to use.

Of course, a slow bus ride meant they arrived at Ostend long after their booked ferry had departed. This meant sitting on uncomfortable seats in a lounge most of the night before eventually being allowed onto a much smaller passenger-only ferry which tossed them up and down as it rode the waves across the channel in the early hours of the morning.

Phyllis's Memories

On 11 July 1983, as a family, we left our lovely home in Ripon, Yorkshire, and travelled by public transport over to Lemgo, North Germany. It was a Saturday, and the first lesson we learned when we tried to shop was that Germany's shops at that time closed at midday on a Saturday. We went to Lemgo to live in Germany for three months, to learn German with cassettes through a Linguaphone course and attend summer meetings at a Bible school, trying as a family to immerse ourselves in German. We had pretty basic accommodation which, when we first arrived, we shared with a family of mice! We were helped by a lovely family living next door to us who advised us and kindly lent basic things that were missing in the house. We used bicycles to get around and to visit places and people.

We returned briefly to our home in Ripon during September 1983 and finally left our lovely house for good with a friend who drove us over to Basel. We needed to dispose of, in various ways, the majority of our furniture and household possessions. My friend and I spent the whole night before leaving clearing out our walk-in larder. It was heart-breaking for me, leaving our home and Geoff. He wasn't coming with us at that point (he was doing his 'O' levels that year); he would be living with good friends of ours in Ripon. Whilst it was thankfully a settled and happy time for him, it made our leaving even more traumatic, and we were also leaving our dear dog behind. She could not be with Geoff as the farm where he was to stay already had dogs. The Lord overruled in an amazing way for our dog to get a new home eventually, but I couldn't get over the thought that we had let our dog down, and I was heart-broken for many, many months about having to leave such a loyal friend. I knew my son was all right and we would see him soon enough, so although the pain of leaving him temporarily was awful, it wasn't a permanent separation.

PART 5

BASEL
1983–1989

Fear not, for I have redeemed you;
I have called you by your name;
You are Mine.
When you pass through the
waters, I will be with you;
And through the rivers, they
shall not overflow you.
When you walk through the fire,
you shall not be burned,
Nor shall the flame scorch you.
For I am the LORD *your God,*
The Holy One of Israel, your Saviour.
— Isaiah 43:1–3

CHAPTER

1

Awayday Ticket?

It has been a joke in the Holder family that when Leonard, Phyllis, and son Daniel emigrated to Switzerland, they crossed the channel on an awayday ticket. This is, in fact, apocryphal. Such a ticket certainly offered the best value at the time, and it seemed unlikely that anyone would worry if the passengers didn't use the return half of their ticket. Leonard suggested in a rather tongue-in-cheek manner that this type of ferry ticket would be their best option, but despite being unconventional, it also became unnecessary when a kind friend who would need to return to Britain again kindly offered to drive them across to Switzerland.

With the family having got back to Ripon from North Germany, there was masses to do. The Holders needed to sort out how many of their possessions they could fit into the limited capacity offered to them in the hired van and then organise the disposal of everything else. There was another major concern, although there were only two weeks before they were due to leave, as yet they had no apartment to go to. The college had promised to find them accommodation but had not been able to come up with anything. It was a matter of urgent prayer, and when he was challenged about it by his wife, the best answer Leonard could give was they would have to camp on the border until accommodation was found! Thankfully, that didn't prove necessary, although it was about three days before they left Britain when they had a phone call from Reinhart saying he had found them somewhere.

Finally, their goods were packed tightly into the van, and Phyllis will tell anyone who asks that thirty-three boxes of Leonard's books took up more of the space than household articles and furniture. Right up to the last minute, they were either selling off cheaply or giving away other household and personal things they were unable to take.

Leonard's parents kindly agreed to look after their beloved Shep, the border collie cross, and the family retained the hope they would one day be able to have her with them again. There were so many unknowns in making this move, and only their confidence in God gave them a degree of peace, although sometimes their faith wavered.

The house was put in the hands of an estate agent, and the Holders recognised that income from this, after repaying the outstanding mortgage, would, unless the Lord provided otherwise, be their main financial support.

Geoffrey was settled into the home of family friends and had already started his final year at Ripon Grammar by the time they finally left. There were tears when the moment of departure actually arrived, and although Leonard can't remember exactly, he thinks it most likely they slept on the floor of an empty house on that last night in Britain. In any case, Phyllis and their friend Sue, who was going to drive the family across the continent to their new abode, spent the entire night packing for the early start and finishing the cleaning out of the walk-in larder and freezer, which were going to be left with the house.

One disadvantage of living in the north of England is the long drive down to the channel port when motoring to the continent. They had one night sleeping somewhere in France, as best as they could in the car, before crossing the French border into Switzerland and locating the address of their rooms in Morgartenring, Basel.

They had hoped the van with their goods would already be there waiting for them, but there was no sign of it. Their rooms were on the first floor, and there was a single gentleman living on the ground floor who had been authorised to let them in and introduce them to their accommodation upstairs. Phyllis refused to call it an apartment as there was access through the middle of it to a smaller flat on the second floor under the roof, where a single girl lived. So effectively, their part consisted of two big rooms, a kitchen, and a bathroom with all rooms opening off the landing, which, as mentioned, also gave access through to the flat on the next floor. The rooms were good, and there was a large balcony accessed from both the living room at the back of the house and the kitchen. Heating was by means of two

First home in Basel
First-floor flat in Morgartenring

oven-type fires on which one could burn wood. It was, of course, completely empty of furniture, although the kitchen was equipped with a stove and fridge.

Soon after they had arrived at this empty flat, there was a ring on the front door, and an unknown man appeared, introducing himself in good English as Pierre Nussbaumer. Although Swiss, he explained that he was married to an English missionary named Violet, and together they ran both a church and a Christian bookshop in Mulhouse, a French city about twenty-five miles from the Swiss border.

He welcomed the Holders to Switzerland but then added, 'I'm afraid I've got some bad news for you. Your belongings have been refused entry across the border into Switzerland.'

He further explained that he and his wife were associate workers with the European Missionary Fellowship, and when the driver of the van had not been allowed across the Swiss border, he had driven to Pierre's home in France, not knowing what else to do. Knowing something of the way Switzerland functioned, he explained that what was missing was a document giving the Holders permission to live in Switzerland.

'I suggest you get in touch with the FETA Bible college tomorrow, and they should know what to do.' Then he added kindly, 'In the meantime, the van and driver can stay with us.'

After a prayer with the family, Pierre gave them his address and phone number and left. After Pierre had departed, Leonard summed up the situation to the others.

'So,' he said, 'we have a flat, and we are here, but we don't actually have permission to be here or any furniture for our new dwelling. Let's trust and pray we can sort things out tomorrow.'

The Swiss gentleman downstairs directed them to a couple of old mattresses in the cellar. These, they dragged up the stairs to the rooms, feeling somewhat depressed and bewildered. They unloaded their car, had something to eat, and slept on the floor, fully clothed.

The next day, Leonard contacted the college and explained their predicament. Within a few hours, it was arranged that he would meet a Swiss student outside the appropriate office in the centre of Basel; he would have a document stating that Leonard Holder was enrolled as a student in the Freie Evangelische-Theologische Akademie. Thankfully, all this went to plan, and the authorities provided a stamped document to show to the border guards who would allow their belongings entry to the country.

It was still necessary for the family to visit the immigration office to register and receive personal residence documents, and this proved to be quite a traumatic experience. In one's own country, one knows one has a right to be there, and then for tourists, most foreign countries make their guests welcome because they are going to spend money, but trying to get residence in a foreign land is quite a different matter entirely. It's almost certainly different if you happen to be a film star or a rich businessman, but the Holder family certainly didn't fall into either of these categories. The first shock was to see that the office was labelled 'For Aliens'. You could imagine Daniel looking at his parents to see whether they had green faces! Swiss offices generally provide plush furnishing and very comfortable seating for waiting guests and clients, but the alien waiting room was extremely basic with hard, bare wooden benches.

Leonard could answer most of the questions put to him satisfactorily, but then came a very crucial question: 'How will you support yourselves financially whilst in Switzerland?'

After a few minutes of thought and a quick prayer, Leonard stated briefly that the family were selling their house in Britain. He hadn't realised how significant this was to the Swiss. To rent accommodation was far commoner at that time than in Britain, and in the Swiss mind, to have a house to sell indicates wealth. It was surely God's overruling that the girl behind the counter failed to ask what sort of money they would expect to get for their house. She simply stated that they would be asked again later about their money situation once the house was sold. This must have been overlooked as during the six years they lived in Switzerland, no further questions were ever asked. Later, they were asked to fill in a form about their income for income tax purposes, and the Christian friend who helped them with this commented that he reckoned the Holder family must have been the poorest in the whole of Switzerland.

One great benefit whilst Leonard was registered as a student in Switzerland was that they were provided with free medical insurance. As Leonard was used to the NHS in Britain, health insurance was not something he, in his innocence, had thought about. It is, however, a considerable expense in both Switzerland and Germany, and to have it free for the whole family proved to be a wonderful provision. They did have to visit a doctor to be signed off as fit prior to getting this cover as any medical condition they already had was not covered by the insurance.

They realised later that God had wonderfully overruled for them in another way. In the BCF which they began to attend, they met several Americans studying in Swiss universities who expressed surprise that Phyllis had been allowed into the country because of her husband being a student. In their cases, their wives had only been allowed to come with them if they too registered and were accepted to study.

The lesson to learn is surely that when, as Christians, we step out in response to God's guidance, although, as Leonard and Phyllis experienced, He doesn't necessarily make things easy, He does make them possible.

Phyllis's Memories

With only what we had taken with us in our friend's car, we settled into four rooms off the second landing of a house on a ring road in Basel. This had been found for us three days before our arrival there. The first night, we slept in our clothes on mattresses found for us by the man who lived on the first floor of the house. However, the mattresses, having been in the cellar of the house, were very cold, but they did prevent us having to sleep on the floor. The only other thing in the room was a very old-style, unconnected telephone lying on the floor.

The next day saw us trying to get the few possessions into Switzerland that had been brought out for us. We were sharing a small removal van with a missionary to Spain which a Christian friend was driving, and it hadn't been allowed over the Swiss border from France the night before. A dear missionary friend from the European Missionary Fellowship helped us with this. The fact that he was Swiss and lived in France helped enormously! The only items of furniture that we were bringing out with us were essentially our beds, Len's grandfather's chair, the boys' small snooker table, and our bikes as we had disposed of the rest of our things. However, we did, in addition, have thirty-three boxes of books with us!

As Len was immediately starting the Bible College Course arranged for him, it was left for Dan and me, along with our friend to go to the Salvation Army second-hand depot in Basel to get some basic furniture and necessities for living and starting a new life. When our friend left to come back to England, it was just Dan and me trying to navigate everyday life, which was a huge challenge and I got very depressed. I experienced significant culture shock with everything being so different, compounded more so by the new language– it was traumatic.

One of the books which I found extremely interesting when we were anticipating moving out to Switzerland was Edith Schaffer's account in her book *L'Abri* of some of the struggles she and her husband, Francis Schaffer, had in obtaining residence and then settling into this country. The Schaffer family's ministry, which attracted many young people to visit them high up in the Swiss

Alps, fascinated me, and it was a blessing to visit L'Abri during our visit to Switzerland in 1973. Interestingly, however, when we ourselves moved out to Basel, we discovered we could identify closely with several of the incidents Edith Schaffer mentions in her book, including teeth problems and experiences with Swiss dentists.

CHAPTER
2

Settling into Life in Basel

Morgartenring, where the Holders' accommodation was located, was a busy ring road around the city. During working days, buses ran by their house every four minutes in each direction. Indeed, after a certain hour, this became every seven minutes; however, additionally, as there were traffic lights immediately outside house number 34, all traffic was constantly having to stop and then rev up to set off again. After the peace of Yorkshire, this constant noise took some getting used to. There was only peace from midnight until five in the morning, when all public transport stopped.

As they needed more items of furniture, they discovered the Salvation Army warehouse, already mentioned, a very suitable place to obtain the required items. Unwanted household furniture, large and small, was donated to be sold for the benefit of the charity. The Swiss, being generally well-to-do citizens, ensured there were good-quality household items at reasonable prices. Once their friend had returned to Britain, the Holders had no vehicle to transport anything they bought, and Daniel and later Geoffrey also retain embarrassing memories of walking through Basel streets, helping their parents carry quite large items of furniture to their new abode. Money had to be used sparingly and even more so before their Yorkshire house was sold. Leonard remembers one incident particularly relating to the purchase of one item of furniture. They had seen a sideboard with cupboards and bookshelves in the Salvation Army store which, to some people, would seem perhaps a bit old-fashioned, but it was excellent quality and ideal for their needs. Although not so expensive, it was more than they could justify spending. Within a couple of days of them seeing this and thinking how practical it was for their needs, an envelope appeared anonymously in their letter box containing the exact number of Swiss francs needed for its purchase. It was clearly from a fellow Christian in the Basel Fellowship, but because of its timing and amount, it could be clearly recognised as a gift from the Lord Himself. Another instance of God's blessing and approbation of the step they had taken in coming to Switzerland was when an elder from the English-speaking Basel Fellowship called to see the Holders and informed them that the fellowship would like to make a contribution towards the rent of their flat. This generous financial support continued throughout the family's stay in Basel and was transferred as support for Geoffrey and Daniel when they were at university after their parents had moved to Germany.

One morning, at about six o'clock, the doorbell rang, and a very Swiss voice informed a very sleepy Leonard that he had come to sweep the chimney. Leonard endeavoured to explain that he hadn't ordered a sweep and certainly not at that time in the morning. All objections were swept aside with the explanation that this was a legal requirement and that a certain sum was needed to be paid in cash. Coming so early was no doubt to try and ensure a fire had not yet been lit, but it was normal for a household to receive notification beforehand of the date and approximate time.

With regard to heating the flat, as the weather got colder, Leonard realised that there was a constant and ready supply of timber to burn available to be picked up in the streets. Fortnightly, the Basel council collected what they referred to as *Sperrgut*. Households were able to leave out in the street bulky items they wanted to dispose of. All manner of things were left out to be collected, including wood and wooden items that could be dismantled. Leonard, with Daniel's help, would walk around after dark the night before the collection, and they would gather for themselves timber to keep the house warm. Although it was a humbling thing to have to do, in this way, the Holder family avoided paying a single cent for their heating during two winters in the Morgartenring accommodation.

Another essential thing to arrange was schooling for Daniel. Comments from a few other British families were that for non-Swiss children, one shouldn't expect much co-operation from the schools. Bearing this in mind, Leonard and Phyllis prayed about finding the right school and investigated the possibilities. Basel offered several grammar schools, each giving a general education up to Matura, which is the university entrance

MNG grammar school, Basel

qualification, but each had a particular specialism. Daniel decided a maths and science grammar school would suit him best, and so Leonard arranged an appointment to see the headmaster at the Mathematisch-Naturwissenschaftliches-Gymnasium (MNG). Unexpectedly, they found him very sympathetic. They explained their position and that Leonard had come to study theology at the FETA and showed him Daniel's reports from Ripon Grammar School. Having looked at the reports, he acknowledged they were very satisfactory and then, turning to Daniel, asked him a few basic questions in German to test his language skills. His parents were agreeably surprised by how their son responded in German, seeing the only German language studies he had done were together with the whole family in Brake.

'Yes, I'm happy to take Daniel,' the headmaster said, looking at the parents. 'But first, he must learn German.' He then picked up the telephone on his desk and spoke earnestly to someone. Then turning to Daniel, he said, 'I've arranged for you to have two hours German tuition every day, Monday to Friday, with a Frau Nabholz.

216

She lives within walking distance of your home. This will be for three months – so until Christmas. You don't need to come to school, but I want you to read German books as much as possible for several hours a day. After Christmas, we'll decide how to take things further.'

Leonard and Phyllis thanked him very much, and taking a note of Frau Nabholz's address, they left the school to walk back to Morgartenring, amazed at what they firmly believed was God's provision for Daniel to learn German at no expense to themselves.

With son Geoffrey remaining in England for that first year, sleeping arrangements had to be organised in their two-roomed flat for parents and one son. After some thought and discussion, they decided they needed to keep the living room free for living and to use the bedroom for all three to sleep. By arranging wardrobes at ninety degrees to one another in one corner, they separated off a secluded sleeping space for their 13-year-old son, and this proved a pretty satisfactory solution under the circumstances. It was clear they would need a bigger flat once Geoffrey was able to join them.

Memories from Phyllis

I experienced culture shock. This is feeling like a little child again, having to relearn so much that you have, for years, taken for granted. A thinking adult who feels completely unable to function in everyday life without help. The world that you have been able to cope in for many years has suddenly gone. Life around you makes no sense anymore, and despite being an adult, you have to relearn many life skills to simply survive day by day. This is not simply language as conversely, when you return to England again after a long period of time, you have to go through the reverse process. I well remember talking to a lady about culture shock. She had been a missionary in Spain for a number of years. She mentioned how she could never explain to anyone who had never experienced culture shock for themselves how it makes you react and behave. She said that she had gone into a supermarket back home in Britain; gazing around, she had just burst into tears! I told her I had done exactly the same thing, whereby she told me what a relief it was to talk to someone who understood. It's the reaction to too much choice and a different ethos of living once again. In a missionary situation when money is scarce and every penny or franc or whatever has to be explained and accounted for – and this has gone on for years on end – to suddenly be presented with too much choice of product and range of expense is more than one can cope with. The mind and senses are overwhelmed as you try to apply your recent understanding and way of functioning to this new situation.

Another humiliating aspect of moving into another culture is, of course, problems in communication. Basic communication necessitates understanding the sounds being communicated; it assumes starting from the same premise – that is, the same way of thinking. Dan told us that when he was getting used to school, there were times when he would understand all the words spoken, but the meaning of all those words put together was a mystery. The other students, hearing what was said, came from the same cultural background so could understand what was intended. Once Dan had experienced more within the Swiss culture, there was increasingly less problem understanding everything.

Interestingly, on speaking with an American couple who had come to Basel to study, they commented that they had felt a greater culture shock in Switzerland than when they had spent time in Africa. They added that this had come quite unexpectedly as they had been prepared for it in Africa but not in Europe. During our time in Basel, we learned that one of the large pharmaceutical firms had, after a lot of persuasion, accepted that they needed to provide counselling and support for the non-Swiss wives of their employees.

We each had a pioneer situation which was very hard. Len's college life was very difficult. The other students were not much older than our own children, and Len couldn't learn as fast as they could. After several hours at college every day struggling to understand all that was said, he had to work for hours in the evening at his homework, learning not only German but also Hebrew, Greek, and Latin – through German!

Dan, meanwhile, was having lessons in German from a lovely lady who inspired him to want to learn, to get to know and understand Basel, and to be ambitious in learning other languages also. Dan's attitude helped us tremendously and particularly when he eventually started properly at the Swiss grammar school. He would remind us when our courage threatened to fail, which it very frequently did, that the Lord had brought us there and therefore would help us. Len and I often felt we couldn't cope and that we were drowning in a bottomless sea, but going back to England was never a serious option, and the Lord helped us through as we clung to His promises and to the conviction of Len's call.

CHAPTER

※※※

3

—

First Year at the FETA

Each new study year at the college began with an opening ceremony at which new students introduced themselves, and this was probably the first time Leonard had to stand at the front of a crowded hall and speak in German. It was unusual for the college to have an English student; in fact, Leonard doesn't believe that another English person had ever enrolled for the full course before, although a few Americans had attended lectures for short periods.

People have often asked Leonard why he didn't study at an English-speaking college, which would have been much easier. His answer was that the main reason was to improve his German and to begin to understand German and Swiss culture as it is reflected in the churches.

Phyllis and their friend Sue, who had driven the Holders out to Basel, attended the ceremony, and not realising how the college leader frowned on women wearing trousers, they both turned up in this forbidden item of clothing. Although nothing was said, it would have been a black mark against the Holders' reputation in the eyes of the college leader.

The FETA had been given university status, and its aim was to give its students a level of theological education as high as, if not higher than, that of the main universities but from a conservative, Bible-believing point of view. Therefore, a good understanding of the old languages – Greek, Hebrew, and Latin – was considered essential. These languages were taught in two stages. The first stage, with exams to pass in all three languages, was seen as necessary before studying the Bible and theology in more detail. Later, there would be more advanced studies in Greek and Hebrew. Because of his limited German, Leonard was permitted to concentrate on Greek and Latin for his first year and to only attend college for these lectures. He needed to allow about an

Basel tram

hour to get door to door, home to college, and this involved first a trolley bus journey, a tram, and finally a six- or seven-minute walk.

Being a mature student, very much older than most of the others – who, in many cases, had come to study straight from school – Leonard decided he would not hesitate to ask questions about anything he didn't understand. Unfortunately, he soon lost the confidence to do this as there was so much of the German spoken which went over his head. He consoled himself by thinking he could read it all up in his textbook when he got home, although the textbook was, of course, also in German. The main homework given involved language exercises translating simple sentences, some German into Greek and then others Greek into German, with the same procedure also in Latin. There was vocabulary to learn as well, all very straightforward for those with German as their mother tongue, but for Leonard, it was a nightmare. There were days when he walked back to the tram stop feeling dazed and despondent. In his mind, he likened the situation to falling into the deep end of a swimming pool and being unable to swim. He said to himself, *If I can't swim, I must simply concentrate on keeping my head above the water.* He saw this as ensuring he completed all the homework, even though for him, everything had to come via English. So German sentences were first translated into English and written down before translating the English into Greek or Latin. The same process was then repeated for Greek and Latin sentences into German. Homework took hours. The latter didn't usually need to be handed in, but students were called on at random to read out their answers, and Leonard felt he needed to be constantly prepared for this. The Latin teacher was a Swiss lady who travelled to the college from Bern for the two days a week she had classes. She was very understanding of Leonard's situation and offered to correct his German sentences to aid his learning of the language. As she pointed out, writing these fairly simple sentences in German and getting them right grammatically was an excellent way to improve his abilities in the language.

There was, however, one homework exercise each week which Leonard found virtually impossible to cope with. This was vocabulary learning. In Latin classes, each week, there was a vocabulary test. German words were read out, and the class had to write the equivalent in Latin. Leonard's mind had to grasp the meaning of the German words, translate them into English, and then think of the Latin word. Before he had got halfway through

Studying in Basel

this process, the next word was sounding through the classroom. He discovered the best thing was to hurriedly write the German word, and then he could go back to it to think about it a bit more. Each week, his score was two or three correct Latin words out of the thirty-odd German words read out. Fortunately, the test was essentially for the students' own benefit, and results didn't need to be handed in.

Leonard can't say that he never had the fleeting thought *Why are you doing this?* Still, he reasoned with himself that this was God's provision to enable him to learn German as well as German and Swiss thinking and that it was the door into whatever God had for him in the future. Also, the verse would come to him: 'No one, having put his hand to the plough and looking back, is fit for the kingdom of God.'[37]

---

37 Luke 9:62.

CHAPTER

4

Home Difficulties but also Encouragements

Phyllis found the situation very difficult in another way. She had had to leave behind in Britain both the house she loved and her elder son, who was just 15. She had also lost her dog and suddenly felt so far away from all her friends and family. It should also be remembered that ease of communication was very much more difficult in the 1980s. There were no mobile phones or Wi-Fi, and access to a telephone was via a call box up the street, with calls to Britain being expensive. Letters were still the main way of communicating, and the post took several days in each direction. Although not really doubting that God had led them at that stage, as she acknowledged later, she was really making these sacrifices for her husband's sake and on the basis of her husband's call. Only later did she feel convinced that she also had a part in this call.

Phyllis also realised later that she was suffering from culture shock. She wasn't understanding and couldn't communicate in the Swiss language, and it seemed that everything she had learned in life was now purposeless as the world around her did things differently. Leonard also felt this to some degree, and it made them feel like babies, needing to start learning how to live all over again.

Leonard had the enormous challenge of his studies, but he did try and support his wife as much as he knew how. It came as a shock to him to learn later of the extent of her despair in those early days. She confessed that on one occasion, when walking through Basel streets, she had been seriously tempted to throw herself under a tram.

Shopping was difficult as they found the Swiss shops so expensive, and their money was in short supply. They then discovered that prices in Germany were very much cheaper and particularly for milk, dairy items, and meat. What soon became their custom was to cross the German border and to walk about a mile to where there was a small Lidl supermarket. Leonard's college was close to the German border, so once a week or so, Phyllis would catch the tram and meet him so that together, they could walk across the border into Germany. However, walking with heavy bags made this a difficult exercise, and then coming back, they were usually stopped by the Swiss border guards and their bags searched. The Swiss had set a limit on the amount of food items that any single person could bring across the border – for instance, three litres of milk per person and a strict limit on red meat. Then when there was a pig disease rampant in Germany, absolutely no pork meat in any form could be brought into Switzerland. All this made shopping more difficult.

Still, their son Daniel was a source of much encouragement to them. He enjoyed his lessons with Frau Nabholz, and she made learning German interesting. Sometimes she took him into the city and explained Swiss life and some of its history to him.

On more than one occasion when his parents were feeling depressed, he was known to say, 'Remember, the Lord has brought us here, and He will look after us.'

Then the Lord gave them a wonderful blessing. Once they had made their new home reasonably comfortable, they would invite friends they made at the BCF back to lunch on a Sunday. There were several single people in Basel for work who had no real home life in their little flats, and they appreciated coming into a family home. One Sunday, they were introduced to a Swiss lady who was interested in English and had been invited to the service by her neighbour. They discovered that Marianne, whilst learning English, had spent time in Fareham, the very town where Phyllis and

Leonard had attended school. This was a real point of contact, and they invited Marianne round to supper one evening. Over the meal table, she asked why they had come to Basel, and they explained about God's guidance and that their faith and trust in God had brought them there. Marianne's response was that no Swiss person would do this, but when she left, Phyllis wished her God's blessing and hoped that she would sleep well.

A day or two later, she contacted them again, saying, 'You know you hoped I would sleep well? In fact, I didn't, and I want to know how to become a Christian.'

Marianne began coming to the Holders for Bible studies, and after this had gone on for a while, Leonard felt he needed to tell her that it wasn't sufficient to simply understand the teaching of the Bible; there needed to be a definite step of faith in acknowledging personal sin and need and to trust Jesus Christ as our Saviour. Very soon, she was able to do just that, and she discovered the joy of knowing she belonged to Jesus.

Phyllis's Memories

There are many stories of how God enabled us and provided for us during these years, although the way was through deep valleys of despair but also mountaintop experiences. A few particular incidents come to mind as I write.

When we first arrived in our new home in Switzerland, I noted that the only thing that was in the living room was a very ancient telephone on the floor. We couldn't afford to get it connected at that time, which made life even more of a nightmare for me, but then somebody in our church fellowship, out of their tithe money, paid for us to have it connected. Oh, the difference this made to our daily existence! It was the Lord showing us kindness through His people and showing He was with us.

Another very significant incident occurred when we were endeavouring to buy furniture soon after our arrival in Switzerland. We found four hundred Swiss francs in our letter box one day! We never knew where it came from, but a perfect piece of furniture for us was found in the Salvation Army second-hand shop in Basel when we went there, and yes, you've guessed it – it was exactly four hundred Swiss francs. We had already seen this lovely piece of furniture on our last visit to the second-hand shop and commented that it would be ideal for us as it had shelving, cupboards, and an able-to-lock bureau. God provided for our exact need in a wonderful way at exactly the right time.

A third incident that I will note here which was huge for us, especially for me, and confirmed God's care of us was in regard to my teeth! I had wisdom teeth problems soon after arriving in Switzerland which clearly needed treatment. Someone had once observed, 'You must be the poorest people I've ever known to try and live in Switzerland,' and consequently, since dental costs were huge, it was a real dilemma as to how to get treatment for my teeth. In Basel, there's a dental surgery known as the people's dental clinic (*Volkszahnklinik*) which is often referred to as the poor man's clinic, where costs are minimal. The dentists were apprentices mostly from other countries, learning on the job! I got a dentist who split my wisdom tooth in half and left half the roots still stuck in my mouth, whereupon he just poured anaesthetic into and on the tooth and walked out of the room! The main clinic had closed by then, and no one was around except Len, thank God, because I was very distressed and in pain. Eventually, the dentist came back and hacked away until he got my tooth out. Len and I then went back on the bus to where we lived; I was in great discomfort and traumatised for a long time. Consequently, I was terrified about having the second wisdom tooth out, but two ladies from the church fellowship we attended who were dental nurses themselves kindly used their tithe money to pay for the second wisdom tooth to be extracted by a very sympathetic dentist at the dental practice where they worked in Liestal, a short train ride out of Basel. Much to my embarrassment, a dry socket infection started up in the tooth cavity, and when I couldn't bear the pain any longer, I apologetically presented myself at the dental practice again and had to have three further appointments for extra treatment to heal the infection. This meant extra money from the two ladies' tithe fund, but thankfully, they expressed no problem with this as they realised it was not something I could have anticipated. God's provision for the payment of treatment and the kindness I received then was something I have never forgotten.

CHAPTER

✻

5

Basel Christian Fellowship

Despite the fact that Leonard's hope for the family was to integrate into the German-speaking Christian scene and have fellowship in a Swiss church, it was clear that in the initial stage after their arrival in Switzerland, they needed the fellowship and support of English-speaking Christians. The BCF was a fellowship with a strong international flavour, attracting English-speaking residents in Basel who wanted a Christian worship service. The leading elder at that time was a Chinese architect named Eric. He had a Swiss wife, and his Christian background lay with All Souls Church, London, and the ministry of John Stott. If Leonard understood the situation correctly, it was his initiative that had brought the BCF into being. Assisting Eric on the eldership was a Swiss businessman who had an American wife and a retired British missionary, Jack, who had worked for many years in Africa with the mission started by C. T. Studd. Jack had lost his first wife in Africa and had subsequently married a Swiss missionary nurse, which was the reason he now, in his retirement, was living in Basel.

The chemical and pharmaceutical companies in Basel employed many from the English-speaking world, and several regular worshippers at the BCF worked with companies like Roche, Sandoz, and Ciba-Geigy.[38]

There were also a number of Swiss believers in the fellowship, but most of these were married to English-speaking partners or, alternatively, had been converted through contact with English people and therefore somehow considered this the language they used when worshipping God. There was one interesting couple where the wife was Japanese and the husband Swiss, but they had met whilst studying English in England, and this had become the common language between them. Remarkably, their children had learned to speak Swiss German with their father and Japanese with their mother and attended church and Sunday school in English. There were also several American, Canadian, and British Christian singles and couples working with the Janz Team (a missionary organisation) and the Child Evangelism Fellowship which had its international headquarters at Kilchzimmer in the Jura Mountains outside Basel. Another small group of regular worshippers were singers with the Basel opera company. Leonard and Phyllis remember a Sunday when an international opera singer who was based for a while in Basel sang a solo in the morning service. Without the need for a microphone, his voice filled the building.

Getting to know these lovely people who had come from such diverse Christian backgrounds certainly served to widen the Holders' experience of the international family of the Lord Jesus. They made some good friends, particularly from amongst those serving with one or other of the Christian organisations with whom they had most in common.

The BCF at that time had no formal membership, but it did have a confession of faith which acknowledged the Bible as the inspired Word of God and that salvation was through faith in the Lord Jesus Christ alone and through God's grace.

Leonard and Phyllis, with Daniel, were warmly welcomed into the fellowship and, as has already been mentioned, soon after their arrival, were offered some financial support to help with the rent of

---

38 In 1996, Ciba-Geigy merged with Sandoz, and the large pharmaceutical company Novartis came into being.

their accommodation. Leonard was also invited onto the preaching rota and very soon was preaching approximately once a month. To ensure consecutive preaching, the eldership decided on a Bible book to study, and the preachers were allocated particular passages to preach from. Leonard remembers one Sunday having to preach from three chapters in the Epistle to the Romans in one sermon, being Chapters 9, 10, and 11; he did wonder whether the eldership wanted to pass over some of the content of these chapters as quickly as possible. What was interesting and very encouraging was many years later, long after Leonard and Phyllis had left Basel, a man of standing in the fellowship who had been a fellow speaker on the preaching rota at that time wrote a letter to the couple on their fiftieth wedding anniversary and thanked Leonard for his sermons. He commented that they had been the means of leading him into the truth of reformed doctrine.

Leonard was also asked to give the children's talk each Sunday. He did different series of talks, including one on some of the main incidents in John Bunyan's *The Pilgrim's Progress*. He also remembers giving several talks on Elijah. The children would come and sit in the front pews, and there was one little boy, Christoph, who would sit wide-eyed, apparently enthralled with the stories. His mother was American and his father Swiss, and when later, his mother brought her two children to visit the Holders in their home, she told them that she had had to explain to Christoph that Leonard was neither God nor Elijah, as he had seemed to think.

She also told them that soon after her second child had arrived, Christoph has seen her putting out the rubbish bag for the dustman and had said, 'Couldn't we put the baby in the bag too?'

'Oh no, Christoph,' she had answered, looking at her elder son anxiously. 'He would die.'

'Then he would go to heaven,' Christoph answered. 'And he would be very happy. And I would be happy too.'

Tragically, for Christoph and, of course, his mother and little brother, his father, who suffered from depression, took his own life a few years later.

The BCF was, at that time, meeting in a Swiss evangelical church building whose Swiss members had an earlier Sunday service. The church building had no baptistery, but the Swiss church practised believer's baptism using a very large bath on wheels which was kept in the vestry. Their practice was to wheel the bath to a position across the door of the vestry so it was visible to the congregation in the church. The bath was then filled with water. At the appropriate moment, the candidate for baptism would be helped into the bath, where he or she would sit in the water. The minister performing the baptism would then kneel outside the bath on the vestry side so the congregation could witness what was happening, and on the candidate's audible confession of his or her faith in the Lord Jesus, he would baptise the candidate by submerging their head forward between their legs. Probably because of the Christian background of the founding elder of the fellowship, the BCF had neither preached nor practised adult baptism, but during the time that Leonard was there, there were requests for baptism, and the elders asked Leonard whether he would conduct these. This, of course, was a great privilege which he was pleased to do. After leading a few baptismal classes to explain the biblical teaching, Leonard remembers baptising at least two young people during the years the family were attending the BCF.

One thing Leonard and Phyllis missed when first coming to Basel was a Sunday evening service. However, they soon discovered that an American couple who were studying at the university held a Bible study in their flat on a Sunday evening. Don was working on a PhD in theology and later went on to lecture at a thoroughly conservative Bible college in Germany. Although the family could walk from their flat to the Sunday morning service, getting to the evening Bible study involved a tram ride, but they were happy to do this, and most Sundays, Daniel came too.

Trams in Basel, like most things in Switzerland, were efficient and punctual. Passengers needed to have a valid ticket before boarding a tram or bus in the city, and this meant buying a ticket from a machine at the bus stop. One could buy a single ticket or a multiple-ride one, which gave eleven rides for the price of ten, but the date and time of each ride needed to be stamped on the ticket by the appropriate machine before beginning the journey. The tram drivers neither sell nor check tickets, so any checking is done by inspectors who roam around the city, jumping on and off trams and demanding to see the passengers' tickets. One can travel for days without seeing an inspector, but if you are caught without a valid ticket, the fine is considerable. The Holders had a friend who, having met her mother at the train station and whilst talking excitedly, jumped on a tram, forgetting to buy the tickets. An inspector caught them, and when neither had sufficient cash for the fine, he got off the tram with them and accompanied them to a bank and waited while they withdrew the money he demanded.

Later, when Don and his wife moved on, Leonard and Phyllis began a Sunday evening Bible study with fellowship in their own flat.

Phyllis's Memories and Comments

We were in a very lonely situation, and meeting with people for fellowship each Sunday was very necessary. The congregation at the BCF varied each Sunday, but we met people from many lands and languages, all wanting to worship in English. It is an interesting fact that if somebody's conversion experience was in English, this is then the language they will often use as their 'religious language' and so will seek out an English-speaking church. So we met a lot of different nationalities, converted to Jesus Christ whilst either in England, America, Australia, or another English-speaking country. There were people in the same situation and circumstances as we were, new to Basel and finding life in Switzerland very difficult, but nobody wanted to show weakness to anybody else, and we all appeared fine on the surface. It was not until years later that many of us discovered that we had all felt at breaking point but had not let on!

Being at this fellowship was good preparation for our later ministry of encouragement in Haus Barnabas. We were meeting people of different denominations and nationalities, learning the important lesson of accepting Christians from a variety of backgrounds with differing styles of worship. The criterion for being a true Christian is personal faith and trust in Jesus Christ as Saviour and Lord, and although it's easier to have fellowship with those of the same doctrinal persuasion, there is, at the same time, a common bond with all who are born again and indwelt by God's Holy Spirit. There is a richness of blessing in meeting other believers at the foot of the cross and not at the foot of the five points of Calvinism or any other 'ism'.

CHAPTER

6

A Local Swiss Home Group

Leonard can't remember quite how they first became acquainted, but a short while after moving into Morgartenring, the Holder family discovered that a family living a few houses away were Christian believers who, once a week, held a home group for Bible study and prayer in their living room. Leonard and Phyllis were invited to attend, and with great hope of having fellowship with Christians who loved the Lord Jesus, they were happy to accept.

In comparison with past experiences of the joy of fellowship with those who loved the Scriptures and had found the freedom in Christ which faith in Him brings, their initial impression of the meeting was rather disappointing. They were happy to accept that part of the contrast was due to cultural differences; also, since a lot that happened was conducted in the local Swiss dialect, much of the content of what was said was lost on them. The leader was actually a medical doctor running his own surgery, but his home apartment was very basic, and there didn't appear to be any comfortable chairs for relaxing in. Their living room was furnished with a largish table and dining chairs at which all of the group sat.

The Holders learned that the group of three or four couples were members of the Swiss state church but had become very dissatisfied with its liberal theology, which left them spiritually hungry. They were no doubt born again believers but had obviously been reading literature by very pietistic writers. In their concern to follow Christ, they had, in the view of Leonard and Phyllis, become very legalistic. This showed itself in their very conservative dress style and the women wearing head scarves in the meetings. They were very sensitive to what they considered to be worldly influences. Whilst in some ways commendable, if taken to extremes, this really means cutting oneself off from the world completely. The leader counselled Leonard and Phyllis against having a television in their home but did concede that their case was an exception when they explained that they needed to hear German and try to follow the Swiss news programmes to improve their understanding of the language and Swiss thinking.

There was one incident particularly amusing to English minds. In the middle of prayer time, the telephone rang. The leader spent ten minutes or so talking in Swiss German whilst the group, being in the same room, sat quietly.

Then coming off the phone, he said in clear German that the Holders could understand, 'Das war Götti.'

The word *Gott* being German for the Creator of heaven and earth and our Father in heaven, it appeared that God had telephoned during their prayer to Him. It was only later that the Holders learned that the Swiss refer to their godparents as *Götti*.

The group were very kind to the Holders, and although somewhat uncomfortable meeting with them, Leonard and Phyllis hesitated to stop doing so. However, the crunch came when the leader came round to their flat one evening and told them the group no longer wanted them to attend their meetings. He explained that he had noticed that Phyllis was wearing a copper bracelet. He believed this was devilish and was inviting the devil into their home. Phyllis explained that someone had given her the bracelet because the copper was thought to help the arthritis she had in her back. She explained that she had no great faith in this and would be happy not to wear it if it offended him, but he was adamant that neither she nor Leonard were any longer welcome in their meetings. Leonard did wonder whether any doctrinal comment he had made at one of the meetings may have been the real cause for this sudden exclusion from their home and meetings, but he couldn't think of anything he had said which could have upset them.

The folk they had got to know at the meeting continued to be friendly to Leonard or Phyllis if they met them in the street, but clearly, this rejection left an uncomfortable feeling.

When Geoffrey came across to Basel during the school holidays, the same family up the road very kindly offered the use of an attic room they had above their flat as a bedroom for Geoffrey and Daniel. Thankfully, although turning Leonard and Phyllis away from their meetings, they were still happy for the boys to use this room. It was very sparsely furnished and without heating, but since the boys only used it to sleep in, it fulfilled a need for which Leonard and Phyllis thanked God.

CHAPTER

7

A Family Crisis and God's Wonderful Solution

In the summer of 1984, Geoffrey, after completing his O-level exams with top grades in most subjects, joined his family in Basel. By this time, his brother, Daniel, had gained a good understanding of German through his lessons with Frau Nabholz and was well established in school. The headmaster had appeared to take a personal interest in him and ensured that he sat next to another pupil who understood English. Jean-Claude had an Irish mother and French father and, through his mother, had a good understanding of English, although he spoke with a very strong Irish accent. The two lads sitting together meant Daniel was able to ask Jean-Claude things he didn't understand. He took it all in his stride and very quickly found he could keep up with the class. An added problem at school was the mixture of languages. Although the lessons themselves are conducted in the official High German, which is the textbook German everyone learns, any additional comments and some discussion can take place in the Basel dialect of Swiss German, which is quite another language to understand and learn. The Swiss don't expect foreigners to speak their dialect, but when one lives in Switzerland, it soon becomes necessary to understand the Swiss dialect when it is spoken, although the Swiss are then happy for people to answer in High German.

Geoffrey had gained a top grade in his O-level German exam, but to be suddenly immersed in his higher studies completely in the German language was a very different matter. The school offered no additional German language lessons, and it was expected that Geoffrey would cope if he worked hard. However, Geoffrey is a perfectionist. His temperament requires that he gets things right, and the ability God has given him normally has enabled him to do this.

In his immutable way, he once made the following comment (quite possibly not an original one): 'I made a mistake once. I thought I was wrong.'

After a few weeks at the MNG grammar school in Basel, Geoffrey, then aged 16, came home and, throwing down his books, said, 'It's no good. I can't do it. I just can't go back to that school.'

His parents were concerned but quite hoped after a good night's sleep he would feel better in the morning, but no. Geoffrey was quite determined. Studying for the Swiss equivalent of A-levels in German was too much for him. When it became clear that this was his final decision, his parents realised the next thing to do was to talk to the headmaster. They telephoned for an appointment and, together with Geoffrey, caught the tram down to the MNG. For anyone who knows Basel, it is the large impressive building facing one, beyond the tram stops and busy road, as one comes out of the SBB Swiss railway station.

It was the same headmaster who had helped Daniel so successfully a year earlier. His comment was that he had seen Geoffrey's work and had no doubt at all that he was at the right level of school and would be able to make the grade. His opinion was that Geoffrey was experiencing culture shock, and his advice was not what they expected.

'Stay at home. Do something you enjoy and come back when you are ready.'

After a week or two at home, Geoffrey decided to try school again.

'I can't just hang around here doing nothing' was his comment.

Still, it only took a few days before, once again, 'It's no good. I can't do it.'

This was now a real dilemma for his parents. People had warned them that taking their children into another country and culture in their teens would ruin their education and consequently their whole lives. Where was God in this? They firmly believed He had led them. They suggested to Geoffrey that he could go back to Britain to do his A-levels, but he – having had a taste of life in Switzerland and, in particular, having seen his younger brother coping well with the German language – had no wish to give up and return to Britain with his tail between his legs.

What was to be done? It became a matter of urgent prayer. One Sunday evening, as all this was happening, Leonard felt he should challenge Geoffrey about his faith. The family had been concerned for some time as to whether their elder son really knew the Lord Jesus in his life. They remembered a comment Phyllis's mother had made some time before.

'Looking into Geoffrey's eyes, there is nothing there,' she had said sadly, meaning, no doubt, all she could see was a look of hopelessness.

That night, having come to the end of himself and confidence in his own ability, Geoffrey very positively committed his life to the Lord, trusting the Lord Jesus as his Saviour. As Phyllis said, if coming to Switzerland was for no other reason than this, it was worth it. She went on to sing an old hymn the male voice choirs used to sing:

When the last day shall come and the roll shall be called,
When the saints meet the Saviour in the air,
When the pilgrim and stranger at last reach their home,
We'll be there, praise the Lord, we'll all be there.

Geoffrey had found a new basis for his life, and he began to find a new sense of peace and happiness in knowing something he had, in fact, been longing to know for some time: he was a child of God and could trust God as his heavenly Father, to help him and guide him. This didn't solve his problems immediately, but the family could now pray about them positively, seeking in this difficult situation to know what God's way forward was.

Then Leonard saw an advertisement offering the opportunity to study for the Swiss Matura, which is the qualification allowing entrance into a Swiss university, by postal study from Zürich. He showed it to Geoffrey, who followed it up and decided this was something he would be confident to do. This was before the time of computers and Wi-Fi, so it would involve receiving study notes and guidance by post, working at home, and posting back his completed work. It was, of course, all in German, but being able to do everything in his own time, with a dictionary at hand, would make it much easier for him.

Geoffrey was very disciplined and motivated; very soon, he was getting full marks on most of the homework he sent in. This was clearly God's answer to Geoffrey's need, and the home student worked in this way for two years, keeping up with the work and making good progress. At the end of two years, Geoffrey decided he needed to go back to school to finish the course. He was, by that time, 18. He had an interview with the headmaster again and showed him the work he had been doing. It was agreed that he could return to school but was advised that

Geoffrey at his home studies

because the school syllabus was slightly different, he would need two years to complete the MNG Matura course. This put him in the same year as his younger brother, which was rather humiliating, but they were able to go into different classes, which they decided was best.

At the end of those two years, Geoffrey's achievement in the final exam was among the best in Basel, and the school recommended him for a monetary award offered by one of the pharmaceutical companies for outstanding students. His prize amounted to several thousand Swiss francs.

Phyllis's Memories and Comments

One of our mountaintop experiences was on a Sunday evening in November 1984. Geoff, by then, was living with us, even though both he and Dan were sleeping in the unheated attic of a house three doors up the road. Incidentally, dealing with this added to the difficulties I was experiencing. I needed to walk up a busy Basel ring road with bedding for my sons, climb to the unheated attic of a strange house to find the beds, change the linen, retrace my steps to our abode, and go down to the basement to wash the linen. In doing all this, I tried to avoid meeting people as trying to communicate was an embarrassment.

During the year Geoff had been back in England, he had written to us every week and continued going to church and youth group, but he was aware that he wasn't a Christian. Now, living with us again and continuing his education in Switzerland at the grammar school, he was finding it nigh impossible to cope. The school had recognised that part of the problem was adjusting to a different culture, but it had left Geoffrey feeling desperate, realising that he couldn't manage his own life in the way he expected to. The crunch came for Geoff on a particular Sunday evening after a Bible study in our home. A young lady was attending the Bible studies at that time, and having come to know the Lord just a month before that evening, she was avidly learning from God's Word, and it had been a very helpful and meaningful study.

Len was talking to Geoff in the kitchen after the study at about midnight, and the subject of Geoff's education was on all of our minds. During the conversation, Len suggested to Geoff that he commit his life to the Lord there and then, and it was clearly the right time as God had evidently been preparing Geoff for this. We all prayed, and Geoff committed his life to the Lord, admitting that he realised he could not live his life relying on his own strength but that he needed the Lord to govern his life and forgive his sins. It was a wonderful time, as was the day a while later, when a Baptist church building in Basel was used for a baptism service. Geoff was one of several being baptised that day by the new pastor at the BCF. It was a great witness to his new-found faith, and I remember how moved I was as I thought back to how we had arrived at this day.

However, Geoff's coming to the Lord did not solve the practical issues immediately as to the direction in which his life should go, but it did mean that he had a spirit of submission as to how the next stage of his education could be worked out. There was never any question about him going back to study in Britain. It never came into question for either Geoff or Dan as their attitude was that if the Lord had placed us in Switzerland, that was where they would continue their lives, and for this, we were always so thankful. We marvel at how God made Geoff and Dan so willing to tread these challenging paths in a new country with a new language.

Two Americans who were training for mission and ministry said to us later that seeing what the Lord had done for us in bringing us and our boys through this difficult period had been a great encouragement for them in helping them to persevere in their pathway with and for the Lord.

CHAPTER

✿

8

New Friends

Leaving friends was one of the hardest things to endure in leaving Britain, and this was particularly so for Phyllis. She comes to life with people and takes a genuine loving interest in them, and the thought of letting them down or betraying them in any way is anathema to her. There were some friends she felt particularly bad about leaving, and this was as much because of the fear they would feel forsaken by her as for her own loss of closeness with them. Some were able to come and stay, although sleeping space was very limited in the Holders' flat.

Leonard remembers one occasion when a couple with three children came, and the whole family was happy to sleep on the floor in the lounge. Daniel had to leave for school early and realised his school bag was under the table in what had become the guests' bedroom. Trying not to disturb the sleeping family, he crept in on his hands and knees to retrieve his bag with the schoolbooks he needed. The problem was a young lady of similar age to himself was sleeping near the table, and when the mother heard a noise and looked up to see Daniel creeping towards her sleeping daughter, she was initially rather suspicious. She soon realised his intentions were innocent, and the incident became quite a joke between the two families.

There were also summer days when the balcony was turned into a bedroom under the stars. This was fine when the weather remained dry, but one night a vicious thunderstorm erupted, and there had to be a rapid evacuation into the kitchen.

Very soon, there were new Basel friends to add to Leonard and Phyllis's 'extended family'. As is always the case, a true friend is someone you can share yourself with, and Leonard has never really needed friends to the same degree as his wife, and his inner thoughts and feelings remain much more a closed book.

Amongst their earliest friends in Basel was an English Christian family. The couple had four children, and the family also attended the BCF. The wife was musical and played the violin as well as the piano. She and Phyllis were able to make music together, and Phyllis very much enjoyed having access to a piano again. The husband was a chemist working with one of the Basel firms. Each year, he was responsible for proofreading a chemistry textbook and, realising the Holders' shortage of income, offered to pass some of this work over to Phyllis. It was a question of checking newly printed type on galley proofs against a typescript and didn't really involve any understanding of chemistry. Phyllis finds concentration difficult with any background noise, and the constant traffic stopping and starting at the traffic lights just outside the window of their room proved such a problem that she would sit up for several hours during the night to work when the street was silent.

After several months in Morgartenring, they were able to get a telephone installed, and one morning, earlier than you would expect, its ringing woke them. It was their new friend, very upset, saying her husband had suffered a severe heart attack in the night and had died before help could get to them. Leonard and Phyllis jumped on what was probably the first tram of the morning and went across to comfort and help the family in any way they could. Of the four children, the two eldest were then in their early teens and the youngest 4 or 5 years old. The husband's father had died in similar circumstances at a similar age, and being aware of this, he had kept himself very fit. He had cycled to work every day, watched his diet, and loved to take the children walking – but all to no avail in trying to protect himself from this family weakness. It was a tragic situation for the wife and the young children, and Phyllis tried to comfort them as much as she could. The husband's mother and brother from Britain came out to Basel for the funeral, and Leonard and Phyllis were able to welcome them into their small flat. They wrote later to say how the Holders' friendship and sympathy had helped them.

Phyllis was able to join a women's Bible study group which was part of the international Bible Study Fellowship. She made good friends with a Chinese lady from Hong Kong who was married to a Swiss banker and also a Chinese Canadian who was very newly married to a medical doctor of the same nationality doing research in Basel. Getting used to different cultures and a different use of the English language is an interesting experience. On one occasion, when they were invited to a meal with the Chinese Canadian couple, the husband returned from work and announced to the gathered company that he needed to go and change his pants! A British person would, of course, have said their trousers. In conversation later, Larry disclosed that the experiments he was currently working on involved rats and that since there was just then a full moon, this confused the animals' normal behaviour. When Leonard expressed interest in this statement, Larry explained that all scientists working with animals avoided taking readings of animals' behaviour when there was a full moon as they often went berserk. This, of course, raised the question of how much the moon's cycle affects human behaviour. Clearly, this was recognised in the past as seen in our English word 'lunatic', *luna* being the Latin for moon.

The Holders invited Larry and Audrey, the Chinese Canadians, to spend Christmas Day with them. They also invited a couple from Germany with a young teenage daughter whom they also knew from the BCF. Over this same Christmas period, Annabel, Leonard's brother's daughter from Australia, was staying with them. This would have been the Holders' second Christmas in Basel, and they made it as joyous an occasion as they could. Annabel's presence was a great help in this. In fact, they made it too joyous for Hans and Petra, with their German and Dutch customs. They considered Christmas Day to be a holy day and were unhappy with the Holders' balloons and general festivities. They enjoyed the meal but then left early.

Another young couple Leonard and Phyllis got to know very well in those early years in Basel were also mixed race. The wife, an extravert, had a Swiss mother and an Italian father and was completely blind; her young husband was English. How they met each other Leonard is not too sure. The contact with British people seemed important to the couple, particularly as the husband was struggling to learn German. The wife was an excellent linguist and was able to converse in German, Swiss German, Italian, or English with equal fluency. Leonard had begun a time of fellowship and Bible study on a Sunday evening after Don's time in Basel had come to an end, and this couple began to attend regularly. Later, she asked to be baptised and was one of the candidates Leonard baptised in the bath at the BCF.

Leonard and Phyllis made a number of other friends during those years in Basel. John and Irene Barfoot were, at that time, working with the CEF at Kilchzimmer and travelled into Basel each Sunday for the morning service at the BCF. Leonard and Phyllis appreciated the fellowship with John and Irene, and it was a blessing to accept their invitation to spend their first Christmas in Switzerland with them. The Barfoot family had a flat in Langenbruck, a little more than twenty miles outside Basel in the Jura Mountains. The CEF centre at Kilchzimmer was in a lovely position in the hills above Langenbruck. Leonard and Phyllis well remember a glorious walk on Christmas afternoon into the hills and a marvellous view of the Swiss Alps. Sometimes the climatic condition has the effect of bringing the Alps much closer, the so-called Föhn wind causing this. This was one of those days, and the view of the snow-covered Swiss Alps was amazing.

One other friend to mention is an Indian lady named Deepa. Deepa is a medical doctor who, whilst married with two sons in India, had a wish to come to Europe for further study. Her husband was also a doctor but working, if Leonard remembers correctly, with the World Health Organisation on diseases which are spread by insects, particularly mosquitoes. Deepa's husband took some convincing that she should leave him and her sons and spend time in Europe, but he finally agreed. Deepa showed herself to be a true Christian believer with a very simple faith in the Lord Jesus, His Word, and His promises. She explained that on coming to Europe, she had expected to find vibrant Christian faith, maybe because most of the Europeans she had had contact with in India were Christians. She was very disillusioned, when on her first Sunday in Basel on attending the English-speaking Anglican service, to find only about a half dozen other worshippers there. She later discovered more people at the BCF, and this soon became her regular church. She was very pleased to accept an invitation to the Holders' Sunday evening Bible study and brought a breath of fresh air into the fellowship. At her request, there was regular prayer for her two sons and husband, who, during her many months away from India, never wrote to her once. This was a real concern to her as she felt he was punishing her for forsaking her motherly and wifely duties at home. Her PhD involved studies on the brain and, when completed, must have been considered a valuable contribution to this subject as she was later invited back to the university to read a paper on it. Deepa spoke of finding a lot of comfort and encouragement from spending time with the Holders, and she related well to Geoffrey and Daniel, saying they reminded her of her own boys, whom she was longing to see again.

Another couple who visited the Holders frequently for a while were newly married medical doctors from Australia. They came to Switzerland to study anthroposophy, an understanding of which they felt would add to the medical care they could offer their patients. They were both the children of Christian missionaries but, as it became apparent, had very little knowledge of Christian doctrine. After even a few days of lectures on anthroposophy, the wife spoke to Leonard and Phyllis about her hesitation in continuing. She felt to accept the spirituality of plants and the belief that they needed to be picked in moonlight when the moon was in a certain phase (to provide the most effective herbal benefit) was far from biblical. She quarrelled with her husband about this as he was prepared to accept what was being taught. She spent several days in the Holders' flat reading good Christian books and eventually decided to return to Australia ahead of her husband. Leonard and Phyllis were so relieved when he agreed to his wife doing this, and the couple arranged to meet again back in their homeland. After a few years, there was an invitation to visit them in the centre of Australia at Alice Springs, where they were working. Further news spoke of a growing family of young children, so it was assumed a good relationship between them had been restored.

Phyllis's Memories

I'd like to mention the Bible studies we had in our flat on Sunday evenings and at other times too and the significant life-changing incidents we and others experienced through such times. God used us, perhaps because we were one of the few families at the Basel Christian Fellowship in close proximity to the city. We only realised later that for the authorities to allow residence for the whole family when only the husband was studying seemed to be quite rare in Basel.

We had people from all over the world coming to our flat at all hours. They wanted to talk about Christian things or delve into Christian books, which we had in abundance. People came in and out as they needed, and there was usually someone there to let them in. Later, during his studies, Len was doing what he called his 'printout'. This was a short explanation of different Christian issues and the exposition of Scriptural texts printed from the computer for people to read and discuss; he also saw this as a tool for evangelism. Some years later, our son Geoffrey took over the idea of producing a paper to help and challenge Christians and produced the BCF's church magazine which he called *Spoke*.

Looking back, it's interesting to see that our open home in Basel was simply a development of what had started in Horley and a foretaste of the ministry we were to have in Germany. We praise God for all those who, over the years, have benefited in a lasting way from the caring and loving hospitality we have been able to provide. Some have come to know and understand Christ's love and redemption personally and have gone on to serve Him.

CHAPTER

9

Exams and a New Flat

Leonard struggled through that first year in Basel. It was a miracle he could keep on top of what was demanded of him in his studies and then, knowing something of what his wife was suffering, doing what he could to support and encourage her once he got home. The librarian at the FETA, a Swiss gentleman named Robert who also attended the BCF, was always very friendly and would often wish Leonard 'a good evening with your family' if they happened to meet at the close of lectures. This wish was surely sincerely meant, perhaps with a hint of regret that he, Robert, himself had no family to go home to, but Leonard found it difficult. He would have loved to have had a quiet evening with his wife and family, but looming before him were several hours of Greek or Latin translation into German and German sentences into Greek or Latin which, at that stage, all had to be worked out in English first.

At the end of the college year, there were exams; these could either be taken in May or at the end of the long summer break in September. Leonard chose to take them in September as that gave him the whole summer to revise. Exams consisted of both a written paper and an oral session, when the examiner could ask questions to delve into the student's understanding of the subject. Leonard was very thankful to pass the Greek exam, but he failed the Latin. This meant that in his second year, he would repeat the Latin and also study Hebrew. He was very thankful to pass both Latin and Hebrew at the end of his second year.

During the second year in Basel, the family had the opportunity to move into a bigger flat. Once Geoffrey had joined his parents and brother, it had become increasingly important to find accommodation where they could all live together. For several months, both Geoffrey and Daniel had been sleeping in the very Spartan attic room of the Christian couple further up the road. For Phyllis, to change bed linens, this involved walking up the road, climbing about forty stairs with the fresh bedding, and coming back with the old. She felt she needed to do this when no one else was about as the couple's friendship with her had been soured and she found needing to try and converse in German an added barrier.

The provision of much more suitable accommodation was from the Lord; this was certainly how Leonard and Phyllis viewed it. The family who had introduced the Holders to Marianne, whom they had been able to lead to the Lord, were moving to a house farther out of the centre of Basel and, knowing the situation the Holder family were in, suggested they could recommend them to the owner of the flat as being suitable tenants after they moved. The flat was described as a three-and-a-half-roomed apartment. This meant in addition to a bathroom and a kitchen, there were three and a half rooms for living and sleeping. The reason for describing one as half a room was because the entrance into it was from the landing outside the entrance to the rest of the flat. Phyllis's initial reaction to it was to feel a bit dubious. It was at the top of a terraced house, up fifty-four stairs, and from the rather narrow balcony at the back, where she would need to hang clothes, there was a significant drop down to the garden below. Would she be able to stand near the railing to hang clothes on the clothesline? This was her fear.

Still, in most other ways, the apartment would suit them ideally. It provided three bedrooms, a good-sized living room, and a kitchen just big enough for the family to eat in. Marianne lived in a flat next door, and Jack Robertson, the retired WEC missionary, and his wife, Helene, were living almost opposite them. The rent was well over double what they had been paying, but by then, they had the money through from the sale of their Yorkshire home, so they felt it right to sign the contract and move.

The family had been given a grade B residence permit to live in Switzerland, which entitled them to study but not to take employment. It was dependent on being accepted and registered at a university or college and needed to be renewed annually. Both Geoffrey and Daniel decided they would like to earn some pocket money and found they could apply for permission to get jobs distributing free advertising 'junk mail'. This was granted to them, so each week, piles of papers

Daniel on his paper round

were delivered to the house, and they were provided with a deep trolley to push around the houses. They each had a different circuit of houses to deliver to, and what was advantageous was that each circuit consisted essentially of blocks of apartments with an accompanying set of post boxes outside each entrance. In this way, Geoffrey was able to earn a large amount of the cost of his postal study course. Occasionally, if the boys were overburdened with homework or weren't well, Phyllis would help them out with the delivery of the papers.

Later, Daniel got a job in the archives of the main Basel hospital and was provided with a small motorised vehicle for moving around all the corridors under the hospital to pick up patients' files as required by the doctors.

The family's second flat in Vogesenstrasse was within easy walking distance of the River Rhine, and there was a towpath along the edge of the water leading into the city centre. It was also the right side of the city for the building used by the BCF and so walking distance to Sunday church. Also, Daniel and eventually Geoffrey too were able to cycle into school.

Having earned a bit of money, Daniel bought himself a bicycle, of which he was rather proud. Although chained and padlocked to a lamp post, one sad day it was stolen. Now the Swiss insist that bicycles owned by their citizens be licenced. After the bike is inspected to ensure it is roadworthy, there is a small fee to pay; the bike is then registered with the authorities, and the owner receives a small sticker to attach to the bike. Daniel reported the theft of his bike to the police and then, after a week or so, gave up hope of getting it back. However, after about a month, a policeman called round to the flat and invited Daniel to come to the police station to identify his stolen bike. It was certainly his bike, and apparently, it had been spotted over the border in France, no doubt by the French police, who recognised it as Swiss by the licence sticker. The father of the boy who had stolen it was at the police station, and Daniel was asked to ensure there was nothing missing from the bike and that it was not damaged. Either the bell or the light was missing, and the police asked the father to pay Daniel enough to replace it. All this was evidence not only of God's overruling but also of the efficiency of the Swiss police and their system.

Memories from Others

Jack and Helen

We first came to know Len and Phyl when they came to the Basel Christian Fellowship. The way they were living in the first months – the flat in Morgartenring – was impressive! The flat was small; Dan, then 13 years old, slept in the same bedroom as his mum and dad but behind a cupboard. We were sorry that their older boy, Geoff, had been left behind in England. There was a lot of adjusting for them all to live in Basel, even small things, like having a wood-burning stove for heating in the flat. Wood was to be found sometimes on the streets, and I can picture Len going around in the evenings to look for some. You once told us, Len, that the first year in Basel was atrocious.

We were glad to see Len invited to preach at the BCF. This was appreciated, as were his talks to the children; he is gifted in that respect.

Some impressions that you have left with us, Len and Phyl: petunias are usually bought as small plants, but Len had a whole balcony full of lovely ones grown from seed. I feel you are a real optimist, Len! You seem to be still very much in love with each other – I remember seeing you in the Casino (a public concert and conference hall in Basel) hand in hand!

CHAPTER

10

An Italian Adventure

Marianne was conversant in Italian, and during the early summer of 1985, she suggested a camping holiday together in Italy. She knew people who ran a campsite near Pennabilli, about twenty miles inland from Rimini, and would love to show her new friends Italy, a country she loved.

This sounded a wonderful idea, but how practical was it when Leonard, whilst living in Basel as a student, didn't own a car? The answer to this initial problem came unexpectedly when another British family who worshipped at the BCF offered Leonard and family the use of their Peugeot 504 whilst they themselves were in England. This was suggested after their son Andy, who was a friend of Geoffrey and Daniel's, had indicated he would rather go to Italy with the Holders than with his parents and siblings to Britain. Geoffrey had already arranged to do a tour of European countries with Wesley, the son of the friends he had lived with during his final year in Ripon. They planned to buy Eurorail tickets, which would enable them to use trains across many countries. This meant that the camping group for Italy would consist of Leonard, Phyllis, Daniel, Andy, and Marianne.

It proved to be a memorable holiday with several incidents the Holders would never forget. The first was before they even left home. For several days before leaving, Phyllis urged Leonard to hunt out the sleeping bags and tents. They knew they had a biggish tent which had a compartment for themselves to sleep in and then a living area all could use. Also, there was a smaller tent in which the two boys would sleep. Marianne had her own tent and sleeping bag. Leonard, thinking he knew where everything was, responded to his wife by saying they would get everything together the evening before they left. When this time came, there was no sign of the small tent. What they didn't know – and only discovered about a year later – was that it was wrapped in the only sleeping bag they had decided they didn't need to use that holiday! So the morning of the holiday started with Daniel rushing off to Migros, the Swiss supermarket, to buy a new two-person tent.

The campsite proved very convenient and included a restaurant which was open to local residents as well as campers. Leonard remembers arriving there early morning after stopping and getting a few hours' rest on the way and being given a welcoming drink of strong black

Camping in Italy

expresso coffee in a tiny cup. One of the first encounters in the restaurant was with an Italian who had recently lost his wife and now spent most of each day sitting at a table with a glass of red wine in front of him. He had apparently claimed he could speak English, which caused his drinking companions to urge him into conversation with the newly arrived English campers. This, he was loath to do, but by sitting with him, some understanding among them all slowly emerged. When hearing he had spent a few years in England, Leonard was just about to enquire if he had enjoyed his time when he realised it had actually been during the war in a prisoner of war camp. During the holiday, more information was slowly divulged, and because of his knowledge of French, Daniel found he could communicate somewhat in Italian by using French words and putting 'o' or 'a' on the end. One evening the gentleman had an old photo with him of a young lady and disclosed that she had been his girlfriend in England. He said they had corresponded at first after his return to Pennabilli, but then his wife had discovered the letters, and communication was forced to stop. He didn't seem to have any bad impressions of England or the English.

Once the campers were installed, they had a time of Bible reading with a short discussion each morning and worked their way through the book of Joshua. This was followed by prayer together.

One morning Marianne suddenly said, 'Could we have a short prayer as I need to go to the loo?'

Of course, the Holder humour twisted this to mean what she had not intended. (The meaning of the request changes depending on whether the emphasis is put on 'short' or 'prayer'.)

For several days, the weather was hot and sunny, just ideal weather for camping and exploring the surrounding area, and then on the first weekend, it rained, not simply a shower or two but torrential rain that continued for hours. The site owners said there hadn't been rain like this in Pennabilli in July for eighty years. They sent staff around the site to dig shallow trenches to help drain water away from the tents. Thankfully, the restaurant on site gave a place of sanctuary from the wet, and playing card games together proved to be the best way of spending the hours. Marianne made friends with an Italian lady called Giusi who had a semi-permanent caravan on the site. Because of the weather, she invited Marianne to sleep in her caravan, which was certainly big enough for two. There was a television screen in the restaurant, and although the Holders couldn't understand the Italian spoken, when the weather map appeared, all of Italy and the surrounding countries were seen to be getting unbroken sunshine apart from a whirl of cloud over Pennabilli. At least that's what it looked like on the screen.

Leonard and Phyllis had an arrangement with their son Geoffrey that he would use the last few days of his Eurorail ticket to come down to Rimini. They would meet him there from the train, and he would have a few days with them on their campsite.

The arrangement had been made hurriedly, shortly before Geoffrey had left to get a train up to Scandinavia nearly a month earlier, so this led to a debate between his parents as to which day he would arrive. He had mentioned a train that arrived in Rimini soon after midnight, but was that Sunday night or Monday night? Phyllis was adamant that it was midnight Sunday, and so the couple set off for Rimini Station soon after 10:30 p.m. for what they calculated was about an hour's run.

The car needed fuel, and Leonard had already seen at least two all-night petrol stations on the road they needed to take, so his plan was to fill up as soon as possible. At the first filling station, all instructions being in Italian, he couldn't get the pump to accept his money so moved on to the next. Here, there was a customer filling up, so Leonard asked him for his help in putting in his money and pressing the right buttons. All went well, and they got fuel in the tank, but after about a quarter of a mile down the road, the car spluttered, lost power, and then stopped altogether. Oh dear! Eleven o'clock on a Sunday night on a dark Italian road is not an ideal time to break down. Then Leonard had a sudden thought: had he filled up with diesel instead of petrol? Using the same pump as the customer who had helped him, he hadn't actually checked what sort of fuel he had used.

'I'd like to walk back to the service station and check what fuel I'd put in the car,' he said to his wife, looking worried.

Thankfully, it had, by then, stopped raining, and a brisk walk back to the filling station confirmed his fear.

As they were sitting back in the car together, Leonard suggested they pray about the situation and ask the Lord for wisdom as to what best to do. After praying and sitting and thinking, Leonard decided that the wisest think to do was to try and sleep in the car until daylight and then hitchhike back to the campsite and get advice from the friendly campsite owner. Remember – these were days before mobile phones, and neither Leonard nor Phyllis spoke Italian.

Phyllis took the situation very calmly but did comment, 'Remember, my dear, what Marianne said when we stopped to rest in the night whilst travelling down. She said Italy was far less law-abiding than Switzerland, and Italians have been known to steal wheels from cars whilst the owners slept.'

'I can't imagine that happening in this remote rural situation,' answered her husband in his usual optimistic way, 'but we will keep an ear open for anyone stopping by us.'

They had thankfully been able to pull into a small layby and, feeling fairly secure, tried to get some sleep.

There was virtually no traffic on the road, but after what couldn't have been more than about half an hour, Leonard saw in his mirror the headlights of a car approaching and slowing down. Being aware of the danger of wheel thieves, both Leonard and Phyllis became alert to possible problems. Instead of travelling by, the car braked and pulled up next to them, and the window was wound down.

'Marianne!' exclaimed Leonard. 'Who told you we were in trouble?'

'Well, since you obviously are in trouble, I guess the premonition I had must have come from God,' answered Marianne, smiling.

What had brought Marianne and Giusi out to look for Leonard and Phyllis was initially an uneasiness Marianne had felt after they had left. This had intensified, and when she mentioned it to Giusi, the latter saw it as a good reason for an adventure.

'We'll go and find them,' she had retorted. 'The rain is stopping, and if we don't find them or they don't need us, we can simply drop off somewhere for a drink.'

Hearing what had happened, Giusi offered a way to sort the situation. 'I'll drive you into Rimini to find your son,' she suggested. 'Then on the way back, I can hitch your car behind mine and tow you back to the campsite. I've got a tow rope in my boot.'

A remarkable deliverance – but there were still problems to face. Leonard decided he should stay with the car to ensure it wasn't stolen. Phyllis acknowledged she needed to go into Rimini to meet her son – assuming, of course, they had got the day right and he would be waiting for them – but Giusi drove so fast and erratically that by the time they entered the town, Phyllis was feeling quite ill. Then finding the station was the next problem. The streets were fairly empty, but Giusi spotted an Italian policeman, pulled up beside him, and, giving him an engaging smile, asked the way to the railway station. Giving a rather unusual answer for a policeman, he directed them up a one-way street, the wrong way, as being the quickest route.

'If one of my colleagues challenges you,' he added with a smile, 'tell him I gave you permission.'

Arriving at Rimini Station, they discovered quite a crowd of youngsters sleeping on benches and at tables in the restaurant area, and Phyllis wandered around, looking for her son. Eventually, she spied a lad who looked like her son asleep on a bench with his head drooped low, but it needed much closer inspection to dispel any uncertainty about his identity. At last, being pretty certain it was Geoffrey, she dared to touch his shoulder and speak to him.

'Oh! I hoped you would eventually arrive,' exclaimed Geoffrey, waking up. 'I'd just decided if you didn't turn up, I'd catch another train to see another part of Italy and come back here tomorrow night.'

By this time, Phyllis was feeling quite ill. Giusi's driving had shaken her up, and with the whole trauma of the night, she now felt sick. 'I'll need to sit down for a bit before we drive back,' she uttered, looking quite white in the face.

The restaurant must have been an all-night affair as it was still open, so they sat around a table together. Giusi was pleased to order herself a beer (Phyllis was quite sure she had had several that evening already), and Phyllis ordered an Alka-Seltzer, which helped to settle her stomach. Feeling a bit better, she was able to explain everything to Geoffrey.

Leonard was dozing in the Peugeot when they got back to him and, having been somewhat worried, was very pleased to see them back safe and sound, accompanied by Geoffrey.

They decided they would need to push the Peugeot to turn it around, facing the right direction, before connecting the tow rope. Leonard, Geoffrey, and Phyllis pushed, whilst Marianne steered the car and Giusi (who was attired in a long white dress) positioned herself in the middle of the road to halt any oncoming vehicles. Leonard could imagine that any Italian driver who had been imbibing freely might well imagine he was seeing a vision of the Virgin Mary, but thankfully, the road remained empty. Giusi's vehicle was a small Fiat and the car to be towed a heavy Peugeot, but thankfully, the route was without any significant hills, and all went well. Driving slowly, they were, at one point, overtaken by another small Fiat with two men whose offer to help was communicated in rather slurred speech. Giusi gave them what for, and they accelerated away. A mile or so later, they and their car were seen in a ditch.

The adventuresome night, with its miraculous deliverance, ended as they drove back into the camp to the sound of the dawn chorus. The campsite owners were extremely helpful, and with Marianne able to explain everything in good Italian, they contacted a local garage who came and towed the vehicle away. The garage did what was necessary and brought the car back later the next day. Leonard was thankful the cost was not exorbitant, and there was no indication of any lasting damage to the car.

The holiday produced several other interesting incidents, including an evening at a local restaurant where Giusi introduced them to the mayor of Pennabilli, who insisted on sharing a bottle of Italian champagne with them. Leonard felt it had been good for Marianne to have had the experience of Bible reading and prayer each day and to have witnessed how God had cared for Leonard and Phyllis through her own premonition, which she could recognise must have come from Him.

CHAPTER

11

Visits from Family and Friends

Phyllis's father had never been very vocal in expressing compliments or showing affection to his daughter, but she heard from her mother that he had spoken proudly of her move to Switzerland with her husband, particularly as he knew how much she had enjoyed Yorkshire and

Phyllis's parents visit

their home there. Although he had never motored on the continent of Europe, he lost no time in booking a visit to them by ferry and then driving through Belgium and Germany. He was, by then, in his 70th year, and Phyllis's mother would have already celebrated her 75th birthday. They didn't find the journey easy and, once arriving in Basel, wisely decided to park the car and use public transport for visiting places in the city.

Phyllis was extremely happy to be able to provide her mother with the fulfilment of a long-held dream, namely, to visit the Swiss

Alps. A family in the BCF, knowing something of the Holders' financial position, had given Phyllis some casual work cleaning and tidying their home whilst they were at work. In addition to having a home on the outskirts of Basel, they also owned accommodation high up in the Swiss Alps having a wonderful view down to Lake Thun with the Eiger range of mountains behind it. Generously, they suggested that Phyllis could take her parents there for a couple of nights. It was early enough in the year for there to be a mass of snow still piled up around the chalet. Phyllis remembers waking to find her parents gazing out in wonder at the sun rising over the peaks of the Eiger, Mönch, and Jungfrau; the chalet and surroundings were blanketed by snow. Her father was so impressed later that, despite there being about two metres of snow behind them, they could sit on the terrace in shirt sleeves with the morning sun smiling warmly down on them.

After enjoying the many new experiences which came out of this visit to their daughter, Ron and May Pittwell had a very frightening experience on their way home. Soon after they were filling up with fuel on the German motorway, a passing car hooted to warn them that something was wrong, and Ron noticed smoke coming out from around the sides of the bonnet. He pulled onto the hard shoulder and, realising that the engine was on fire, got his wife safely out of the vehicle and hurriedly began to unpack the luggage in the boot onto the tarmac. He had scarcely finished when the whole car went up in flames and smoke. All they could do was to stand back and watch in alarm and fear.

A couple of motorists pulled in to offer help, and eventually, the police arrived. Being unable to speak any German made communication difficult. Thankfully, Ron had five-star AA breakdown insurance for Europe, and the police helped him contact the right people. The insurance included getting the driver and passenger home after such an incident, and they were offered the use of another vehicle. However, Ron decided he was too shaken after what had happened to drive home in an unknown left-hand-drive vehicle and requested a chauffeur, which was also possible under the insurance cover. All this took time, but eventually, they arrived safely at the port of Calais.

However, here, their driver informed them that he would need to leave them and dropped them and their luggage off. This annoyed Ron greatly as the insurance cover was supposed to get them home, but maybe they were expected to contact the AA again in Dover for an English driver. The result of this drop-off at the port meant that two elderly pensioners were left standing on the dockside with several cases and loose bags, which were impossible for them to handle themselves. In their need, God sent them help.

A friendly English tourist driving into the port stopped, lowered his window, and said with a questioning look, 'You don't appear as though you intended to be foot passengers?'

They explained to him what had happened, and he very kindly loaded their bags into his car boot and made room for them in the back seats of his vehicle. Ron then found a way of telephoning Phyllis's sister, who sent her husband, Alistair, to Dover to pick them up and drive them home.

Quite understandably, Ron vowed never to drive on to the continent again, but an additional problem was that he had also always vowed nothing would ever induce him to get into an aircraft! Phyllis's mother sadly reflected to herself that this single delightful occasion of visiting her daughter in Switzerland was going to be the last. However, politicians are often known to make U-turns, and changed circumstances can make most people rethink a stand they have made in the past. So a year or so later, to the delight of his wife, Ron returned home from town and lay two air tickets from Heathrow to Basel on the table.

Many family members and friends with their families visited the Holder family during their years in Basel. Both of Leonard's brothers, then living in Australia, spent time with them, combining this with a visit to family in England also. Sue, who had kindly driven them out to Basel, came for a visit with her mother and younger brother. They wanted to see more of Switzerland, and Phyllis took them into the Alps for a couple of nights and was treated to an unforgettable mountain trip up to the Jungfraujoch, which, at 11,371 feet, is described as the top of Europe. On another day, the three visitors booked a personal flight over and around the Alps in a small plane from Basel Airport.

Providing sleeping space for guests in their small apartment was always a challenge, but Leonard and Phyllis gladly gave over their bedroom for the guests and slept on a pull-out sofa in the lounge, and at times, Daniel or Geoffrey would also give up their bedroom. Leonard and Phyllis had always, since the start of their marriage, seen hospitality and an openness for friendship as part of their service for God, and it was also something they enjoyed which often gave them as much blessing as they hoped it gave their guests.

Using the word 'hospitality' reminds Leonard of a reported incident when a visitor from India had written back to his host and hostess thanking them for hospitalising him!

CHAPTER

12

Changes

The Bible warns us that the Christian life is a battle, not first and foremost against our fellow human beings ('flesh and blood') but against satanic forces, ('rulers of the darkness of this age, against spiritual hosts of wickedness in the heavenly places').[39]

We also know that these attacks are used by our heavenly Father for our sanctification and often to awaken us to dangers both around us and sins within us which would threaten and hinder our service for Him. They can also be a means of redirecting the course of our lives.

In the early part of 1986, Leonard had a summons to see Professor Külling, the rector at the FETA, where he was studying. He had absolutely no idea what this was about. It was during the period when the college was closed for a short spring break, so there was a strange emptiness about the building as he found his way to the rector's office. He was astonished to learn the reason for this interview. In essence, he was informed that reports had come through to the college about him and his wife which were causing concern to the college leadership. It was clear that Leonard's

---

39 Ephesians 6:12.

genuine astonishment at these accusations baffled the rector. The accusation that his wife was planning to leave him was, to Leonard, a complete mystery. He was aware that because of the pressure of the move to Basel and the culture shock, she was suffering; there had been periods when she had been extremely unhappy, and he could well imagine that in a moment of despair, she could have made such a statement to friends with whom she had felt she could talk freely, but there were so many positive things in their marriage that he couldn't take it seriously. Professor Külling declined to say how he had gained this information but said he would let the matter rest for the immediate.

There would seem to have been a tangle of complicated factors which led to the malicious reports reaching the college; Leonard and Phyllis never tried to question the people they had thought of as friends who they felt quite certain had initiated the rumours. Someone must have harboured extremely hard feelings, perhaps even hatred, against the Holders because during the following three years or more, every now and then, the Holders' telephone would ring at about two o'clock in the morning. This continued even after they had moved across the border into Germany. There was never anyone prepared to say anything understandable on the other end of the line, but Leonard always tried to answer the phone in an agreeable tone of voice, even when often awoken from a deep sleep.

Finally, at the end of his third year, Leonard left the college, and at the same time, he also considered it wise to move on from the BCF. There was quite a close link between the college and the BCF, and at the time, Leonard felt that moving on from the one was also the time to move on from the other. It had always been the Holders' intention to involve themselves in a German-speaking fellowship as soon as they were able, and although it was circumstances which, at the time, were extremely distressing that forced them into this decision, they later could recognise it was God leading them into new experiences which were for their good and would make them more usable in His service.

CHAPTER

13

Pastures New

The aforementioned events took place in the earlier part of 1986, and Leonard's studies at the FETA ended at the end of May that year. After thought and prayer, Leonard decided to apply to the theological department of Basel University to continue his studies, but his application was rejected. He realised that this could have simply been because he had been at the FETA. At that time, there was not a good relationship between the two as the leader of the FETA openly criticised the university's approach to theological studies.

Someone then suggested that he could apply to Zürich University. This, he did, and happily, he was accepted. Although this meant an hour's train journey from Basel, it did enable him to continue his studies and, what was perhaps even more important, enabled him to extend his residence permit in Switzerland so that the boys could complete their secondary school education in readiness for university.

Theological studies at the university were very different from those at the FETA and very much more relaxed. Leonard was working towards the *propaedeuticum* examinations in theology. This level in theology would be similar to a BA degree in Britain and halfway towards the final examinations, which would be equivalent to an MA degree. The latter is the qualification a student needs before advancing after practical experience to ordination into the Swiss Reformed Evangelical Church. Zürich University accepted Leonard's examination passes in Greek, Latin, and Hebrew, but he needed to study further in the New and Old Testaments, church history, and philosophy.

Zürich
with the Grossmünster

Zürich is a remarkably interesting place to study theology. Ulrich Zwingli became pastor in the Grossmünster (cathedral) in Zürich in 1519. Through expounding the Bible and preaching reformed doctrines, he exposed the unbiblical practices and teaching of the Roman Catholic Church, which led to the canton of Zürich and then several other cantons culminating in a break from Rome. Although being independent of Luther in Germany, the reformation in Switzerland ran simultaneously with the better-known German reformation.

Modern theologians feel that in many aspects, they have advanced beyond the teaching of Zwingli, and a belief in the inspiration of the Holy Scriptures is no longer considered a prerequisite to a study of biblical theology. The Bible is approached from a critical point of view rather than with a sense of awe that one is studying God's revelation to man.

Leonard enjoyed Zürich as a city and was also able to spend time between lectures studying and reading on the banks of the city's lake, combining this in the summer with an occasional swim. The schedule of lectures and seminars he needed to attend was spread out during the week, and he was able to restrict making the hour's train journey between Basel and Zürich to, on average, three times a week.

Phyllis and the two boys continued attending Sunday services at the BCF for a while, but Leonard began to attend the nearest Swiss state church, Johannes Kirche. Services there were very different from those at the BCF. There were three pastors, and Leonard had some hope that one of them was a true believer in Jesus as he preached a more Bible-based sermon. He met a young man at the service named Markus who was a junior schoolteacher and spoke of using material from the Swiss branch of the Scripture Union in some youth work he was involved in. He expressed interest in coming to the Sunday evening Bible study Leonard and Phyllis were still running, and it was good to have fellowship with him. The influence of the liberal theology that was being taught in most of the churches became apparent when once during the study, Leonard referred to a verse in the prophecy of Jeremiah in the Old Testament. Markus commented on this that he didn't feel the prophecies of Jeremiah should be considered any more inspired than the writings of Martin Luther King Jr, the African American preacher of the twentieth century.

Soon after Leonard began to attend the Johannes Kirche, a few of the members who clearly were not satisfied with things in the church tried to get a group together to discuss ways the services could be improved which they could then suggest to the pastors. Both Leonard and Phyllis felt it would be interesting to attend the first organised meeting about this. There were about a dozen people in attendance, and all were asked to think what they personally would expect from a church service. Each was given a smallish piece of paper to write their thoughts on, and these were then hung on small tree which stood in a pot in the corner of the room. One by one, people came out and read one of the written comments to the group, and these were then discussed. Leonard had thought carefully of what to write to describe his expectation from a worship service. It had to be simply a few words, so he wrote, 'Gott besser kennenzulernen' (to get to know God better). The other comments were more practical, more about people's thoughts on the structure of the service or innovations which might attract bigger congregations. These were read out and discussed. Although one of the pastors was present, he didn't express an opinion. Then when Leonard's comment was read, there was complete silence. No one knew what to say at all. Leonard owned that the comment had come from him, and after a few minutes' silence, someone made the suggestion that it would be good if Leonard could explain to them all at the next meeting what he meant by his desire to know God better.

Leonard saw this as a wonderful opportunity to bring some serious spiritual thought to the meeting and spent considerable time working on the paper he would read. It would need to be in good, understandable German, and thankfully, there was a lady by the name of Christine, whom the couple had met at the BCF, who had very kindly offered to help Leonard with any written German he needed to do. He was already meeting her from time to time in the staff restaurant at Roche, the pharmaceutical firm where she worked, and she corrected some of his written work.

In his paper, Leonard began by indicating the importance of knowing God in the sense of Jesus's words in John 17: 'This is eternal life, that they may know You, the only true God, and Jesus Christ Whom You have sent.'[40] This led to reference to the teaching of Jesus that no one can come to the Father except through Him[41] and to the apostle Paul's testimony that he counted everything else in his life as worthless compared with the experience of knowing Jesus Christ.[42] The conclusion is therefore clear that to 'know' Jesus Christ is to know the full Godhead – Father, Son, and Holy Spirit – and that this knowledge begins with a faith which embraces Jesus Christ as our Lord and Saviour. To 'know' God is far more than merely knowing about Him; it is to have a relationship with Him through trust and prayer and experiencing His Word speaking to us in our lives. We experience God's communication with us first and foremost through the Bible, and this is what he, Leonard, meant by saying his greatest wish when attending a church service is to worship God in spirit and truth and to hear God's voice speaking through the preaching of His Word – thus to know God better.

---

40 John 17:3.

41 John 14:6.

42 Philippians 3:8.

The group's response to Leonard's reading of his paper was silence, even an embarrassed silence. They turned to the pastor who was there for his comment, but he said nothing. Maybe in his kindness, he didn't want to embarrass Leonard by saying this was old-fashioned pietism. What was interesting and encouraging was that one of the group members rang Leonard the next day and asked whether she could have a copy of the paper he had read as it had disturbed her.

After a while, Leonard decided it would be more helpful for him to travel a little farther across Basel to one of the more 'evangelical' churches in the city.

CHAPTER

14

Summers Whilst in Basel

The Holders' second flat in Basel was on the fourth and top floor of a terrace of old houses converted into apartments but void of even a single lift. With the flat being immediately under an uninsulated roof, it got very hot in summer. Thankfully, there was a balcony at the back of the flat which enabled them to sit in the open, looking down on a communal garden. However, the balcony had a glass roof, and after midday, once the sun got round to the back of the house, it became unbearable to sit out there until the evening.

The friends in Germany who had come to one of their early Christmas celebrations had given the family a yellow canary. It had flown onto their balcony, obviously having escaped from somewhere. They, however, already had a budgerigar so didn't want another bird, and their daughter brought it surreptitiously across the border into Switzerland in a cardboard box as a gift for the Holder family. Daniel was able to find a discarded canary cage amongst *Sperrgut* left for the council to collect in the street, so another family member was welcomed into the home.

He (or she) had been named Pete and sang so beautifully that sometimes this brought tears to Phyllis's eyes. He was with the family for about three years, and it was a sad day when they found him dead on the bottom of his cage. After some controversy on how best to dispose of the body, Leonard's suggestion of simply putting it wrapped up in paper in the dustbin was overruled, and Pete was taken out to a wooded area and buried under a tree.

To keep up with his studies, Leonard needed to continue to read and revise during much of the long summer break from lectures, finding a delightful way of doing this by either sitting by the Rhine or, on really hot days, at an open-air swimming pool, where an occasional plunge into cool water helped things along.

One summer there was an urgent phone call from Phyllis's father saying her mother had taken a turn for the worse in her depression and he really could no longer cope. He had purchased them plane tickets and a hire car at the airport; could they please come home at once? Since the boys were quite old enough to look after themselves, Leonard and Phyllis hurriedly packed a suitcase, and when their sons returned home from lessons, they were informed their parents were off to the UK for an unspecified time. It was not an easy time, and clearly, Leonard and Phyllis couldn't stay with May Pittwell indefinitely. Soon after their return to Basel, Phyllis's father sold the family home and bought a bungalow near his second daughter's home in Oxfordshire.

Leonard and Phyllis had friends who had moved out from Britain to work in a missionary capacity in Austria. For a few weeks during another summer, they responded to an invitation to stay in their friends' apartment, leading the Sunday morning worship service whilst their friends had a break back in their home country. Although they intended to minister predominantly to Austrians, a Sunday service in English attracted British tourists, and Leonard and Phyllis met a few most interesting holidaymakers. One lady on holiday with a German friend informed them that she came from a small village in Hampshire which they would never have heard of. When pressed further, she divulged that she came from Locks Heath and was amazed when Phyllis informed her that she had not merely heard of it but that it was her own home area and that she had attended Locks Heath Junior School. Of course, following this, they soon discovered they knew many of the same people.

The Holders had a day out with another family with two teenage children who had come to the Sunday service. While they walked in the Zillertal Mountains, fellow German-speaking walkers would greet them either with the Austrian greeting 'grüß Gott' or the more normal German greeting 'guten Tag'.

The father, wanting to respond in the correct manner, greeted the next passers-by with the words 'gut Gott', whose response brought derisive laughter from his teenage son, who, amidst his chuckle, said, 'Dad, you can't say "good God" as a greeting.'

Leonard and Phyllis knew that at times, they also embarrassed their children with their faux pas when speaking German.

Another very interesting encounter whilst in Austria was with a charming Austrian young lady married to an Englishman. The husband came from a Christian family, and in fact, his grandfather had been the missionary doctor who had aided Gladys Aylward in China when she collapsed with typhus fever after crossing the high snowy mountains with a group of children to escape from the Japanese soldiers. However, although the husband himself was not a believer, he knew enough of the Bible to be very concerned when his wife began to attend Jehovah's Witnesses' meetings. He approached our British friend with the request that he should please instruct his wife in true biblical Christianity. Monika very soon embraced the truth that Graham explained to her. She was moved by the Holy Spirit to trust Jesus Christ as her Saviour and was then baptised by Graham. She would regularly attend the Sunday services clutching her husband's Bible, but he himself, as far as Leonard knows, has never come to a personal faith himself.

CHAPTER

15

Studies in Zürich

To suddenly become a student in a Swiss state university at the age of 40 amongst youngsters, many not much older than his own children, was an eye-opening and challenging experience for Leonard. He would, of course, have got more out of the experience if the lectures and seminars

View of Zürich

had been in English, but after three years at the FETA, his grasp of the German language was now reasonable enough to follow much of what was said. In fact, he felt more at ease with the German theological language than everyday German when shopping. There were a few German words over which his mind had to quickly adjust its thinking, and one of these was the word *sinnvoll*. An English mind, at least a Christian one, will immediately interpret this as 'sinful', where in fact, this word in German means 'sensible'.

Another German word that can cause confusion between German and English speakers is the English word 'eventually'.

When British people say they will do a job eventually, there is no hint that they won't do it, but simply, it must take its place in a line of other duties. However, when a German uses the word *eventuell*, he is saying that he may or may not do it at all. It has the sense of 'maybe' or 'perhaps'. There are several other words between the languages that can cause confusion. Another example is the German noun *Mist*. To the English mind, this is the water vapour which can hover over fields in the evening as the air cools. However, *Mist* in German is the word for dung. A *Misthaufen* is a dung heap. One can understand that Rolls Royce would need to change the name of their high-class Silver Mist vehicle when selling it in Germany. Two other words also need explanation. *Gift* in German means poison, and *hell* means light!

Leonard had a good grasp of Bible knowledge, but in his studies of the New and Old Testaments at university, to pass the exams, he had to get his mind around the critical approach of modern theological studies, which, sadly, for many young Christians wanting to study the Bible, has destroyed their faith in its divine inspiration.

Church history was another subject which Leonard had read quite widely, and in the university studies, apart from some more general lectures with recommended books to read, students were encouraged to select a few characters from past church history to study in greater detail. Leonard chose Augustine of Hippo, the Scottish reformer John Knox, and the English preacher of the sixteenth-century Reformation Hugh Latimer. By reading about these in English, he was able to get quite a good understanding of these characters and the age and circumstances in which they lived, but of course, the final exams had to be in German.

Philosophy was a new subject for Leonard. He had read some of Francis Schaffer's books, but philosophy was not a subject covered in general education, certainly not covered in Leonard's grammar school education. To his shame, he had to confess to his professor that he had absolutely no knowledge of John Locke, the English philosopher. The professor teaching the subject commented that he had always imagined that the works of John Locke would be on the bookshelf of nearly every British home. Leonard was encouraged to make John Locke one of his special studies and so had to delve somewhat into empiricism. To the uninitiated person like Leonard, this teaches that all knowledge is based on experience derived from our senses. Leonard tried to get his mind around this and other philosophical concepts, quickly seeing that philosophy is really man-centred, where the mind and experience struggle to understand our own humanity and the world around us. The Bible teaches that true knowledge has been revealed from God and must be received by faith from the teaching of His Word. King Solomon, the man who had been given special wisdom by God in answer to his prayer, tells us under the inspiration of the Holy Spirit, 'The fear of the Lord is the beginning of wisdom.'[43]

The teaching of John Locke (1632–1704) was taken further by the Irish philosopher George Berkeley (1685–1753). He taught that material things only exist when registered by our senses. Then to safeguard against the objection that they must therefore disappear when no one is sensing them, he added that God sees everything constantly, so they don't vanish when no human is looking at them.

Noel Fleming wrote a rather humorous limerick about Berkeley's theory:

The Tree in the Quad[44]

There was a young man who said,
'God must think it exceedingly odd
if he finds that the tree continues to be
when no one's about in the quad.'

'Dear Sir, your astonishment's odd.
I am always about in the quad.
And that's why the tree continues to be
since observed by,
yours faithfully,
God.'

---

43 Proverbs 9:10.
44 'Quad' is quadrangle, which is the courtyard, usually enclosed by buildings within a college campus.

Leonard and his boys discovered that examinations in Switzerland have an equal if not greater emphasis on oral sessions with the examiner. Each of the subjects Leonard was examined on, both at the FETA and Zürich, involved a written paper and an oral examination. If the examiner wanted to fail anyone, it would be easy for him to quickly discover areas of the subject in which the candidate was weak and concentrate on this. Thankfully, in Leonard's experience, they wanted, if possible, to pass the candidates and so probed to find areas they knew and asked more questions on these. With God's help, Leonard was able to pass each subject except the New Testament. He had concentrated his study and revision on subjects that were new to him and had not given so much time to the New Testament. He found it somewhat ironic in the light of his university studies – and perhaps it was also a message from God – that the passage given him in Greek to translate into German was from Paul's letter to the Colossians: 'Beware lest anyone cheat you through philosophy and empty deceit, according to the tradition of men, according to the basic principles of the world, and not according to Christ.'[45]

After five years of study, Leonard decided enough was enough. He registered with the university for one further year, essentially to ensure that the family could stay in Switzerland and that the boys could complete their Matura, after which, if they wanted to attend university, they could do so in their own right and not under the umbrella of their parents' residence.

The years of study at university level in German had been of interest and had been exceedingly hard going; moreover, Leonard didn't sense he had become a more knowledgeable person as a result. The whole experience of the move – living in Basel, being together as a family, and meeting a very wide range of different people from different nationalities and backgrounds – had taught the whole family far more than a university education ending in a top-grade qualification ever could. Also, they had proved God's gracious provision for them through it all.

---

45 Colossians 2:8.

One morning, as the family sat around the breakfast table, Leonard's younger son had looked at him with a smile and asked, 'What do you want to do when you leave school, Dad?'

The morning meditation for 28 July from 'My Utmost for His Highest' by Oswald Chambers is both a challenge and a blessing:

After Obedience – What?

And straightway, He constrained His disciples to get into the ship and to go to the other side.

— Mark 6:45–52

We are apt to imagine that if Jesus Christ constrains us and we obey Him, He will lead us to great success. We must never put our dreams of success as God's purpose for us; His purpose may be exactly the opposite. We have an idea that God is leading us to a particular end, a desired goal; He is not. The question of getting to a particular end is a mere incident. What we call the process, God calls the end.

What is my dream of God's purpose? His purpose is that I depend on Him and on His power now. If I can stay in the middle of the turmoil calm and unperplexed, that is the end of the purpose of God. God is not working towards a particular finish; His end is the process – that I see Him walking on the waves, no shore in sight, no success, no goal, just the absolute certainty that it is all right because I see Him walking on the sea. It is the process, not the end, which is glorifying to God.

God's training is, for now, not presently. His purpose is for this minute, not for something in the future. We have nothing to do with the afterwards of obedience; we get wrong when we think of the afterwards. What men call training and preparation, God calls the end.

God's end is to enable me to see that He can walk on the chaos of my life just now. If we have a further end in view, we do not pay sufficient attention to the immediate present: if we realize that obedience is the end, then each moment as it comes is precious.

CHAPTER

16

Last Year in Basel

Leonard and Phyllis's last year in Basel could almost be a book in its own right. It was significant for each of the four Holders.

Geoffrey and Daniel were both concluding their education at the MNG grammar school, and it was the custom that once the final Matura examinations were over, each class would have a holiday together. This was referred to as the 'Matura Reise', and the class themselves would plan it together and would save for it over the last couple of school years by putting money into a designated fund.

As the pupils progressed through the school towards their final year, numbers in each class would shrink, the reason being that unless each passed the grade every year, he or she couldn't move up but was forced to repeat a year. This was obviously adhered to strictly as it was said that most pupils stayed back for a repeat year at least once during their education. Daniel's class had just eleven pupils remaining for its final year, and they chose to make a trip to Russia for their Matura Reise. This was in 1989, the era of more openness under Mikhail Gorbachev, and closer links with the West were slowly emerging, but it would be 1991 before this really happened. The group of eleven students made their own arrangements, and no member of the school staff accompanied them. They visited three cities: Moscow, Kiev, and Sochi on the Black Sea. They were provided with an attractive young Russian lady as their guide who had a duty to control what places they visited. It seems, however, they were able to escape her jurisdiction without too much difficulty. Amazingly, six of the group were Christians. They had contacted the Slavic Gospel Mission before travelling and were supplied with some Russian Bibles and New Testaments with addresses of 'underground' Christian fellowships in each of the towns they were to visit.

Daniel remembers one incident in particular when, unable to find the address they were looking for, they asked a taxi driver. He, either unable or unwilling, could give them no help, but just then, a pedestrian passing by overheard their request and, after the taxi had moved on, indicated they should follow him. He turned out to be one of the members of the fellowship and led them to a house they would have never found by themselves. The literature was received with enthusiasm, as were the couriers from Switzerland. One group were singing when the lads arrived, and they could add their voices in their own language to the beloved hymn 'What a Friend We Have in Jesus'.

Geoffrey's class made the more conventional choice to head towards sun and sea and spent a week sailing around the Greek islands in three sailing boats skippered by professionals. Whilst many of the class were intent on cavorting on the beaches and in the night clubs on the islands they anchored at, Geoffrey also made sure he had time to himself and ended up with a fine series of interesting photos. Back in class later, he made a display and took quite a few orders from those who hadn't bother taking pictures (this being the time before mobile phones and digital cameras). He informed his parents later that one of the girls had fallen in love with the Greek captain of the girl's yacht and did not return home with the rest of her classmates.

Geoffrey's education had been delayed by a couple of years because of the circumstances already described, and he was nearly 21 by the time he passed his Matura, which incidentally isn't an unusual age for students at Swiss grammar schools. The Matura is a highly prized achievement and involves passes in a range of subjects, languages as well as science, each at a level as high as, if not higher than, the English A-level standard.

The Holder family made another visit to Austria in the earlier part of 1989 to stand in for their missionary friends, and whilst they were there, Leonard's knees and ankle joints began to swell, giving him pain. Christian friends there encouraged him to see an Austrian doctor who advised him to return to his own GP as soon as possible. Once they were back in Basel, the doctor they were registered with referred him to a rheumatologist. Later, Leonard discovered that this specialist was one of the leading men in this field in Europe. After blood tests and X-rays, he diagnosed a form of rheumatoid arthritis.

He explained that there were two forms of this, a so-called positive form and a negative form. Leonard had the negative form, which, he explained, under treatment, could clear up completely within about three months. Alternatively, it could develop further into a chronic form of the disease. He put Leonard on a very strong anti-inflammatory drug and explained that without this, most of his joints would become inflamed and be permanently damaged. He said that he would be keeping a close eye on the development of the disease through testing his blood at least once a week. Under the treatment with the drug, the swellings went down, and the pain decreased. The doctor had his own surgery in part of his home, not too far from where the Holders were living, so Leonard went to see him for blood tests regularly. When, after some weeks, there was no improvement, the doctor became more anxious and decided he would try to 'clobber' the disease with a couple of large infusions of what Leonard thinks was cortisone straight into the blood stream.

After the next visit following this additional treatment, he delivered the good news that the blood was showing a decrease in whatever it was the body was producing to fight the disease, which indicated he was winning. A week later, he informed Leonard that he could cut the dose of the medication by half and, after another week, stop it altogether.

Then with a smile, he added, 'I don't expect to have to see you again, and I'm very hopeful the disease will never return.' Praise the Lord it hasn't.

Whilst Leonard was struggling with this illness, the Lord gave him and Phyllis a special blessing. An American family worshipping at the BCF were returning home for a few weeks and asked Daniel if he would be interested in living in their apartment and looking after their cat whilst they were back in the States. This didn't suit Daniel as it would make a longer journey for him getting into school, but he suggested that his parents might be prepared to help. Leonard and Phyllis recognised this as God's provision. The apartment was on the outskirts of Basel in a quiet position with scenic views, and the couple concerned also offered them the use of their car, even giving them some petrol money to run it. The cat was a long-haired pure white animal who was used to living completely indoors. After a few days' rebellion, he adjusted well to his minders.

There was one other major health incident that same year; Phyllis developed gynaecological problems. Her doctor decided that a hysterectomy was necessary, and when she became aware that this would be the last few months that Leonard would be registered as a student and therefore entitled to free health insurance, she kindly said that she would get this arranged within the next few weeks.

Phyllis was quickly given an appointment in the *Frauenklinik* (hospital for women) in Basel and found herself in a ward with three other ladies. None spoke English, and so Phyllis was forced to try out her German. Up to that point, she had lacked confidence in speaking although had absorbed a lot of the language. Clearly, in her subconscious, she accepted she was in a German-speaking environment as the nurse told her that when she was coming out of the anaesthetic, she was chatting away furiously in German. Thankfully, there was no indication of cancer, and healing proceeded in the expected manner.

The way forward for Leonard and Phyllis was very uncertain. They had been praying for many weeks to have some indication from God as to the next step in His plan for them. As summer drew to a close in 1989, they had spent six years in Basel, years of much testing and many new experiences, but they had never doubted that all had been under the control of their Lord and Master. After several tentative enquiries, they decided that what they needed was time in a purely German environment. Leonard had studied immersed in the German language, but the family had not had the opportunity of actually living in an everyday German situation. The Swiss spoke the Swiss dialect, and since many in Basel happily speak English and prefer this to the official German language, they would readily revert into Leonard and Phyllis's mother tongue instead of allowing them to practise the German language they were trying to assimilate.

Accordingly, Leonard wrote to a number of addresses across the German border, families who were advertising holiday apartments, requesting the possibility of renting their accommodation for a full year. How this developed will be the subject of further chapters.

Phyllis's Memories and Comments

When we got to Germany, it was easier for us to live in so many ways. However, our experiences with the Swiss and Swiss schools had been exceptional, and because Len was a student there, we had the advantage of great medical treatment. In 1989, I had a hysterectomy at the women's hospital in Basel, and Len had experienced an acute rheumatism flare-up which had been treated successfully by a top rheumatism specialist in Basel. It was an acute form of rheumatism flaring up periodically or never reappearing; thank God the latter seems to have been the case for Len.

I can look back and see that God's hand was in everything that happened, although that was sometimes the last thing we were conscious of. God had brought this to my mind very often whilst we were in Switzerland and particularly when in the four rooms off a landing. The verse in 1 Timothy 6:17 says that 'God gives us richly all things to enjoy'. My response, I'm sorry to say, had been 'Lord, you must be joking' and 'You do have a sense of humour', but God *was* faithful and always saw the bigger picture for us, of course. And so it was with my hysterectomy operation. I went into the hospital in Basel very quickly once it became expedient for me to have the procedure, and I was in a small ward with three others.

I had barely spoken German during our time in Switzerland as the Swiss people I mixed with preferred to speak English, but in that ward, I found myself conversing with a Swiss lady in basic German. I was told after I came out of the anaesthetic that I had been talking in German non-stop whilst unconscious, which made me realise that I *could* speak German if I stopped being self-conscious about it. This thought was great comfort to me once we were actually living in Germany and I was forced to communicate in German as a necessity; indeed, that was one of the main purposes for being in Germany at that time.

One of the things I look back on as being particularly significant to me during my hospital experience was a Scripture text calendar up on the wall in the ward; I thought that was unusual. I took to reading the verse for each day, and on one such occasion, the nurse who was often on the ward at night, seeing I was struggling a bit, looked at me with a smile and asked whether I had read the Scripture text for that day. Following that, we often commented on the day's text, and after I had been discharged, we invited her to our home for a coffee. We learned she was a German nurse from Berlin.

One of the verses God gave me during my hospital time was Psalm 138:3 – 'In the day when I cried out, You answered me and made me bold with strength in my soul.'

CHAPTER

17

The Boys on Their Own

Conveniently, Geoffrey and Daniel both graduated from the grammar school the same year. They both got good grades in their Matura examinations, and in fact, Geoffrey's achievement was considered exceptional. The school put him forward for an award being offered by one of the pharmaceutical firms in the city, and he was presented with a cheque for several thousand Swiss francs.

Geoffrey's first wish was to study medicine, but as the family had been informed that there were limited places for this and the privilege was reserved for Swiss citizens, he didn't hold out a lot of hope of being accepted and had applied to study biochemistry as a second choice. Accordingly, it came as a surprise and wonder when he heard that Basel University had indeed accepted him for a course in medicine. It was quite likely that the high recommendation from the school had brought this about, but the family recognised the hand of their heavenly Father revealing His power to bring about His purpose for those who trust Him.

Daniel applied to study theology with a view to becoming a pastor in a Swiss church. He decided against the FETA and applied directly to the Basel *Evangelisch-reformierte Kirche*, which, in many ways, can be compared to the Anglican Church in Britain. At that time, the Basel Church had its own Bible school for its students to complete a couple of years study before they were passed on to the theological department of Basel University.

At the interview, Daniel was asked about his financial position. He explained his parents' position, and the answer came back – 'It is impossible for you to live like that in Basel!'

Daniel responded by saying that as a family, they had lived like this for six years. Those interviewing him conferred together and came back with the offer of giving him a financial grant from a special fund.

The way was being prepared for Leonard and Phyllis to move on. Being accepted for study in Basel, their two sons could obtain the necessary Swiss residence permission to remain in the city on their own merit. Also, with financial support from both the state church and the continuing contribution from the BCF plus income from their part-time jobs, they had the financial means to pay the rent on the family apartment and pay university fees, which are minimal compared with current fees in Britain. They invited another friend from the BCF to live with them to share the expense of the accommodation.

After Leonard and Phyllis had sold their house in Ripon and paid back the outstanding mortgage, they had around £17,000 to take out to Switzerland. At the exchange rate as it was in 1983, this gave them more than fifty thousand Swiss francs. Knowing this had to be considered as the basis for their living during Leonard's studies, they drew on it sparingly. With support from the BCF and occasional gifts from Christian friends, although Switzerland is an expensive country to live in, this sum sustained them for the six years they needed it. When the way began to open up for them to move across the border into the Black Forest in Germany, Leonard decided that they really needed a car. The family supported this idea, and on a couple of occasions, Leonard and Daniel cycled across the border to look for second-hand cars in Germany. There was the equivalent of around £1,000 left in their Swiss account, which they felt they should use to buy, tax, and licence a car, and this would then throw them completely on the Lord for their subsequent support.

When children finish school and college and start university, it is normal, especially in Britain, for them to leave home. Somehow it always seemed that in the Holder household, things have worked back to front. During October 1989, the parents packed a few belongings into suitcases, left their Basel home for their sons, and moved across the border into Germany, to a sparse but adequately furnished holiday apartment for which they had a contract for twelve months.

Phyllis's Memories and Comments

During the time the boys were at school and Len was at Bible college, we experienced anguishing times, hard times, despairing and very low times, but it was tempered with amazing experiences of God's help and miraculous provision for us.

Both boys went to university in 1989, and as, by then, they could stay in Basel on their own residence permits, we could move into the Black Forest to consolidate our German, leaving the boys living in our family flat.

PART 6

GERMANY ESTABLISHING A MISSION WORK 1989–2002

*You did not choose Me, but I chose you
and appointed you that you should go
and bear fruit and that your fruit should
remain, that whatever you ask the Father
in My name, He may give you.*
                                    — John 15:16

*For we are His workmanship, created in Christ
Jesus for good works, which God prepared
beforehand that we should walk in them.*
                                    — Ephesians 2:10

CHAPTER

1

On the Move

Leonard never had a wish to live in Germany. Despite his never having experienced the fighting or the bombing, never remembering hearing his parents speaking against the German nation and obviously being born at the end of the Second World War, in his subconscious, Germany was still the enemy. Switzerland was the country he had felt God had called him to, and really, he knew very little about Germany. However, clearly, Germany was the country of the German language, and if Leonard and Phyllis were to work in a German-speaking environment, they needed to spend time in such. This was certainly Leonard's thinking at the end of 1989. A time in Germany, he thought, would be just another step towards some form of service for God in Switzerland or even perhaps Austria.

Of the ten letters Leonard had written to the different addresses he had found in a holiday accommodation directory for the southern Black Forest, only one responded. A family in the village of Schlechtnau, between the little towns of Schönau and Todtnau, offered him the possibility of renting a holiday apartment for twelve months at a very reasonable rate.

It was a lovely autumn afternoon in the middle of September when Leonard and Phyllis first ventured into Germany to inspect the apartment that had been offered to them. Not yet having a car, they caught the train from the Badische Bahnhof, which is the German station in Basel for German trains arriving and departing from Switzerland. Passengers needed to show a passport when entering and leaving the station as they were moving from one country to another. This was then a new experience for Leonard and Phyllis as although living so close to Germany, apart from a brief nip across the border to the German shops, they had only very occasionally ventured into the country that actually, through the EEC,[46] had far closer connections with Britain than Switzerland.

The train ran up a single-line track which divided into two tracks at stations to allow passing. Our adventurous couple watched the names of the small stations with interest as the train stopped at each one.

'This one looks to be called Ratbait,' murmured Leonard, expressing astonishment, having briefly caught sight of the station name as the train pulled alongside the platform.

Once they could see the sign again, Phyllis corrected him. 'No, you silly. Look, its Raitbach. I guess a *Bach* must be the German word for a stream similar to the word "beck", used in Northern England.'

Soon, the train arrived at the end of the line at a station called Zell im Wiesental.

'That's right,' commented Leonard, looking across to his wife as they clambered out of the train. '*Tal* is the German word for "valley", so this is the valley of the River Wiese. Clearly, the Wiese must be the river the track has been following most of the way up here. It's pronounced "veeser", not "weeser" or "wiser".'

A few yards away from the railway line in the station yard was a bus stop, and our couple followed most of the train passengers across to it. Within a few minutes, a very smart red bus arrived, bearing the destination 'Titisee' on the front.

---

46 The European Economic Community. The EU, the European Union, was only formed in 1993.

The passengers waiting for the bus simply crowded on with no semblance of a queue, which meant that the Holders, being more used to English politeness, got on last.

'Schlechtnau, bitte,' said Leonard as he handed the driver their tickets, which with German efficiency served for both the train and the bus.

After about half an hour, the driver called out, 'Schlechtnau!' and Leonard stood up and pressed the bell.

As the bus pulled up, the door opened, and he and Phyllis jumped off and looked around them with interest. It was a beautiful countryside. They were in a long valley, with the fast-flowing Wiese River running close beside the road, and on either side, a

Village of Schlechtnau

hillside rose steeply. A few largish detached houses were scattered around on both sides of the river and also on the lower slopes of the rising valley sides.

The address they were looking for was in Bergstrasse (Mountain Street). They soon found it, and almost immediately, the narrow road rose steeply ahead of them. After an abrupt U-turn, they found the house they were looking for and rang the bell. A voice called down from a balcony above asking them to come around the back. The house was built into the hillside, and the back entrance was on the first floor, which opened directly into a garden, also therefore at a higher level than the front.

First home in Black Forest
In Schlechtnau

The apartment they had come to see was on the ground floor with an impressive front door opening into an entrance hall. A good-sized room opened off each side of the hall; one room contained a large double bed, a wash basin, and basic bedroom furniture, and the other was the living room. There was a dining table with four chairs, a couch which pulled out to make a further double bed, and kitchen units along one side. Each room had a large window with a wonderful view straight across the valley to the hillside opposite. The road on the valley floor was completely invisible. At the back of the apartment was a good-sized bathroom which, because the house had been built into the hillside, was actually underground. It had a small window which opened into a narrow shaft with an overhead grid at ground level. Outside the front door was a large paved forecourt with a short steepish drive leading down to the road they had walked up.

The apartment was basic but cheap, and for Leonard and Phyllis, who loved the countryside and had been confined in a city for six years, it was in an idyllic location.

They agreed to have it, and the wife of the family took them into the back garden and brought them out coffee and cake. She told them she was a junior schoolteacher in the neighbouring town of Todtnau and that her husband was an engineer working for a firm in the same town. They had two junior school–aged boys, the youngest of whom was a pupil in the class she taught. They had built the house after they got married and were very proud of it. There was a second apartment under the roof which they also rented out to holiday guests. Leonard informed her that they were in the process of buying a car, and she said they could keep this on the forecourt outside their front door or perhaps well over on one side if they didn't want to lose the view. It all sounded ideal, and Leonard and Phyllis both felt very strongly that God had provided this for them as their next temporary home in the purpose He had planned for them.

Before the couple returned to Basel, they decided to call and see the nearest larger town, Todtnau. They were very impressed with the layout of the town, with its large market square surrounded by coffee and ice cream shops, small guesthouses, and a bank. At one end, dominating the whole square, was a very large church, set up on a rocky base well above the square itself. Two high towers gave the church a very distinctive character. Leonard later learned that a fire had destroyed the original church and much of the town in

1876, and subsequently, most of the town they were now seeing had been rebuilt.

On looking through the window of one particular café and spying a wonderful array of cream cakes, they decided they must just sample one of these together with a coffee before they caught the bus and train back to Basel. As they were eating, it suddenly occurred to Leonard that they would need to pay in deutschmarks (DM) and not Swiss francs. The previous day, he had emptied his Swiss bank account, withdrawing the cash in German marks to buy the car they were considering. His account had provided 3,000 DM (about £1,000), but unfortunately, the bank had given the money in the form of three one-thousand DM notes, quite suitable for buying a car but not for two cups of coffee. Leonard apologised to the waitress when she came round for the money and showed her one of the large denominator notes. She must have thought the couple to be very rich British tourists; little did she know. After talking to her boss, she came back to say sorry, but they couldn't take such a large note; did Leonard really not have anything smaller? Then having a brainwave, Leonard offered Swiss francs.

'Oh, that'll be fine,' she said with a smile. What a relief!

With the couple having settled on somewhere to live in Germany, the next move was to buy the car. Leonard and Daniel had viewed several models and, although not fully persuaded, came home and told Phyllis they had settled on a red Mazda. However, when they went across the border again to settle the purchase, sitting alongside the red Mazda was a blue BMW. It was a few years older than the Mazda but about the same price.

'You need the BMW, Dad!' exclaimed Daniel, looking at it enviously.

'It's older and has done more miles,' answered Leonard, hesitating.

'But BMWs keep their value and are extremely reliable,' retorted his son. Then he spied the gear stick. The knob at the end of the gear stick had been replaced with a billiard ball. 'Dad! Look at that billiard ball. You've really got to buy the BMW. I'd love to drive a car with a billiard ball gear stick.'

To buy and register the vehicle, the car sales manager informed them that they needed an address in Germany and a German bank account. Leonard could now give him their new address in Schlechtnau but said he would have to come back to him with details of a bank account.

Leonard paid a deposit for the BMW; the garage agreed to renew its TÜV (German equivalent of MOT) and, once they had a bank account, would tax the vehicle and suggest an insurance company. Soon, it was all sorted, and after moving into their new home, Leonard and Phyllis got the bus and train back down to Lörrach, the district town, and picked up the first vehicle they had owned since Ripon days, six years earlier.

There is one other interesting incident to recount. When they had paid and picked up their car, the owner of the car sales room asked them if they knew anyone who might be interested in a British-registered Renault. He had taken it in part exchange for a new car from a British person who had moved out to Germany. It had sat in his yard for some months, and he was eager to get rid of it. It had been first registered in 1982, and Herr Holder, he said, could have it for 300 DM (equivalent to £100). Leonard said he would see if he could find anyone interested and would be in touch.

The book value for this vehicle was over £1,000, and Leonard mentioned the offer to a few friends whom he felt might be interested. A friend of a friend in Yorkshire expressed interest, but the problem was getting it across to him. Then Geoffrey and Daniel mentioned that they had received an invitation to a wedding in the south of England, and Leonard had a bright idea.

'If you wanted to drive the Renault I told you about across to Britain, we could charge the expense to David, who wants to buy it,' he suggested with a smile.

Geoffrey had recently passed his driving test and, although having had very little driving experience, thought this a great idea. A lady friend, another friend of the bridal couple and a member of the BCF, had also been invited, and the boys suggested to her that she could travel with them and help with the driving.

There were various arrangements to make, including booking an MOT in Britain for the vehicle once it entered the country.

The garage assured them that the vehicle was fit to travel the five hundred miles or so to England, but a quick look under the bonnet revealed cobwebs around everything. The bonnet was closed back down quickly, and thankfully, the engine started easily.

On the evening of the day the journey was happening, Leonard received an urgent phone call.

'Dad, a red light appeared on the dashboard, and as we didn't know what to do, we kept going. Then the radiator boiled, and the vehicle came to a halt. We are on the outskirts of Paris.'

Geoffrey went on to assure his father that everything was now fine. They had stopped just outside a garage, and on inspection, they were informed that the car needed a new radiator and water hoses. The garage could do this the next day and had suggested a small bed-and-breakfast place where they could stay overnight. All three would have to sleep in the same room, and their friend had agreed to this. To them, it seemed to add to the excitement of the whole adventure. Geoffrey's greatest concern was the expense of putting the vehicle right. Leonard told him to get it done, and he would speak to David, who was buying the car. David was prepared to pay the expense of getting the car across to Britain and also these necessary repairs; he would come down to Surrey to pick the car up.

The following evening, the parents had another phone call from their sons. They had reached the coastal port of Dieppe, and the roar of the wind could be heard over the phone line. It was a rough night crossing to Newhaven. Unfortunately, once in Britain, the car failed the MOT on a whole list of points, but David came south, picked the car up, and did most of the necessary repairs himself. He, despite the various setbacks, felt he had a bargain with the car and ran it for a good number of years.

Phyllis's Memories and Comments

Our first small apartment was in Schlechtnau, a tiny village about thirty miles up the Wiese Valley from Basel, having Lörrach as its district town.

I well remember our first visit to Schlechtnau. We took the train halfway up the Wiese Valley to Zell and then the bus, which wound round corners for miles, it seemed, with the hills and mountains getting ever nearer and higher as the valley narrowed. I remember thinking how strange it was to have such a contrast of scenery so close to Basel. My first reaction to being in the countryside again was almost like a 'townie', finding it a bit scary in this seemingly enclosed valley! We seemed to be heading directly for a mountain, which, in reality, we were as at the end of the valley is the Feldberg, the highest mountain in the Black Forest, at nearly 1,500 metres (approximately 4,800 feet, so higher than Snowdon and Ben Nevis, our highest UK mountains).

I had no way of knowing then that this mountain would become very familiar to us in years to come and be a huge part of the attractions we could offer our guests at Haus Barnabas!

We walked up the winding little road on the right-hand slope from the bus stop, finding the small apartment, which we ended up renting for two years, in Bergstrasse, Schlechtnau. It really was a very small basic ground-floor apartment of a house on a slope, but we could sit out in the garden to enjoy an amazing view. Being able to purchase a second-hand car again, we could soon explore the wonderful countryside around us.

The car served us well, but as winter approached, we soon learned the difficulty of driving up to our apartment in the snow. The first time we experienced this and found ourselves unable to move, our landlord sent his two boys to sit in the boot of the car, legs dangling over the back, to give sufficient weight on the rear wheels to get the necessary grip on the icy road. We realised then why cars in the Black Forest need winter tyres once the snow comes. It's quite amazing what a difference these make when driving on snow.

CHAPTER

2

The Black Forest

Leonard and Phyllis had no knowledge of the Black Forest before moving there. Some years later, one of their guests commented that the Black Forest was one of the best-kept secrets in Europe. Another guest confessed that he and his wife had only booked a holiday in the Black Forest because it was a lot cheaper than their previous year's holiday in Switzerland.

'We thought of it as a second best,' he said. 'But it's not. Our experiences here in this southern Black Forest – with its mountains and valleys, lakes, chalet houses, delightful restaurants – have been just as enjoyable, if not more so than Switzerland.'

The Wiese River has its source on the southern slopes of the Feldberg mountain. The Feldberg, at approximately 1,500 metres above sea level, is one of the highest mountains in Germany. It is higher than anything Britain can offer, including Ben Nevis in Scotland at 1,345 metres. The village of Schlechtnau, as we have said, lies in the Wiese Valley, which runs down to Basel. Here, the river enters the Rhine, and its waters make their long journey up to Holland and the North Sea.

Leonard and Phyllis soon discovered that their new neighbours spoke a dialect not dissimilar to the Swiss language they heard all around them in Basel. The difference was that very few in the more rural areas of the Black Forest were eager to speak English and expected to speak the official High German to visitors coming to them. Youngsters learned English at school but usually, unless they had spent time in an English-speaking country, were very hesitant to converse in it. Black Forest residents also recognised that High German or 'written German', as they referred to it, was their national language and, apart from local situations, the language they were expected to know and use.

Leonard and Phyllis felt a sense of freedom in their new environment. On analysing the grounds for this, they decided there were two main reasons. First, experiencing the wide expanse of fields and woods made them realise how hemmed in they had felt living in a city, but there was more than this. Switzerland is a very restrictive country. Someone had taken great delight in informing them soon after their arrival in the country that there was a law for everything. Also, there were people, mostly older ladies living alone, who would take great pleasure in phoning the police if they saw anyone transgressing. Any noise after ten o'clock at night was a common cause for complaint, usually not to the person causing the noise but directly to the landlord of the accommodation or to the police. Landlords, it seemed, had the legal right to turn people out of their rented accommodation if neighbours complained about their behaviour.

Thankfully, the Holder family had experienced none of this. Phyllis had heard from a friend who had lived in the country several years that she knew several Swiss housewives who had committed suicide on having to return to their home country after experiencing a more relaxed atmosphere whilst living abroad.

The other major reason for a greater sense of freedom in Germany under the EEC, as it was then, was that British citizens had a right to live and get employment there. In Switzerland, residence permission for the Holders was dependant on registration at an educational establishment, which was granted for twelve months at a time and forbade paid employment. There was a constant risk of being thrown out of the country, and even a driving offence could lead to expulsion.

However, registration in Germany was necessary, and Leonard soon learned that he needed to make a visit to the town hall in Todtnau to complete the necessary forms. The girl on the information desk was very friendly and helpful. She filled the form in for him, asking him the required questions about his nationality, marital status, address in Germany, etc., but then the crunch question: his financial support and employment.

'What is your profession?' she asked.

Leonard thought for a while and then commented that he had been in publishing and also a farm secretary, but at present, he was a self-employed Christian minister having studied theology in Basel.

'Are you an *evangelische Pfarrer* [Protestant minister] or a *katholishe Pfarrer* [Catholic priest]?' she asked, and the implication was 'Are you employed by one or other of these recognised German churches?'

Leonard had to acknowledge that he came under neither of these categories. He didn't like to say he was a missionary as he thought this might be offensive within this strongly Roman Catholic region. He simply had to repeat that he was an independent, self-employed, Free Evangelical pastor. Later, when asked, and looking back to his time in Horley, he would say he had been ordained as a pastor in a Baptist church.

'I'm very sorry,' the young lady responded. 'I don't have a box to tick for that. I suggest you go away and have a think as to how you want to be employed here in Germany and come back again soon. You are allowed three months in the country as a British tourist.'

Leonard and Phyllis can't remember being greatly perturbed by this situation. It seems they were getting used to needing God to make the way smooth for them.

Phyllis's Memories and Comments

It was during our time in the flat in Schlechtnau that we first met one of our future daughters-in-law. Dan brought her to meet us on his 21st birthday. We learned later that Martina, being from East Germany originally, had not known what to expect of English people and English parents, having some preconceived ideas.

Thankfully, she soon discovered that we were not like the people she had envisioned, and we loved her right from the start.

There is one thing that stands out in her memory about her first meeting with us as we were showing her around the area. Whilst enjoying a stream alongside an historical water-powered log-cutting saw we were visiting, she slipped into the water, much to her embarrassment. I also remember getting a good view of the rather rare black woodpecker for the first time when out walking with Martina near the village of Wieden.

CHAPTER

3

The Basis for a Residence Permit

Their first months in the Black Forest seemed like a holiday. Phyllis was still getting over her hysterectomy operation, and Leonard was still recovering from that acute attack of rheumatoid arthritis. They explored the area with great interest and particularly remember one excursion up

Lake Titisee

to Lake Titisee. This was one place they knew already. A few years earlier, when a friend had visited them in Basel, they had hired a car and taken tents to a campsite on the lakeside. It had been interesting and quite fun but not a roaring success as although it was August, with sunny days, it had been high-pressure conditions with a wind coming from the east, and at an altitude of more than eight hundred metres, the nights had been exceedingly cold. In fact, Daniel, who was with them, had commented that he had camped on a glacier in Switzerland and been warmer! Still, that autumn afternoon, now as residents of the region, the couple hired a paddle boat and enjoyed coffee from their flask in the middle of the lake.

On another day whilst walking around Todtnau, Leonard decided it would be useful to have a map of the area and, with this in mind, went into a little store that seemed to offer everything under the sun. On requesting a local map of the immediate area, the elderly gentleman serving them asked whether they were on holiday.

When Leonard informed him that they were, in fact, living in Schlechtnau, he questioned, 'Sind sie ein Reisefuhrer?' (Are you a tour operator?)

Having bought the map, Leonard thought over this question as he walked home. It seemed a very sensible question when addressed to a British person in a predominately holiday area. *Could this be God's guidance?* He had prayed about how they could register with the authorities and also how they, as foreigners and evangelical Christians in a very insular, rural Roman Catholic community, could hope to have any meaningful contact with their neighbours as a witness for Jesus. He could begin to see that this might provide a way forward, answering both needs.

After thinking and praying about this a bit more together, Leonard went back to the town hall.

'I would like to register as a tour operator,' he stuttered with a questioning look.

The young lady retrieved his application paper from a file, glanced through it, and, looking up with a smile, replied. 'Yes, that's good. It's one of the possible means of employment here. Sign here, and I can give you a five-year residence permit. You will be hearing from the tax office about registering with them in due course.'

The later statement didn't sound so pleasant, but at least they now had the right to be living in the Black Forest. Their intention in coming into Germany was not at all with the aim of setting up a business, but if this was God guiding them, it was actually rather exciting.

It was, by then, the second half of October, and since they couldn't expect to be entertaining guests on a tour-operating business until the next year, there was plenty of time to work on preparations. In the meantime, they had to live; buying their second-hand BMW had used up all their funds. Leonard believed firmly that if the step they had taken was of God, then He would supply their needs. He was also very conscious that there were many more worthy causes for the Lord's money and therefore decided he wouldn't actually request financial support but, simply like George Muller and many other nineteenth-century missionaries, pray for the Lord to meet their needs as He saw fit. The tourist business might be God's way to provide part of this provision, but he didn't have great expectations for it and saw it more as the way to satisfy the authorities and provide a point of contact with local people than a money provider.

Different Scriptures encouraged Leonard and Phyllis at that time, and verses from Psalm 37 were very relevant, particularly verse 3: 'Trust in the LORD and do good. Dwell in the land and feed on His faithfulness.'

When Leonard and Phyllis originally left England for Switzerland, they had approached Phyllis's home assembly, who knew them both pretty well, as to whether this could be considered their home church, and they agreed. Phyllis's father, Ron Pittwell, was then an elder of the assembly, and when the couple moved on from Leonard's theological studies in Switzerland into the Black Forest, this was seen as the beginning of their practical service for God, and Ron made a suggestion to them. They should consider forming a charitable trust in the UK through which gift-aided funds could be channelled to them for their support and for missionary expenses. Also, although not openly requesting funds, they should write newsletters to let interested friends know what they were doing.

Leonard was pleased that the initiative for this came from someone other than him, and it was also clear that any charitable trust would have to be set up by trustees in Britain and not by himself. He agreed wholeheartedly to the principle of the suggestion and was delighted when three of the elders of Phyllis's assembly agreed to be founding trustees. They also suggested inviting Leonard's brother-in-law to join with them.

Leonard prayerfully thought through the aims and objectives of the ministry, he felt that God had called him and Phyllis to in German-speaking Europe, and these were formulated into the aims and objectives of the trust, which he suggested should be called Bible in Action.[47]

Thinking back now, Leonard can't see how the couple managed financially during that first winter except to say that he doesn't remember being worried about it, and each month, there was enough money to pay the rent. With them being careful about how they spent money, there was sufficient money for their needs, and they lacked nothing.

He remembers quoting in a newsletter as a testimony to God's faithfulness words from Luke's Gospel: 'Jesus said, "When I sent you without money bag, knapsack, and sandals, did you lack anything?" So they said, "Nothing."'[48]

Residing in Germany in November 1989, Leonard and Phyllis witnessed the reaction from their area in the south of the country to the reunification of East and West Germany. They remember walking around the town of Todtnau at the time the Berlin Wall was collapsing, and East German citizens were flooding across the border.

In one shop, which seemed to stock everything and which they referred to as the 'big man's shop' because of the size of the owner, the radio was shouting out events as they happened, and the 'big man' was heard to utter in their direction with great emotion, 'These are our people. These are our people.'

Later, there was a more cautious note in their enthusiasm when it was realised that they were having to pay an extra tax to correct some of the deficiencies in the east after about forty years of communism. Another point of view was expressed by guests from the former east bloc who were staying in the other holiday apartment in their house. Having experienced life in East Germany personally, they commented with some feeling that there should

---

47 The aims and objectives of Bible in Action Trust are given at the back of the book in Appendix 1.
48 Luke 22:35.

have been bloodshed. The old leaders will be back just where they were before, they said, simply under another name and system.

Phyllis's Memories and Comments

Very soon after we came into Germany, a piece of history was made when the communist regime collapsed and East Germans starting streaming into West Germany. East Germans were breaking free over the wall of division, knocking it down, taking souvenirs from the wall, and trying to be reunited with their loved ones whom, for forty long years, they had been separated from. Some townships and villages had been divided in half, often where a river came down the middle of a community. As I write this story, we are in lockdown because of the COVID virus, which has separated many from loved ones and families, but thankfully, we are not expecting this to last for forty years!

I stood in the middle of the square in Todtnau in 1989 when this history was being made, and people were out with their radios, some in tears, saying, 'These are our people being released.' It was hard to believe it was really happening after so many years. This enthusiasm for reunification emanating from the Germans in the west lapsed somewhat when they were forced to pay extra taxes to finance updating the east. Also, many in the east who had believed in communism or had simply accepted it and now found they had to fend for themselves without being so cushioned by the state felt themselves struggling, and there were apparently many suicides. People continued to be suspicious of each other, not knowing who to trust as the state had had its spies everywhere. Years later, when people were allowed to go and view the Stasi files, many were totally shocked as they discovered that the people that they thought had been their friends had actually been reporting their activities to the secret police and that some they had regarded with suspicion had, in reality, been faithful friends!

CHAPTER

✺

4

Christmases in Britain

Phyllis's parents were concerned to have their family together with them at Christmas, and when they felt unable to entertain their daughter and family themselves, her father, for a number of years, would arrange to bring Phyllis and family back from Europe and book Christmas at a Christian guesthouse for both of his daughters as well as their husbands and families.

Thinking back over a series of Christmases, Leonard and Phyllis can see a very interesting development, particularly in the lives of their sons.

One summer in the latter years of their grammar school education, both Geoffrey and Daniel volunteered to assist at an English-language Christian camp run for German youngsters wanting to improve their English skills. There, they met a young American lady who was working as a housemother for children living in the boarding wing of an English-speaking school, principally for missionaries' children: the Black Forest Academy. For a couple of years, the Holder family's home in Basel became like a second home for this young lady, and she would drive in to spend time with them on her free days. In fact, at her suggestion, she and the four Holders would spend an hour or so on her day off in Bible study. Leonard remembers working through and discussing Paul's Epistle to the Colossians together. At one stage, there was quite an attraction between her and the Holders' elder son.

One year, to the American friend's delight, Phyllis's father suggested including her in the Christmas arrangements, which, that year, was to Sandown, on the Isle of Wight.

Phyllis's father had a special interest in the Aaron Hotel in Barmouth as, for some years, he had been acquainted with the Christian couple who had wanted to own and run it, and when they were looking for finance to get started, he had given them an interest-free loan. This gave a good Christmas venue for the family groups for a year or two.

After the Aaron decided not to run Christmas house parties, the next venue was a Christian guesthouse in Bournemouth, Dorset, on the south coast of Britain. Here, the family met some interesting fellow guests, including one young man who subsequently, for more than thirty years, has provided very practical support to Leonard and Phyllis's work in Germany.

One of the Holder sons became very friendly with the daughter of key workers at the guesthouse. The friendship developed so far until it was decided by one of the pair that it should stop, at which point it was no longer considered diplomatic for this guesthouse to be the Christmas venue for the Pittwell–Holder–McCann families.

At this same Bournemouth guesthouse, the other Holder son informed the family that he had received a self-made Christmas candle from a young lady with whom he was studying and whom he rather fancied. Words inscribed on the candle in colourful contrasting candle wax said, 'I like you.' He decided that before any friendship should develop, he should state clearly his Christian beliefs and doctrinal position, which he did during that Christmas break, in a long letter written in German. His parents seem to remember that after being very formal, he closed the letter with the words, in English, 'I like you too!'

The friendship did develop, and the following Christmas, the young lady in question was also invited to join the families' celebrations. That year, the venue was in Wiltshire, in a hotel in a delightful country village. Christmas Eve was a clear frosty evening, and most of the group from the three families attended a Christmas Eve midnight service at the village Anglican church. It was quite a moving experience. The village church, decorated for Christmas, was filled to capacity, and the birth of our Lord and Saviour Jesus Christ was remembered and celebrated with appropriate Bible readings and the singing of Christmas carols. At about two in the morning, as Leonard and Phyllis were getting to sleep, there was a knock on their bedroom door, and there was Daniel, their younger son, with a beaming face.

'I couldn't wait until the morning to tell you!' he exclaimed. 'I proposed to Martina on a moonlit bridge over the little river in the village, and she accepted me. We're engaged to be married.'

Marriage of
Daniel and Martina

CHAPTER
5

Black Forest Holiday Services

Leonard and Phyllis decided to call their holiday agency business Black Forest Holiday Services. The German tax office sent them forms to fill in, part of which required them to give an estimate of their expected annual income. All Leonard could do was to give a guess as to the number of guests they would attract, and then in simple terms, the business's income would be the difference between what the guests paid and what the Holders paid out to the landlady or hotelier providing the accommodation. There would also be the cost of some advertising, telephone calls, and postage to deduct before arriving at the net profit that the tax office was interested in. It was all a huge guess and very ambitious. Leonard also declared that he was a Free Evangelical pastor and that there would be some income in support of this role. The tax office must have thought him very naive, but there was no follow-up from them after he submitted the forms.

To offer a holiday package, it was necessary to prepare information about the area, and this necessitated fetching leaflets from the local tourist offices, visiting some of the places of interest, and writing relevant details in English. There was, at that stage, very little information about the Black Forest available in English apart from details of a few very popular tourist spots.

Then Leonard decided they needed to be able to offer a Sunday worship service. He considered finding a room in a restaurant or guesthouse they could hire, but then a very bold thought came into his mind.

'Darling,' he said to Phyllis rather hesitantly, 'do you think we dare approach the small Protestant church in Todtnau about using their church premises?'

After a short hesitation, his wife responded. 'I guess there's no harm in trying.'

They discovered that the church was run by an ordained couple, man and wife.

Their first response when Leonard said they were wanting to hold an English-language service was 'But there are no English-speaking people here.'

Leonard explained about Black Forest Holiday Services and his wish to offer a holiday package to British people which would include a Sunday morning worship service.

After consulting with their church committee, the answer was an agreement with a couple of conditions. Could Herr Holder give some evidence that he was an ordained Free Evangelical church minister, and could they ensure that the service was advertised as widely as possible? Also, under the deeds of the building, they were not permitted to hire it out, so there could be no charge for its use for an English-language service. The building would be available from approximately ten forty-five on a Sunday morning after the German service had concluded at about ten thirty.

The pastors were extremely helpful, and Phyllis was introduced to the small pipe organ, which she then played very efficiently for the services, and Leonard was shown how to ring the church bells, which echoed around the town and informed that they could light the candles if they wished.

Leonard wrote a letter in German for the trustees of Bible in Action to sign, giving his credentials as a bona fide pastor, ordained in 1972 as pastor of the Baptist chapel in Horley, and this seemed to satisfy the Todtnau church. When advertising the services, he would name himself as Pastor Len Holder.

Running from December that first year, they began to advertise Black Forest Holiday Services, offering holiday accommodation with Christian fellowship. They intended the Sunday services to run from May through to September and produced leaflets advertising this, placing them at the beginning of the summer season in several local camp sites and information offices.

Also, to prepare the way for their guests, they produced an introductory letter which they personally took round to a selection of homes offering rooms with breakfast or holiday apartments and also small guesthouses. The letter introduced Black Forest Holiday Services and offered the possibility of providing English guests. The landlady or hotelier would be asked to quote for specific guests for specific dates, and Pastor Holder would be available in the event of any language difficulties with the guests.

In this way, Leonard hoped to introduce himself in an acceptable way into the community. Several worthwhile conversations ensued, and he was always sure to mention the Christian nature of the enterprise and that a Sunday service in English, open to everybody, would be offered during the holiday season in the Todtnau Evangelische Kirche[49] following their normal German service.

The first service they held was actually on Easter Sunday that year. Through the contact with guesthouses, they heard of a family on holiday from the UK who would appreciate a service, and the opportunity was too good to miss. So it was that Pastor Holder's bells first pealed out over the quiet town on that Resurrection Day. Still, the congregation was small: four Holders, their American friend, and the visiting family. It was a large family from Wales, as it turned out, and they all went back to Bergstrasse afterwards for the afternoon.

Leonard and Phyllis had not originally considered their move into the Black Forest to be a long-term affair, but it seemed that

---

49 Evangelische Kirche is the state Protestant Church in Southern Germany, roughly equivalent to the Lutheran Church in other parts of Germany.

God had orchestrated circumstances which, when followed through, caused them to lay foundations for a possible long-term ministry.

Phyllis's Memories and Comments

Life goes in stages or as a series of different 'lives', which is the way we have sometimes referred to it. We were now embarking on another one. We were tour operators in Germany!

Doing what we hadn't been trained for was no strange thing for us. Most of our lives, we had learned things in the school of life as we went along rather than specifically having formal training. God had opened for us a new venture which we recognised as a means of serving Him and sharing the Gospel. We embraced it with enthusiasm. Please note my use of the word 'we'. God had now enabled me to see that I was not just supporting my husband in his calling. This was a joint venture in which we were partners.

Realising that a number of homes around us were offering either bed and breakfast or self-catering holiday apartments, we decided that for a start, we should encourage British Christians to come on holiday in the beautiful Black Forest and that finding them accommodation would give us access into local homes and give an acceptable point of contact with a range of different people.

Some of the dear people we met during those days still remain friends of ours today. One such family had self-catering accommodation in the beautiful village of Wieden, high up in the hills. From the balcony of one of their flats was a stunning view across the beautiful Wieden Valley

A family home with a self-catering holiday apartment in Wieden

with, on a clear day, the Swiss Alps visible in the far distance. They were a lovely indigenous Black Forest farming family, and our contact with them in those early years was part of the confirmation we needed to stay on in the area after our time in Schlechtnau came to an end. We enjoyed great times with them. They were so helpful to us. I gained more confidence in my German when speaking to them and also learned interesting local dialect! It was a great grief to me that as we got busier with our second Haus Barnabas and it began to take up all my time and energy, I gradually had less and less time to see these dear people or do anything much more than work in the house.

As I write now, the lovely lady of the family – who, together with her husband and daughter, was a friend for many years – has sadly recently passed away. One memory of visits to her was the drinks she plied us with. This was her way of showing hospitality, and it seemed churlish not to accept the small glass of beer she expected us to drink. We soon learned not to drink it too fast as an empty glass was not allowed and refills came unexpectedly. Sometimes we could persuade her that coffee was a better option for us, and the cakes she made were delicious.

Often with many of our Black Forest contacts, on agreeing on a deal for our guests to come to their home, a bottle of schnapps was produced, and we all clinched the arrangement with a tiny glass of this intoxicating liquor, which could be downed with one swallow. Christians have different views about drinking alcohol, and Leonard remembers hearing a story of a conversation between two Christian ministers.

One, on seeing the other accept a glass of schnapps, commented, 'I don't know how you as a Christian can drink that stuff.'

The other answered with a smile, 'Like this, my friend,' and he threw it back with one gulp.

As we look back on our pathway through our years on the continent, we can see so often that God led one step at a time. We have always found the words of Abraham's servant when he was searching for a bride for Isaac – 'I being in the way the Lord led me' – to be most pertinent to our experience, past, present, and future.

CHAPTER

6

Early English Teaching

During that first season with Sunday services in the Todtnau church, Leonard and Phyllis would regularly find it necessary to wait a short while outside the building until the German congregation had left. Waiting with them most weeks was a German lady who had come to pick up her mother, who regularly attended the German service. One Sunday she asked Leonard if he could teach English. He had to confess that he had not had any experience of language teaching.

'But surely, anyone can teach their own mother tongue' came the quick response.

When Leonard asked her what she had in mind, she informed him that she was responsible for arranging a programme of adult evening classes in the town and that she would love to be able to include an English language beginner's class taught by a genuine Englishman. After thinking and praying about it, Leonard enquired further as to what would be involved. On learning that there was a detailed textbook for students and a teacher's manual to go with it, he agreed to give it a go. The autumn course would consist of ten evening sessions, one a week, beginning in September. For the course to take place, it would require a minimum of six students to apply.

Interestingly, very shortly after agreeing to take the course in Todtnau, Leonard had a phone call from a Herr Asal asking whether he would be prepared to lead a similar course in the town of Schönau! Would he teach two English language classes in this little town south of Schlechtnau – a beginner's and also another class for those who had already completed an initial class? Leonard agreed and then began to realise what a wonderful opportunity God was giving him of getting involved in the local community and also earning a bit of money.

Because only four students applied for the advanced group in Schönau and this was too few for the authorities to pay a teacher, Leonard offered to teach this group privately. The advantage of this was that he and Phyllis could get to know these students more personally as they would come to their little home in Schlechtnau for the lessons. The group consisted of two farmers' wives, the wife of a forester, and the owner of a wholesale drinks business. These were all older people, and the reason they wanted to learn English was very interesting. One of the farmers' wives, whom the Holders got to know best of all, had had her schooling during the Second World War and, for some reason, had always wanted to learn English, but within Germany during the war, her education was limited, and she spent a lot of her young teenage years as a milkmaid on a farm in the far east of the country, fleeing when the Russian troops ravished the country. After the war, she was settled together with her parents in the Black Forest, where she eventually married a young farmer. There's little money to be made from a small hill farm, and her husband also had a job in a factory, leaving her with much of the responsibility of running the farm. One evening she came to the class with her arm bandaged. A goshawk had attacked her as she tried to protect her chickens from its attempts to fly off with a succulent dinner.

Like most of the population in this area of the southern Black Forest, Elizabeth was a Roman Catholic. Leonard and Phyllis got to know her and her husband fairly well, even being invited to her 60th birthday celebration, and conversations with her indicated she had a living faith in the Lord Jesus. Her character and life certainly reflected the fruit of a born-again child of God.

The forester's wife's interest in the English language stemmed from experiences she and her husband had had soon after the war, when a corps of Royal Engineers from the British Army had been sent into the area to help get things going again. At least one soldier had worked closely with her husband in the forest; they had become good friends and had remained in contact. It seemed that she and her husband had occasionally visited England to spend time with this man and his family and, with retirement coming up, were hoping to repeat this. Leonard and Phyllis were invited one afternoon to their rather isolated home up a track in the forest for 'Kaffee und Kuchen'.

In regard to the presence of the British Army in the Black Forest after the end of the war, it is interesting that a plaque (on a rock face by a small footbridge over a deep gully around the back of the Belchen mountain) states that this was constructed by the British Army in the 1950s.

In the years immediately following 1989 and the fall of the Berlin Wall, many families came across from Eastern Europe into West Germany, and some settled in the Black Forest. One day Leonard had a telephone call requesting whether he would be willing to give extra English lessons to one or two youngsters, now in German schools, needing to catch up with their English language skills. The authorities had allocated funds for this but at a level quite a bit less than that which a qualified teacher would expect to receive. Leonard agreed to do this, and two students living within easy distance of Schlechtnau came to the Holders' home for private one-to-one lessons for several weeks. There was a lad from Poland, living with his father in Todtnau, and a teenage girl from Romania, whose family had been given accommodation in the Schönau region. It wasn't easy for these families from the east to settle in the west, and the Polish lad, who was used to city life, found the Black Forest very dull.

Speaking of his contemporaries at school, he one day commented with some scorn, 'They go to bed at 9:00 p.m.'

English teaching took off over the following years, and the income from this became quite a proportion of the income God provided for them – but more about that later.

CHAPTER

7

British Holiday Guests

Through the adverts in the *Evangelical Times* and one or two other Christian papers, the Holders began to get enquiries for holiday accommodation in the Black Forest, not in large numbers but sufficient to enable them to begin to gain experience in supplying what their guests would require.

One of the earliest bookings was from an elder in a north of England church, and he and his wife were accommodated in the Waldeck Hotel, one of the more expensive options Black Forest Holiday Services was offering. This couple returned several times in following years, and during later visits to the north of England, Leonard had the opportunity to preach in their church.

Interestingly, unknown to this couple, a young lady from the same church who had completed her A-level exams and was wanting some summer work in Germany before studying German as one of her university subjects wrote asking whether Leonard could find her some form of employment in the Black Forest. Leonard and Phyllis were able to do this as several small hotels were regularly looking for extra kitchen help. The job offered accommodation with the employment and, on the face of it, appeared to be a very satisfactory solution, but sadly, it proved disastrous. Not only were the management very hard on their staff, but also, the young lady in question had been ill and found the workload required of her too demanding. Leonard and Phyllis supported her as best they could, negotiating fewer hours and running her between Todtnauberg and Schlechtnau when bus times made this difficult by public transport. When at last, it was clear the work was not suitable, she moved in with the Holders until her planned return flight in late summer. This established a close friendship which continues now thirty years later.

Another couple who came on holiday that first year had a background in the exclusive Brethren denomination, which they had left many years earlier. Rather remarkably, when another couple, holidaying in Titisee, came to that particular Sunday service and names were exchanged, there was a realisation that both gentlemen had spent their childhood in the exclusive Brethren in the same area of Britain. They were soon conversing about families they both knew and the severe difficulties they had both suffered when their parents and themselves had left the denomination.

Families from Phyllis's home church
visit for Sunday worship and fellowship

Advertising the English service in tourist offices and camp sites brought a number of very interesting and different tourists into the service. Leonard included on the advert an invitation to bring a packed lunch and offered the opportunity to picnic together.

Leonard and Phyllis then, after the service, led those who wanted to join them to one of a selection of suitable picnic spots, and this time together enabled them to converse with their guests and to get to know them in a more relaxed setting. After the picnic, they would then lead a guided walk. A favourite spot was the Todtnau waterfall, and children loved to paddle and play in pools at the base of the fall.

These Sunday gatherings served to introduce them to a range of Christians from different home areas, mostly in Britain, and different denominations. Some have remained friends over many years and have invited Leonard and Phyllis back to their homes or home churches and, in some cases, to speak about their ministry and advertise their holidays.

One Sunday that first year, a family of four came to the service and afterwards picnicked with them. Subsequently, they returned most summers over several years. Although British, they were living in Belgium, and Allen was head of the English department in a rather prestigious German school in Brussels. He was also an elder in a French-speaking church where a majority of members were Africans from the former Belgium Congo. Although speaking English at home, their two children were attending French-speaking schools. This family proved in God's purpose to play a significant role in Leonard and Phyllis's life.

Some years later, Leonard was invited to take a major part in the weddings of both children. He flew to Oslo to take the wedding of the son when he married an African young lady whose family had settled in Norway. This was a delightful wedding in a Lutheran church, with the ceremony and programme full of African customs with music and dancing. The daughter was married in an Anglican church in England, and Leonard was asked to give the address after the vicar had heard their vows. The bridegroom was a music teacher and welcomed his bride into the church and down the aisle with a musical accompaniment on his violin. As you will learn, the parents later joined Leonard and Phyllis in the Black Forest.

The Sunday services followed by picnic lunches and fellowship provided interesting encounters with many lovely people. One week in the Holders' second summer, they had found self-catering accommodation for the head of a surgical department (in a British hospital), together with his wife and two daughters. At the close of the Sunday service, the wife very politely asked Leonard whether he could possibly trim his moustache before the following Sunday. She explained that she was deaf but was skilful at lip reading as long as she could see the speaker's lips clearly. This reminds Leonard of another guest who commented with a smile that she was unable to hear unless she had her glasses on!

As part of the holiday service, Leonard and Phyllis were pleased to care for any practical needs of their guests, and during the week following the Sunday service mentioned above, the father of the family rang during the night, expressing great concern for their younger daughter. She had extreme stomach pains, and he feared it was a serious appendix problem. Did Leonard know how to get a doctor? Leonard was able to find the phone number for the doctor on duty, give him a ring, and then drive the father with his daughter to the doctor's home surgery. In the event, it was a female doctor, and it was obvious she had got out of bed specially to see the patient. The decision was that the cause of the pain was most likely the consequence of drinking water from one of the Black Forest streams. These, although fast flowing and looking sparkling clean, can often get contaminated through cattle drinking and urinating further upstream.

Another family coming to a Sunday service that summer consisted of husband, wife, and adult daughter with her partner who were all holidaying together in a caravan. Only the parents had come to the service, and they stayed for fellowship for the rest of the day. During the week, they returned unannounced (remember, these were days before mobile phones) and invited Leonard and Phyllis out for 'Kaffee und Kuchen'. They later acknowledged that the Sunday service and fellowship had saved their holiday from disaster and perhaps their marriage too. The husband was a long-distance lorry driver and therefore away from home a lot, and his wife was unaccustomed to having so much of his company. Suddenly, being forced together in the close confines of a caravan, with the daughter and partner as well, was proving too much to bear, and before finding blessing through the service and the fellowship, they had been on the point of returning home.

Todtnau boasts a large, very elaborate Roman Catholic church and a small, very much simpler Protestant church building, where Leonard and Phyllis were able to hold their services. It was very suitable for non-conformist services, having a small two-manual pipe organ, complete with foot pedals, which Phyllis was able to play, also a simple desk to preach from with a table from which communion could be served. At that stage, however, with no settled nucleus of Christian believers, Leonard didn't include communion in the services. Hymn sheets were printed each Sunday to sing from, and although the congregation was never large, the acoustics in the building were excellent and the singing enthusiastic.

A neighbour living near the church once commented to Leonard, 'You English really sing well. On a Sunday morning, we always open our window to hear you.'

The pastors were happy about the building being used by the so-called English pastor and one morning commented in a very thrilled way that one of their members had seen an advert for the English worship service in their Todtnau church in a London newspaper. Leonard had

Todtnau church

to think about this and decided it must have been the *Evangelical Times* he was referring to. He later discovered that a member of the Todtnau church committee had a sister in London who was a believing Christian worshipping at Cole Abbey Presbyterian Church and that she was no doubt the source of this information.

One summer the pastor contacted Leonard to say he had been notified that a coach of American tourists was expected in the town, and the tour leader was asking if it was possible to have at least part of the church service in English. The request was whether Leonard would be prepared to give a sermon in English following the pastor's own sermon in German at their normal Sunday service. Leonard was, of course, happy to oblige.

Phyllis's Memories and Comments

As holiday guests started to come to us in 1990, we established a pattern of care for them. We would direct them to our small apartment in Schlechtnau, where, on their arrival, we would offer them a much-needed cup of tea and refreshment. We would then discuss their accommodation with them, trying and get to know a bit about what they wanted from their holiday with a view to helping them to achieve this. Our special 'information pack' written in English soon began to be put together, giving details of places of interest around and the bus and train connections to explore them. Soon, guests who had come by car would be leaving their vehicle behind and venturing onto the buses, thus getting more acquainted with the German way of life. British people have traditionally been cautious of anything 'foreign', and often, unless they could take their own language and usual way of life with them into another country and live with the familiar, they weren't really comfortable and happy.

Once our visitors had been refreshed, we would take them to their accommodation, introduce them to their hosts, answer any queries on either side, and assure them we were at the end of the phone should problems arise. Guests were told they would be very welcome to come and find us any time they needed, which they often did. Usually, a good relationship soon developed between the guest and the host family, both eager to enjoy the new experiences they were having. Most found it great fun to try to understand one another, often using gestures when the spoken word was unintelligible.

We always tried to match the nearby accommodation with the specific needs of the guests, and this meant in the early months that we were visiting a lot of bed-and-breakfast and self-catering properties to ascertain what was available. Of course, availability during the holiday dates requested could sometimes be a problem.

By car, we drove a wide area advertising the Sunday services in the Todtnau church. Two particular campsites where we placed advertising notices were in Kirchzarten, towards Freiburg, and another at Staufen, at the end of the Munstertal. We also placed advertising leaflets in several tourist information offices in the neighbouring villages and towns.

Over the years, we had wonderful fellowship with many people, including quite a few Dutch families. The Dutch language has many German-based and English-based words. Because of this, some of their language was understandable to us when praying together as each used their mother tongue.

Later, when Dutch families visited our Sunday services in our lounge in Haus Barnabas, one of the adults would sometimes translate the sermon into Dutch to make sure the children understood as well.

CHAPTER

8

German Believers

On discovering that Todtnau produced a weekly paper providing local news, adverts, and information from local firms, Leonard enquired in the town hall as to the possibility of the paper including a notice of their English service. He was directed to a particular office in the building and found a very friendly man behind a desk who was most interested in hearing about the service. He informed Leonard that there was no charge for church adverts. He agreed to publish the notice Leonard had written out and include it in the paper every week the church service was running.

The notice brought the fact of the service to the attention of the whole community, and this led to an encounter with the Holders' first local evangelical Christian believer, a young lady by the name of Monika.

Monika had a good grasp of English and came to one of the Sunday services. She introduced herself as a born-again believer, saying she was a member of a church in the Freiburg area. She was very happy with a suggestion Leonard made of meeting one evening in the week for fellowship and a Bible study; this soon became a regular weekly event.

Like most, if not all, of the established families in the area, Monika came from a Roman Catholic background. She spoke of her grandmother, with great respect, as a prayerful Christian lady and also felt her mother had a real faith in Jesus. Her elder sister was the first in the family to find the freedom of a faith in Christ, which delivered her from the unbiblical rituals and rigidity of the Catholic Church. Through her sister's witness and whilst away from home, Monika also came to know Jesus. She was thrilled to meet Leonard and Phyllis and commented that she had been praying that God would send an evangelical witness into the area.

Monika had three brothers and, once she started coming to Leonard's Bible studies, was concerned to bring one or more of her brothers with her. Although they often promised to come, there was always some reason why they couldn't.

Through her church connections, Monika later went across to America and, whilst working with a church there, met and married an American Christian. She frequently returns home to see her mother and family and has continued to have contact with Leonard and Phyllis over the years.

One Sunday a very interesting young German couple came to the service. In conversation afterwards, Leonard and Phyllis learned that they had recently married, and because the lady's family home was in Todtnauberg and they liked the idea of setting up home in such a beautiful situation, they were praying and looking to God for guidance as to whether they could settle in the Todtnau area. At that time, they were renting a flat in Lörrach, the area's district town, where the husband had been brought up and worked as a male nurse in the hospital. The husband had been brought up in a Christian family and knew and loved the Lord. He had met his wife whilst she had been in hospital and had given her a Bible. After her discharge, she had taken the Bible home and read it, and the Holy Spirit had opened her eyes to a need of a personal saviour. Further contact with the male nurse who had been instrumental in giving her God's Word had led to marriage. Now as they had prayed about moving into the Black Forest, they considered there were three points that needed to be settled – first, finding a suitable apartment; second, being able to get a job in Freiburg, where the closest hospital was; and third but no less important, finding Christian fellowship. Later, they decided that meeting Leonard and Phyllis provided the answer to their third point, and very soon, the other two points were also satisfied.

Through many changing circumstances, all three of these believing Christians played an encouraging role in Leonard and Phyllis's life and ministry over the following thirty years.

Another more elderly couple came briefly into Leonard and Phyllis's life in those Schlechtnau days. They originated from the former Czechoslavia, and the husband, having fought in the Second World War when his country had been incorporated into Nazi Germany, had a war pension and was given the right to settle in Germany. Leonard was convinced they were a genuine born-again couple, but the husband's view of the nation of Israel, which seemed to dominate his whole Christian thinking and conversation, soon made fellowship difficult, and their contact with Leonard and Phyllis sadly ceased. Leonard remembers the husband once maintaining that evangelising the Jews was unnecessary as they were the elect and, in the light of Romans 11:26, all of Israel would be saved.

The couple had a daughter living in Israel, and Leonard remembers driving them to Zürich Airport for their flight to visit her. It was the first time he had driven the route taking him over the Black Forest mountains before dropping down steeply into Switzerland. It was early on a Sunday morning, and from the height they were motoring, there was suddenly a breath-taking view of the sun rising over the distant Swiss Alps. It was the first time Leonard had witnessed this, and on his return journey, he stopped the car and sat for some time, admiring and praising God for the splendour of His creation.

CHAPTER

9

Sunday Fellowship

For several years before the Holders were established with a large enough meeting room of their own, they very much appreciated having the use of the Protestant church building in Todtnau for a Sunday morning service. The initial permission to use the church was for an English-language service for English tourists. Leonard felt that requesting it for this use would not indicate any wish to be in competition with the regular German-language service. Later, when there was some interest from a few local German folk, Leonard got the pastor's permission to have a German translation and to run a dual language service.

A few German Christians came regularly in those early years. One lady acknowledged that the main reason she liked to come was the later starting time of the service. She also came to a week evening Bible study for a number of years until after her husband retired when the couple moved away from the area.

One Sunday an elderly lady living in a care home came to the service. She was obviously an active member of the German church, and interestingly, on the Sunday she came, the pastor of the church came and sat with her. During the following week, Leonard received a letter in the post from the lady saying how wonderful she had found the service. She compared it very favourably with services in her own church, pointing out that Leonard just stood there without a gown, he spoke with enthusiasm explaining the Bible, and the congregation stood up to sing hymns which were uplifting, having bright tunes and sung with fervour. However, having written like this, she then didn't appear again, and Leonard wondered whether her minister had advised her against coming, but on enquiring, the Holders were told that the time of their service didn't fit in with the midday mealtime in her care home.

Phyllis's Memories and Comments

I was very pleased to be able to play the two-manual pipe organ for our church services. The meeting room in the church building had wonderful acoustics, which was a real help with a small congregation. The singing rang out well, and most of our guests were used to singing enthusiastically anyway. Our experience of German services revealed that the congregation remained seated for the hymns and didn't appear to expect to raise their voices in praise. We used the church during the summer months and, having the windows open, were informed that our singing was appreciated by some of the local residents, with one lady telling us she always kept her own window open to listen.

As most of our congregation were on holiday, they were in no hurry to leave and lingered to talk and to get to know one another. Realising this, we soon began to advertise a picnic after the service, recommending guests

Todtnau church (interior)

bring food with them, so this picnic time became a memorable part of many guests' holidays. Before we had a suitable lounge of our own to gather in, the time together after the church service provided a valuable opportunity for fellowship and to encourage one another as Christians. Right from the start, we realised Christian encouragement should be a key part of our Haus Barnabas ministry.

In addition to our own holiday guests, people joined with us on Sundays from other holiday accommodation and local campsites. Occasionally, folk travelled in for the service and fellowship from quite a distance. Through this, we learned the value of true fellowship in Jesus with Christians from a range of different denominations. This is easier outside of a home situation, where there can be suspicion among different churches. We all have our own ideas of what and how we worship God, often simply from the influence of our upbringing, and it is a steep learning curve to think through what is necessary and what is merely habit.

We had a few different picnic venues, and a favourite for quite a time was the grassy area just below the car park by the Todtnau waterfall. After the picnic, those who felt able walked up to see the waterfall. This has several impressive drops and, depending on the time of year, varying amounts of water. Its roar can be heard

Todtnau waterfall

from quite a distance as you make your approach along a forest path. Children can enjoy paddling in the lower pools, and more active folk climb a path and steps beside the falls to admire the view from the top.

The toilet facilities in those earlier days at this picnic spot were fairly basic, and the 'Da' of the 'Damen' had dropped off the sign for the ladies' toilet, leaving the sign reading 'men'! This confusion had to be explained.

Another picnic venue was on the outskirts of our neighbouring village of Geschwend. Here, there were picnic tables in an open grassy area beside a small tributary of our River Wiese. Unfortunately, there was very little shade, but it was a good place to picnic with a suitable walk to follow. One memory from this site was that of a particular guest who, whilst preparing to take a photo, stepped back to get a better position and disappeared unceremoniously down the other side of the bank towards the river. He reappeared a short while later, dusting himself down but none the worse for his abrupt disappearance!

Then there was Knopflesbrunnen, which we visited occasionally. This is at the top of a higher range of mountains behind Utzenfeld. Access is by means of a rough and very steep mountain track, but once there, the views around are spectacular.

One memory from here is of a student helper – who later became our future daughter-in-law and the worthy mother of three of our grandchildren – running down the slopes, singing, 'The hills are alive with the sound of music!'

CHAPTER

10

An Enormous Step of Faith

The Holders had a contract for their apartment in Schlechtnau for twelve months. They were able to pay their rent promptly each month, and at the end of the twelve-month period, nothing was said about moving on. However, after two years, their landlady indicated that she was wanting to make changes and asked if they could please vacate the apartment at the end of the month. This meant they had four weeks to find somewhere else to live.

Although initially, Leonard and Phyllis had had no thought of the Black Forest being their established home, things had so developed that they now felt convinced that unless the Lord indicated otherwise, this is where He would have them live for Him.

As Leonard thought things over, he was convinced that every part of every country of the world needed the Gospel preached and demonstrated by Christians living godly lives: salt and light in the community, as Jesus had said.

The area where they were living was religious, and the customs and rituals of the Roman Catholic Church were embedded into their annual calendar, but apart from a few exceptions, there was little evidence of a living faith in the Lord Jesus, and a personal relationship with Him was sadly missing. The sixteenth-century Reformation in Europe under the leadership of Luther hadn't affected this part of Germany as at that point in history, it was part of the Habsburg Empire. Leonard also realised that if they were to have any influence for Jesus in the area, this would require a long-term commitment and settling there as their permanent home.

Accordingly, needing to move from Schlechtnau, the couple began to look for another apartment to move into. The local weekly newspapers often had adverts for available apartments (as many people rented their homes), but just at that period, nothing suitable was cropping up. Some of their local friends tried to advise and help, and several pointed out that there were apartments available in the Reiterhof in Utzenfeld. Leonard resisted investigating this as the Reiterhof was an enormous building, and he imagined having an apartment there would be like living in a block of flats.

The building was constructed during the war years using Russian prisoner-of-war labour. It was designed as the office and distribution centre for the Finstergrund mine and no doubt included accommodation for prisoners-of-war mine workers. The Finstergrund mine itself is situated in the hills a couple of miles away from Utzenfeld, with access from the Wieden Road. In medieval times, it yielded silver and lead but more recently had been an important source of fluorite and baryte. These have a wide range of uses in industry and would have had great importance during the war years. The material was brought down to Utzenfeld by conveyor belt, where it was sorted and then transported by rail down to Basel and up the Rhine to the industrial centres of Germany. The rail line, which ran up to Todtnau until the second half of the 1960s, ran immediately in front of the Finstergrund building.

When the mine was closed as being no longer financially viable, the huge building – which is not unattractive, unlike many industrial buildings today – remained unused for several years before a local builder purchased it and converted it into an equine centre. There are stables on the ground floor of the main building and, in addition, a new stable block alongside it. Also, another block provides a large inside riding yard with a restaurant attached, giving a view into it through large plate-glass windows. Behind the building is an impressive outside arena for the exercise and training of the horses. Above the stables in the main building are guests' rooms and self-catering apartments.

Leonard and Phyllis had no idea what sort of apartments were being advertised to rent in the Reiterhof, but as already said, they didn't imagine they would be particularly attractive or suitable. However, when nothing else appeared to be on offer, they decided they should at least go and view them.

They were asked to meet a Herr Schwörer at the back of the building, and he showed them into a side entrance, up steps to a self-contained area of the house, which he told them had been used as dormitory accommodation for young people, complete with an entertainment room. He explained that there was

Reiterhof in Utzenfeld

insufficient demand for the premises as youth accommodation, and the planned intention was to convert the area into two separate large family apartments. He had a plan with him showing the intended design of each, and if the Holders were interested, they could choose which one they wanted.

Leonard and Phyllis looked around the rooms as they then existed. There were two very large rooms, approximately eight or nine metres in each direction. One of them was obviously used as an entertainment room. Although it had windows on two sides, dark green walls and large beams painted dark brown gave it an oppressive feel. Disco lights on the low ceiling would have provided the right atmosphere for evening entertainment. The second large room had a large ensuite bathroom and, at one end, opened onto a balcony with a view into the village and the surrounding hills.

In addition to these two very large rooms, there were two two-roomed apartments, each with an ensuite bathroom and a balcony looking out onto a large tennis court and the horse arena at the back of the house. Finally, there were two further ensuite rooms, one small, suitable for a single bed, and the other large enough for a double bed or two singles.

Although Leonard and Phyllis had had no idea what to expect in the Reiterhof, it certainly wasn't this. Herr Schwörer explained that the work on the major alterations planned, to form the two apartments, was scheduled to start the following Monday, and he mentioned the price for renting one or other. Leonard asked whether he could take the copy of the plan home so they could think about the situation, and he promised to be in touch.

As Phyllis later told the story, after they got back to their apartment in Schlechtnau, Leonard sat down with the plans and went very quiet.

After an hour or so, he went to find Phyllis and, looking rather embarrassed, said, 'Darling, I think we need the whole of this. If we had one of the planned apartments, it would really be too large for just the two of us, but if we had the whole complex, we could use it as the centre for our ministry. We would have rooms to accommodate guests ourselves, and if redecorated in a light colour, that entertainment room would provide a lovely lounge for Bible studies and a general sitting area for our guests.'

'But, Len,' exclaimed his wife in alarm, 'how could we finance that? Remember, all those rooms are empty. We shall need to furnish them before we could do anything. And if the rent is twice what they are asking for a single apartment, that's an enormous price. Also, at the moment, there is no kitchen.' Then she added with a smile, 'However, there are five bathrooms!'

'I haven't overlooked all those things,' answered Leonard. 'It would be a tremendous step of faith, and we would need to be sure this is what God wanted for us. But if it's His purpose, He can easily ensure we have what we need.'

'It's certainly true that He looked after us in Switzerland,' responded Phyllis. 'It certainly hasn't been easy. In fact, many times, I just longed to give it all up and get back to Britain, but we were always able to pay the rent, and God has really blessed our sons, and it would seem He has blessed other people through us.'

'I'll give Herr Schwörer a ring,' said Leonard after thinking for a while. 'I'll simply say we might be interested in renting the whole premises and ask what this would cost. We must then pray and ask the Lord for some reassurance from Him that this is His will and that He will provide for us.'

Herr Schwörer was delighted about their enquiry. He said he would get back to them with a definite rent, and also, if they did decide to rent it as one entity, his men would redecorate the whole place through in whatever colour scheme they wanted. However, he would really need an answer, yes or no, by Monday morning as by then, his workmen were scheduled to start work on the premises.

Oh dear! An urgent decision was necessary, and how could they be sure it was the right thing to do? Communication with friends in Britain was not easy, and how could anyone so far away advise them anyway? The natural human approach would be to make a decision on the basis of funds available and income expected and set this against the cost of the venture, but they had no funds and no settled regular income at all. From a human point of view, it was utterly foolish and reckless even to contemplate renting such premises, and yet there were so many biblical stories to prove that God honoured steps of faith made in His name and under His guidance.

Leonard and Phyllis prayed, seeking the Lord to reveal to them whether this was His will or not and, if so, to strengthen their faith to sign the contract that would be presented to them.

It was the end of the season, and they had planned one more Sunday morning service in the Todtnau church, even though the previous Sunday, no one had come. That Sunday morning, a single gentleman came into the church. He was an Asian man, and they later discovered he was from Singapore and was in the Black Forest on business. He was staying in Titisee and had seen the notice about their service in the information office there.

They had a short time of worship together, and Leonard shared the message he had prepared. They then invited the man back to have some lunch with them, and this led to him inviting them back to his hotel for an evening meal.

During the time they had together, they felt able to share with him the burden of the decision they had to make by the next morning. The gentleman was a man of faith and spoke of the work he was doing with the Full Gospel Business Men's Fellowship in Singapore. He encouraged them strongly to trust God and venture forward in faith. As they left him in Titisee, he stood on the steps of the hotel and, putting his arms around them both, prayed for them. Leonard and Phyllis don't remember his name, and there has been no contact from him since that Sunday evening, but they felt strongly he was God's messenger, sent to confirm to them the step of faith they were about to take.

With some trepidation but believing this was God's guidance, Leonard and Phyllis signed the contract to rent the whole premises of self-contained rooms in the upper story of the green wing of the Reiterhof building. They were agreeing to a monthly rent of about four times what they were paying for their apartment in Schlechtnau.

Their sons, Geoffrey and Daniel, had been following with interest all that was happening and were concerned about them, knowing they had to vacate their apartment. Daniel rang from the holiday he and Martina were having in Greece.

'How are things going, Dad? Have you found another apartment yet?' came the enquiring voice over the phone.

'Yes, son. We've just signed a contract for another place. It's effectively a small guesthouse with an enormous lounge.'

'Wow, Dad! What's it costing?'

When Leonard told his son the rent they needed to pay, Daniel turned to Martina next to him with the comment 'Dad's flipped'.

CHAPTER

11

Furnishing an Empty Guesthouse

With the Holders having agreed to take the whole premises on offer
in the Reiterhof, the building firm from whom they were renting
it got to work immediately with redecorating. Leonard and Phyllis
walked around the rooms with a chart of paint colours, deciding
how they wanted it. Most if not all the ceilings were panelled
with dark wood, so they chose very light colours for the walls.
The workmen themselves commented on how incredibly different
the large lounge appeared once the dark green and brown was
eradicated.

The first furniture came from a completely unexpected source.
That next Sunday lunch time, their son Geoffrey telephoned them
from Basel excitedly.

'Dad, the care home attached to the church where we worship
are changing much of their furniture. There's masses of stuff spread
out in their garden, and it was announced in church that they are
happy for anyone to take what they want. Why don't you come
down this afternoon to see if there's anything you want for the new
premises?'

Leonard and Phyllis did just that. What was most relevant for
their needs were lounge chairs. These were the sort of chairs you

find in public reception rooms, and being Swiss, they were of good quality. They put about twelve or so of these on one side together with four or five simple relaxing chairs. There were a few bedside cabinets, but it was the chairs that were the most significant as they immediately made it possible for a group to sit together in their new spacious lounge. They stayed in the Basel flat with their sons that night, hired a small van the next morning, and drove the first items of furniture for their new home, provided for them free of charge, up to Utzenfeld. Although they had not as yet taken possession of their Reiterhof rooms, they were able to store the chairs etc. in an odd corner.

They decided they would convert the small single room into a kitchen and realised that they would really need this before they moved in. Each week, an advertising paper called *Schnapp* appeared in the local supermarkets and could be picked up free of charge. Leonard suddenly had the idea to search this for possible items of furniture, and lo and behold, there was a kitchen for sale. Someone in Freiburg was exchanging their kitchen and offering their old one, complete with oven and fridge, at a very reasonable price. The dimensions stated seemed a good fit for their small room, so he phoned the number given and arranged to call and see the already dismantled kitchen and hopefully pick it up the next day. Geoffrey agreed to come and help his father, and so they motored into Freiburg and hired a small van for a few hours. The kitchen units and all components looked in very good condition, and so Leonard clenched the deal as a cash purchase, and he and Geoffrey loaded everything into the van.

Then the 'fun' really started! It was pouring with rain in Freiburg, very heavy rain, but as they climbed over the mountain into the Black Forest, the rain turned to snow. The road was soon covered, and cars were turning around as drivers realised things were going to get more difficult. Leonard and Geoffrey kept going, thankful that there was a lot of weight in the van. The road got steeper and steeper, and the snow continued to come down heavily. Although it was building up steadily on the road, the tyres continued to grip enough to keep the vehicle moving, but then as they turned a corner, in front of them was a red light with one-way traffic for a short stretch because of road repairs. They were forced to stop, and when red changed to green, it proved impossible to get a grip on the road to start off again. The lights turned back to red and then green and then red again. In desperation, Leonard suggested that Geoffrey should get out and try to push the vehicle as best he could. There was no other traffic at all, which made life simpler. Finally, with Geoffrey's force from behind, the van edged forward, and although the light was now red again, Leonard ignored this and was able slowly to get past the restricted stretch of road. Realising if he stopped, he would have the same difficulty starting off again, he slowly continued up the hill, leaving his son to follow on foot. Thankfully, they were then close to the summit, and with the road becoming more level, Leonard felt it safe to stop for his son to catch him up.

'Wow! That was tricky,' exclaimed Leonard as Geoffrey clambered in beside him. 'Thanks for that push. Let's hope things will now be easier.'

However, descending from Notschrei at the top of the mountain towards Todtnau proved to be an even worse experience. The compressed snow had become like an ice rink, and on beginning the descent, they now came across a line of traffic coming up the hill which was unable to move because the first vehicle was stuck. Leonard braked slightly, and the van began to slide. The back slued, and they approached the stationary upcoming vehicle broadside. As they slid slowly towards the bonnet of the car facing them, there appeared little Leonard could do. Then through God's preserving care, their van came to a halt a few inches from the front bumper of the stationary car.

Leonard continued cautiously down the hill, but with the vehicle insisting it wanted to slide towards the metal barrier beside them, this was far from easy. As they lost altitude, the snow gradually turned back to rain, the road surface lost its slippery surface, and everything became easier.

After unloading the van and having a bit of lunch, Leonard and Geoffrey undertook the journey back to Freiburg to return the hire vehicle. Amazingly, the snow had stopped, the roads were clear, and travelling was easy. This being still October and probably the first snow of the season, the white stuff that had caused so much trouble disappeared as fast as it had arrived.

Remarkably, the kitchen units fitted into the small room amazingly well. It was necessary to get another worktop as the arrangement of cabinets and sink needed to be different, but with the help of Leonard's brother-in-law who had come with Leonard's sister for a holiday at that precise time, the moving all went well. Their landlord sent in a plumber and an electrician to complete the work without charge to Leonard and Phyllis.

Leonard with a Sunday Black Forest gateau in Haus Barnabas kitchen

A substantial gift from Britain enabled the purchase of many additional items of furniture and necessary fittings, and it was, of course, possible to bring many household utensils up from their apartment in Basel and more still after Geoffrey and Daniel gave up living there the following year.

There are several other stories which could be related in regard to the equipping of the house. What became crystal clear to them was that God is so gracious in meeting His children's needs, none so much as those relating to steps taken in faith in His name under His guidance. This provision which they have been so grateful for over the years through generous gifts from brothers and sisters in Christ has been very humbling for Leonard and Phyllis and the means of bringing them into fellowship and often closer friendship with many lovely people.

Leonard and Phyllis decided it would be helpful and good to give their new premises a name. Various possible names floated through their minds, and one or two were suggested by their boys; eventually, they settled on Haus Barnabas. The New Testament character Barnabas was a missionary working with the apostle Paul in the first century, but the New Testament tells us the name means 'the encourager', and it was a nickname given to him because of this God-given gift which the early apostles recognised in him. Now with the development of their hospitality work, which could now become more personal (with guests actually staying in their own home), together with their desire to present the Gospel by being vital, living witnesses of their faith in the local community, they considered the name Barnabas very suitable.

There have been a few misunderstandings during the years. For example, one person once referred to the guesthouse as Haus Barabbas, Barabbas being, of course, a very different biblical character. Also, occasionally, letters have arrived addressed to Herr Barnabas.

CHAPTER

12

Early Haus Barnabas Guests

It was early the following year before guests began to come to the newly opened Haus Barnabas. Leonard had produced a coloured single-sheet brochure advertising Black Forest Holiday Services with an enticing photo of Lake Titisee on the front. His sister in Britain kindly agreed to answer phone enquires and post out more details and a booking form to enquirers.

If Leonard remembers correctly, the first guests, in the spring of 1992, were a group of young people from Westminster Chapel, London. They self-catered, using the new kitchen, and wanted a few days of hill walking. There were two significant factors in regard to these particular young people which both Leonard and Phyllis felt to be more than merely a remarkable coincidence. God appeared to be linking their new bold venture with aspects of their earlier lives in Britain.

First, Leonard had appreciated the ministry of Dr Lloyd Jones, who had ministered at the London chapel these young people came from, attending some of the doctor's Friday evening Bible lectures on the Epistle to the Romans whilst he had worked in London prior to his marriage. Second, they realised as their guests were introducing themselves that one of the young ladies was the daughter of Phyllis's best friend when she first began school forty-two years earlier. It had been some years since Phyllis had seen her friend and her family, and since the daughter was now calling herself by her second Christian name, it wasn't immediately obvious who she was.

Other interesting guests in those early years included a young man from Fraserburgh in Scotland named John. He arrived in a heavy tweed suit which he immediately realised was far too warm for the climate of the southern Black Forest. He quickly bought himself a pair of light shorts but, not realising the strength of the sun, got himself severely burnt. He spoke of his holiday as a great adventure and something to tell the grandchildren about, which, as a comment from a single lad in his twenties, seemed rather interesting.

Also from Scotland but from the islands further north, two sisters came for a fortnight. One was a schoolteacher on the Island of Tiree who taught Gaelic, her mother tongue. Her sister was married, and she and her husband wove Harris tweed as a cottage industry on one of the Hebridean Islands. One morning the married sister came down to breakfast with an amused smile on her face.

'I phoned my husband,' she said, laughing. 'We chatted away for a while, comparing how we both were and what the weather was doing. Then sensing something strange, I realised the person I was talking to wasn't my husband at all. I apologised and finished the call abruptly. I've no idea who he was, but clearly, he must have been from the same area as he spoke Gaelic with the same intonations as my husband.'

Her sister found this a great joke.

These two ladies also found the strength of the sun more than they were used to, and Leonard and Phyllis can still remember the delightful sight of them under the wide-brimmed hats they had bought, sitting beneath a tree on the Knöpflesbrunnen during a Sunday picnic.

One of the sisters wrote later, thanking the Holders for the holiday and saying how God had used the daily devotions and spiritual input and, in particular, a very helpful conversation with

Phyllis to prepare her for the unexpected and tragic death of someone close soon after they had returned home.

Several of the guests who came to Haus Barnabas in those early days have remained long-term friends. David and Margaret Harman, who were travelling with another couple for a holiday in Austria, stayed for a night or two on their journeys. They then became regular guests and supporters, becoming trustees of Bible in Action Trust and later providing Leonard and Phyllis with a residence address in their home and a base for them to use during their visits to Britain.

When two other couples arrived, Leonard and Phyllis realised the second couple, who hadn't personally made the booking, were known to them from their days in Horley. John, as a young man, had occasionally preached at Horley Chapel during the years before Leonard became pastor. On renewing contact with Leonard and Phyllis, he and his wife, Faith, became firm friends and, for a number of years, came out to Haus Barnabas for several weeks during January and early February to lead Bible studies and Sunday services, thus freeing Leonard and Phyllis up to visit churches and friends in Britain to promote their work and advertise the holiday opportunities in the Black Forest.

Another booking that proved to have a lasting significance for Leonard and Phyllis was from a family with five boys. They catered for themselves using the house kitchen and, during their holiday, mentioned they were wanting to move out to Germany. The husband, Chris, had studied German alongside his engineering course at university and was keen to use this in his career. The couple discussed this with Leonard and Phyllis, and the question was asked whether, if the family could find accommodation in the Utzenfeld area, this would be a help for the Holders in their local witness in giving them support at their Bible studies and Sunday service. This appeared a positive suggestion to Leonard and Phyllis, and Chris and his wife, Nicola, said they would go home and pray about this possibility.

The move happened surprisingly quickly and proved to be an interesting chapter in the Haus Barnabas story, more of which will follow in due course.

Finally, in thinking back to a few other earlier guests in Haus Barnabas in the Reiterhof, two more elderly single people are worthy of a mention. They will now both have departed this life, so Leonard has no hesitation in giving their names. A lady named Rachel had come to a meeting in Northern England when Leonard was showing pictures, talking about the Black Forest and the 'home from home' they could offer, and she booked to come for a holiday that summer. In the comfortable atmosphere of Haus Barnabas, Rachel was able to unburden her heart about the very recent death of her husband. They had married late, and through the more spiritual thinking of her husband, Rachel's faith in the Lord Jesus had been revived and nurtured. Shortly before his death, they had attended the Keswick convention in the Lake District of Britain and learned a hymn by Timothy Dudley Smith which was new to them. Her husband had loved the hymn, and for the first time since his promotion to glory, she felt able to choose it so they, as a small group, could sing it together at their Sunday evening fellowship gathering. With tears pouring down her face, she sang with full confidence and inner joy:

Safe in the shadow of the Lord,
beneath His hand and power,
I trust in Him,
I trust in Him,
my fortress and my tower.

My hope is set on God alone,
though Satan spreads his snare,
I trust in Him,
I trust in Him,
to keep me in His care.

Some guests are more challenging than others, and amongst the former was a middle-aged man from Newcastle. He was a somewhat tricky character and had lived with his parents until their recent death. He had been reading avidly the writings of Smith Wigglesworth, sometimes referred to as 'the apostle of faith', and was keen to exercise faith in his own life. Unable to accommodate him in Haus Barnabas, Leonard found him a room with breakfast in the village. His landlady, Lisbeth, understood extremely little English and her guest no German. Over breakfast, he talked to his landlady continuously with little regard for the fact she understood nothing he said. Eventually, Lisbeth called in Joyce from over the road, who was a British lady.

Joyce listened for a while with little opportunity to give an answer and, after a while, turned to Lisbeth and, speaking in German, commented, 'Don't worry, Lisbeth. He's not saying anything significant. I suggest you simply smile and nod occasionally.'

This guest really needed a holiday in which his days were organised for him. Leonard directed him on outings using public transport, but he would return early, commenting that every town looked the same and no one spoke English!

On his first day, he approached Leonard, saying he had forgotten to bring his cheque book and hoped Leonard could lend him some cash. Although hesitating to do this, Leonard realised that without any money, their guest would be unable to do anything. Leonard was assured that there would be a cheque in the post as soon as he got home. The main cost of the holiday had already been paid, so Leonard began to advance money for daily needs. Then suddenly, during the two weeks of the holiday, the bank notified Leonard that the holiday payment cheque had bounced! Oh dear!

After thinking and praying about the situation, Leonard sat down with their guest one evening, broaching the delicate subject of the cheque, whereupon with great remorse, the following story was related. His parents had recently died, and there was a considerable sum of money coming to him. His sister had warned him not to book a holiday until the money was there, but he was too impatient. Having read Smith Winklesworth, he felt he should book his holiday in faith. Although knowing the money was not in his account, he had written out the cheque to pay the holiday invoice in faith that somehow God would ensure the money would be there when needed. He was very apologetic. He had no intention to cheat or deceive and assured Leonard he would pay all that was owed as soon as he could.

Recognising that their guest's mind worked in a rather simple way and that he did have a desire to trust God, Leonard decided he needed to have patience with him, to trust him, and to continue to help him have a good holiday. In due course, a few weeks after he returned home, a new cheque arrived to cover all the expenses, which, this time, the bank honoured.

This rather unusual guest loved to talk to the ladies. Having met a village lady at the Haus Barnabas Bible study and then seeing her come into the Sunday service in the Todtnau church, he decided she was his friend and hurriedly moved to sit almost on top of her in her pew. Thankfully, she was very understanding. Another British guest in Haus Barnabas was a nurse, and she was concerned about this guest as well and tried to help him, particularly so when she realised he was diabetic and seemed to be ignoring any dietary restrictions. Her concerned attention was misread, and one day, on a group outing, spying a delicious cream cake in a baker's shop, he offered to buy it for her.

'Oh no, thank you,' our nurse friend said. 'I have to watch my weight and mustn't have cakes like that.'

'But I like my women plump' was the prompt answer that came back.

Our nurse's husband kept a sharp eye on our guest after this episode.

On another outing, Leonard included a brief stop at a very ornate church which was part of a nunnery. The main buildings housing the nuns with their surrounding gardens could be seen through an entrance gate, clearly signed as out of bounds for visitors to the church. The sign was, of course, in German. Having looked around the church – which incidentally had, in one corner, a memorial to a wartime priest whom the Nazis had taken into the forest and shot for speaking out against Hitler – Leonard decided it was time to move on. Later, someone commented that they had noticed the most adventuresome of the party looking inquisitively through the gate, and now he was nowhere to be seen. Seeing a nun coming out of their private area, Leonard explained the situation and asked permission to go in and look for the missing guest. Thankfully, he was not hard to find as his loud voice, with its distinctive Geordie accent, was issuing forth from a summer house in the grounds. Leonard approached cautiously, and there was the English gentleman, sitting in the centre of a circle of nuns, holding forth to a bemused audience who clearly had no idea what he was saying. Leonard apologised in his best German and led the intruder back to the waiting group of other Haus Barnabas guests.

The Grand Ballon, at 1,424 metres in altitude, is the highest peak of the Vosges range of mountains in the Alsace region of France across the border from the Black Forest. On a visit to the historical village of Riquewehr, Leonard was thankfully able to dissuade this same guest from purchasing a picture postcard to send to the office where he worked, advertising the Grand Ballon but illustrated by a well-endowed topless French lass. After Leonard had patiently suggested this was not really a suitable card for a Christian to send, the card was, with some obvious regret, returned to the rack.

Our friend from Northern England certainly made a strong impression on everyone he met. His German landlady was amused by him, and they managed to communicate to some degree by gesturing. They agreed somehow together to each take steps to learn the other's language before there was a return visit. When Leonard picked him up for the trip back to Zürich Airport, the departing gentleman gave Lisbeth a big hug, which she accepted happily.

Phyllis's Memories and Comments

Our visitors, in the main, found it exciting to explore a different culture but with a safety net of having us to help them out of dilemmas, inform them of what they needed to know, and speak the language for them to people when necessary. Over the years, we've had some interesting situations to deal

Guest breakfasting on balcony

with. Some have been amusing, but occasionally, there has also been the need to correct a misunderstanding. As I have often said to different ones, planning is good and right, but through experience, as soon as human beings are involved, inevitably, plans need to change, and the intended approach to things can go right out of the window!

CHAPTER

13

Bible Meetings in Haus Barnabas

Having got themselves settled into their new accommodation, Leonard and Phyllis began to put a weekly advert in both the Todtnau and the Schönau papers inviting all interested to a Wednesday evening Bible study and a Sunday morning service in their new lounge. The Todtnau church was only used for services in the summer months.

One afternoon there was a ring at the door, and an Utzenfeld lady introduced herself and asked whether she would be welcome at a Bible study. Leonard invited her in, and as they conversed, she shared the fact that her husband had recently died from cancer, and during his last few days, they had prayed

Bible study evening with guests and local believers

together. She confessed she knew next to nothing about the Bible but was eager to know more about the Christian faith. She began to come regularly to both Bible studies and the Sunday services and, as the weeks went by, confessed that it was her faith in God and the fact that she could bring everything to Him in prayer that kept her buoyant and enabled her to be a supportive mother to her two teenage children after the loss of her husband and their father. One day she commented that her parents had expressed amazement at this, and she knew that they were watching for her to collapse under the strain, not understanding where she got her strength from. A hymn that she frequently chose was 'Father, I place into your hands the things I cannot do.'

Sadly, after a couple of years, when Leonard and Phyllis really believed that this, their first village contact, was truly born-again and progressing in the Christian life, she informed them that there were to be changes in her circumstances, so she would need the baby cot she had previously lent the house to use for guests with youngsters; eventually, she had a little daughter.

Whilst Leonard and Phyllis had been extremely encouraged to watch her increasing commitment to the meetings in Haus Barnabas and what they truly believed to be evidence of her faith in Christ, they knew enough about the weaknesses of human nature and the power of the prince of darkness from whose kingdom every convert to Christ is being set free not to judge her for what had happened. She confessed to them that she had considered an abortion but had rejected this as a sinful, cowardly way out of her predicament. Her teenage daughter became hostile to her because of the situation and moved out of the house, but Leonard and Phyllis and others gave her what support they could. She continued to come regularly to the meetings until the care of her baby in a one-parent situation made her attendance increasingly irregular.

Later, when the father came to live with her, having left his own situation in a neighbouring village, her attendance slowly ceased altogether apart from the odd occasion when she would come, often breathless, to a service, saying, 'I had to get away to have some time for myself.'

Another woman who would come occasionally to Bible studies had recently moved into the area. She professed to have been converted through a Free Evangelical church in the area where she had previously lived. The minister there had encouraged her to seek out a church with a born-again minister, and she told us that she had spoken to the minister in the Todtnau church and asked him point blank whether he was born again.

'I knew from his answer, avoiding the question, that he wasn't,' she told Leonard.

This lady had quite a history. What she told Leonard and Phyllis (they really had no reason to doubt the truth of her story) was that her father was now in prison for shooting her abusive husband. She had learned to lock herself and her young daughter in her bedroom when her husband was out late, knowing that when he came home after drinking, he was invariably vicious and abusive. The situation was a great concern to her own father, and one evening he was with her when the husband returned and, during a serious argument, had taken out a revolver and shot her husband, killing him. This lady had her own business as a beautician and had moved up to a neighbouring village, but she herself had a real problem with alcohol and also seemed to find it impossible to live without a man. She never came regularly to the meetings but would often ring to talk to Phyllis, particularly when she was depressed and mostly the worse for drink. Leonard and Phyllis did their best to help her but sadly without any noticeable effect.

There was one particular Bible study evening which Leonard and Phyllis found quite bizarre. The above-mentioned lady arrived with a man friend who began to maintain he was a Christian because of his baptism in the Catholic Church and his reasonably good living. The other, earlier-mentioned lady was also at the Bible study that day, and both began to bring arguments against this, pointing out the necessity of a personal faith in Jesus Christ. This would have been very encouraging except for the fact that neither of the two ladies were living a moral Christian life. One was carrying an illegitimate child, and the other was drinking heavily and associating with different men friends. The situation drove the Holders to prayer and challenged Leonard to try and ensure his preaching ministry had the right balance between faith and Christian living. Ultimately, we know it is only the power of the Holy Spirit that can change a person's heart and give them strength to lead a moral life.

Living in Utzenfeld was an English lady by the name of Joyce. Her presence was brought to Leonard and Phyllis's attention in several ways long before they met her. One of the garden gates, as one walked through the village, bore the sign 'Please shut the gate'. Invariably, it was left open, perhaps because the Germans didn't understand the message.

Then in conversation with a couple Leonard had got to know through English teaching, the following comment was made: 'There's an English lady in the village, you know. Joyce is the wife of a farmer, and it's common knowledge that she always talks to her cows in English!'

Joyce was quite a shy person and made no attempt to continue a conversation when Leonard greeted her in the local shop. Incidentally, another villager claimed that the Utzenfeld village store was probably the first shop in Germany to offer self-service. When Joyce arrived in the 1950s, she spoke no German and so would go around the shop shelves helping herself to what she needed. Recognising her problem, the shop provided a basket for her to use for this.

One Sunday morning, shortly before the start of the morning service, Joyce was seen pushing her bicycle up the steep drive to the entrance to Haus Barnabas. Leonard and Phyllis were thrilled, and very soon, as she began to come regularly to the Sunday service, they established a good relationship with this very interesting lady from Sittingbourne in Kent.

Joyce's story is very different from that of either of the other ladies mentioned. She was an only child, and her father was an elder in a Congregational church in Sittingbourne. During the war years, she was sent to work as a land girl on a farm near Egerton in Kent where, interestingly, the farm manager was a member of Union Chapel, Bethersden. Also working on the farm were two German prisoners of war, and Joyce, it seems, fell in love with one of them, a young man named Helmut Behringer. At the end of the war, Helmut was sent home to Germany, to his family, who farmed in the village of Utzenfeld, in the Black Forest. The couple remained in contact, and in the early fifties, Joyce left her homeland and parents and emigrated to Utzenfeld, where she and Helmut were married. One can only imagine how difficult the situation must have been for Joyce, and her courage is to be admired. She spoke no German and found herself living in the Behringer family home, where only the local dialect of Alemannic was spoken. Only her husband could speak sufficient English to communicate with her, and he was also working full time in the local mine. One can imagine what pleasure it would have given Joyce to speak English to the cows she was caring for and milking every day. The situation must also have been a disappointment and perhaps embarrassment too for Joyce's parents in England. The war was just over, and the Germans had been the enemy, causing much destruction across Britain, and many families were mourning the loss of their young sons and husbands. Being an elder in the Congregational Church, no doubt Joyce's father and mother too would have prayed for their daughter. Leonard can't help wondering if one reason God had sent him and Phyllis to Utzenfeld was in answer, many years after their death, to the prayers of Joyce's parents.

Leonard and Phyllis never quite knew how it was spiritually with Joyce. She came regularly to the Sunday service, cycling through the village on her bicycle. She never joined in with the singing and once commented that all her life, she had never sung and didn't think she could. She commented to a guest that she came to the service at first because of the English contact, and on reporting this, the guest felt she was strongly implying she now came for more than this. By the time Leonard and Phyllis appeared on the scene, Joyce's three children had married and produced grandchildren for her and Helmut, and very shortly, great-grandchildren also appeared. All of her family were baptised in the Catholic Church in the Behringer tradition, but Joyce herself remained aloof from the RC Church. She supported the ministry of Haus Barnabas financially through the offering box each Sunday and once or twice, when kept away from the services through illness, passed an envelope to Leonard containing her offerings for the weeks missed. There is one very remarkable incident in regard to this. Joyce had not been able to attend the services for several weeks, and one Sunday morning in the middle of the sermon, when Leonard was preaching on Elijah and the way God provided for his servant by sending food by means of ravens, there was a shout from the reception area in Haus Barnabas. Phyllis went to investigate and was handed an envelope by a relative of Joyce who had been visiting her. In the envelope was a gift of three hundred euros from Joyce. It came at a needy time for Haus Barnabas and gave strong proof that the God of Elijah is the same today.

There was one hymn which Joyce chose several times when there was an open opportunity for the congregation to suggest hymns to sing:

There is a green hill far away,
outside a city wall,
where the dear Lord was crucified,
who died to save us all.

In Joyce's younger years in Britain, the BBC would always play this hymn before the 7:00 a.m. news on Good Friday, and hearing it sung again in Haus Barnabas no doubt revived memories for her. Leonard and Phyllis really hoped, however, that the words meant more to her than memories.

There was no other good enough
to pay the price of sin.
He only could unlock the gate
of heaven and let us in.

Joyce died in 2017, and Leonard was invited by her family to take the funeral service. The chapel attached to the cemetery in Schönau was packed with family, friends, and Utzenfeld village folk. The whole service was, of course, in German, and after reading a selection of appropriate Bible passages, Leonard gave a brief summary of Joyce's life and then homed into this hymn which – at Haus Barnabas, he said – is referred to as 'Joyce's hymn'. Leonard explained its meaning in German, which is a wonderful explanation of the Gospel, and then Phyllis and their colleague Deborah sang it, with Deborah playing the guitar. Leonard read verses from Paul's first epistle to the Corinthians at the graveside and was equipped with a microphone linked to loudspeakers on the trees around.

There were various encouragements following this funeral address. Joyce's family were very appreciative and also mentioned that a couple of different people had said to them that they had had second thoughts about coming but were so glad they did. Another lady in the village telephoned the next day to thank Leonard very much for his sermon. Leonard and Phyllis continue to pray that seed sown through God's Word during their ministry in Utzenfeld might even yet bear fruit.

CHAPTER
✻
14
—

Interesting Contacts through English Teaching

Leonard had a few older students in his English classes who had experienced the war years. Interestingly, none whom Phyllis and Leonard met expressed any problem with British people; rather, whether they said it or not, there was a sense of gratitude that Britain and the Allies had liberated them from the oppressive power of Hitler and Nazism. There was also an appreciation and even admiration of the friendliness of the British. An owner of a furniture business on the point of retirement engaged Leonard to teach him English because a brief visit to the UK had given him a strong desire to spend more time there in his camper van.

'You British are so friendly,' he said, smiling. 'Everyone addressed me as *du*, meaning, of course, "you".'

To understand the significance of this comment, it must be realised that the German language, as also the French, has two forms of our British word 'you'. The normal form in German is *sie*, unless you are a child, animal, or close friend, and then the word *du* is used. The *sie* form enables the Germans to keep a distance from one another in their relationships, and progress into a '*du*' relationship is considered cause for a celebration. Having said this, the younger generation seem more willing to lapse far more easily into '*du*' relationships.

On another occasion, a tradesman, in conversation, commented with some enthusiasm on the British sense of humour.

'I was in London,' he said, 'and in looking for somewhere to stay the night, I went into what appeared to be a bed-and-breakfast guesthouse.

'The young man I saw called his father, and the first thing the father said was "Are you German? Have you lost anything?"

'"Not that I'm aware of," I answered.

'"How about a war or two?" came back the reply.'

He went on to say that it was all said in a very friendly way, and the man then provided him with a bed for the night and was extremely helpful and friendly, with no sign of animosity because of his nationality.

A man in his eighties joined one of Leonard's language courses. Kurt was a very interesting old man. He was Protestant rather than Catholic but, after the passing of his first wife, had come to the Black Forest to marry a lady who played the organ in the large Roman Catholic church in Schönau. Getting to know Leonard as his English teacher, he would occasionally come to one of the Haus Barnabas Sunday services. He once made a comment which Leonard interpreted as being complimentary.

'Len,' he commented in an appreciative tone as Leonard shook hands with him after the service, 'I can see you are not simply a *Beamter*.' (A *Beamter* is a civil servant paid by the state.) The comment no doubt indicated how Kurt considered some of the ministers in the churches he had attended.

Kurt invited Leonard and Phyllis to his home for afternoon coffee and cake and to meet his wife. He had bought his wife a small pipe organ for her to practise on for the church services. He explained that so as not to disturb the neighbours, they had had to soundproof the room. Knowing that Phyllis played the organ in the Todtnau church for their service, Kurt's wife suggested she would play some of her music if Phyllis would like to play some of hers.

She played something from Bach, and then when Phyllis played a couple of the hymns they often sang in the service, 'To God

Be the Glory' and 'How Great Thou Art', she said with a hint of astonishment, 'Do you sing that? But that is nice!'

After they had enjoyed the afternoon refreshment, Kurt took Leonard into his study and showed him his Bible.

'I read this every morning,' he said.

He went on to explain that he didn't sleep too well as he had tinnitus in his ears, which kept him awake. He got up about 5:00 a.m. and had a Bible daily reading plan that he used. This gave Leonard the opportunity to talk of his own love for the Bible, and he certainly got the impression that Kurt was a born-again man who loved Jesus.

Kurt was not afraid to talk about the war. He commented that his grandchildren had often asked him how he could have worked for Hitler and supported him. His answer was that when he was a young man, most of Germany saw Hitler as a saviour. He provided the nation with work, and few had any idea what this sudden employment was leading to. Kurt's home had been in the eastern part of Germany, and as the war was coming to an end, his wife and children had to flee westward as the Russian army moved in. One young child died because of the extreme conditions the family had faced on that journey, and then after he himself was dismissed from the army, it took him weeks to locate where his wife and children were.

Kurt worked hard at his English learning and enjoyed the challenge; other members of the class were very helpful to him. He had problems with his heart, and when Leonard heard he had had a heart attack and been rushed to hospital, he went round to see his wife.

'I've had a strange experience,' she said. 'I thought with Kurt away, I would read the Bible passage allocated for the day in his little booklet. It was a reading in the fifth book of Moses, and you'll never guess what one of the verses said.'

'Tell me,' answered Leonard with interest.

'You know our family name is Ruben,' she said. 'As you can guess, I was really reading the Bible for some comfort with Kurt being rushed to hospital, and there before my eyes was it written,

"Ruben lebe, und sterbe nicht." [Let Reuben live and not die.[50]] I couldn't believe it.'

Leonard had a brief prayer with Frau Ruben and thanked the Lord for the encouragement this Bible verse had given her and prayed that Kurt would quickly be able to come home again.

Kurt did get over the heart attack, and the Lord gave him several more months with his wife there in Schönau before he was called home to glory.

Another of Leonard's students approached him after one of the lessons and asked whether he knew of a family in England with a son of similar age to her own with whom there could be an exchange arrangement. She explained that her son Jo was eager to go to Britain to improve his English, but she herself was not too happy about this. She felt that too often, when pupils went on an exchange made by the school, they spent too much time talking together in German and made little progress in English.

Leonard was able to make arrangements for her son to stay with a Christian family in Dudley. They had been on holiday in Haus Barnabas the year before and had a son of similar age to Jo.

The outcome was that soon after Jo returned home, he began coming to Bible studies in Haus Barnabas. Leonard was very encouraged with the amount of Bible knowledge he had. Jo told him that the Catholic priest would come to the school for religious knowledge lessons and would teach them the Bible.

One evening Jo rang Leonard, asking whether it would be convenient to come round to talk to him. He very quickly got to the reason for his visit. He wanted to know how he could be born again. It was clear that what he had learned from the Bible had convinced him that his baptism into the Roman Catholic Church was not sufficient for his salvation. After Leonard had read John 3 with him and explained that it was a personal faith and trust in Jesus Christ and His redemptive work on Calvary alone that could ensure eternal life, he suggested they should pray together.

After Leonard's prayer, Jo prayed and very clearly and deliberately expressed his trust in Jesus Christ as his Saviour.

---

50 Deuteronomy 33:6.

Leonard remembers him expressing this trust in Christ as illustrated by a rock climber trusting himself completely to the rope he was using to scale a rock face. This was a thrilling moment for Leonard and a tremendous encouragement in the face of the many discouragements. Very soon after this, Jo left home to study medicine in Freiburg but would often come to Sunday services when he was home for the weekend. He began also to bring along a girlfriend, a friend from his school days who was also studying medicine. It appears he had influenced her as she too expressed a commitment to Christ. Eventually, Leonard and Phyllis were invited to their wedding in the Catholic church in Todtnauberg, and then eventually, the couple took over a doctor's surgery in a Swiss Alpine village.

CHAPTER

15

Support in Haus Barnabas

A Christian family coming from Britain joined Leonard and Phyllis in Haus Barnabas during the winter of 1993. As mentioned earlier, this came about after they had enjoyed a summer holiday in Utzenfeld, and it was also the first step in fulfilling the husband's dream, since university days, of working in Germany. It was agreed that they could live in Haus Barnabas over the winter months, using the kitchen and looking after themselves. In the spring, once guests wanted to come, they agreed that they would find accommodation elsewhere.

Leonard and Phyllis valued the Christian fellowship and found it particularly encouraging to have their support in prayer as the four eventually allocated a time to regularly pray together for the village and surrounding area.

It was, however, very tough going for the family. Their five boys ranged in age from about 3 up to 12 years and were sent to local German schools. Unfortunately, for several years, the husband was unable to find the employment he was hoping for. The wife was a qualified nurse, and these were in demand, so quite quickly, she was able to get a job on the district providing nursing care to mostly elderly folk. Her problem was that her German was still very basic, and she had a daily fear of finding herself in a situation where she would need to contact a doctor and be unable to do so because of the language. She once commented that one older man scarred by war found it extremely difficult to allow a British woman to kneel before him and tend his feet.

The family looked after themselves, and taking over the kitchen, they generously paid for Leonard and Phyllis to have kitchen units of their own along one wall in the large room they used as bedroom, personal sitting room, and office. After living in Haus Barnabas for six months over winter, the following May, they were able to rent a big enough apartment for themselves in the village. Eventually, after a couple of years, the husband was able to get employment as a stress engineer in a firm based at Basel-Mulhouse Airport. At this point, they also decided to move across to the Rhine Plain, where they found fellowship in a larger church and the boys had other Christian young people. Leonard and Phyllis appreciated it very much when the parents arranged to continue their prayer times with them. For many months, one evening a week, they would motor the fifteen miles or so across the mountains to join with Leonard and Phyllis to pray for the spiritual needs of Utzenfeld and the surrounding Black Forest villages.

Although the husband was not a man for public speaking, he was gifted in speaking of Jesus and his own personal faith in one-to-one situations. This led to one very significant development for Haus Barnabas when, at a meeting arranged by the authorities for unemployed people seeking jobs, he met another English man and invited him to the Christmas carol service in Haus Barnabas. The story of Eric deserves another chapter.

CHAPTER

16

Eric

Since Eric is now in glory with his Saviour, Leonard feels able to recount their experiences with him in some detail.

Eric originated from St Helens in Lancashire, and various members of his family had been employed at the Pilkington glass works. His parents separated when he was still young, and he lived with his father in St Helens. There was obviously no contact at all with his mother as he was already an adult when he discovered he had a brother who was living with their mother in the London area.

Eric joined the RAF training as an electrician, and during a posting in Germany, he met and married a German girl. Eventually, after leaving the RAF, the couple settled in Germany and produced three daughters, and Eric practised his electrical training in a German firm.

At some point, Eric separated from his wife, and Leonard knows his daughters later accused him of deserting their mother. After his firm moved him down to Southern Germany, Eric moved in with a German lady who was interestingly from a Sinti background. She would speak of her father as an accomplished violin player, but her family suffered badly under the Nazis. Soon after he had arrived in the Black Forest region, Eric's firm made him redundant, and it was at this point he was invited to the Christmas carol service Leonard and Phyllis were arranging.

Although open to all, it was particularly the students in his language classes that Leonard had in mind when arranging the programme for the evening. The programme was conducted in German, and in addition to some German carols, Leonard included several English carols, using the opportunity when translating the English to explain the Gospel. Bible readings were in German. Eric obviously appreciated the evening, and it was probably the fact of being reminded of English carols after many years in Germany which played a part in this enjoyment. However, during the next couple of days, he telephoned and enquired about the time of the Sunday service. Having come once to the Sunday service, he subsequently attended almost every Sunday without exception for many years.

Leonard and Phyllis slowly got to learn more of his situation, but he kept remarkably quiet about the lady with whom he was living. During the summer, the services were still held in the Todtnau church, and because of this, they were more formal and structured. Between the end of September and the following June, they were held in the lounge of Haus Barnabas, where the chairs were arranged in a circle. Leonard encouraged a time of open prayer in the middle of the service prior to the sermon, which was either in German or English or both depending on who was in the congregation. It was many years before Eric prayed publicly, but he would often ask questions or add a comment in the middle of the sermon. Leonard didn't discourage this as it showed he was listening and revealed what he was thinking. It also gave the opportunity to explain things further. He had a unique little phrase he would use when he had understood something new:

'Len, I've just had a GBO!' he would exclaim.

To anyone new in a service, it was necessary to explain that a penny had dropped about something for Eric and that a GBO could be interpreted as a 'glimpse of the blooming obvious'.

In the early days of Eric coming to Haus Barnabas, he once began to talk about evolution over millions of years. Leonard remembers it being pointed out to him that there were many eminent scientists who accepted a young earth created by a wise Creator. The whole subject of creation began to interest him, and he was lent a number of books to read. Soon. Eric readily embraced a literal interpretation of Genesis 1 and, for a while, loved to talk about it. He considered a big bang as quite a plausible way for God to have got creation under way and wrote his own theory of how it could have all happened.

For some months, Eric hardly mentioned the partner he was living with, but one Sunday she came along with him. Eric's partner had a little dog called Lady, and once Leonard and Phyllis agreed that they were happy for Lady to come to the service with her, she began to attend regularly.

Sunday service in Haus Barnabas
with Eric in foreground

Lady would arrive in her basket and would remain very quiet and attentive during the service. Her owner maintained she must be a Christian dog as she obviously enjoyed coming to church.

Leonard has been known to comment, 'We had our Lady at the service this morning.'

One evening Eric called to talk to Leonard. He had obviously had a disagreement with his partner and said he was thinking of leaving her. Leonard had to think hard as how to advise on this in a way that honoured God as they were not married. After a silent prayer, he felt it right to tell Eric it would be wrong to leave because of a disagreement. They had been together for about five years, and Leonard considered that before God, this constituted a commitment which needed to be honoured.

Eventually, the couple agreed to marry. This was simply to be a registry office wedding in the town hall where the couple lived, but for different reasons, the date kept being postponed.

Leonard and Phyllis were invited to be the witnesses of the couple's legal commitment to each other, but the evening before it was due to happen, Eric rang Leonard, saying, 'I told the town hall we want our pastor to say something at the wedding. Is this all right with you?'

The female official marrying them went through the legal requirements at speed and then handed the gathered company of about fifteen relatives and friends over to Leonard. He read a few Bible passages about marriage, which he had also printed out to distribute to the assembled folk, and then, particularly addressing the newlywed couple – who, in fact, had already had several years of living and coping with each other – indicated a few words of wisdom that God Himself had given in His Word and encouraged them to respond to our Lord Jesus's promise: 'If anyone loves Me, he will keep My word; and My Father will love him, and We will make our home with him.'[51]

Eric's wife later confided in Leonard that she hadn't married Eric out of love but in obedience to the Lord. Their relationship was often turbulent, but in Eric's latter years, his wife proved beyond any shadow of doubt her devotion to him.

After the wedding, one of the relatives approached Leonard, asking him whether he would bury her. After regaining his composure, Leonard suggested she come to the services in Haus Barnabas so he could get to know her prior to the solemn occasion of her funeral. Eric was able to give her a Bible after this, but Leonard heard no more from her.

Eric and his wife's development in the Christian faith grew slowly. Leonard remembers Eric saying to him after a service one Sunday, 'You appear to speak far more about faith than our Christian duties, Len.'

Encouragingly, a few weeks later, he came back with a further comment: 'I understand it now, Len. We need to have faith in Christ first, and then we serve Him out of love, not duty.'

The subject of baptism cropped up occasionally in the preaching, but Leonard decided not to put any pressure on Eric about this, so it was a real joy when, one day, he asked whether it would be possible for Leonard to baptise him. His wife also talked

---

51 John 14:23.

to Leonard about being baptised. This was a big thing for her as her identification as a Roman Catholic was important to her, and she had been baptised into the Catholic Church as an infant.

She expressed a great desire to be baptised as a believer but added, 'I don't want to become a Baptist.'

Leonard pointed out that to be baptised as a believer was an expression of her faith in Christ and a desire to follow Him and that this was completely independent of any particular denomination.

For the baptism, they were able to use a guesthouse in a neighbouring village which had a swimming pool. The owners were believing Christians from further north in Germany and allowed them to use the swimming pool without charge on the understanding that the baptism congregation could be served with refreshments afterwards at the normal rates.

It was a significant occasion for Leonard and Phyllis's ministry in the Black Forest as there were several local people there, and it was an opportunity for Leonard to indicate the link between baptism and faith as shown in the Scriptures: 'He who believes and is baptised will be saved; but he who does not believe will be condemned.'[52]

As each of the two candidates came out of the water, the small group standing around the pool sang a chorus by Dave Bilbrough which Eric loved – 'I am a new creation, no more in condemnation. Here in the grace of God I stand.' Eric was baptised first when the chorus was sung in English, accompanied by guitar, and, following the baptism of his wife, sung again in German.

Soon after her baptism, Eric's wife had a remarkable experience. She had smoked most of her life and had tried, without success, to give it up several times. However, on returning home after a Sunday service, she later reported to Leonard that she had heard a voice behind her which made her turn to see who was there.

The room was empty, but she had clearly heard the voice saying, 'Waltraud, if you don't stop smoking you, will die.'

Believing this was God speaking to her, she threw the packet of cigarettes in the rubbish bin and amazingly found she had the

---

52 Mark 16:16.

strength of mind and body to stop smoking. Soon after this, she needed an operation to deal with the narrowing of specific veins, and the doctor commented to her that if she had still been a smoker, she would probably have died.

After many years, the couple moved farther away and, without a car, ceased coming to the Haus Barnabas services. Leonard and Phyllis and the Haus Barnabas team maintained contact with them, and Leonard took Eric's funeral in 2017. This gave the opportunity to preach the Gospel of salvation through Christ alone to a number of Eric's family, namely, his brother from London and three daughters from his first marriage, who all claimed to be atheists.

A comment by one of Eric's daughters after the service illustrates so clearly the thinking of most of the world. In response to Leonard's comment during the services that it was the death of Christ and Eric's faith in Him that was the only ground on which God could receive him into heaven, the daughter said, 'But surely, my father wasn't as bad as that.'

CHAPTER

17

Tourist Trips to Britain

Leonard can't remember where the idea first came from, whether from himself or his students, but during the years he was teaching, he and Phyllis took at least four groups of his English language students at different times to Britain.

Leonard and Phyllis drove the groups of five or six mature German students across France to Calais, where they boarded the ferry to Dover. They usually stayed one night in a hotel before reaching Calais and, on a couple of occasions, were treated to an enjoyable evening meal by Christian friends in Belgium. As well as introducing his students to some of the sights of Britain, Leonard planned for there to be the opportunity for Christian witness. On the Sundays, he mentioned he wanted to go to a morning church service and that the group would be very welcome to come with him or simply have a morning free. Most members of the different groups were interested to experience an English service and opted to go along with Leonard and Phyllis. Although they were never sure how much they understood of the English, there was one notable service when attending an Evangelical Anglican church. The minister distributed printed notes of his sermon to all who were interested as they left the church. Each of the group took a copy, and then as they sat together that Sunday evening, they asked Leonard to work through the notes and explain everything in German.

Also, as they travelled, Phyllis put a range of different music cassettes in the car's stereo, including one or two Christian ones. One particular Christian cassette was very popular, and several of the group asked whether Leonard could get them a copy as a memento of the holiday. The song was one by Bryn and Sally Heyworth:

What kind of love is this?
That gave himself for me.
I am the guilty one,
yet I go free.
What kind of love is this?
A love I've never known.
I didn't even know his name.
What kind of love is this?

Leonard took the groups to different parts of Britain that he and Phyllis knew and where they had friends. These included the Portsmouth/Southampton area, Weymouth and the Dorset coast, and North Wales. In contacting friends in these areas, they were invited into different homes for an evening meal and sometimes more than once. The group were extremely impressed by the friendliness and kind hospitality they received, and invariably, grace was said before each meal. One lady remarked to Phyllis that she had noticed all the people they visited were believing Christians as she had noticed different Scripture texts around. Another lady commented as they returned to Germany that she had no idea how Leonard and Phyllis could live amongst the German Black Forest folk, who were so cold and unfriendly in comparison to their friends in Britain.

On most of the visits, the groups wanted to spend at least one day in London, and one group expressed a strong wish to attend a London musical. Leonard tried to get tickets for *Les Misérables* but without success but then had the brainwave to ask a friend who worked in London if she would be able to get tickets for him.

Surprisingly, on telephoning the ticket office, she discovered a group booked for one of the stalls had just cancelled, and she was able to purchase tickets for Leonard and his German students. To sit together in one of the stalls looking straight down on the stage was a London experience the group would never forget.

On another occasion, Leonard was able to recruit the services of a friend who drove tourist coaches and was experienced in driving around the main attractions of London. They picked him up from his home, and sitting next to Leonard in the front of the vehicle, he was able to navigate them around the London sights, acting like the perfect tour guide.

Leonard and Phyllis discovered they saw Britain through different eyes when coming as tourists. Good use was made of each day, and places visited during the different trips included Nelson's ship, *Victory*, in Portsmouth; Arundel Castle; the sea front and narrow shopping lanes in Brighton; the Dorset coastline; and Caernarfon Castle in North Wales as well as a walking tour around the city of Chester led by a friend residing there. Visits to several beaches were of particular interest to the German tourists who lived at least five hundred miles from any coastline. They collected shells like little children, and Leonard remembers one lady standing on the beach, facing the sea, and expressing wonder and delight as a strong sea breeze blew through her hair.

'At home,' she said, gasping as she braced herself against the salty air, 'I'm rather afraid of wind, but this is marvellous.'

They experienced the delight of meals in English pubs, which completely changed their opinion of British cuisine. In every way, the British tours were considered a great success by Leonard's students. There were indications that the exposure to the evangelical form of Christianity they experienced, both in the church services and through the lives of Christians visited, made an impression. One lady informed Leonard that after the holiday, she knew she wanted to take the Christian faith more seriously and debated whether to attend Haus Barnabas services or be more involved in her Catholic church. She chose the latter. Two or three others began to occasionally attend Haus Barnabas services, but once they were back in their home environment, this sadly didn't last very long.

Many Germans take life very seriously, and one lady commented as they arrived back in the Black Forest that she had laughed more that week than in the whole of her life.

On a couple of occasions when Leonard was somewhat unsure of the route they were taking, he was heard to comment, 'We'll just see what happens.'

There was great astonishment expressed by one passenger at this remark. It would appear this way of thinking was a complete anathema to her. On one trip, there was also disbelief and alarm when Leonard informed them, when asked, that he had no road map with him. These were days before satnavs, but the parts of Britain visited were all quite well known to Leonard and Phyllis.

There were several interesting incidents, but one rather humbling one was when they were around a meal table with a family who had holidayed in Haus Barnabas, one of the German ladies asked the two teenage children what they had liked best about the Black Forest.

The answer came back – 'Len and Phyl.'

CHAPTER

18

British Students

A good number of students and young people have come as short-term helpers to Haus Barnabas over the years, and this chapter will mention two very significant language students whom God sent in the early years.

Students of languages at universities are required to spend time in the country of the language they are studying, and for Ruth, this meant Germany. After receiving a letter asking whether it would be possible for her to spend this time in Haus Barnabas, Leonard suggested meeting up in Britain prior to any firm arrangement. This first meeting was in the car park of a Baptist chapel in Dunstable where Leonard was due to preach one Sunday evening. A fourteenth-century proverb states, 'Great oaks from little acorns grow,' and neither Leonard and Phyllis nor Ruth and her mother had any idea what would develop from that first fleeting encounter in that Bedfordshire car park.

Leonard had informed Ruth and later other language students who wanted to come to Haus Barnabas that unfortunately (apart from Bible studies, when local people were involved), since most of the guests staying in the house were English speaking, they would need to find ways to involve themselves in life outside of the house to gain experience of the German language. Ruth did this very well. She contacted the grammar school in Schönau and requested permission to attend some of the classes with the sixth-form pupils. Later, she also helped with English lessons in another secondary school in the town.

During Ruth's year in Haus Barnabas, a relationship developed between her and the elder Holder son. Geoffrey, by this time, was well advanced in his medical studies and still living in Basel, but he would visit Haus Barnabas frequently and find Ruth's company congenial; they would chat together for hours. This led to something closer than mere friendship, and they were married at Stanmore Chapel in North London, where Ruth's father was pastor, in December 1995, shortly after Geoffrey's final medical exams in Basel. Leonard was pleased to take the ceremony while Ruth's father gave his daughter away.

Marriage of Geoffrey and Ruth 1995

Marriage unites together more than just the two people involved. It brings two families together, and this is particularly noticeable when obviously, you share the same grandchildren. When Leonard first heard that Ruth's father was the pastor of an evangelical church, he somehow imagined him to be a rather awe-inspiring figure. Any illusion of sanctimony in Pastor Colin soon vanished, and Leonard has a vivid memory of masses of black smoke billowing into the Black Forest sky from behind a pile of builders' gravel in the yard behind Haus Barnabas. The London pastor was vainly attempting to discretely dispose of old car oil, left from an oil change, by burning! Thankfully, neither the police nor the fire service came to investigate, but his wife suggested Haus Barnabas should disown him if challenged about the event. The two families have enjoyed each other's company over the years, and the rather unique Pastor Colin has successfully led a number of weeks of ministry in Haus Barnabas since that first encounter.

Another significant development arising from this coming together of the two families was the invitation to use the church hall at Stanmore Chapel for Haus Barnabas reunions. These became an annual opportunity for past and potential guests and friends to meet together with Leonard and Phyllis. The afternoon included a presentation of holiday photos, a catch-up of news of Haus Barnabas, a short time of prayer, and a final short Bible message, often given by Pastor Colin.

The second student helper from those early years, whose initial summer visit had long-term significance for Haus Barnabas, made an unfortunate introduction by missing her flight. However, she was able to travel on the following one and arrived safely at Basel Airport later that day. She was studying both French and German at the University of Essex and had selected French as her major subject. With her having already spent a year in Lyon, France, it was still required of her to a have a few months in Germany. A previous attempt to fulfil this duty, working as an au pair in a German home, had not worked too well, and she hoped this second attempt through a few weeks in the Christian environment of Haus Barnabas would be a better option. Many voluntary helpers at Haus Barnabas over the years couldn't resist applying for a revisit, and Deborah Rule returned for the next summer after successfully graduating. She had set her heart on the thought of serving God somehow in France, but after she completed a 'Teaching English as Foreign Language course' at Cambridge, Leonard spoke to her about the possibility of returning to Utzenfeld to help him in the increasing opportunities of teaching English in the Black Forest. This, she did, and after reluctantly giving up the idea of France, she is still serving God in Haus Barnabas twenty-five years later. Her language skills play a major role in the running and witness of the house.

CHAPTER

19

Other Interesting Guests

Having learned that a number of enquiring guests were not coming to Haus Barnabas because it only offered bed and breakfast with no evening meal, Leonard decided something needed to be done about this. After thinking it through, they began to offer an 'evening meal package'. This involved either Leonard or Phyllis, sometimes both, taking guests out for a meal at local restaurants for three evenings, introducing them to German restaurants and menus, with the idea of giving them the confidence to go out two evenings in the week by themselves. The remaining two evenings, Leonard and Phyllis prepared an easy evening meal in the house, mostly cold ham or smoked salmon with salad and boiled potatoes. This worked very well, and eating together for five days in seven enabled Leonard and Phyllis to get closer to their guests in relaxed conversation around a meal table.

Sunday evening fellowship also became a significant part of the holiday for many guests. After a more formal Sunday morning service, the evening fellowship was very relaxed. Most Sundays, the time revolved around hymn singing. Guests chose the hymns to sing, and Leonard encouraged them to share their reason for choosing a particular hymn, pressing them to share past experiences in which that hymn had played a part. He would also invite at least one person to share with the group how God had led them to faith in Him.

On picking up a single British gentleman from the airport, by way of conversation, Leonard asked him what his hobbies were. This can sometimes give an idea of the sort of places to recommend to guests during their holiday. The answer the gentleman gave was quite unexpected.

'My hobbies are explosives and hot air balloons,' he responded, looking at Leonard with a smile.

He went on to explain how he had found a way of combining both of these interests. Using a simple plastic rubbish bag opened out to give a single sheet of plastic, tying a string from each corner, and bringing the four strings down and tying them together at a suitable distance below the plastic, one can form a simple umbrella-type construction. The potential hot air balloon is then completed by soaking a wad of light cloth in methylated spirits and attaching it to the joined strings below the plastic. Once the methylated spirit-soaked cloth is set alight, the resulting hot air will cause the whole structure to rise into the sky. It will need a couple of people to hold out the upper canopy as the methylated spirit-soaked cloth is lit below and then to let it go as the hot air rises and takes the whole structure heavenward.

'In addition,' said this unusual Haus Barnabas guest, 'I like to fix a chemical to the top of the plastic which will ignite when warmed.'

Leonard thinks he mentioned magnesium – or was it phosphorus?

Then he added with a gleeful smile, 'The whole thing goes up in flames high in the sky.'

Later, it turned out the guest had brought with him all that was needed to perform such an experiment.

One evening, after one of the Haus Barnabas meals eaten out in the delightful Wiese Restaurant in the centre of Utzenfeld, the guests had wandered home with full stomachs. Fully satiated with Black Forest fare and washed down with beer, wine, or apple juice, they agreed enthusiastically to witness an exploding hot air balloon. All went well with the preparation, and soon, the 'balloon' was rising from the open space behind the Reiterhof. High up, it suddenly burst into flames and dropped back rapidly to terra firma. Seeing the flames, Leonard was suddenly aware that a breeze could waft the burning balloon into the forest and get an infamous Haus Barnabas into the local history books for burning down the Utzenfeld Schwarzwald. Thankfully, it was a still evening, and the flaming contraption landed safely on hard soil only a few feet from the group of watching guests.

Another couple from this earlier period were interesting for completely different reasons. The wife was German by birth, from a village not far from Utzenfeld, and one of the objectives of the holiday was to visit her home area to show it to her English husband. Leonard sensed she had come to Haus Barnabas with a rather critical spirit. Perhaps her thought was *What right have these British people to run a guesthouse in my homeland?* but contrary to her expectations, she expressed delight at the strength of the coffee served at breakfast and congratulated Leonard and Phyllis on the Black Forest gateau dished up for dessert on Sunday. However, the most remarkable incident in connection with their visit was an encounter with other guests at the Sunday service in the Todtnau church. This second couple had arrived latish on the Saturday and, as they were self-catering, had not met the others at breakfast. Whilst sitting in church a few rows behind the English husband with the German wife, the second husband recognised the shape of the back of the man's head in front of him and could hardly believe his eyes! It was a close friend from the past with whom he had shared a flat twenty years or so earlier in London when studying and attending Dr Martyn Lloyd Jones's ministry at Westminster Chapel. Their circumstances had caused them to drift apart, and one couple had also spent several years in Australia. They recognised such an encounter like that on holiday to have been God's gracious providence for them.

Several groups of guests came from time to time, mostly wanting to self-cater. One group Leonard remembers well was a group of Chinese Christians from a Chinese church in Britain. They decided to hire bikes to get around, but because there were only two or three available, they came cycling back with three people on each bike, which would have upset the German police had they been spotted.

Another guest whose first visit proved to be the beginning of a continuing partnership in the work arrived at Haus Barnabas in the closing years of the twentieth century. Timothy Brooks felt God's call to work with Leonard and Phyllis and to marry their co-worker Deborah. The couple married during the year 2001 and settled in a small flat in another part of the Reiterhof building.

Over the years, God sent to Haus Barnabas a number of interesting guests with considerable significance both within the Christ's church or with connections to famous names within the wider world. One of the earliest was the daughter of the evangelist used mightily by God in the Hebrides Revival of the mid-twentieth century, Duncan Campbell. When later, during a theme week on revivals, the house considered the events brought about through the outpouring of God's Holy Spirit on the Isle of Lewis, it was a joy to remember they had entertained the daughter of the leading evangelist, with her Swiss pastor husband in the first Haus Barnabas twenty years earlier.

During Leonard's teenage years, the minister of Above Bar Church, Southampton, Leith Samuel, was having a wide influence in the evangelical world through his preaching and writing. Leonard and Phyllis remember welcoming him and his wife into their little Schlechtnau apartment before taking them to accommodation they had booked for them. They remember marvelling at Leith Samuel's pastoral gifts when, after a short relaxed conversation over a cup of tea, he had taken the couple's circumstances very much to heart and succinctly brought these to the Lord in a brief prayer before leaving.

Amongst several other well-known Christian ministers, one other stands out for a special mention. Having retired from a pastoral position in a large church, he lost a beloved and supporting wife and was making the first holiday without her company. His family was concerned for him as he was still mourning the loss of his wife, and they feared two weeks by himself in Germany might be more than he could cope with. He confessed this to Leonard in a personal conversation and commented that he had discovered that one of his caring children had slipped an air ticket into his bag for a return flight to Britain dated halfway through his holiday, to use if he needed. Thankfully, he 'survived' and, it is hoped, enjoyed the hospitality and fellowship of Haus Barnabas for the full fortnight, and the team in the house felt it a privilege to have him as a guest.

One further guest to mention informed Leonard as he drove her from the airport that she had once been a nurse and carer to the famous physicist Stephen Hawking. Later, in conversation in Haus Barnabas, she mentioned that occasionally, Stephen would ask her to read passages from the Bible to him. After his death in 2018, Stephen Hawking's ashes were buried in Westminster Abbey.

CHAPTER

20

A Remarkable Experience

In the year 2000, Phyllis's mother died. Her father had died two years earlier, and for the last period of her life, her mother had suffered severely from depression. A very distressing consequence of the mental depression was a strong persuasion that she wasn't a Christian. It appears that all sorts of unwanted wicked thoughts would flood into her mind, leaving her to believe she had committed the unforgivable sin and was without hope before God. This unfortunately is not uncommon for Christians to experience when they are suffering from clinical depression. Her mother was consequently very afraid to die, and Phyllis had promised to do her best to be with her at the end. So when the message came from the nursing home that they feared the end was imminent, Leonard and

Phyllis's mother
May Pittwell
1909–2000

Phyllis left Utzenfeld immediately and drove across to Oxfordshire. They arrived in time and, for the next two days, shared watches day and night at her mother's bedside with Phyllis's sister and husband.

The end came on a Sunday evening. It was a beautiful evening a week before Easter, and a blackbird was coming and going, building its nest in a bush just outside the window. Phyllis and Leonard were at the bedside, and Phyllis had been playing hymns her mother had loved and singing some of her favourite songs. One her mother loved her to sing was 'At even when the sun had set' to the tune 'Jude'. Her mother was no longer showing signs of recognition or communicating but no doubt knew her daughter was there. As she showed signs of distress, the nurses left to bring her morphine, so only Phyllis and Leonard were at her bedside as her breathing changed to a rattle, and then suddenly, she moved, raised herself in the bed, opened her eyes, and, looking beyond her daughter, uttered a joyful 'Ooh'. Then her breathing faded out rapidly, indicating clearly that her spirit had left her body. She appeared so peaceful in a way she had not been for years, and Phyllis and Leonard were convinced that in her dying moments, she had either seen angels or the Lord Jesus Himself appearing to take her home.

The whole experience so moved Phyllis that she would later describe it as the greatest moment of her life, and she often said that at that moment, sitting by her mother's deathbed, she sensed the ladder from heaven down to earth that Jacob saw had come into the room. It left her with no great desire to continue living but to go herself to be with Jesus.

She later realised that the song 'The Holy Hills of Heaven Call Me' by Dottie Rambo wonderfully describe the experience she witnessed at her mother's deathbed.

This house of flesh is but a prison!
Bars of bone hold my soul,
But the doors of clay are gonna burst wide open
When the angels set my spirit free.
I'll take my flight like the mighty eagle
When the hills of home start calling me.

By way of contrast, when they were talking to a missionary who had worked in Africa, the comment was made that this friend had witnessed the opposite when sitting by the dying bed of someone who didn't know Jesus as their Saviour and who had died expressing anguish and fear. The apostle Paul wrote,

> Giving thanks to the Father who has qualified us to be partakers of the inheritance of the saints in the light. He has delivered us from the power of darkness and conveyed us into the kingdom of the Son of His love in whom we have redemption through His blood, the forgiveness of sins.[53]

It's a very serious and dreadful thing to die without knowing the forgiveness of our sins through faith in Jesus Christ.

Phyllis's father had died suddenly and unexpectedly just two years earlier. He had felt unwell for about two weeks, which was very unusual for him, and Phyllis or her sister had spoken to him every day during this period. He died on a Saturday, and the evening before, Phyllis had one of the most remarkable conversations with him that she had ever experienced, made more remarkable because the phone call that evening nearly didn't happen. Leonard and Phyllis were under pressure from their guests, and the suggestion was made that she leave it until the next day. It is wonderful is see how the Lord intervened in the situation and prompted her to make the call and thus to speak to her father on his last evening on earth. The conversation they had that evening cleared up many of the misunderstandings they had had about each other over the years, and they parted very affectionately.

Her father was taken to hospital the next morning and died whilst being examined. He had always resisted seeing a doctor, and part of the reason for his sudden death was untreated diabetes.

Phyllis marvels how the Lord graciously undertook in regard to her parting with both of her parents. Although missing them terribly, she herself could not have devised or arranged a more satisfying way to experience their departure to glory.

---

53 Colossians 1:12–14.

CHAPTER

21

'Enlarge the Place of Your Tent'

It was discovered after the death of her mother that Phyllis's parents had left their children a considerable sum of money. Phyllis initially invested her share, but after a while, she and Leonard began to wonder whether it should be used to further their ministry in the Black Forest, to which they were fully committed. One evening, when close friends and supporters of Haus Barnabas were with them, the four together had a time of prayer together when they really sensed God's presence directing their thoughts and prayers.

A major subject on their minds was the future of the work, and as Leonard tore off the calendar which had a Bible text for each day, the reference was Isaiah 54:2, which reads, 'Enlarge the place of your tent and let them stretch out the curtains of your dwellings; do not spare, lengthen your cords, and strengthen your stakes. For you shall expand to the right and to the left.'

What did this mean? What was God preparing them for?

A little while after this, Phyllis was having afternoon coffee with a friend in the village who was secretary to the mayor. She happened to mention that the Engel Gasthaus at the top end of the village was for sale. There was no outside sign indicating this, probably because if it were made public, the ongoing business would decline. Phyllis mentioned the availability of Gasthaus Engel – which, translated, means the 'Angel Guesthouse' – to Leonard over their evening meal and suggested they should maybe consider the possibility of buying it. Leonard was, at first, rather sceptical as he knew the money that they had would be far less than that required to make such a purchase. However, a few days later, on his way home after a teaching session in Todtnau, on the spur of the moment, he decided to stop at the Engel and talk to the owner.

The owner was clearly eager to sell. He was suffering severely from back pain and was only able to continue running his business by having two pain-killing injections a week. He ran the guesthouse/ restaurant together with his wife and one additional staff member. His speciality was the restaurant, and his

Gasthaus Engel
Utzenfeld

meals had an excellent reputation. He advertised that he could provide meals for groups of up to one hundred. The restaurant consisted of two large rooms with adjoining doors. The rooms had low ceilings, and the windows looking out to the front of the building were of coloured stained glass with very wide window ledges, indicating that the stone walls were nearly a metre thick. Leonard later learned that the building dated back to the mid-seventeenth century and claimed to be the first hostel in the whole upper Wiese Valley. There was an extremely large kitchen, and in addition to the two restaurant rooms mentioned, there was another smaller room on the ground floor which, in English terms, would be referred to as the 'snug'. As required for a restaurant, there were public toilets, which, rather imaginatively, were labelled *Bübli* and *Mädli*, meaning 'Little boys' room' and 'Little girls' room'. The house also offered sleeping accommodation, and so upstairs, in addition to the owners' own living accommodation, were six guest bedrooms, five of which had an ensuite shower and toilet.

On that first visit, Leonard didn't suggest an inspection of the house; he merely wanted some idea of how much the owner hoped to sell it for. It became clear that the owner would be happy to come to any suitable arrangement for a sale, and Leonard decided to put all his cards on the table. He mentioned that his wife had recently inherited from her parents and mentioned the figure they had available as cash. Although a fraction of what the owner felt the house and business was worth, he was not dismissive but suggested Leonard should talk to the bank. He also expressed a willingness for a down payment linked with an arrangement for subsequent monthly payments coming out of the proceeds from the ongoing business.

Arising out of this initial conversation with Herr Kaiser, Leonard sensed the glimmer of a possibility that God was opening the way for them to have Gasthaus Engel for their work and witness. He returned home to inform his surprised wife that he had taken this initiative despite his initial scepticism, and they quickly arranged a time with the owners to inspect the guesthouse more carefully.

The building was large, and in addition to the two furnished floors, a large cellar housed the heating equipment and a laundry room. Within the large roof space, there were three further floors ripe for development whenever finance was available. The owners had bought the building in the mid–1960s in poor condition and had redesigned it completely. The main restaurant had attractive wood panelling and large artificial beams built around an original wood-burning *Kachel* oven. The main heating of the building came from the large oil-fired boiler in the cellar, but the tiled *Kachel* oven was still usable as an additional source of heat to create an extremely cosy atmosphere in cold winters.

Restaurant in
Gasthaus Engel

Built onto the side of the original rectangular building was a new entrance and reception room. Lying outside, behind this, was a large barn-like shed, within which was a concrete bunker housing a few pigs which the owner fattened using boiled restaurant waste as part of their diet. Alongside this was a well-constructed gable-roofed double garage with a loft area above it. The garage loft was accessible from a flat open terrace which ran across the top of the reception room and barn. Patio doors from two of the rooms on the first floor led onto the terrace.

The owner explained to Leonard and Phyllis that in addition to the building itself, the property included a large garden area and a significant part of the forest running up the steep hillside behind the house. The total area of the property was 4.20 acres.

The guesthouse/restaurant was still running as a business, and since the owners were retiring, they wanted to include all the furnishings and equipment as part of the sale.

Wow! As Leonard and Phyllis walked away from this first viewing, they gasped at the possibility that God was perhaps going to enable them to take over this property as a new centre for their work in Utzenfeld, but they also knew it would be an enormous challenge and responsibility.

On talking to two separate banks, Leonard learned that neither were lending money for the purchase of guesthouses in the Black Forest. Trade had dropped back in recent years, and to put it bluntly, there were now too many guesthouse/restaurants for the demand, and many were struggling financially. Initially, this appeared to put an end to all thought of purchasing the Engel, but then Leonard had another idea. There was an increasing demand for English teaching, and in addition to the continuing evening classes, Leonard was already employed by one of the larger local firms to give English tuition to its employees both in Todtnau and once a week in Freiburg. It occurred to him that they could establish a language school as part of the business side of the Engel and use the potential income from this to satisfy the bank.

Leonard and Phyllis talked over all their thoughts with their co-workers Timothy and Deborah, who agreed to add their personal money into a partnership to purchase and run the Engel. After continuing prayer together, committing all their thoughts to God for His overruling and guidance, they spoke again with the owner of the Engel, the bank, and also an accountant.

Eventually, there was an agreement. A certain amount was to be paid to the owners as cash, consisting of Holder money and Brooks money, plus a loan from the bank for each partner, enabling the contribution from each couple to the partnership to be topped up. The ownership of the Engel would then be divided accordingly, maintaining the proportion indicated by the original personal cash each couple could contribute. In addition to the cash paid, the Holder/Brooks partnership agreed to pay the retiring owners an agreed sum each month by way of a pension for the remainder of their lives. This payment was considered a business expense. The agreed purchase price included all furniture, furnishings, and equipment.

Interestingly, shortly before everything was settled, the bank manager called round to see Leonard and Phyllis. He was a personal friend, being the husband of one of the ladies to whom Leonard had taught English and who had accompanied the Holders to England on one of the tourist trips. Leonard, however, was out, so he spoke to Phyllis alone.

'Are you sure you want to do this?' he asked in a concerned tone. 'I could invest this money for you, which would provide you with a most comfortable future. To buy a guesthouse will just bring work, worry, and possible financial disaster.'

Phyllis told Leonard about this when he came in, but the bank manager's concern hadn't seemed to change her mind. They both felt that the way things had moved in regard to the purchase of the Engel was of God, and they had to trust Him for the future.

PART 7

'HAUS BARNABAS IM ENGEL' 2002 ONWARDS

Therefore, do not worry, saying, 'What shall
we eat?' or 'What shall we drink?' or 'What
shall we wear?' For after all these things, the
Gentiles seek. For your heavenly Father knows
that you need all these things. But seek first
the kingdom of God and His righteousness,
and all these things shall be added to you.
Therefore, do not worry about tomorrow, for
tomorrow will worry about its own things.
Sufficient for the day is its own trouble.
— Matthew 6:31–34

C H A P T E R

1

Language School

Since a language school was regarded as an important means of financing the new Gasthaus Engel, it needed to be established. Over the years, a frequent summer visitor to Haus Barnabas had been an English teacher living and working in Belgium, and after much thought and prayer, Leonard wrote to him, suggesting the possibility of him coming to the Black Forest to set up and run the proposed school. After much prayer and consideration, Allen accepted, so the King's School of Languages was set up later that year.

An official opening of the school was arranged with an open day for the village. This was a wonderful opportunity for interested local people to come into the house and see what was happening in Gasthaus Engel, which had been a significant building in the village for several centuries. The day started with an English breakfast for the early

Early language school students with Allen Broome

visitors, and then during the morning, people could come in and look around the premises. Leaflets about the language courses on offer were available to peruse and take away. Gospel leaflets were also made available, as were details of the Sunday services and Bible studies, including a statement of Haus Barnabas's theological position as a Free Evangelical fellowship. Later in the day, there was a formal meeting when the mayor of Utzenfeld made a speech welcoming the language school as part of the village. Allen then gave details of his plans for the school, and Leonard spoke of the spiritual ministry of the house. The mayor and parish council members who were present then presented a bouquet of flowers to the ladies.

In a conversation following the meeting, one member of the parish council pointed out to Leonard that not so many years earlier, the strong Roman Catholic influence within the village would have prohibited any acceptance of a Lutheran church, let alone a Free Evangelical one. On another occasion, a lady who came to their Sunday service, having expressed delight at their presence there in the church in Todtnau, informed Leonard that when her grandfather had first settled in the town as a Lutheran believer, he had needed to carry a gun to protect himself from some of the resident Roman Catholic citizens. Another older lady also told them that as a girl, she had had a Lutheran boyfriend, and her parents had forbidden him to come into their house.

A lot of work was put into getting the language school off the ground, and there were many encouragements, but with much of the teaching being one to one, this meant hours of teaching with less income than with groups. Allen came as an employee of the language school, and at the end of the first year, it was clear from a financial point of view that there needed to be changes. Recognising the potential for language teaching in the Wiesental, Allen agreed to take over the school completely, thus separating it from the guesthouse business, which now had come under the title of 'Haus Barnabas im Engel'. It was also soon realised that it was necessary for the language school to have its own premises, and in a remarkable way, suitable rooms became available to rent immediately opposite Gasthaus Engel.

Although relieving Haus Barnabas of the financial burden of a language school which was taking far longer to get established than the optimistic business plan had imagined, Leonard and Phyllis, together with Timothy and Deborah, were left to find the means of meeting the large ongoing monthly amounts needed to cover not only running costs but also the commitments made for the purchase of the building. Also, with them having brought in Allen to do the teaching, there was no longer the income they had received themselves for this. This became a cause of great concern, and how God provided for them is a subject for further chapters.

Still, the language school did bring some additional guests into the house. With the Holders having advertised weeks of intensive English learning, with the possibility of accommodation in the English-speaking Haus Barnabas, several very interesting non-British guests entered the Gasthaus Engel household.

One of the first was a Christian young lady with German parents who had been brought up in Kazakhstan. Leonard was very interested to learn of the migration of large numbers of Germans into Russian-speaking Eastern Europe in previous centuries. For Christians, one reason for emigrating eastward was the restrictions they, at that time, faced in Germany and, by comparison, the freedom to worship as they wished further east. As we all know, this situation soon changed, reversing the whole situation, so after the collapse of the Berlin Wall and the possibility of migrating back into Germany, many did just that.

In the present day, there are Christians meeting and worshipping in the Russian language in many areas of Germany. The young lady who came to Haus Barnabas had an interest in working with children and had completed a course with Child Evangelism but, not having learned English during her school days, felt the need to remedy this deficiency. For a few years, she became part of the Haus Barnabas 'family' and also started a children's club. Sadly, Roman Catholic parents were very suspicious of this, and it was unable to continue very long.

There were also several very interesting German young people who came for weeks of intensive English language learning as part of their preparation for the mission field. One incident that stands out for Leonard and Phyllis arose when a mother brought her teenage daughter to improve her English. The mother was very scared of spiders, and in some strange way, it almost seemed that the spiders could sense this. It's really impossible to keep spiders out of the Engel guesthouse as the building is on the edge of the forest and, in late summer, these eight-legged creatures of varying sizes seek shelter for the winter. After discovering a spider in their bedroom, the mother threatened to find other accommodation. Then that evening at supper, Leonard was sitting opposite the mother at the table when a spider dropped from the ceiling onto the tablecloth between the two of them. Thankfully, Leonard was able to immediately put his hand over it and surreptitiously dispose of it, but the whole experience was very strange as it had never happened before nor did so again.

The story of another language student deserves a longer account and is the subject of the next chapter.

CHAPTER

2

'For Such a Time as This'[54]

In a remarkable way, the story of this chapter begins some years before Leonard and Phyllis had any idea they would settle in the Black Forest.

Living locally in the Black Forest, a young girl had experienced a very disturbed childhood. Because she suffered from epilepsy, her parents kept a strict eye on her, and she was forced to spend hours alone in the confines of the family garden with her dog as her only companion. She learned to love all the natural life she discovered around her, and this love of birds, flowers, insects, and spiders remained with her into adult life. She had an elder brother whom she loved and admired, but her life was shattered when he took his own life. The attitude of the Roman Catholic priest to her brother's suicide also turned her against the church despite the fact that her mother's family were deeply religious and she had several aunts who were nuns.

One of her mother's closest friends became a loving aunt to her, and this lady was a member of the small Protestant church in Todtnau, where she played the organ for the services.

---

54 Esther 4:14.

One day, as her life was drawing to a close, this caring 'aunt' said, 'You must look out for a man named Len Holder. He will be able to help you.'

Since this happened some years before Leonard and Phyllis had had any thought of living in the Black Forest and they can see no way in which this lady could have known them if she had really said this name, it was clearly of God Himself. However, whatever name it was the aunt had said, when the name of Pastor Len Holder was seen in the local paper advertising worship services, this was identified as that mentioned by her aunt several years before. She hesitated for a long time to come to a service, but when she saw that Haus Barnabas was offering day courses in English, she decided this was an opportunity to meet these English people and this unknown Len Holder.

Leonard and Phyllis were actually away the first time she came, but she had several hours of English with Allen and met Timothy and Deborah. This was the breakthrough she needed, and she began to attend Bible studies and services. Timothy was leading the services with Leonard away, and she said later that what struck her forcefully was that this young man, who was about her own age, clearly had a strong faith in God and such a good understanding of the Bible.

At that time, she was working as personal secretary to a blind man who ran a charitable organisation for the blind and visually impaired. She was the only employee, and the demands on her were varied. To make herself more versatile, she had taught herself Braille and acquired the means to punch Braille script onto suitable paper. She had also gained a deep interest in blind people and their needs. Then soon after she began to come to Haus Barnabas for Sunday services, the source of income for her boss to run the office dried up, and she was suddenly without a job. She applied for several jobs but, whilst unemployed, would come and do voluntary work in Haus Barnabas. Then suddenly, Leonard received an enquiry from Poland from a blind gentleman asking to come to talk about the possibility of bringing a group of blind and visually impaired Polish men and women to the house. Later, it became clear that this gentleman had heard about Haus Barnabas through our new enthusiastic voluntary worker via her boss.

The Polish group was an amazing financial provision. It was a European Union (EU) project with the aim of benefiting the blind and visually impaired. Wojtek was delegated by a Polish charity to organise the project. He had been completely blind from birth but was very talented and ran his own business supplying computer hardware and software for the blind and offering courses in its use. The project was to run for nine weeks, and it could be arranged to take place in Haus Barnabas's quiet time in the winter months. The criteria for receiving finance for this project stipulated that it needed to be held in a different EU country from that of the participants, and the main aim was to give new experiences to those chosen to take part and to provide courses to help make them more employable. Wojtek and his wife would organise and lead the courses, with the emphasis being on teaching them to use computers. Leonard was asked about providing English teaching, and he agreed to do this at no extra charge if he could be permitted to use Bible texts as a basis for at least some of the teaching. Leonard and Phyllis realised that their enthusiastic voluntary worker's experience with blind folk would be invaluable in helping to care for this group, so they offered her employment in the house.

Wojtek brought three different groups to Haus Barnabas over an eighteen-month period, and the income thus provided got the business out of a very sticky financial situation. Someone commented on hearing about this, that God, in His unique and wonderful way, provided financially for Haus Barnabas through some of the poorest people in one of the poorer countries of Europe. Experiences of these blind Polish groups will form the subject of the next chapter.

Having been the indirect means of bringing these Polish groups to Haus Barnabas and contributing valuable assistance during their residence there, their new employee continued with them for several years. She would travel in from Todtnau each day and attended most, if not all, of the Sunday services and Bible studies. For many months, she struggled with personal faith and had many questions, but finally, one day she felt God really spoke to her, and for a while, she found peace and happiness knowing herself to be a daughter of God. She was very keen to be baptised and, with her love of nature, was adamant that this should be in the river. Leonard had already baptised one couple in the river and had located a suitable spot within easy walking distance of the house. The date chosen was Palm Sunday, even though at that time of year, there was still melted snow coming down from the higher slopes, and the water temperature couldn't have been more than five degrees. In her enthusiasm, the candidate wanted her baptism to be announced in

Baptism in Wiese River

the local paper, and the occasion was a very happy and encouraging time. One of the Polish groups was in the house at the time, and following the morning service, a group of about twenty-five walked up to the chosen spot by the river to witness the baptism. Leonard put on an additional pair of trousers to help keep out the cold, and the two went into the water to near waist height. On confession of her faith, Leonard quickly immersed the candidate under the water in the name of Father, Son, and Holy Spirit, and then both were helped back up the bank as the spectators sang songs of praise.

Later, it became increasingly difficult to justify having a paid employee in the house, but Leonard and Phyllis were loath to let their friend go. However, subsequent events forced change, and she eventually moved away from the area to be near her sister in North Germany. Still, in a remarkable way, this lady became a significant member of the team and was clearly God's provision for the ministry of Haus Barnabas at that time, and she would later occasionally call by when visiting her native Black Forest.

CHAPTER

3

'In My Dreams, I Can See!'

The separation of the language school from the guesthouse work of Haus Barnabas, whilst clearly a wise move after the experience of the first year, fully frustrated the business plan for financing the purchase of Gasthaus Engel. However, to be thrown back completely on God's provision for the work of His kingdom creates a very definite exercise of faith, and this dependence on God for the provision of their daily needs was no new experience for Leonard and Phyllis.

One weekend, when several of the trustees of Bible in Action Trust were visiting, Leonard decided that the Sunday service should be the occasion to make a definite prayerful act of consecration of the house and its ministry to God. The declared aim of each of the four partners in the ownership of Gasthaus Engel and the society in Germany they had set up to run it was to 'seek first the kingdom of God and His righteousness'. In the pursuit of this aim, they could plead the promise of Jesus in Matthew 6:33 that 'all these things would be added'.

When Wojtek came to talk about the possibility of bringing the blind group to Haus Barnabas, Leonard pointed out to him the Christian basis on which the house was run, and he commented that he had read this on the website, and it was partly this that had attracted him. There was a fixed budget offered by the EU per participant and strict requirements to be adhered to. Leonard was able to agree a price with Wojtek within that budget, and ways of meeting the EU's requirements were also discussed and agreed upon. Leonard's offer of providing English language tuition as an extra was accepted enthusiastically.

Knowing that the house held a public worship and Bible ministry every Sunday morning, Wojtek commented that because most of the group would be Roman Catholic, he didn't think this would interest them, and some might want to attend mass in the local Catholic church. However, a day or two after the first group's arrival, he came back smiling, saying most of the group would like to come to the service. He offered to interpret the service and sermon into Polish as long as he could do this from English as his knowledge of German was very limited. What this meant in practice was that most Sundays, everything said needed to be in three languages, but it was a wonderful opportunity to present the Gospel and Bible teaching to a wider congregation.

Miraculously, God provided the house with a Braille printer and the software to convert Word documents into Braille and to print all the little raised dots onto suitable paper. A British friend had seen this equipment offered for auction on eBay and sat up all night to acquire it. The cost was then divided between him and another friend. With this equipment, Leonard was able to provide the Sunday hymns in Braille for the totally blind, in addition to very large normal print for the partially sighted. Similarly, he was able to print Scripture passages from an online Polish Bible.

It was so encouraging to see some of the group members be enthusiastic about the Bible, and both Leonard and Phyllis sensed that some of them really knew and loved the Lord Jesus. One lady asked whether they could practise singing the Sunday hymns on a Saturday night in readiness for the service, and a majority of the group came to these practice sessions. This, of course, gave Leonard the opportunity to explain the meaning of the hymns and songs. Hymn singing was usually led by Deborah on the guitar, and in her absence, Phyllis would play the house's electric organ, which she had inherited from her father.

Each morning, five days a week, Leonard would provide English tuition. Each lesson would start with a few verses from the Bible printed in Braille and large type. He would explain the meaning of the text in simple English and then take up different points of grammar and sentence construction, after which he would revert to a standard English language textbook. Many of the group had some basic knowledge of English from school but some not, and Deborah had a separate class for these complete beginners. When the lessons were over, there was a coffee break, when many of the group would sit around a table to chat to Phyllis, who would try and encourage them to use some of the new words they had learned. There was usually one of the group who knew enough English to translate into Polish for the others. Following the coffee break, their courses with Wojtek and his wife kicked off.

With each of the three groups staying nine weeks, there was plenty of time to get to know them fairly well, and as is always the case, some group members stood out more than others.

One young man had a very sad story. He had been a sportsman representing Poland in the Olympics and had married a beautiful American girl who had given him a daughter, but following an evening of drinking, he had been involved in a serious car accident which had left him completely blind. This changed the whole course of his life.

His wife left him, taking the daughter with her, but as he himself said, 'I can't blame her. No one would have been able to bear living with me then.'

He attempted to take his own life several times but was just beginning to accept his new situation as a blind person when he came to Haus Barnabas with the project.

One happy memory of him was an evening when the group were choosing hymns and songs to sing.

He called out, 'Can we sing "Thank You, Jesus"? We love that one.'

We pray that these words might have really come from his heart:

Thank You, Jesus. Thank You, Jesus.
Thank You, Lord, for loving me.

You went to Calvary,
There, You died for me.
Thank You, Lord, for loving me.
You rose up from the grave.
To me, new life You gave.
Thank You, Lord, for loving me.
Thank You, Jesus. Thank You, Jesus.
Thank You, Lord, for loving me.

Several of the group came from very poor homes and obviously very much appreciated and enjoyed the comparative comfort of Haus Barnabas and also being with other blind young people. One young lady who clearly came from a more well-to-do home found a lot of enjoyment in being allowed in the Haus Barnabas kitchen. The reason behind this was that it was decided that as part of the course, the participants should be involved in practical aspects of running the house. They laid the tables for the meals and cleared away afterwards and washed up. To witness blind people doing all this is very interesting, and although it was ensured that a sighted person or one with sufficient sight was there to help, unfortunately, there were still regular breakages. The young lady mentioned above was very inquisitive, and nothing could persuade her not to test what was in every container by popping her finger in and tasting the contents, which was rather alarming.

There are clearly a limited range of employment possibilities for blind people, but one profession that is open to them, certainly in Poland, is that of a masseur. Several of the men who came on the course had trained in this and had jobs in health clinics. One man who had worked as a masseur had some sight, but it was very limited. He had sufficient sight to oversee the washing up when it was his shift, and Leonard remembers seeing him kneeling in front of the dishwasher with his eye about an inch from the controls. He liked to go for a walk by himself, and one evening he found himself locked out. Not being able to locate the bell push, he managed to climb up to the terrace on the first floor and alert Wojtek, who was working in his bedroom. No one knows how he managed to get to the first floor, and he refused to divulge this, but to Leonard's knowledge, it has never been attempted since.

Several of the young people who came had been blind from birth, but with others, it was due to accidents. One attractive young lady had lost her sight through a road accident when in her late teens. During an English lesson, to encourage conversation, Leonard prompted the group to talk about dreams they had had. This young lady commented that she enjoyed her dreams because in them, she could see, but then she added poignantly that it was so distressing to wake up and find herself blind.

The priest on the board of the charity Caritas in Poland who had negotiated the projects with the EU visited Haus Barnabas whilst the groups were there. No doubt he needed to put in a personal report to the EU as to the way the project was running. He interviewed each of the participants to enquire how they felt the courses were helping them and if there were things they felt could be improved. Leonard was extremely encouraged when this very friendly Polish priest reported back to him that almost without exception, one aspect of the programme that they enjoyed most was the Christian atmosphere in the house and the Sunday services. Of course, it's possible that some, knowing they were speaking to a priest, wanted to please him by saying they liked the religious side of the programme, but this certainly wouldn't have been so with them all. The priest also commented to Leonard that although he realised the house wasn't Roman Catholic, he found the atmosphere very Christian, and he was very happy for the groups to be there.

CHAPTER

༈

4

—

More Polish Experiences

Part of the agreed programme for the three different groups from Poland involved an outing each week to places of interest. Thankfully, by this time, with Timothy working with Leonard as a driver and with two people carriers, together with Wojtek's wife's car, which she had driven across from Poland, there was sufficient vehicle capacity for even the largest of the three groups. Blind guests need different venues for outings than the usual guests visiting Haus Barnabas, and also, there needs to be a sufficient number of people with enough sight to lead the totally blind. The fifth member of the team, with her experience of working with the blind, was clearly God's provision for the work during these weeks.

By searching online, it was possible to find suitable places to visit, and one of the more unusual but very appropriate venues was a centre for breeding and training dogs for the blind. This occasionally had open days to help create interest and financial support and, when approached, were happy to arrange a specific date to welcome the group from Haus Barnabas and show them around. Normally, visitors are discouraged from actually touching and petting the dogs, but under supervision, the guide who showed the group around allowed those who couldn't see the animals to feel and stroke them. There were puppies at various stages of development, and several more mature animals were beginning their training on a specially laid-out course. The centre was situated on the outskirts of Basel, and following some initial training, dog handlers took animals into Basel City to experience real-life situations. The outing was a great success, and several of the blind project participants expressed a great wish to have a guide dog. Sadly, this was unlikely to be possible as the animals are expensive to breed and train and demand far exceeds supply.

There were visits to several cities, and on an outing to Basel, Leonard was directed to a tactile plan of the city so the group could feel how the city was laid out and read Braille wording indicating the more important features. Something very much appreciated also was a crossing of the River Rhine on one of the ferries, powered by the current alone and guided by a cable up to a stronger cable high above the river. The ferryman was extremely friendly and helpful and allowed a few of the group to hold the tiller and feel the pull of the current.

A visit to the city of Strasbourg coincided with the annual Christmas market with all its bustle and exotic smells. This trip also included a tour around the city by boat, negotiating the waterways through the older parts, and included a taped commentary with some history of significant buildings through headphones in a choice of languages. Strasbourg has a park and ride system, whereby paying the car parking fee provided a free ride into the city centre by bus or tram for up to nine people.

A further trip to Strasbourg had a completely different objective. Wojtek, the organiser and leader of the group, had contacts with the Polish government and has, on occasions, been chosen to interpret from English into Polish for the prime minister. When the Polish member of the European Parliament was due to give a speech in a sitting of the EU parliament in Strasbourg, Wojtek received an invitation to attend and to bring all the project participants. Leonard and Timothy were needed as drivers and carers and so could also get a seat in the public gallery of the splendid auditorium. It was a very interesting visit. The Polish MEP showed the group around some of the magnificent parliament buildings and then gave them a talk on the way things functioned. His own opinion was that this second parliament building in Strasbourg was a complete waste of money, as was the need for the MEPs to move to and from Brussels and Strasbourg and to have an office in both places. The only reason for this, in his opinion, was to appease the French.

There were very few MEPs in the auditorium for the sitting of parliament that the group attended. Leonard and Timothy sat with the Polish group in the public gallery, and headphones enabled everyone to hear the speeches in the language of their choice.

After the Polish MEP had made his speech, the Polish group clapped and cheered, which caused the chairman to look across to them, and his warning echoed around the vast hall: 'Quiet, please, in the public gallery.'

One of the matters being discussed was the application by an Eastern European country to join the union. An English MEP who clearly had a poor view of the EU made the comment that he couldn't understand why a country which had so recently escaped from the Soviet Union should now wish to join another union which could restrict their newly obtained freedom.

There appeared to be more MEPs in the bar than in the conference hall, and the comment was made that most only sit through sessions if they have obtained the right to make a speech, and they would leave again soon after their bit was over. Apparently, members can listen to speeches that apply to them online later.

As is the regular custom in Haus Barnabas, after the Sunday morning service and a lunch together, there is the possibility for a guided walk, and a favourite location for this is the Todtnau waterfall. One Sunday afternoon Leonard drove a small group of the Polish blind to the lower reaches of the waterfall. It was winter with snow and ice around, but the path to the bottom of the main fall was clear enough to negotiate. There was plenty of water coming down the rocks, and the sound of this was very satisfying for those who had no visible enjoyment of it. Rather foolishly, as it turned out, Leonard suggested the group might like to climb the steep steps which ran alongside the fall. This was greeted with great enthusiasm. As they climbed, Leonard realised how the frozen snow with ice on the steps was making the climb really treacherous.

Thankfully, there was a good strong handrail for much of the climb up, but the steps were very slippery.

With help from the sighted and partially sighted, there were thankfully no accidents, but Leonard whispered to the other member of the team who was with them, 'There is no way we can come back down these steps. It's far too dangerous.'

Thinking and praying about the situation, Leonard decided that really, the only way was for the whole group to continue climbing up the path and steps which led up beside a second fall of water to the village of Todtnauberg above the falls. He would himself retrace the steps carefully back down to the car and drive round the road to the top to meet and pick up the group. He continued with the group until the more dangerous parts of the ascend were negotiated and then returned to the car. God be praised that all got safely back to Haus Barnabas in time for the Sunday evening meal.

Interestingly, this incident was one of the highlights of the group's time in Utzenfeld. The following year, a Polish television company produced a programme about these projects for the blind in Haus Barnabas, and the team that came to film the location wanted to visit and film the waterfall which some of the blind participants had climbed in the snow. Thankfully, there were no recriminations from the health and safety authorities.

5

A Bridge Too Far?

The opportunity to share the Gospel and to bring Bible teaching to the Polish young people was a wonderful experience, and after many years, Leonard and Phyllis are still in touch with a few of them. During the year following their visit, Wojtek arranged a reunion for the participants from the first group in a youth hostel in Southern Poland near the Slovakian border and was very emphatic that Leonard and Phyllis should come as their guests. It proved to be a most interesting and worthwhile experience. Driving across Germany into Eastern Poland, the couple spent a few nights in a hotel in Kielce, which was Wojtek's home city with his wife and young son. They then motored south to the venue for the reunion, visiting the beautiful city of Krakow on the way. The youth hostel had been hired for three nights and a small range of activities planned. Leonard remembers the weekend as the first and only occasion he has ridden, high up, on the back of a large horse and been led around a circuit of lanes.

Also included was a specially arranged mass in a very ornate church. Leonard and Phyllis sat at the back of the church as observers. It was interesting to note that the procedure of the mass was in line with the Orthodox form of Christianity rather than Roman Catholic because, although then within Poland, this area had once been part of Slovakia. The priest departed into the 'sanctuary' behind an ornate screen decorated with icons depicting Jesus and the saints where the altar was situated out of view. Here, he consecrated the bread and wine and then emerged to give this to the people. After those very interesting days, Leonard and Phyllis motored back to the Black Forest through Slovakia and Austria.

Although a wonderful provision from God, the profit element of the income from the EU for the Polish groups, after satisfying immediate needs by bringing the payment of bills up to date, left very little for the continuing running of the house. Also, the money had not always been there before the group arrived, which created difficulties as supplies needed to be bought in.

There was one remarkable incident at the commencement of one of the courses. It was the largest group, which, together with the leaders, numbered nearly twenty guests, who all needed to be provided for and fed. The money hadn't arrived, and the bank account was in the red. As was their custom, Leonard and Phyllis and the Haus Barnabas team took this situation to the Lord rather than make it publicly known. However, an English guest whom they had accommodated in the village but who came in for meals and fellowship must have noticed the concern and perhaps overheard something said. After breakfast, he took Leonard on one side, drove him down to the local bank, and, withdrawing five thousand euros, presented it to him as a gift from the Lord.

During the main holiday season, things could normally run quite happily as far as finance was concerned, but with most guests paying in advance, by the end of the season, income came in far more slowly and then finally virtually ceased. Bills kept coming in, and there was also the need to order oil for the boiler. The boiler was a greedy monster, and linked to it in the cellar was a twenty-thousand-litre oil tank. In heating water for both the central heating and for the general hot water use in the house, it was consuming, on average, about fifteen thousand litres of oil per year. One year in particular, things got very frightening financially, and Leonard was tempted to think that buying the Engel was simply a 'bridge too far'. However, in his quiet times with the Lord, as his prayers became more and more earnest, his heavenly Father constantly gave him reassurances through the promises of His Word, which gave him a good measure of peace in his heart that all was well.

Then adding to the unpaid bills which were mounting up, although Leonard always managed to pay the local small firms, came demands for a substantial tax payment from the German Finanzamt. On referring the tax bill to their accountant, Leonard was assured that it was wrong, and he was advised not to pay it, which, of course, was a wonderful answer because there was no money to do so. However, although the accountant took the matter up with the Finanzamt, the demands didn't stop coming and eventually turned into a threat of prison. Leonard kept most of the details of the financial situation from the other members of the team whilst sharing for earnest prayer the fact that money was urgently needed. In a non-specific way, this was also mentioned in a newsletter to friends and for prayer at the Sunday services. Much prayer was lifted up to their heavenly Father, who had promised that if they sought first His kingdom and righteousness, all needed things would be provided. A number of gifts came in, but the need was so great that these did little more than keep food on the table. The oil company agreed to accept payment by instalments, but Leonard was aware that much of the oil in the large tank being used was yet unpaid for.

One day a German friend who came regularly to the services casually asked Leonard for details of the Haus Barnabas bank account. A few days later, as Leonard looked at the bank account balance on his computer, he couldn't believe his eyes. There, to his great amazement, were funds sufficient to clear all their outstanding debts. He couldn't control his emotions or restrain the tears which ran down his face. He ran to find Phyllis, and together, they praised God with overflowing hearts for His wonderful provision.

Then another year, there was a similar situation. It was New Year's Eve, and Haus Barnabas had a group in the house with a speaker leading a brief devotional time as the old year came to a close. The thought was expressed that most had something they had planned or even promised to do during the year which they had not managed to achieve. A few moments were then given to commit these unfinished tasks to God, for Him to forgive and make good all these human failures. As Leonard thought over his failures and unfulfilled aims, there was one major item on his mind. The house accountant had been very patient in regard to the payment of his invoice. He had spent many hours on Haus Barnabas affairs the previous year, and his invoice for nearly four thousand euros had, with his understanding, not been paid for several months. When Leonard had last seen the accountant, he had indicated to him that he would aim to pay the outstanding bill before the year end. Now that point had come, and there was not sufficient money in the account to pay even a fraction of it. Without sharing this with anyone else, this was the matter Leonard brought to his heavenly Father during those moments of quiet prayer as the year drew to a close.

The group left early the following week, and after Leonard and Timothy had returned from delivering them to Basel Airport, Leonard happened to look in the offertory box, which lay, as usual, on a table in an inconspicuous corner at the end of a corridor. To his amazement, in it was sufficient money to pay the accountant's invoice. He and the Haus Barnabas team were so humbled to experience God's wonderful provision through His children and the answer to that New Year's Eve prayer that only God knew about.

When God leads, there is no 'bridge too far', even if the circumstances may sometimes tempt one to think otherwise.

CHAPTER

6

A Home for The Homeless

One Monday morning Leonard was working at his computer at a table in the large lounge, with its view up the valley to the mountainside rising above the neighbouring village of Geschwend, when he heard someone come into the reception area. When anybody worked downstairs, it was customary to leave the door of the house unlocked, and there was a little handbell on the reception desk for incomers to ring. As he went to investigate, Leonard was interested to see a largish bearded gentleman who addressed him in good English but with an Eastern European accent. The man introduced himself as Gabriel and explained he was from Hungary but had been working in Germany for a few years and had been attracted to the Black Forest, where he hoped to obtain another job. He had just agreed to rent a flat in the village and had seen the advert in the local paper giving everyone a warm welcome to a worship service in Haus Barnabas on Sunday mornings. However, having noticed this too late to attend that Sunday, he thought he would call by to make himself known.

Leonard made Gabriel and himself a coffee, and they sat and chatted. Gabriel explained that he was an engineer by profession but had been working in another area of Baden Württemberg in a more mundane manual job to earn his living. He explained that he was a Christian believer, and because of this, along with some political involvement, he had felt himself persecuted by the Hungarian authorities. This had caused him to leave his wife and two sons in Hungary and flee to Germany. Later, Leonard realised that Gabriel had what could be described as a persecution complex, and whether this fear was justified or not, he wasn't sure. For instance, when he was in Haus Barnabas for any length of time, he asked whether he could hide his little yellow car with its Hungarian registration plates around the back of the house, where it couldn't be seen from the road. He also spoke of his fear that via Google, all his computer work was being recorded and his movements followed. During that first chat, Leonard recognised him to be a fellow believer and brother in the Lord Jesus and assured him of a welcome in the house.

Gabriel had drawn plans of an engineering invention which had something to do with the purification of water. He would have loved to have made a model of it, but unfortunately, his circumstances didn't make this possible. He was quite convinced of its viability and usefulness and was taking steps to try and convince the German authorities of its value.

After a few weeks in his rented accommodation and no employment in sight, he approached Leonard, asking whether he could move into Haus Barnabas, requesting a quote for the use of a room on the basis of him preparing his own meals in the kitchen. Leonard and the team were wary as to where such an arrangement would lead if he continued to be without employment, but Gabriel had been attending the Sunday services and Bible studies regularly, and they decided they should agree to this arrangement as he was a Christian brother. However, quite understandably, the situation deteriorated. Gabriel tried in vain to interest the authorities in his invention. His money dried up, and after paying for his room for a few weeks, he explained the situation and suggested he would be content with a non-guest room often used for staff on the next floor under the roof. He had brought his limited furniture into the cellar and made a little nest down there to eat the meals he cooked in the main kitchen. Having spoken to the minister of the church in Schönau, he was able to get the necessary paper qualifying him to get supplies from a food bank in Schopfheim. He continued to attend devotional meetings with the house team and the guests and, from time to time, was invited to join in the family's communal meals and, of course, the fellowship meal with guests on Sundays.

Understandably, his mental health deteriorated, and he began to spend hours in his room, away from everybody. Timothy also had his office in the roof space, and one day he came downstairs with a written message that Gabriel had slipped under his door, requesting help. Leonard was out that afternoon, so Phyllis cautiously went in to see him, wondering what to expect. Other team members remained within calling distance in case she needed assistance. She was able to talk and encourage him and pray with him. He clearly was extremely depressed but was adamant he didn't want to go to a doctor.

After this, Leonard went up to see him every morning and would read Scripture and pray with him. The team also ensured he had the food and drink he needed. Then suddenly, one Sunday morning Gabriel decided he needed to see a doctor. This was quite a relief, and Leonard assured him he would introduce him to their own doctor in Schönau on Monday morning.

That Sunday, Leonard and Phyllis were celebrating their fortieth wedding anniversary and were meeting up with their sons and families in Geoffrey's home; it was about 11:00 p.m. before they got home. As they went up the stairs, there was Gabriel in his outdoor coat, coming down. He informed them that he had decided to drive back to Hungary. He had already packed his little yellow car and was ready for heading off.

Although in some ways, this was a relief, both Leonard and Phyllis were rather concerned about him beginning a journey of more than a thousand kilometres at midnight in his state of mind. However, he was adamant that he should go, so they both put their arms around him at the bottom of the stairs and committed him to the Lord's safe keeping. During the following year, Gabriel returned with a friend for a couple of nights to pick up some of the personal belongings he had left behind. So ended another interesting experience in Haus Barnabas.

The second person to mention was very different and only occupied a bed for a single night.

It was Christmas Eve, the first Leonard and Phyllis had experienced in Gasthaus Engel. They were alone as Timothy and Deborah and their baby son, Thomas, had gone back to England for the festive season. They were together in the *Stübli*, which is the small 'snug' next to the main, much larger lounge. Phyllis had come out of hospital a few days earlier, having had gallstones removed. Suddenly, there was a knock on the window, and Leonard went to investigate. Standing at the back door was a young man who had been introduced to the Holders some little while before. He was German, and his parents lived lower down the Wiese Valley towards Basel. He had studied at a Bible college in England and, whilst there, had spoken of his call to missionary work at a church where friends of Haus Barnabas attended. It was then through these friends that he had been introduced to Haus Barnabas. Leonard welcomed him in, and he came and sat with the couple in the *Stübli*.

He obviously felt that he needed to give an explanation for his sudden appearance on *Heiligabend*, as the Germans call Christmas Eve, and after being offered something to eat and drink, he sat quietly for a little while and then confessed that he had had an argument with his parents and walked out on them. He had walked the ten miles or so up the valley and asked whether he could stay the night. Leonard and Phyllis agreed to this but suggested it would be good if he were to telephone his parents so they knew he was safe. When he hesitated to do this, Leonard offered to do it for him, to which he agreed. It all seemed rather strange, but the Holders asked him no further questions, and since it was, by then, quite late, they showed him to a bedroom, and they all retired for the night.

The next morning, the situation appeared even stranger when they discovered that their guest's room was empty and he had vanished. During the morning, Leonard decided he ought to ring their visitor's parents once again just to check that their son had returned safely home. He hadn't, but before evening, the parents returned the call to say all was well.

After this incident, the Christmas Eve visitor would very occasionally come to a Haus Barnabas Sunday service, and it slowly became clear that he was suffering from schizophrenia. The mission work he had set his heart on became impossible, and the Holders understood that he needed to spend time in a clinic.

Their last encounter with him was most peculiar. He arrived early for a Sunday service, and Timothy provided him with a cup of coffee and had a brief chat as he was arranging the chairs for the service. Then immediately after the opening prayer, the young man stood up and, in

Leonard preaching in a Haus Barnabas Sunday service

quite an accusing way, read a Bible passage from Paul's first epistle to Timothy: 'In latter times, some will depart from the faith . . . forbidding to marry and commanding to abstain from foods which God created to be received with thanksgiving by those who believe and know the truth.'[55] Then after the service, he approached Leonard, saying that he was shocked and extremely upset that Timothy had told him before the service that it would be wrong for him to get married. On asking Timothy about this, the Holders' co-worker was adamant that the subject of marriage had never even been mentioned in the brief conversation he had had with this visiting member of that morning's congregation, and for him to have made the statement of which he was accused was unthinkable. The visiting friend was clearly not in the right frame of mind to talk amicably and rationally, but he did comment that he had stopped taking that 'rat poison' he had been prescribed by his doctor.

---

55 1 Timothy 4:1–3.

CHAPTER

7

Café Engel

With the aim of encouraging local villagers and passing motorists into Haus Barnabas, Leonard and Phyllis applied for the necessary permission to place tables outside of the building and to offer drinks and cakes to the public at specific times. There was, of course, always the option for visitors to sit at tables

Café Engel

inside the restaurant, but displaying tables outside in good weather advertised the fact that they were open for business.

They offered a wide range of drinks and ice cream as well as a selection of homemade cakes and scones baked by Deborah and stored in the freezer until needed. At times when Haus Barnabas had more staff to run the café, they were able to make more of it, but although it was always very much a side-line, it resulted in several very positive encounters with customers. One elderly lady in the village would often call during her afternoon walk, pushing her rollator, when she could see the café was open. She preferred to sit inside, and if Leonard was on duty in the café, he would call his wife to sit and chat to her, which the couple sensed was as much the reason for her visit as the apple tart and coffee which she would regularly order. Phyllis occasionally managed to steer conversations onto serious subjects and, at times, passed on Scripture tracts.

There was one occasion when three people came into the café, and after they ordered and received their eats and drinks, their conversation together became very heated. Leonard's procedure when on waiter duty was to work in the neighbouring room, where he could keep an ear open for repeat orders or new customers coming in. Two of the customers arguing were a couple, probably married, and the third seemed to be the father of one of them. From the raised voices Leonard could hear, the impression he was gaining was that the older man had recently lost his wife, and the younger couple were reasoning with him to pull himself together, make changes in his life, and get on with living. Of course, Leonard had no idea of the circumstances behind the situation, but it seemed to him that the older man was still very much in mourning and the younger ones were not showing him any sympathy or understanding. As it went on, all the force was coming from the younger couple, and the older man was clearly extremely emotionally distressed and close to tears.

Leonard showed his face, as any waiter should do to check that everything was all right with the food and drink, and the older man ordered another drink. As Leonard brought him his order, he felt compelled to say something. He commented that he realised there must be problems between them, introduced himself as a pastor, and asked whether they would allow him to pray for them. They looked at him in amazement but agreed that they would like that. So Leonard, in simple language, sought God's help for them in their circumstances, whatever these might be, and prayed that they might experience God's love and grace in the Lord Jesus.

The older man looked very appreciative, and when they left, the lady thanked Leonard very much, commenting that she had never before experienced a café where she was served by a pastor who had prayed for her. She added that they would return. However, it was clear from the way they spoke German that they were not local people, and they never appeared again.

There was another, quite different situation when an older man came into the café and ordered a coffee. When it was obvious that he wanted to say something, Leonard sat with him to hear his story. Looking around him with interest, he said he was extremely interested to come into Gasthaus Engel again as during the war, he had been evacuated with his mother to this very guesthouse in the Black Forest, to which Leonard added, just to himself, *Obviously to get away from British bombs!* The man went on to say that the layout of the rooms had changed a great deal since those years in the 1940s, but he was pleased to see that the Kachelofen heating was still there as that had been the main source of heat for them and they had spent many hours sitting around it on cold winter evenings.

Gasthaus Engel in the 1940s with the owner, guests, and staff

Being built in the first half of the seventeenth century, the house has a long history. A few years ago, Leonard had email correspondence with a man living in a neighbouring village who sent him a few old photos of the house taken in the war years. He commented that the house had been owned by his grandparents and that it had been his home in his early childhood. He had also added that he noted Leonard and Phyllis were using the house for Christians and Christian groups, which would have pleased his grandparents.

Many customers coming into the café have been rather intrigued by the fact that it is run by English families. This has aroused curiosity and given the opportunity to explain the Christian emphasis of the work of the house, and some customers have been happy to take a copy of John's Gospel.

One afternoon four motorcyclists arrived in the café and, after removing their leather jackets, ordered a large pot of English-style tea, which is an item on the menu. One of the men explained that he was from a particular town in England and had met up with German friends for a touring holiday. He expressed surprise and delight in discovering this unexpected opportunity of obtaining a cup of good English-style tea in the middle of Germany's Black Forest. Most British guests visiting Continental Europe know from experience how different the tea is once one crosses the English Channel. It's generally made with a small dip-in tea bag, using less-than-boiling water, and is drunk without milk. To enjoy a cup of it, one must remove from one's mind any expectation of a cup of tea from the homeland.

Having poured himself a cup of the darkish brown beverage from the very large white porcelain teapot (and he didn't say, 'Shall I be mother?'), he suddenly commented, looking expectantly at his host, 'This would be complete with a couple of custard cream biscuits!'

To his amazement, Leonard went back into the kitchen and emerged with a small glass plate bearing a number of these very British, very sweet delicacies.

There are various clubs in the village of Utzenfeld which, as is their custom, hold gatherings in the local restaurants. They will order and eat a meal and then chat together over drinks. The Haus Barnabas team were delighted to be asked to occasionally host these evening gatherings. With the café having passed

Local club meeting in Gasthaus Engel

approval of the first group, two village groups of up to a dozen members began coming three or four times a year. The 'Pensioners Club' was run by a retired businessman who would book four dates well in advance for the following year. The secretary of the second group had another approach and would ring to book a date a week or even a few days before the occasion. After enjoying a fairly simple hot meal (fish and chips was a favourite), the group would sit for a couple of hours with drinks, chatting. This proved to be a wonderful opportunity to get to know these representatives from the village as they welcomed one of the team to sit with them, a role that Phyllis felt best able to take on. This often led to some interesting conversations which could be very enlightening as, being mostly older folk, they would often share wartime experiences. Several had come into the Black Forest, fleeing as refugees from farther east, before the invading Russian army. There was occasionally opportunity for some spiritual input into the conversations, but sadly, this mostly resulted in a hushed silence.

Appreciative remarks were sometimes made, indicating that the reception these German village folks experienced in 'Haus Barnabas im Engel' was much warmer than was customary. Several came to regard Leonard and Phyllis as their personal friends, and some of the elderly ladies would greet Phyllis with a hug when they arrived and expected the same when leaving.

Utzenfeld village ladies
in Haus Barnabas

One evening one of the gentlemen approached Leonard and asked him if he was a *Pfarrer* (the word used in German for a pastor or priest). He commented that there was a dispute amongst some of group about this. Leonard explained that he had not been ordained by either the Catholic or Protestant Church but had studied theology and had been a pastor of a Baptist church in England.

'Do you preach at the services you hold here in the Engel on Sundays? he was asked. When Leonard responded positively to this, the man gave a satisfied retort (clearly indicating which side of the discussion he had been on): 'Then you are a *Pfarrer*.'

A majority in Utzenfeld and the surrounding villages would profess to be Roman Catholic, and for many of the older inhabitants, their faith was something they took seriously. Leonard knew the Saturday evening and Sunday morning masses were well attended. Services with a mass for a dead relative are held regularly, and Leonard was shocked the first time he had read in the local paper a church announcement reminding the parishioners that on All Souls' Day, they had the opportunity to free a loved one from purgatory by visiting their grave and praying a prayer approved by the pope. There was also an invitation to come to church and make confession before a priest to prepare them for this solemn duty and privilege.

Although most of the villagers have hesitated and refrained from coming to a Haus Barnabas Sunday service – imagining, no doubt, that this would be a denial of their Roman Catholic faith – several of those who have come into the house with their clubs, on getting to know the team as individual people, have been happy to come alone to special meetings. The Haus Barnabas carol service has, over the years, been very acceptable. Between singing carols and reading the appropriate Bible passages, there has been the opportunity to explain the reason Jesus Christ came into the world and the response of faith we need to make to Him if He is to be our Saviour.

One year a local Christian lady who had been trying to help and encourage refugee youngsters who were being housed in a guesthouse in a neighbouring village brought three young African Muslim men to the carol service. The service was conducted in German, and these lads' grasp of the language was limited, so it was great to be able to explain the Gospel to them in more detail in English later. The lady who had brought them and had their confidence was able to do this very adequately.

CHAPTER

8

Groups and Theme Weeks

Over the years, a number of very interesting groups have spent time in Haus Barnabas. One such, celebrating a significant birthday, was organised by a lady from Norfolk. She had invited a number of her friends to book to spend New Year in Haus Barnabas with her and informed the Haus Barnabas team that she was praying there would be snow as she loved it. It was a very successful house party, and our God, who controls the weather, graciously answered His daughter's prayer. In fact, when the snow kept coming throughout January, it was suggested that prayer should then be made for it to stop!

One of the guests celebrating the birthday was Marilyn Baker, the blind Christian singer, and a very enjoyable part of the birthday celebration was her singing and leading the group in worship through song. Because the group were so satisfied with the occasion, a New Year house party with Marilyn Baker became an annual fixture for several years. They were very enjoyable occasions, and the week included a public concert by Marilyn, with a programme of her songs intermingled with words of testimony revealing her love and devotion to Jesus. Marilyn's companion and co-worker Tracy also made a valuable contribution to the devotional times, and most years, there was snow, adding to the guests' enjoyment of the group holiday. As time went by, the house parties moved away from New Year, but Marilyn and Tracy continued to advertise and organise a house party most years in Haus Barnabas, to the pleasure of Leonard, Phyllis, and the team. On one occasion, a local German Christian friend, on mentioning to her pastor's wife that Marilyn Baker was singing in Utzenfeld, encountered utter disbelief.

'I heard her last in the Royal Albert Hall in London' was the retort. 'They must be just playing her music.'

One year Leonard got a phone call from one of the leaders of Sportsreach. This is a Christian organisation which brings young people together for football and netball, using the opportunity to evangelise. Sue was enquiring about the possibility of bringing a group of girls to Haus Barnabas for a retreat of

Sportsreach girls in Haus Barnabas lounge

several days and asked if there was a suitable field in the village for football. She was very satisfied with the response, and after the suitability of the premises was confirmed with a quick visit, a date was arranged. A very lively group of fourteen young ladies and two leaders arrived from Yorkshire one summer's day, and they had an active holiday of football, walking, boating, and swimming, with evening Bible times. This was then repeated several times during the next few years. Leonard was able to arrange football matches with ladies' teams in a couple of neighbouring towns, and after each match, the leader brought both teams together, sitting around her on the grass pitch, and shared the testimony of her faith and the message of the Gospel, offering New Testaments in German to anyone interested. Leonard or Deborah interpreted the message into German, and a few German girls asked for New Testaments.

There was one interesting incident after a match in Schönau. The goalkeeper for the British girls had not defended too well, which, diplomatically but unintentionally, had enabled the German team to win. Seeing this, an elderly gentleman went up to the goalkeeper, asking whether he could give her some tips. He introduced himself as a previous coach for the Schönau men's team and proudly added that he had coached Jögi Löw. This little town of Schönau in the Black Forest is Jögi's birthplace, and he went on to play international football for Germany before being the national team's very successful manager for many years. The splendid football stadium in Schönau has now been named after him.

Many secular clubs and associations have their Christian equivalent, and for a couple of years, members of the Christian Walking Club visited Haus Barnabas for a walking holiday. They very much enjoyed the area and entered well into the fellowship and ministry provided in the house, but a limiting factor hindering further bookings was the small number of rooms. Being mainly single men and women, they preferred single rooms. Haus Barnabas only has six guest bedrooms, and although they all have an ensuite toilet and shower room and will accommodate at least two people, with four rooms large enough to take extra single or double bunk beds, single guests are not always happy to share in this way. When single people have been willing to share, there have been interesting episodes of guests taking their duvet into the lounge to sleep when disturbed by their companion snoring. It has often been possible to use extra rooms for sleeping within easy walking distance in the village, but Lisbeth, the hostess of the most convenient of these small local guesthouses, has sadly given up offering bed-and-breakfast accommodation because of her increasing age.

Guests out walking have come back with interesting reports of experiences they have encountered. These include seeing unusual birds, such as the black woodpecker, which is unknown in Britain; flowers which they needed to identify in one or other of the books on the Haus Barnabas shelves; a striking fire salamander, with its bright orange streaks along the back of a black body; nude bathers in one of the mountain lakes; a group of mountain horn players practising in the forest; cows chained to the back of a tractor and being driven along country lanes; and large flocks of sheep following their shepherd across the open hillside, to name but a few.

One summer an older couple so enjoyed their holiday that they asked about the possibility of bringing their children and grandchildren back for a family holiday over Christmas and New Year. This proved most successful. The group filled the house with three families in addition to the grandparents. The grandfather had been a missionary doctor in Africa but sadly was now suffering from some degree of Alzheimer's.

One morning, coming down to breakfast, he looked at the large table where his children and grandchildren were seated and, smiling, happily murmured, 'Am I on earth or in heaven?'

There was plenty of snow on the mountains that Christmas, and all the youngsters hired skiing equipment and spent most of every day on the mountain slopes.

Over the years, Haus Barnabas has hosted a good number of theme weeks covering a range of different subjects. For several years, 'Reformation Week' drew guests interested in the sixteenth-century Reformation in Europe. The programme combined visits to Reformation sites within travelling distance and evening lectures. Zürich was a very important city for the Swiss Reformation. The city's Grossmünster (Zürich's cathedral church) was the centre from which the influence of Ulrich Zwingli's expository biblical preaching began to influence many cantons of the country. Also, very close to the 'Münster' is the house where the Anabaptist movement really took off. Here, in 1525, George Blaurock, believing that Christian baptism was for believers in Christ and not infants, requested Conrad Grebel to baptise him. Also, in Zürich, by the River Limmit, is a plaque indicating where unrepentant Anabaptists were drowned at the command of the city council and Zwingli's 'reformed' church.

A longer but very interesting day's trip is to the village of Wildhaus in the Swiss Alps, where Zwingli was born in 1484. His father was a mayor in this Alpine village, and his place of birth has been preserved as a museum. By booking ahead, one could arrange for a short lecture on Zwingli, which added interest to the visit. There was an incident arising from one of these visits when one of the Haus Barnabas guests left her handbag on the wooden bench outside the Zwingli house. In the attempt to recover this, it was remembered that a hotel immediately opposite Zwingli's house had the unusual name of Friedegg. On telephoning the hotel, it was discovered that one of their guests had found the bag and handed it in to reception. Very graciously, the hotel management was willing to post the bag back, extracting some money from a purse in the bag for the postage.

Zwingli's birth house in the Alpine village of Wildhaus

On several of these occasions, the lectures and video films giving information about the German and Swiss Reformation were supplemented with a series of lectures by Dr Bernard Kaiser on Luther's Reformation based on his five 'solae': Scripture alone, faith alone, grace alone, Christ alone and God's glory alone. One year the emphasis was on John Calvin, with a few lectures on Calvin's teaching from Ian Jemmett. That year, with a group of guests from Scotland, one of the day's outings was a drive in the house's two vehicles to Geneva, where Pastor John Glass of Eglise Evangélique Internationale de Genève showed the group around the Calvin sites in the city.

Bird-watching weeks have had mixed success. Although there is a very interesting range of bird species in the Black Forest, these are often difficult to observe as the forested areas are extensive and the birds comparatively few and mostly rather secretive, unlike many garden birds. The greatest interest came from visits to the vine-growing terraced slopes of the Kaiserstuhl on the Rhine Plain. Having discovered the best areas to visit, Leonard was able to lead small interested groups to see the extremely colourful bee-eaters and, on a couple of occasions, also hoopoes. Another of the visits during a bird-watching week was often to Mainau, the Isle of Flowers, on Lake Constance. Here, in addition to the range of interesting aquatic birds to be seen on the lake, the floral beauty of the various gardens, together with the tropical house and butterfly house, provides added intrigue.

A further, very important annual group holiday, the family week, deserves a chapter of its own.

CHAPTER

9

Family Holiday Weeks

A Christian couple who began coming regularly as guests to Haus Barnabas were very active in children's work in their home area of Essex in Southern England and also in taking some of their youngsters to Christian camps each summer. During one visit, they mentioned a particular family in which the parents wouldn't send their four children to camp because, as the father said, they liked to do things together with their children and couldn't afford a separate holiday for simply their offspring.

It was agreed that the desire of parents to spend time with their children was to be commended, and the seed thought was voiced – 'Why not run a holiday for parents with their children in Haus Barnabas?'

Daytime outings could be enjoyed by all of the family, and an evening programme for the children would allow the parents to have time for themselves. This was agreed as a wonderful idea, and the couple concerned had enough initiative and enthusiasm to set it in motion.

The first of these family holidays was fairly small, but the parents whose opinion had initiated the idea were pleased to bring their four children, and what developed out of it clearly proved it was of God.

The group arrived by train on a Saturday in August, and so their first day started with a worship and ministry service in the Haus Barnabas lounge. The father of the family had previously informed the leader that he was not interested in any of the spiritual aspects of the holiday and so took his eldest son for a walk during the time of the Sunday morning worship. Everyone else attended the service, which was adapted, as far as Leonard felt possible, to try and keep the interest and meet the needs of each age group.

Arrival of Haus Barnabas family holiday guests

Each morning, before breakfast, Leonard led the customary devotional time with Bible reading followed by a short period of open prayer. This was intended mostly for the Haus Barnabas team, together with the leaders of the holiday group, but miraculously, by the middle of the week, the father who had wanted nothing spiritual began attending. Also, in the middle of the week, the mother of the family developed severe toothache. Leonard rang the local dentist and took the sufferer along to the surgery.

As they sat in the waiting room and then in the dentist's surgery, where Leonard stayed with his guest to translate if necessary, she turned to him and said with some feeling, 'I don't know why you are doing this for me. Nobody does this. In the pub, before we left, our mates laughed at the thought of us going to a Christian place and commented we would be thrown out within a few days. When we get back, I shall tell them how it really was!'

On the last evening of the week's holiday, everyone spent the time together. Leonard and Phyllis prompted each to say what they had enjoyed about the week, and the children shared something of what they had learned from their evening programme.

At the end of the evening, the father approached Leonard, thanked him for all that the Haus Barnabas team had done for them, and then added in a questioning way, 'I realise my life has got to change.'

Leonard was able to respond in a simple way, commenting that it was only a personal faith and commitment to the Lord Jesus that could bring about a lasting change in his life. He also advised him to talk to David, the leader of the holiday, once he got home with a view to attending church and learning more about the Bible and the Christian faith.

Once they got home, both husband and wife enrolled in an alpha course and, by the end of the year, were asking for baptism. The husband suggested that it would be good to be baptised in the Black Forest, where his path to faith had started, but it was agreed that it would be better for his own pastor to baptise him. The occasion was chosen for a time when Leonard and Phyllis were back in Britain, and Leonard felt honoured to be asked to participate in the baptism.

However, arising out of this came another interesting development in the Haus Barnabas story. The eldest son of the above family was unable to get a job after leaving school and, aided by unhelpful companions, his life soon deteriorated into drug taking and alcohol. When a certain incident ended with a court case, Christian friends got him a good solicitor and, with the cooperation of other Christians, put together a programme to present to the court which would show he was willing to follow a positive new lifestyle. This was successful in keeping him out of prison. The plan was for him to move away from the influence of his home area, live with a Christian family, and attend an evangelical church. As a second stage, Leonard and Phyllis and team agreed for him to come as a voluntary helper to Haus Barnabas for three months.

Praise the Lord that during the first stage of this programme and through the influence of the family and pastor with whom he was staying, he committed his life to the Lord. The plan for the second stage was for him to come to Haus Barnabas, together with his parents and siblings, for that year's family holiday and then to stay on afterwards as a voluntary helper, but things went drastically wrong. Through the influence of another young man in the holiday group, he had a couple of evenings in the village pub. Sadly, this brought back the urge for alcohol, and he acquired bottles of spirits, which he drank secretly. One evening it was realised that he had lost control of himself through drink. The lad was known to become vicious when drunk, and after prayer, the leader of the holiday decided it was necessary to move around the sleeping arrangements, so the young man had a room to himself. Two of the leaders then took turns sitting on guard outside his room throughout the night to ensure he didn't disturb any of the other guests. After a second drunken episode some days later, it became clear that there was no way he could stay on in Haus Barnabas and work with the team serving holiday guests.

Still, wonderfully, God had a purpose in allowing this lapse in the conduct of this young convert, and following real concern and prayer, the family holiday leader was able to arrange for him to move up to Scotland and to come under the care of a youth pastor with a similar background to his own in a Glasgow church. Within a strongly disciplined but caring environment, he was able to have structured Bible teaching and, over a period of a few years, to complete a Bible college course and begin preaching.

A couple of years later, our young friend returned to help in Haus Barnabas as a changed person. He loved the Lord, loved to serve Him, and devoured good theological books. However, as he confessed, drug taking seems to affect the brain in different ways and leaves its marks. Also, urges towards alcohol and cigarette smoking re-emerge when one is deflected from a close daily walk with the Lord Jesus.

On a further visit, as a helper at another family week, he felt strongly one evening that he should offer to share his testimony with the holiday group, particularly for the benefit of the teenagers present for whom he had a burden. All felt his testimony, in which he gave all the glory to God for His amazing grace, to be a very powerful message. Afterwards, however, our young friend was unable to sleep, feeling his total unworthiness and being tempted to believe he was a complete hypocrite in the things he has said. The next day, it was discovered that he had fallen out of the roof skylight of his bedroom on the second floor. Tragically, this has left him paralysed from the waist down. He continues to rejoice in the Lord, and we must trust that his heavenly Father has a continuing purpose for him in His service. The above incident resulted in a visit from the police to investigate how it could have occurred, but thankfully, the conclusion reached was that it was an accident for which Haus Barnabas could not be blamed.

There has been a range of strange incidents in relation to these family holiday weeks, and one cannot help thinking that at least some of these were the result of satanic opposition to the power of the Gospel in Haus Barnabas. The different groups have generally come by train; attention is drawn here to just three different occasions when their journeys have been interrupted. One year, the day before they travelled, part of the railway line in Germany collapsed when the ground subsided, causing a considerable delay. Buses had to be laid on to take all passengers around the impassable stretch of line. On another occasion, when their train pulled into the station, it was announced that it needed to be taken out of service as a gun had been fired at the train, smashing a window.

On a third occasion, the group had already boarded their final train bringing them up the Wiese Valley to Haus Barnabas when an announcement asked everyone to disembark as the train couldn't run. A thunderstorm had brought down a tree across the railway line, effectively creating a barrier to the upper region of the valley. It was already late in the evening, and the railway officials had no answer to the group leader's urgent and persistent questioning as to how to get this group of about twenty people, including young children, up to Utzenfeld. The cost of hotel accommodation in Basel would be phenomenal, so eventually, a station official ordered five taxis for them with the promise that they could reclaim the cost of these from the railway. On arriving at Haus Barnabas in Swiss Mercedes taxis, four passengers to a vehicle, the drivers demanded payment of the best part of £200 per taxi for the thirty-mile journey. The leader had no option but to pay on his bank card, trusting the rail company to recompense him. Sadly, his claim for this was disputed. After several months of waiting for a response to the form he was asked to fill in, together with the taxi payment receipts sent to the Deutsche Bahn head office, the railway company wriggled out of responsibility for the cost despite their officials having ordered the taxis for the group. No repayment was ever forthcoming.

Still, the couple organising these holidays put in much hard work, time, patience, and prayer, and the Lord has added His blessing. One year a man who was not a Christian but had a believing wife and a daughter who was active in the church agreed to join his wife in a Haus Barnabas family holiday. His wife had been praying for him for some years, and a few years earlier, he had attended a spring harvest weekend where he had been drawn towards a step of faith but had some serious questions which worried him. What is

Family holiday guests

difficult to understand is that when he got back to his wife's church and began attending and asking his questions, the elders warned the congregation not to talk to him as they felt the questions might undermine their faith. It rather seems they didn't feel able to answer his questions themselves either. In any case, it became clear that God had been preparing him for this holiday.

During evenings on the holiday, when the group met together for devotions and singing, he sat quietly, saying nothing, but finally, one evening he chose a hymn to sing and eventually commented, 'All week, I've sat here, watching you all and listening, and I've compared myself to someone standing at the top of a diving board watching you all swimming around and enjoying yourselves, but I've been uncertain how to jump in.'

This gave everyone the opportunity to talk to him freely and encourage him to pray and trust himself to our Lord Jesus. After his return home, he was eventually baptised and then, feeling a real attachment to Haus Barnabas, came back with his wife and also his daughter and family for several years afterwards.

During one of the family holiday weeks, a dramatic thunderstorm hit Utzenfeld during the Sunday morning worship service. The first awareness of an advancing storm was thunder in the distance, and then as it gradually became darker and lights had to be switched on, the time lapse between flashes of lightning and the roar of thunder got increasingly less. Then the rain came – heavy, viciously heavy rain – and it became so dark outside that the street lights came on and it appeared more like midnight than midday. Leonard and Phyllis's nephew was leading the service that Sunday, which freed the couple up to sit at the back of the room full of parents and children. A teenage girl sitting immediately in front of them was visibly terrified and was physically trembling in fear at each bright flash of lightning and deafening, often prolonged crash of thunder. Hearing sounds of human activity outside, Leonard and Phyllis went to investigate and discovered a group of motorcyclists and a woman cyclist taking shelter in their porch. They were invited to come into the house and sit in the restaurant and offered cups of coffee. The motorcyclists, who were leaving pools on the tiled floor as water ran off their leather clothing, were from further afield, but the woman was local and introduced herself as the wife of a man in Schönau whom Leonard had done English translating for.

The storm must have continued for the best part of an hour, during which time the service continued in the lounge and the German 'refugees' sitting in the restaurant were clearly aware of what was happening. This provoked questions which Leonard and Phyllis were happy to answer and to explain what the house stood for and who the group was in the neighbouring room. A humorous comment was made later that perhaps the Holders should pray for regular thunderstorms on a Sunday to bring a congregation in!

CHAPTER

10

—

God's Provision for House Maintenance

After the Holders had rented the earlier Haus Barnabas for eleven years, owning Gasthaus Engel meant there was suddenly a new responsibility to care for the upkeep and maintenance of the premises. The structure of the building dates back to the first half of the seventeen century, and although the previous owner had made drastic changes, all these improvements were about forty years old when Leonard and Phyllis, with Timothy and Deborah Brooks and baby Thomas, moved in.

One of the first problems noticed was dampness in a bedroom wall. This became more obvious after rain and dried stains indicated it had been a long-term problem. The outside walls are almost a metre thick, and there is a wide overhanging roof immediately above the window, so it was difficult to see how the rain could be getting into the wall. It was obvious that the previous owner had also never solved the problem. Redecorating the room with fresh emulsion covered the problem for a while, but like sin in the human heart, the root cause needed to be discovered and dealt with. The previous owner had constructed two rooms under the roof above the bedroom where the problem was manifesting itself, and it was only discovered after several years that a roof light in one of the rooms was letting in rainwater. Dripping down behind the inner wall, this water was invisible until it soaked into the stonework of the outer wall and revealed itself as dampness on the bedroom wall beneath. Further inspection in the roof behind the partition wall constructed there exposed a small but significant section of one of the main roof timbers which had rotted slowly away because of rain dripping on it for twenty years or more. Leonard feared the possibility that this situation could have caused dry rot, which could spread around the roof timbers in a dangerous way, but he was greatly relieved when an architect friend advised him that as long as there is plenty of air circulating, there need be no fear of such. There could be wet rot, but this is far less dangerous. When John, a builder friend from North Wales, offered to come and do any needed building jobs for the house, Leonard explained this situation, and John kindly arranged to come out with a colleague. Together, they got into the roof from the outside with the aid of scaffolding, corrected the source of the problem, dealt with the roof timber, and, as an extra, added a further roof window to provide for an additional attic room.

In another bedroom, dampness was causing mildew on the wall to the outside in the ensuite bathroom. The best advice from a couple of builders who examined it was that it was caused by the lack of ventilation. Although this sounded feasible, leaving the window open more frequently failed to cure the problem. The answer came in a remarkable way. A guest who was staying in that particular room for a few nights came down to breakfast after a rainy night and commented that he had noticed the problem on the bathroom wall and thought he knew the answer. After breakfast, he took Leonard outside and, looking up at the roof, commented that he was pretty certain one of the tiles was cracked. This had always been considered a possible cause, but no one had been able to identify the damaged tile.

'I think I can see it,' said the guest, who, incidentally, was someone previously unknown to the Haus Barnabas team and wasn't a professing Christian. 'I think there is a tile there that is broken at the top, just under the upper overlapping tile, where water running down the roof can get in. The crack is almost invisible from below, but perhaps we can get access to it in the roof.'

This proved possible, and finding a suitable replacement tile in the lean-to outside the back door, the friendly guest, who clearly had been sent to Haus Barnabas by God, extracted the culprit tile, which was broken exactly as he had thought, and set in the new one. He later explained that roofing was his profession. Haus Barnabas has never seen him or heard from him since.

On two other occasions, there were issues with dampness on inside walls which clearly didn't come from rain getting in. Leonard called in a local firm, who suggested that the cause of the problem in both of the separate incidents was probably a broken pipe running down on the inside of the affected walls. The foreman suggested that Leonard inform their insurance company as this sort of problem could be covered by the house insurance. The problem was exactly as he had predicted, and thankfully, the insurance company paid up for most of the cost, which included redecorating the wall after the breakages had been fixed.

An amusing incident occurred when a young man who had come to help for a week was asked to put up a small rack on one of the walls. On drilling the wall to set in the screw, he bored straight through a hidden hot water pipe. With his finger over the small hole, trying in vain to stem the fierce spurt of hot water, he called loudly for help. Turning off the main water cock didn't help immediately as there were two stories of hot water above to drain out first. The village plumber was summoned and came promptly.

His first words were 'Well done, lad. That was a bull's eye!' Who said Germans don't have a sense of humour?

The boiler in the cellar was powered by oil and served to provide heating and hot water. Oil was stored in a twenty-thousand-litre tank in a walled-off section of the cellar. Being old, the boiler was not particularly efficient in its use of fuel, and also, since Germany was demanding increasingly cleaner exhaust fumes from boilers, for several years, the only way the dear old boiler could pass its annual cleanliness test was to get it serviced and cleaned immediately before the testing inspector did his job. For a couple of years, it failed but managed to scrape through in a retest after being serviced.

Clearly, it needed to be replaced. One year, the house opposite was having gas put in from a gas main that ran along between the houses under the road, and the firm installing this offered Haus Barnabas a good price to bring gas into their cellar at the same time as the road was being dug up. The team, anticipating the day when it might prove possible to change their boiler, accepted this offer in faith.

A frequent guest and friend of the Haus Barnabas team was a director at Rolls Royce, a combustion engineer, and he took a professional interest in the house's boiler. Having investigated whether it would be possible to make it more efficient, he advised getting a quote for a new one and suggested he could be willing to help finance it. One of the few businesses in the village of Utzenfeld happens to be a plumber and heating engineering firm. The firm understood the Haus Barnabas heating system, and interestingly, the owner, who was about to retire, commented that he had worked on the installation of the old oil boiler as one of his first jobs as an apprentice in the mid-1960s. Any new boiler needed to have enough capacity not only to heat the complete house when outside temperatures dropped to minus twenty degrees Celsius but also to supply all the hot water required for a house full of guests wanting to shower. The quotation was very detailed, but the price for removing the old boiler and supplying and installing a new gas-fired heating and hot water system was not much short of twenty thousand euros, which seemed enormous. Our British friend, who understood these things, analysed the quotation with the help of a colleague who spoke German and agreed it could be accepted and said he would pay half of the cost if Haus Barnabas could pay the other half. Amazingly, when this was mentioned in a prayer letter, another kind supporter of the house's ministry sent a cheque for the remaining half of the cost. This was a wonderful provision from God. and having a much more efficient gas boiler also had the added financial benefit of reducing the annual heating bill.

Wood carving has been a traditional hobby for Black Forest farmers during the long winter months and, on passing this acquired skill down in families, has created small home industries for the benefit of tourists. It has also meant that nicely carved noticeboards are often displayed outside homes and guesthouses. The Haus Barnabas team felt over some years that it would be an added attraction for their house to have such a noticeboard. This was occasionally mentioned when talking with guests, and one faithful supporter of the house and ministry took this very much to heart. On her 80th birthday, she requested that instead of presents, she wished her family and friends to make donations towards the cost of carving such a noticeboard for Haus Barnabas. When this money arrived, Leonard was able to

Notice board with traditional Black Forest carved lettering

arrange for a woodcarver they knew to create a suitable board as shown in the illustration here. The letters are carved to stand out of their wooden base and painted white. On giving the text in John's Gospel to be included on the board, Leonard inadvertently wrote it down incorrectly for the woodcarver. It must be admitted, however, that the false order of words (which some of you might notice) provides for a pleasing arrangement of letters on the board. Our builder friend from North Wales kindly built the framework whilst on holiday, and he and others erected it for vehicle drivers and pedestrians to see as they pass the house.

CHAPTER

11

Testimonies of God's Amazing Love and Grace

It has been a regular part of the weekly programme in Haus Barnabas to have an open time of fellowship on a Sunday evening. Leonard usually led this meeting but made a point of having nothing prepared, unlike the morning worship and ministry service, which is more formal.

Also, unlike the morning service, this evening time together was never advertised to anyone except in-house guests to attend, which gave a greater sense of freedom to share personal experiences together. Many have commented on the openness they have found in Haus Barnabas, and comments made by guests indicate that this is lacking amongst Christians in many churches. Occasionally, guests have initially felt uneasy and even embarrassed by this openness.

Leonard and Phyllis remember a comment from one guest who, after leaving at the end of his holiday, had said to himself, 'I'm never going back there again. It makes me feel too exposed.'

He did, in fact, come back, and the reason for this unease later became obvious. Experience has shown that people find it difficult to share with others things that they are ashamed of, either in their own lives or in the lives of their families. Of course, this is not only understandable but sometimes also wise. Certain things in our lives can only be shared with others whom we trust implicitly. Perhaps less now than in earlier years, divorce in the family can be such a subject. Leonard and Phyllis remember an occasion when, while they were around the meal table, one guest confided with some hesitation the fact that their son's marriage had broken up. Immediately, another couple disclosed that this had happened to their daughter also. Being able to share with one another the trauma of this, the disappointment, and the soul-searching it had caused them as to their own failure in the upbringing of their children had helped both parties.

Still, the spiritual blessings that Christians have received and times when God has been very close and real to them are also rarely spoken of in some churches. Haus Barnabas Sunday evenings were the time when guests were encouraged to share experiences together, and Leonard would, as sensitively as he could, ask questions to try and bring out spiritual thoughts and ways in which God had blessed them. He would encourage guests to say why they chose certain hymns, knowing that very often, behind the love of a particular hymn was an experience of God's blessing. Sometimes he would ask particular people directly how they had first found faith in Christ. Both he and Phyllis remember one couple who were thrilled about the opportunity to share their testimony.

The wife began by confessing that she and her husband had separated because her work had become too much of a priority in her life. This was prior to either of them becoming Christians. Then without warning, she was suddenly made redundant and felt that her whole life was falling apart. As she was clearing out her desk on the last day in her office, a business colleague called in from another firm. Noting her distress and hearing the reason for it, she hesitantly recommended that she seek Jesus as a friend who could give her a new direction in her life. Although she had made no response at the time, the comment placed a seed in her mind and heart, and eventually, she telephoned the colleague, saying she would be happy to go to church with her. The friend then had to confess that her own Christian commitment had slipped and that she wasn't just then connected with a church, but she agreed that they could find one together to go to. This led to our Haus Barnabas guest finding Christ and beginning a new life with Him. After a while, she began to think about the man who was still her husband but whom she hadn't seen for several years. She had no idea where he was or how to contact him but began to pray for him.

The husband then took up the story. He was into ballroom dancing and, after a late night on Saturday, would often sleep most of Sunday. One Sunday morning, unable to sleep, he had an inner urge to go to church. He had no idea what had caused this urge, but on getting himself dressed, he then realised he was too late for a service at the parish church. Then he remembered receiving through his letterbox an invitation to Sunday services at a Free Evangelical Church. He hunted out the leaflet to find out the details, and since denominations meant nothing to him, he decided to go. The service had already started, but the kind face at the door assured him this was no problem and directed him to one of the few vacant seats. On sitting down, he looked at the person next to him and, in total amazement, recognised the woman he was still married to but hadn't seen for many months. Wonderfully, this incident led to his conversion, and within a short while, the two were back together and praising God for His grace to them both. As they said, that holiday in Haus Barnabas was intended to be a second honeymoon for them.

There have been a few guests who, having had a Black Forest holiday, have organised a group from their church or circle of friends to bring out to Haus Barnabas. One group who have come several times are from the church at Penrhyndeudraeth in North Wales. On one of their visits, the leader received a message that prompted a special time of prayer from all in the house. Someone they knew very well in the church had had a very serious car accident. He had been driving down to Cardiff in the south of Wales for, if Leonard remembers correctly, a conference organised by the Open-Air Mission, with which he was working part time as one of their evangelists. The accident was so serious that he was not expected to live.

Remarkably, two or three years later, the person concerned was fit enough to come with the group, and he shared with the other guests present the amazing experience of his heavenly Father's providential intervention in regard to that accident. That prayer in Haus Barnabas and those of many others also had been answered in a wonderful way even before they were made.

A young man driving his father's very powerful car at speed had hit his vehicle with tremendous force on the corner of a narrow road. He himself now has no memory of the incident. Unconscious, he needed to be cut out of the crushed vehicle by firemen and flown by helicopter to one of Wales's main hospitals. The following, he learned from others later. God's first provision for him, he said, came from the fact that three very significant people arrived quickly on the scene: a nurse, a doctor with experience in motorway accidents, and a local farmer. The hospital told him that without the quick action of the doctor, he would have certainly died on the spot, but amazingly, no one since has been able to identify who this doctor was. To this, he raised the question 'Could he have been an angel?' He was, in any case, God's messenger and agent to save His servant. Then the farmer present was able to provide the location and direct the rescue helicopter to the closest suitable field in which to land.

The next remarkable 'coincidence' – which, without doubt as Christians, we can recognise as God's provision for His child – was the fact that when the helicopter arrived at the hospital, a team of specialised surgeons had just completed an operation and were leaving the operating theatre after flying down from London to treat a celebrity. He thought it was a famous footballer or rugby player who had had a serious incident on the pitch. Seeing the almost impossible condition of our Haus Barnabas guest, they recognised this as a challenge and went back into the theatre to work on him. If Leonard remembers correctly, it was an eight-hour operation as almost every organ in his body was damaged and several bones broken. He was kept unconscious for many weeks and needed several additional operations. He commented that one of the surgeons later came to see him and said that knowing how he was when he had been brought into the hospital, his healing was a miracle.

Another fact that he attributes to God's grace related to the answer a nurse gave him. Our friend had had a very chequered past and, prior to his conversion, was often drunk and had been banned from several pubs because of his behaviour and his coarse language. When nurses said to him that whilst unconscious, he had often talked aloud, he feared what sort of language had come out of his brain and mouth when he couldn't restrain it.

'What did I say?' he asked with some trepidation,

'Oh, you were preaching to us' came back the answer.

Our friend commented that his calling following his conversion was open-air preaching, and shortly before the accident, he had asked God for a way to be able to leave his business as a builder and concentrate full time on serving his new Lord and Master. Eventually, after a recovery period of many months, he has been able to do this. Maybe the accident, followed by the miraculous recovery, was first the devil's attempt to stop his witness and then God's intervention to show His greater power and care for His servant. He is now serving the Lord in any way he can, both as a builder and an open-air preacher.

There have been many other testimonies of God's love and grace – but, just to share, one further account of a family incident. One Sunday evening a lady felt able to share the following. It began, she said, following one of the weekly youth meetings. Unusually, the youth leader accompanied her daughter home and asked to speak with her parents. She explained to them that their daughter had spoken to her confidentially and in tears, confessing she was pregnant. She said she was very much ashamed and was fearful of having to tell her parents. After talking awhile, she had agreed for the youth leader to come home and be present with her as the revelation would take place. This was obviously an alarming shock for the parents, but the mother, the Haus Barnabas guest, agreed to help care for the baby, enabling the daughter to continue her education. This had all happened several years earlier, and after a difficult number of years (the granddaughter now being in her teens), the grandmother acknowledged that the two had an extremely good relationship. They both loved the open air, and the granddaughter enjoyed going for long walks with her grandmother, and they both had a passion camping in the most remote settings. As she concluded her testimony, the grandmother acknowledged God's grace to her in this family situation, which, initially, had appeared to have been such a tragedy.

One of the voluntary helpers in Haus Barnabas had suffered with back pains for several years and had frequently been off school with this problem. One Wednesday evening the Scripture passage being considered during the weekly time of fellowship and Bible study was the passage in the Acts of the Apostle where we read of Peter's response to the lame man asking for money: 'Silver and gold, I do not have, but what I have, I give you: In the name of Jesus Christ of Nazareth, rise up and walk.'[56] It was clear that our young assistant was in pain, and during that day, she had frequently needed to lie on the floor to relieve her aching back. Knowing this and in the light of what the group had been studying, Phyllis felt strongly that she should suggest specific prayer for their young assistant. One of the couples with them that week had lived in Hong Kong and, having been impressed by the work and witness of Jackie Pullinger there (well known for her book *Chasing the Dragon*), very enthusiastically seconded this proposal.

Our young friend was happy about this, so standing around her, several prayed, reminding the Lord of what He had done through His servant Peter many years before and seeking His hand of healing in this situation. The girl concerned also prayed, and Leonard remembers how she told the Lord she would love to be free from pain but that she was happy for whatever He saw was best for her.

The following day, when asked how she was, the youngest Haus Barnabas team member was happy to report that she had slept well and that that morning was without pain. As far as Leonard and Phyllis know, the back pain never returned. The Lord is good, and His sympathy and power are the same today as they were in biblical times.

On numerous occasions, guests and visitors coming to Haus Barnabas have commented that they have very much valued

---

56 Acts 3:6.

the peaceful and loving atmosphere within the house. Another comment Leonard and Phyllis remember being made by a young German lady who had come to learn English was that she felt safe in the house, and this comment has been repeated by others. The Haus Barnabas team love to think that these appreciative comments reflect the presence of God's Spirit in the house.

CHAPTER

꙰

12

Voluntary Helpers in Haus Barnabas

Over the years, a steady stream of university students and others, younger and older, volunteered to provide help in Haus Barnabas for shorter and longer periods. In fact, as this began to happen, Leonard and Phyllis sensed that part of the service God was seeking from them was to bring the influence of Scripture and the family atmosphere within the house, to the benefit of the helpers whom He sent to them.

The first person who came in this capacity stayed for at least a year whilst studying German at university. She married the Holders' elder son and has since produced three grandchildren for Leonard and Phyllis. Another early student, Deborah, returned long term after completing her degree and an intensive

Deborah and Timothy Brooks with Tom and Esther In 2012

course in teaching English as a foreign language. She has proved an invaluable co-worker in the house and now, on the retirement of Leonard and Phyllis, is together with her husband, running Haus Barnabas. Their two children – Tom, now 18, and Esther, 16 years old at the time this is written – have grown up in the house and have proved a great asset to the work in many ways.

Over the years, voluntary helpers in Haus Barnabas have fulfilled a vital role in the smooth running of the house. Although there are far too many to mention individually, each has nevertheless played a unique role in the story of the house and, together with many Haus Barnabas holiday guests, on becoming friends with Leonard and Phyllis, have proved the means under God of great personal encouragement,

Leonard and Phyllis with
student summer helpers

influence, and blessing in the Holders' Christian walk. Continuing contact with specific friends goes on to mean a great deal to Leonard and Phyllis, and an introduction to the church fellowships of some has proved a great blessing.

Most helpers have combined service in the house with afternoons out enjoying the Black Forest, and many have also spoken of the blessing they have found through the fellowship and Bible ministry they have experienced in Haus Barnabas. The resident team are indebted to so many for all their unstinted help in a huge number of ways. Guesthouse running, with the related kitchen work, involves endless washing up after helping to lay and clear tables; room service, including striping and remaking beds; and cleaning, involving the use of dusters, brushes, mops, and vacuum cleaners. What would seem miraculous is that many of our helpers have applied to return year after year.

Other voluntary helpers have come to undertake specific jobs. These have included reconstructing a dry-stone wall, felling trees and other garden work, painting outside window shutters, and redecorating corridors and rooms. A very supportive friend from Northern Island has come more than once specifically to spring-clean the house and wash the many curtains. A builder from North Wales came to construct and erect a new noticeboard and, on another occasion, to commence work on the Holders' new flat over the double garage. Other supportive friends have financed, in part or in whole, specific projects or replacement equipment.

During the main holiday season, which obviously was the period in which the most help was needed, the limited number of guest rooms in the first Haus Barnabas made it difficult to accommodate another staff member. This problem was solved by arranging book shelves in an L-shape in the corner of the large lounge and making space for a narrow bed behind it. It was also thought wise to rig up a curtain over the entrance to this private little sleeping domain. There were a few occasions when guests unwittingly caused some concern for the young lady secluded in her makeshift boudoir. On at least one occasion, a guest, unable to sleep, came searching for a book to read, having no idea a member of the Haus Barnabas team was trying to sleep a few inches behind the bookshelves. Also, on a couple of occasions, guests brought their bed duvet into the lounge to sleep on the sofa there, confessing afterwards that they were unable to get to sleep in their room, being disturbed by the snoring from a holiday companion sharing a twin room with them.

There were also several male helpers over the years. One who came to the first Haus Barnabas was recommended by a Christian friend who later, without any comment from the Holders to prompt it, apologised for sending the lad after hearing a bit more about him. Some sincere Christians can become quite fanatical in their pursuit of a spiritual life, and there are many ways one can become like the Pharisees of Jesus's time. Another lad, from a difficult non-Christian home, had made a profession of faith after being involved in outreach from a local church through football. After leaving school with no qualifications, he was recommended to Haus Barnabas as a helper and stayed for the best part of a year. He was a reliable worker on the jobs he could undertake, washing up being his speciality. He happily joined in on the spiritual aspects of the daily and weekly programme and, on returning home, asked for baptism at his local church.

On planning for a year out from studies, a young teenager from a Christian home asked to come and help in Haus Barnabas for about three months as she wanted to spend part of her year in Germany and the other part helping at a mission station in Africa. During that period in Haus Barnabas, her best friend from school, who hadn't had a Christian upbringing, came to visit her and later contacted Leonard and Phyllis, requesting the opportunity to spend time in Haus Barnabas as a helper herself. She was a quiet, thoughtful girl and fitted well into the routine of the house, returning for several weeks each summer during her university days. She appeared to really appreciate the devotions, Christian fellowship, and ministry in the house and would often be waiting with her Bible for these to begin. Although not for the want of encouragement, she never seemed to settle into a church in Britain where she felt comfortable. As Phyllis and Leonard have done for many past helpers and holiday guests, they maintained the contact, and this young lady is one of about six past helpers who have returned to visit, bringing boyfriends or husbands to introduce to the Haus Barnabas team.

One young lady to mention in particular, after coming to help during most of her holidays whilst at sixth-form college, returned again for what was initially intended as a gap year before university. She was a much-valued member of the team and, having a good grasp of German, entered wholeheartedly into the work and witness of the house for quite a while. The whole team were extremely sad to lose her when, after a period of illness, she eventually returned to England to marry and have a family of her own.

A most interesting young man in his twenties came from Russia. It never became clear how he had come to faith in the Lord Jesus, but he was constantly listening to sermons on his computer from the States and had developed a good understanding of Orthodox Christian doctrine. It didn't appear, however, that he had had the opportunity for Christian fellowship either in a church setting or in a family environment. His mother had left the family home when he was younger, and he was living with his father and an uncle. It seemed that he was used to feeding himself as he needed from the fridge as it soon became clear he was not accustomed to sitting at a table with others. Although he had a good grasp of English, it was sometimes not obvious that he had understood what other members of the team said to him. These different factors meant he was not the easiest of the voluntary helpers who came to Haus Barnabas, but believing all are sent by God for a purpose, the house took him under their wing as best they could.

When the time came for his return to St Petersburg, he departed to Basel to pick up his bus ticket as this means of transport, which must have taken hours and hours, was the cheapest. The last bus up the valley comes through Utzenfeld at 11:00 p.m., and Eugene was not on it. Having been expecting him back long before this, Leonard decided he should notify the police. They were as helpful as could be expected and said they would enquire from the Swiss police whether anyone of his description had been involved in an accident in Basel. At least one guest in the house was aware of the situation, and when, the next morning, she heard voices coming from Eugene's bedroom, there was a sense of relief that the wanderer must have returned. However, it very soon became apparent that the voice was that of an American preacher and that there was actually no living person in the room at all. He obviously used this means, by a timer set on his laptop, to wake him up. Eugene returned midmorning and appeared astonished that everyone in Haus Barnabas had been concerned about him.

'I needed to catch the train up to Karlsruhe to collect my bus ticket from the office there,' he explained casually. 'When I got back to Basel, I had missed the last train up to Zell, and so I sat by a radiator in the station all night.'

Leonard and Phyllis decided that this lack of awareness that anyone would worry about him most probably arose from his life experience in Russia.

A couple of years later, Haus Barnabas had a further visit from their Russian friend. He emailed asking whether he could come and stay with his 'bride' at the cheapest rate possible. This provoked a lot of interest, and a date and price were agreed, and in his return email, Leonard confirmed they were reserving him and his wife a double room.

'But she's not my wife. She's my bride' was the answer that came back.

Clearly, the use of language was causing a confusion, and Leonard wrote again, offering him two single rooms.

When the couple arrived, it was soon discovered that the young lady was from Canada. They had met online, and since she was unable and unwilling to travel to Russia and he was prohibited from travelling to Canada, they had needed to meet in Western Europe in a country that was open to them both. It took a while to ascertain how far their relationship had developed, but there were clear indications that he was far more enthusiastic about it than she was. Leonard sat down with them both and tried sensitively to help them talk the matter through together. The young lady was adamant that she had no wish to live in Russia, and Eugene could see no way he could get a residency permit for Canada. Any possibility of a marriage relationship together appeared to be fraught with difficulties.

The next day, Eugene asked Leonard whether he would 'engage' them. This clearly put Leonard in a difficult position, requiring quick thinking.

'Eugene,' Leonard responded, 'it's Sunday, and we have a time of fellowship this evening. If you and your girlfriend come and join us in the lounge, we will all pray for you and for God's wisdom and guidance for you both.'

In the event, neither of them came into the lounge that evening, and nothing more was said about an engagement. Phyllis had an opportunity to talk to the young lady from Canada. There was reason to think she was probably a born-again believer, but her mother had died, she was out of touch with her father, and it seemed she had no one to love, care for, and advise her. The very occasional email from Eugene made no further mention of an engagement or marriage.

One Sunday morning, just before Christmas, a young lady came breezing into the service at the last minute, saying she had run down from Todtnauberg, where she was staying. After the service, she informed the small group worshipping that morning that she was American and had been attending an intensive German language course. She acknowledged that she was a believing Christian and said she liked to search out small Christian groups to worship with wherever she went. On learning that the Haus Barnabas team were putting on a carol service that same week, she requested whether she could come to help with the preparation for this. Leonard and Phyllis felt she must be an angel sent from God! Her next engagement in the new year was a Bible course at a Bible college near Lake Constance, which has connections with Capernwray Hall in England. After a year or so back in the United States, she offered some voluntary help in Haus Barnabas and later informed the team that she had become engaged to marry an Austrian Christian whom she had met on the Bible course. After spending a little time in Austria, she requested Leonard to marry her and her fiancé, Herbert. The arrangements were rather complex. The legal registrar wedding had already taken place prior to the requested Christian wedding, so there was complete freedom in arranging the form and location for the latter. With the couple's love of the mountains, they wanted their nuptial before God to take

Marriage ceremony
in Austrian cave

place in a mountain cave. Leonard agreed, saying he would be happy to fit in with the arrangements, and he and Timothy motored across to Dornbirn for the day, which was a three-hour drive in each direction. To reach the cave involved a bus ride into the mountains and then a twenty-minute climb. Because of the rather inaccessible location, the group gathering to witness the marriage were exclusively younger people, and the majority of them made no profession of a Christian faith. It was a very interesting occasion; the singing of two worshipful hymns rang through the cave, along with Bible readings and a short Gospel message from Leonard, before hearing the couple repeat their vows to each other – everything in German, of course.

CHAPTER

13

Haus Barnabas Animals

When the Holders and Brooks took over Gasthaus Engel in 2002, the resident pigs had been sold off, leaving two empty pig pens. These were within a reinforced concrete 'room', constructed inside the 'barn' between the double garage and the house. It had its own supply of water, which was led down through pipes from a stream high up the hillside. Hence came free water, completely independent of that supplied by the authorities at cost through a meter. Effluent drained out into a large cesspit under the carpark. It had all been very well organised with usual German efficiency. Although Leonard would have loved to get back to a bit of pig farming, it was not a priority, and he never seriously thought about it.

The animals that *were* left by the previous owners were three feral cats. They had been fed exclusively on restaurant waste, lived, moved, and had their being outside the house, and kept away rodents. These three considered Gasthaus Engel, with its garden and forest, their domain and only reluctantly allowed feline strangers to share their feeding bowls. There appeared to be a big ginger tom, who roamed the village claiming the right to impregnate a harem of females. Two of the Haus Barnabas cats were female, the third being a less mature tom of one of them. On asking the previous owners whether their cats were going with them, there was a very distinct negative answer.

'If you don't feed them, they will go away' was the answer Leonard received when enquiring about their future.

Fulfilling this rather naive answer was easier said than done. True, the two older, more experienced cats were able to hunt and survive, but the smaller one got thinner and thinner, and it seemed cruel not to feed it. Of course, having started, it needed to continue, meaning the Haus Barnabas team were adopting three feral cats. Soon, it became obvious that the two females were pregnant. The one they had named Peggy, having produced her litter, brought her offspring and laid them carefully under the open-sided barn outside the back door. They were pretty little things, and it was distressing to see them coughing and spluttering and slowly dying from cat flu. The litter of the second female shared the same fate with the exception of a ginger tom. Further litters fared somewhat better, and when the house was feeding seven or eight cats, it was decided something needed to be done. At that point, the additional staff member from Todtnau was working with the team, and with her concern for animals, she offered to bear half the cost of having then all neutered. An arrangement was made with a local vet, but the problem then was catching the cats. Through subtle means, six were captured, but with them not being used to being handled or confined, the noise they set up was ear-piercing. A secure garden shed was used to confine them until they could be taken to the vet, one or two at a time, and operations carried out. Eventually, all were rendered incapable of reproducing, and the only growth in numbers was when occasionally, one or two other strays joined the Haus Barnabas cat commune. Losses also occurred as now and then, cats vanished, perhaps finding more congenial food providers or, alternatively, being killed on the road.

There was one interesting episode when one morning a guest alerted the team's attention to the corpse of a black cat by the garden gate. Now the black cat was a favourite of the cat lovers in the house, and it was a sad day to see him lying there dead. Mourning his loss and considering where best to bury him, they turned to see the house's black cat smiling down at them from the garden wall. The dead one obviously came from another cat family. With everyone trusting it was not a beloved pet of a lonely old lady but treating it with respect as one of God's creatures, it was buried in the garden and the grave covered with heavy stones to stop any roaming foxes from digging it up.

Phyllis took a real interest in the cats and cared for their needs as much as was possible. One or two became reasonably tame, but with the exception of a stray that joined the group and must have had a more civilised background, they showed no wish to come into the confined space of the house. Later, on the death of another feline friend, one of the helpers asked Leonard if he would say a prayer at its graveside. Not able to

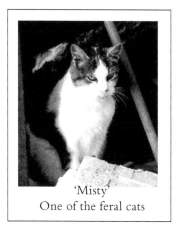

'Misty'
One of the feral cats

think of any biblical basis for prayer over a dead animal, Leonard had to think quickly. He knew that the lady gained a lot of pleasure from her pets and had taken a real interest in the Haus Barnabas cats, so he saw this as the perfect opportunity to thank the Lord for all the miracles of His creation and thanking Him particularly for the enjoyment of pets and, in particular, for the life of the animal they were then burying.

Stone marten

A few other species of animal made Haus Barnabas their home. Unfortunately, not all showed the same reticence to enter the house as the feral cats did. The stone marten is a common animal in the Black Forest. This creature is closely related to the pine marten found in Scotland and which is being reintroduced into Wales. However, while the pine marten is happy to produce its young in holes in trees, the stone marten chooses barns and the attics of old houses.

The previous owners warned the Holders about these creatures, and since the Engel has a large (mostly unused) roof space and because large areas of the eaves are open to the elements, there really is no way of keeping them out. They have ruined the fibreglass insulation by burrowing into it and, where possible, pulling it out, but having said that, they are interesting creatures. One year in particular the young had a habit of playing on the open terrace as dusk fell and were very interesting to watch. Sadly, they had the unfortunate habit of using a ledge outside the patio door from one of the bedrooms as a toilet, which necessitated clearing up each morning. They are, in general, very secretive, and it's quite a rare event to actually see one, but it has been necessary at certain times of year to warn guests that if they hear the sound of running feet above the ceiling whilst lying in bed, the culprits are these squirrel-like creatures from the forest outside.

In recent years, creatures of a different species of fauna have been making their winter home in the Haus Barnabas roof. The first time he saw one of these, Leonard had no idea such creatures existed in the wild in Europe. It was the size of a very small squirrel, with a furry tail and a cheeky little face as it peered down at the host

Siebenschläfer
(Edible dormouse)

of the house from the top of a cabinet. Leonard imagined it was an escaped pet and caught it in a large box. On his showing it to Deborah, it jumped out of the box and ran up a curtain. Leonard was able to entice it out of a window but not before getting nipped. Fearing possible infection, his wife sent him off to the doctors for a tetanus injection. On searching a reference book, the conclusion was reached that it was an 'edible dormouse' – a *Glis glis*, to give it its Latin name. The German name is *Siebenschläfer*, which translates as 'seven-sleeper', indicating that it likes a long winter sleep. Apparently, the Romans found them a delicacy to eat. The *Siebenschläfer* is a protected species in Germany, so as summer turns to autumn and these rather attractive animals come into the guesthouse without booking, the habit has become to catch them in cage traps and let them go a mile or more away in the forest. The photo shows one having been released and escaping up a tree.

However, Haus Barnabas also has a *long-term* resident guest of the non-human variety. In 1990, Leonard agreed to look after a red-eared terrapin for a missionary family when they went back to Canada. Its name was Ben Hur, having its chariot on its back; it was 4 years old. It has acquired a rather larger tank to live in since it was welcomed into the Holders' first Black Forest home in Schlechtnau and, as of this writing in 2021, is still playing an active role in the routine of the Haus Barnabas annual programme. It lives in the reception area of the house in its tank between Easter and October and is fed tiny dried shrimps with the occasional dead fly or succulent scrap of meat. In the winter, the creature sleeps in the cellar in a smaller tank and, for these five months, requires no food. Without suggesting that it is a transgender reptile, it can be said that in the mind of its host family, it changed from male to female. It was introduced as Ben Hur, a male, but after a few years, it laid an egg. Oh! To be now recognised as a female, it required a change of name, so for the last twenty years, 'she' has been known as Benita.

The forest around is a home to a number of other wild animals, although most are rarely if ever seen. It is reported that there are lynx in the Black Forest, but the Haus Barnabas team have only ever seen these in a small local zoo. Wild pigs are occasionally seen, along with, much more frequently, red squirrels. Deer are common, and Leonard and Phyllis had a very close encounter with one a few years ago. As they were returning late at night, a deer suddenly stepped into the road in front of their car. They hit it, and as they stopped and looked back, there it was, unconscious on the tarmac. Leonard went back, picked it up, carried it away from any other traffic, and laid it on the grass verge, which, incidentally, was covered in snow. It was a traumatic experience for both Leonard and Phyllis, but they didn't feel there was anything more they could do for the poor creature. However, on reaching home in Haus

Barnabas, Leonard remembered hearing that one was legally bound to report such an accident. The policeman he spoke to on the phone informed him that he should wait by the animal until a police vehicle came. So back Leonard went to the scene of the crime – if crime, it can be called. He parked his vehicle at the side of the road, with its headlights shining on the animal. He was interested to see that it had regained consciousness and was sitting up. After ten minutes or so, it jumped up and ran back up the rocky slope from whence it had come, and then of course, the police arrived.

'The animal was there, sir,' said Leonard rather sheepishly. 'But it seems to have recovered well from the traumatic experience of being hit by my car and has now run off.'

Leonard could almost imagine the police wanting to say, 'Well now, without a body, we can't treat this as a murder, so guess you are off the hook.'

However, all he did was take down Leonard's personal details and request that he now stay until the forester arrived as the man with the gun had been notified to put a suffering animal out of its misery if this proved necessary.

The forester wasn't sorry the animal had recovered. He commented that since it had run up the rocky slope and not down the other side, this would indicate it had only been stunned and was essentially uninjured. This was confirmed by the fact there was no sign of blood on the snow where Leonard had placed it.

Interestingly, all of the above happened on Easter Saturday, and after the shock of Leonard thinking he had killed the animal and then to watch what appeared to be a resurrection was a wonderful illustration of Easter morning.

C H A P T E R

14

Into All The World

Several guests who come to Haus Barnabas testify of having pictures come into their minds as they pray. Some of these portray biblical truths in a pictorial form, which help to give a better understanding of them. John Piper once said that one of the greatest problems he had in his Christian life was to bring biblical doctrine that he understood and believed in his head into his heart and emotions. He commented that poetry and therefore hymns with a melody help to do this. Many have also found that when the Psalmist exclaimed, 'Bless the Lord, oh my soul, and all that is within me, bless His holy name!' he is surely seeking that his emotions be stirred by the truth he believes with his understanding. This stirring of our faith and emotions in regard to the character and nature of God and His grace towards us enables us to better worship in spirit and in truth, which Jesus says is the only form of worship acceptable to our heavenly Father.

However, while some visionary pictures can be prophetic, clearly, only the actual unfolding of what is seen in this way can confirm that the picture seen is from God and has been interpreted rightly. One morning one of our guests mentioned that they had seen in their mind whilst praying a picture of Haus Barnabas surrounded by a hedge, but then the hedge was broken down, and the house could be seen from far away. They had felt that God was showing them that the influence of His Word and the Gospel of His grace would extend out from Haus Barnabas into all the world beyond simply the Black Forest villagers.

Interestingly, soon after this, three different groups of Polish folk came, and over the years, guests from many countries have come to stay in the house. Also, the *Daily Manna* readings which Leonard has put together are being circulated widely each month throughout India.

It has been the custom in the house for Leonard and Phyllis and other team members to sit with the guests for the evening meal together, and this and the times of devotion together give opportunities to encourage guests to share their story.

One young Malaysian couple, Joey and Lois, arrived by bus from down the valley. When asked how they had heard about Haus Barnabas, they said they had been doing an intensive course at Spurgeon's College in London and seen a leaflet about it there. This had prompted them to break their journey back to Malaysia with a stop in the Black Forest. The story of their conversion was remarkable, illustrating how God works in unexpected ways. Joey had been handed a Bible by a missionary but, having absolutely no interest in Christianity, passed it on to a girl acquaintance. She was in the process of packing to move across to America, probably for study, and took the Bible with her. Then later reading some of it, she was motivated to find a Christian church, where she met with the Lord and found faith. She then said she wrote to the young man who had given her the Bible to tell him what had happened. However, as it would appear. quite

Joey and Lois
at bus stop following their visit

independently, he also had been converted. The two corresponded, and after a while, the man got permission to move across to the United States, and the two attended a Bible college and eventually got married. Together, they started a Chinese language church but then suddenly, out of the blue, felt very strongly that God was challenging them to go back to Malaysia to witness for Him in their home country. This meant giving up their home and the Chinese church fellowship they were leading and going back to an unknown situation. They had been back a couple of years when they came to Haus Barnabas and were both teaching in small Bible colleges. Because of the political situation, the colleges were as secretive as possible in the Malaysian jungle.

In conjunction with India Link Ministries (ILM), several Indian pastors have spent time in Haus Barnabas, often coming to join the special ministry weeks. Joseph Paul runs a children's home, and after his wife died tragically, ILM financed him to come with his young daughter and have Christmas in Haus Barnabas. He explained that he had been moved and challenged by God to open a children's home after he had come across a baby boy left to die on a rubbish dump. God has blessed his work, and there is now a thriving children's home.

A couple from Israel have visited several times. The husband was brought up in Golders Green, London, in an Orthodox Jewish family and, as a young man, went out to Israel to live and work in a kibbutz. His wife was also brought up in Britain and had a Jewish mother, although this fact was hidden from her and never spoken of. As an adventurous young woman, she decided to walk around the Mediterranean Sea with a donkey. Eventually, she arrived in Israel and, without knowing her Jewish heritage, felt very much at home there. She met the man who became her husband in the kibbutz she'd settled at. With him being attracted to her, his approach to get to know her better was to suggest he taught her to drive a JCB digger! Their first home after they married was very close to neighbours from the United States. They were three Christian lads who seemed to play guitars and sing Christian songs all day. Eventually, through their influence and prayers, the wife was converted, but the husband was very sceptical as Christianity appeared to him to be denial of his Jewish faith. However, the Lord touched him, and he too came to believe in Jesus Christ as his Messiah and Saviour.

Leonard was interested to know why they referred to themselves as Messianic Jews and not Christians. The answer seemed very satisfactory. Within the state of Israel, to be classified as 'Christian' is to be identified with the Orthodox Christian Church, whereas the term 'Messianic Jews' enables them to retain their Jewish identity whilst acknowledging they have embraced the historic Jesus of Nazareth as the Son of God, their Messiah and Saviour. Another extremely encouraging disclosure was the fact that when these guests first found Jesus, the population of Messianic Jews in Israel was small enough for them to know nearly all of them. However, they said, twenty or so years later, Messianic fellowships had proliferated to such a degree that they now exist all over Israel and include a good number of Arab believers.

One year a young Nigerian refugee who introduced himself as Geoffrey and explained he was a born-again believer came to the services for a few weeks until he was suddenly moved on by the authorities. Geoffrey explained that he has been brought up by Christian parents in Southern Nigeria, but after the death of his parents, his uncle sent him to Northern Nigeria. Geoffrey later realised he was being sent into a danger zone for Christians, probably so that his uncle could take possession of the family's property. He was in a church service when a bomb exploded. Many of the congregation were killed, and he had quite a severe head injury. Through various means whilst still a teenage lad, he was able to escape from Nigeria and eventually was accepted as a refugee in Germany. His experiences appeared to have brought him closer to the Lord Jesus and deepened his faith, and the hymn he loved and chose to sing at Haus Barnabas fellowship and Bible study evenings was the following:

When peace like a river attendeth my way,
When sorrows like sea billows roll,
Whatever my lot, thou hast taught me to say,
'It is well, it is well with my soul.'

It is well with my soul;
It is well, it is well with my soul.

Though Satan should buffet, though trials should come,
Let this blest assurance control:
That Christ has regarded my helpless estate
And has shed His own blood for my soul.[57]

Before Geoffrey was moved on, the Haus Barnabas team presented him with a signed copy of the Mission Praise hymn book to take with him.

One weekend Haus Barnabas had the privilege of providing hospitality and fellowship for a Christian couple with a baby daughter from Iran. Leonard and Phyllis remember their story: having found faith in Jesus Christ, they had been forced to flee their home country and had met in a refugee camp in Turkey. As a married couple, they had eventually been accepted for entry into Germany and, whilst living in a refugee hostel on the outskirts of the Black Forest, had found fellowship in a Free Evangelical church. They had suffered much deprivation for several years, and a friend in the church had recommended Haus Barnabas as a weekend treat for them. She came to an arrangement with Leonard, making a financial contribution herself to enable them to come Friday evening to Monday as a gift.

It was encouraging to hear their story, and Phyllis took them very much to heart and continue to pray for them. One thing that remains very much in the Holders' memory is the happiness which exuded from their chuckling baby girl. Their daughter was clearly a great blessing from the Lord for them, and Phyllis later commented that her happiness must be a reflection of the peace the parents had together within the difficult circumstances they had come through.

Two most interesting ladies were amongst several visitors from the United States. These two guests were booked on a Reformation tour in Luther country but, having some extra days, were recommended to come to Haus Barnabas. What was of greatest

---

57 By Horatio Gates Spafford (1873).

significance was that one of the ladies had originally come from Sussex in England and had lived as a girl in one of the neighbouring villages to Perching and Edburton, where Leonard's great-great-grandfather Eli Page had farmed. Her Sunday school teacher from her childhood had sent her a copy of Leonard's book *Selina of Sussex, 1818–1886*, which she had enjoyed, and it was only after having booked to come to Haus Barnabas that she realised the link.

Several guests also came to Haus Barnabas from Australia. Leonard's brother John and his wife, Christina, sent one of their older employees for a little tour of Europe, and she stayed in Haus Barnabas for a few days. One thing Leonard remembers is her writing from a high-class hotel in Prague, saying that none of the hotels she stayed in cooked scrambled egg as well as she enjoyed them in Haus Barnabas!

Chacko Thomas – who, for a number of years, together with his wife, Radha, had been the spiritual leaders on the Operation Mobilisation ship *Logos* – having had a brief holiday break in Haus Barnabas, accepted an invitation to return to lead Easter meetings. During their time on the *Logos*, Chacko and Radha seem to have been parent figures to many of the young people who spent time on the ship. Although there was not a large gathering that Easter, Haus Barnabas was pleased to welcome to the meetings

International guests at Easter conference

Christians from Germany, Switzerland, Bolivia, and Sweden, and with Chacko coming from India and Radha from Singapore and with the addition of one or two British guests, it proved to be a very international gathering.

On another Easter, Tom Lori, the Jewish evangelist working with the Messianic Testimony in Europe, spoke at the weekend conference in Haus Barnabas. One evening during the following week, Tom also spoke in German at a public meeting arranged and advertised under a title something like this: 'Why I, as a Jew, Believe That Jesus Is the Son of God'. In his testimony, Tom shared how, when fighting in the Israeli army in the Six-Day War in 1967 and seeing Egyptians die in the Sinai desert, he was convicted by God to question what would happen to him if he was killed. The Jewish rabbi he spoke with had no answer that could satisfy him, but later in Britain, a Christian family befriended him, and after overcoming his scruples about attending a Christian church service, he heard the gospel of God's love in Jesus Christ, which spoke so powerfully to him that he embraced Jesus as his Saviour. Eventually, after completing a Bible college course, he felt God's call to share this message with his Jewish compatriots. The emphasis of his preaching is to expound the Old Testament Scriptures in the light of the New Testament that Jesus Christ is the promised Jewish Messiah.

CHAPTER

༯☙༯

15

—

Providing Support
and Fellowship

When Leonard and Phyllis left Britain in 1983, communication with their family and friends was slow and difficult. For several months, they had no telephone line into their apartment, and Phyllis remembers having to walk out to a public phone to ring her parents and occasionally one or two particular friends, all at such an exorbitant cost. Years later in Haus Barnabas, with Wi-Fi and WhatsApp and mobile phones, talking with friends and family in any country together with visual contact has seemed miraculous.

No doubt most Christians have, at different times, been able to support and help others and also often received encouragement and practical help themselves. We are all needy people, and part of our calling as followers of Jesus is to 'bear one another's burdens and so fulfil the law of Christ'.[58]

Phyllis takes a real personal interest in her friends, and there are several people with whom she is in contact very regularly, either by phone or text. Others seem to find a degree of security knowing

---

58 Galatians 6:2.

where Phyllis and Leonard are and that they would be available to speak to if needed. Leonard is often amazed at the way his wife is able to answer phone calls in an engaging and enthusiastic voice either day or night, whatever their own circumstances might be.

To hear a cheerful, friendly voice on the phone can, in itself, bring comfort when one is feeling low. Leonard remembers a blind person telling him once that he always sensed Leonard was smiling when he spoke to him. He described it as a smiley voice!

Phyllis often will pray with her friends about their needs whilst on the phone to them.

Phyllis's Reflections

The variety of guests we've had over the years from such a mixture of backgrounds has led to some lively discussions and arguments over some very controversial subjects. We have endeavoured to only give an opinion if asked. There's a current saying, 'go to the other side of the bottle', meaning to 'think outside of the box', to be prepared to think beyond our own beliefs and remain open to understanding a different point of view. What this means in practice is not being dismissive of anyone holding a different viewpoint to our own. Applying the wise saying 'There is usually at least one thing more you don't know' should keep us from making rash judgements and becoming overcritical.

Being accepting of those who hold differing opinions from our own and still maintaining a genuine interest in their lives can be a huge learning curve. Christians can be a right 'motley crew', to coin a phrase one of our pastors used; every living, local church fellowship is made up of sinners saved by God's grace. We all have equal standing before God through Christ's death and resurrection, but we come from different backgrounds and life experience (some of us carrying more 'baggage' than others), which affects our thoughts, habits, opinions, and relationships. If we remember that God loves our Christian brother and sister as much as He loves us and has forgiven our failures, this helps us to be more accepting of others. There's a well-known saying: 'We should love the sinner but not their sin' – easier said than done!

God has sent many different people to us in Haus Barnabas over the years, and we have needed to learn to apply the above principles in relation to both our guests and our staff. We have encountered differences in how we communicate, mannerisms, attitudes, and how we approach things, differences in how we interpret Scripture and how we view controversial subjects like prophesy, preaching, the Holy Spirit, baptism, abortion, and homosexuality. We also know that Christians and Christian families are not exempt from problems such as bulimia, anorexia, alcoholism, self-harm, and divorce, and some have found it comforting to be able to talk through such situations.

As we have listened to the needs of others and sought together the Lord's mind on various issues, we are very conscious of the challenges involved in such ministry. We are all sinners before a Holy God, needing His atoning forgiveness for our transgressions and His help to forgive one another. We are all only His people through the merit of Jesus. A right view of Jesus and our sin as well as a desire to love, serve, and please Him through His Holy Spirit in us are the foundation for living out an authentic Christian life. A willingness to treat other Christians and their views with respect before God should be the basis of showing the world that Christians can live peacefully with one another even if they experience a difference of opinion on something. We are sure many of those reading this will know people who, because they didn't behave or live up to an acceptable, expected model for church membership or fellowship, have been left on the fringes, feeling disillusioned and rejected.

We have dear friends who we felt had a true conversion experience but, coming from non-Christian backgrounds, didn't fully understand or follow the expectations of the churches of which they had become part. As a result, they were disillusioned when met with animosity, misunderstanding, non-acceptance, and hypocrisy from those they had looked to for the guidance and encouragement they most needed. This led to a drifting away and a rejection of the pathway they had started to follow. They now live often impoverished and embittered in soul and mind through the rejection they suffered, having utter distain towards the people they had hoped would nurture their souls. Years of disappointment and emptiness have made them develop a hard outer shell, which only God's Spirit can penetrate. Genuine care and acceptance of people by caring for them where they are at is so needed by people – being willing to truly befriend, care for, pray for, and gently lead them to the feet of Jesus, no matter what.

Loving care is needed when people reach rock bottom before their cry for help is realised and acted upon. We have had various friends ring or come to us over the years; some were drunk, some had overdosed, some were self-harming, some had personality disorders, and some were experiencing gender confusion. All need understanding and practical help, not rejection. The Lord has not rejected us with our multi-faceted needs and failures, and we must be His representatives whilst on this earth to direct people to a Saviour who can change and make us poor sinners more like Jesus. Experience teaches us that our witness to others is of no consequence unless we are truly their friends. There is a song saying, 'If I can help somebody in this world today, my life is not in vain' – what a challenge to us all!

Such were the crucial lessons we believe God taught us over the years; indeed, putting it all into practice has been an ongoing challenge, with varying degrees of success. We have needed God's guidance for each situation we have addressed, including those never encountered before. We know we have often failed, but God has dealt with us very graciously when we have been slow to learn and apply His wisdom. We are reminded of Ephesians 2:10, which says, 'For we are His workmanship, created in Christ Jesus for good works which God prepared beforehand that we should walk in them.'

CHAPTER
𓆃
16

Anniversaries

Anniversaries are a time to think back and celebrate God's goodness. Christian believers should always be able to recognise their heavenly Father's goodness for two reasons. First, God is Himself good, and second, whatever our circumstances might be, His Word promises us that for those who love Him, all things work together for their good.[59] Whilst experiencing one of the worst and most testing times in her life, Phyllis felt God directed her to the Scripture verse that states 'the living God gives us richly all things to enjoy'. When things are difficult, such a Scripture is very challenging, but the Old Testament prophet Habakkuk indicates the solution to what could be considered a great contradiction.

After describing the destruction of Jerusalem and the devastation of everything life depended on, he stated, 'Yet I will joy in the LORD, I will rejoice in the God of my salvation.'[60]

In June 2017, Phyllis and Leonard celebrated their fiftieth wedding anniversary, and on this occasion, it didn't take a high degree of faith to realise how much they had to celebrate. Haus

---

59 Romans 8:28.
60 Habakkuk 3:18.

Barnabas has limited guest accommodation, but they were filled with the couple's relatives for the occasion. Leonard was thrilled that his elder brother from Australia felt able to come, accompanied by his daughter, along with Leonard's sister from England, with her husband, as well as Phyllis's cousin and her husband. Sadly, her sister was hindered from joining them as she was having treatment for cancer. They praise God that this was able to be successfully dealt with. Several other cousins and long-standing family friends were invited, but most were unable to come.

The main celebration was over two days. Initially, in Haus Barnabas, when with their children and seven grandchildren and the invited guests, Leonard showed a fascinating PowerPoint presentation of family photos taken over the years. These ranged from early snapshots of the couple as babies and youngsters through their courtship and marriage, the entrance of their two sons, and their lives in Ripon and Yorkshire, concluding with scenes from Basel and the Black Forest. Being reminded of the whole journey before and throughout the fifty years of marriage gave great reason to praise God and to enjoy a celebratory meal together.

The following day, their son Daniel – with Martina, his wife – had organised a wonderful, worshipful programme in the Riehen Dorf Kirche, over the border in Switzerland, where they are the pastors. It included musical contributions by their gifted grandchildren, Bible readings and prayers, and the communal singing of two very significant hymns: 'How Great Thou Art', often referred to as the Haus Barnabas anthem; and 'All the Way, My Saviour Leads Me', one of their wedding hymns. This was followed by a garden party in the grounds of the manse. Their eldest grandson, Barnaby, had acquired a drone, which he used to take a group photograph as it hovered in the air above them.

Family group at Leonard and Phyllis's
golden wedding celebration

Although golden weddings can't be so uncommon, Leonard and Phyllis were quite amazed at the local interest their fiftieth aroused. A reporter from the *Badische Zeitung*, a local daily newspaper, came to interview them, and a photograph of the couple together with a very faithful report about them and their ministry in Haus Barnabas was published. The mayor of Utzenfeld called by with two congratulatory certificates, one signed by himself on behalf of the village and a second from the president of Baden Württemberg, the wider county in which Utzenfeld is situated. The *Ministerpresident* wished them health, happiness, and God's blessing on their future life together. Numerous local Germans with whom the couple had had contact also sent their congratulations, and several brought flowers or other presents. Leonard and Phyllis felt honoured by all this and realised they had been well accepted by the community in which, at this point, they had been living for twenty-six years.

A year later, Geoffrey celebrated his 50th birthday, which he made a very grand affair. He wanted to use the milestone to get people together, not just to have a party but also to think about God's goodness over time and raise many voices of praise and thanks. He hired the Kilchzimmer centre for the weekend, enabling close family and friends to stay there over the Friday and Saturday nights, and then many more friends were invited for a programme of talks and activities, with a celebratory meal on the Saturday. There was then a worship service on the Sunday morning when

Geoffrey's father-in-law, Pastor Colin, preached from the text: 'Our times are in His hands'. The weather was beautifully sunny and warm, and the location of the centre in the Swiss Jura Mountains provided for spectacular views. The whole weekend was such confirming evidence of God's blessing on the Holder family. Not only had He provided financially for Leonard and Phyllis's sons, but also, He had graciously given them a living faith leading them to honour and glorify God in their celebrations.

CHAPTER

17

Blessings a Hundredfold

Jesus answered and said, 'Assuredly, I say to you, there is no one who has left house or brothers or sisters or father or mother or wife or children or lands, for My sake and the gospel's, who shall not receive a hundredfold now in this time—houses and brothers and sisters and mothers and children and lands, with persecutions—and, in the age to come, eternal life. But many who are first will be last and the last first.'

As Leonard and Phyllis look back and take stock of how things have developed as the years have gone by, they are delighted to be able to testify that their heavenly Father has been completely faithful in fulfilling the above promise, given through the lips of the Lord Jesus and recorded by Mark in verses twenty-nine to thirty-one of the tenth chapter of his Gospel. The persecutions have not been so obvious as those suffered by many followers of Jesus, but much of the time, they have sensed a strong spiritual opposition to their work. Many hopes have been frustrated, and there have been a few times when they could commiserate with David of old when he commented, 'Even my own familiar friend in whom I trusted, who ate my bread, has lifted up his heel against me.'[61]

Leonard remembers one local German Christian who supported and contributed to their local witness for a while, speaking seriously to him with the suggestion that he was wasted in this spiritually barren Black Forest backwater and should be looking for other, more productive fields of service.

Their heavenly Father's blessing on the family has been remarkable. He is so gracious. The twenty-seventh of December has always been an important family day in the Holder household. During the years in Britain, it was a special day over the Christmas period to celebrate with Phyllis's parents as it was also their wedding anniversary. In recent years, it has also proved to be the most convenient day for Leonard and Phyllis to get together with their two sons and families. There have often

Leonard and Phyllis with
their seven grandchildren
2011/2012

been guests in Haus Barnabas who need service and fellowship over Christmas itself – also, their pastor son and his wife have a Christmas Day church service to attend to on the twenty-fifth – so the day after Boxing Day suits well as a family get-together.

During recent years, Leonard has looked at his two boys and remembered those early days when the family first came to Basel. He remembers going around the streets to gather wood for burning to keep them warm in the winter. He remembers the apartment they first had, where they never really felt private. The girl living upstairs was entitled to come through their hallway to gain access to her apartment. These and many other incidents were amongst the

---

61 Psalm 41:9.

initial struggles as the family began their journey in what Leonard firmly believed was God's guidance.

However, as he looks at the boys now, with their capable and devoted wives and their very gifted children, he has been known to brush a tear or two from his eyes. God has been so good. He and Phyllis have an enormous house, which, although often a burden to own, is also a great privilege. Their elder son is a medical doctor with a well-paid position in pharmaceutical development, and he and his wife, Ruth, own a spacious dwelling in the Swiss Jura Mountains within travelling distance of Basel. Geoffrey's three children are a credit to him and his wife and are loving grandchildren to Leonard and Phyllis. On the spiritual front, Geoffrey also has studied theology to the level of an MA, holds a firm conservative, reformed view of Scripture, and is a welcomed preacher in Swiss Free Evangelical churches. He has written, amongst other things, an exposition of Ephesians 2 in German, in a form to be accessible to non-theological readers.

Their younger son, Daniel, and his wife, Martina, are pastors in the Swiss Reformed church in Riehen, Basel. The manse they live in could almost be a British stately home. Their four children are all naturally gifted in different ways and are beginning to branch out, each in his and her own direction but reflecting the strong Christian influence of their upbringing.

In recent years, it has become clear to Leonard that his original call to Switzerland has been worked out in the lives of his two sons. It's wonderful to realise – and no doubt has been seen very often – that when parents respond to God's guidance, their Lord and Master has a purpose in this for their children for future generations.

However, the hundredfold blessing includes not only houses and the family blessings mentioned but also a multitude of new spiritual family members. Leonard and Phyllis's co-workers in Haus Barnabas have become like family to them. Also, many who came as helpers and guests have become valued friends and spiritual brothers and sisters.

In retirement now from active involvement in Haus Barnabas, Leonard and Phyllis long to see the work and ministry of the house continue, with both an effective local witness and also bringing encouragement and Bible teaching to Christians from all over the world. This is their daily concern and prayer.

Postscript:

We believe most sincerely God planned Haus Barnabas as our ministry for Him, and we have aimed to run it for His glory. As this book reveals, we have sought first to be witnesses to the Lord Jesus and His Gospel both within the locality and to all of whom He sent to us and second, in following the example of Barnabas of old, to bring biblical encouragement to believers.

However, we would hate the testimony of this book to indicate in any way that we are special, sanctified people. We feel honoured to have been called to serve a holy God, but looking back, we recognise that some of our words and actions both in preaching and counselling and in our daily lives have, at times, reflected our human ignorance and foolishness. Nonetheless, we can testify that we are daily looking to our Lord for needed grace and for the forgiveness of our failures. Under His guidance and discipline, we are still a 'work in progress' and anticipating with joy the full sanctification He has promised when He releases us from this frail and sinful life.

We would like all readers of our book to feel the challenge to seek God's will for their own lives and to follow His leading in faith and trust. We are all unworthy of the great privilege of serving our holy God, but we can trust Him for the needed grace and the enabling of His Holy Spirit as we walk step by step with Him into the unknown.

Len and Phyl

APPENDIX 1

Aims and Objectives of Bible in Action Trust

The practical aim of Bible in Action Trust and its workers is to prayerfully propagate the biblical Gospel by faithfully expounding the Word of God in a clear and relevant way through preaching, literature, and personal witness.

Our Basis

This aim is based on our conviction that

1. the sixty-six books of the Old and New Testaments are the Holy Scriptures, being, in their original form, inspired of God to the extent that the human authors' choice of individual words has divine significance, the Scriptures being, therefore, God's unique, inerrant, and infallible objective revelation in written form; and
2. each personal subjective communication which God graciously makes to mankind through His Spirit will normally come by means of the Scriptures and, without exception, will agree with both the spirit and letter of His written revelation.

Our Objectives

In prayerfully pursuing our aim based on the above doctrinal convictions, we have the following expectations, which we state in the trust's objectives:

1. that men and women will be saved, i.e. brought into the possession of eternal life, through the Word of God becoming to them through the power of the Holy Spirit, the seed of regeneration, and leading them into a personal faith in Jesus Christ;
2. that Christians will be nurtured and built up in their faith through a deeper understanding of the truths of the Word of God; and
3. that falsehood and error, through which Satan deceives both non-Christians and Christians and holds them in varying degrees of bondage of spirit, will be exposed through the light of God's truth.

Bible in Action is concerned to have a part in the church's ongoing obedience to our Lord's great commission recorded for us in Matthew 28:19–20: 'GO, make disciples of all nations . . . teaching them to observe all things that I have commanded you.'

The work is interdenominational in as far as we welcome fellowship with all Christians who acknowledge the lordship of Jesus Christ and the authority of the Holy Scriptures.

INDEX

A

Aachan 202
Aaron Hotel 309
Above Bar Church 382
Aenon 30
Aldershot 21
Alice Springs 247
All Souls Church 227
Alps 131, 140, 189, 213, 245, 261-2, 314, 328, 430
Alsace 350
Alton 72
Andover 55
Arctic Circle 175
Arundel Castle 374
Attard 48
Australia 104-5, 184, 231, 244, 246-7, 262, 381, 470, 477
Austria 184, 272-3, 281, 291, 346, 413, 458

B

Baden Württemberg 416, 478
Badische Bahnhof 292
Balcombe Road 96
Barclays Bank 159
Barmouth 309
Basel 140, 191-2, 196, 200-3, 205, 208-10, 212-16, 218, 220, 224-31, 235-7, 239-40, 243-53, 260-2, 265-7, 270-2, 277, 279, 281-3, 285-7, 292, 294-5, 297-301, 303, 308, 334, 339-40, 342, 365, 377-8, 409, 415, 419, 437, 456, 477, 481-2
Basel Christian Fellowship 191, 227, 247, 251
Basel University 266, 285-6
Beaconsfield 170
Bedfordshire 111, 376
Belchen 318
Belgium 140, 202, 260, 321, 372, 395
Belgrave House 64, 66-7, 77, 96, 100, 106, 111, 124
Ben Nevis 176-7, 298-9
Bennett's 2, 4, 23
Bergstrasse 293, 298, 313
Berlin Wall 306, 318, 397
Bern 222
Bethel Evangelical Church 181, 197
Bethersden 355
Bible in Action Trust 306 n. 47, 346, 403, 485
Bible Study Fellowship 244
Bishops Waltham Gospel Hall 94
Bisikon 140
Black Forest 12, 139, 286-7, 291, 298-300, 303-5, 308, 311-15, 317-19, 321-2, 327-8, 333, 337, 340, 344-7, 350, 355, 360, 365-6, 370, 373, 375, 377-8, 380-1,

387, 390, 395, 399-400, 402, 413, 416, 423-5, 429, 431, 435, 443-4, 447, 453, 461, 463, 466, 469, 477, 481

Black Forest Academy 308

Black Forest Holiday Services 311-13, 319, 344

Black Sea 280

Blossom Gate 169

Bodenseehof Bible School 140

Bolivia 470

Bournemouth 309

Brake Bible School 197

Brighton xix, 2, 6, 8, 14, 17-18, 21, 29, 38, 97-8, 101, 103, 374

Bristol 65, 70-1, 80

Bristol University 70

Britain 1, 4, 6-7, 13-14, 27, 47, 50, 104, 125-6, 141, 154, 176-7, 184, 207-8, 211, 214, 217, 223, 238, 241-2, 244, 253, 266, 272, 285-7, 292, 296-7, 299, 305, 308-9, 320-1, 336-7, 342, 344, 346-7, 356-7, 359, 362, 364, 372-6, 381, 383, 429, 435, 455, 467, 471-2, 481

British Conservative Party 180

Brook Lane 123

Brussels 321, 410

Bucks 170

Budleigh Salterton 108

Burma 6

Bursledon Brick Works 29

Bursledon Bridge 27

Bury Place 87

C

Caernarfon Castle 374

Calais 261, 372

Camberlot Road 22

Cambridge 111, 115, 378

Canada 457, 463

Canton Zürich 126

Cape Town 3-4, 21

Capernwray 140

Capernwray Hall 458

Cardiff 447

Caritas 407

Catisfield 108

Chapel Lane 124

Charlwood 90-1, 124, 128

Charlwood Chapel 90 n. 21, 91

Child Evangelism Fellowship 140, 228

Christian Alliance 170, 176, 181

Christian Walking Club 429

Church of England 179

Church Street 17

Ciba-Geigy 228 n. 38

Clifton Farm 22

Climping 65, 67

Climping Camp 64-5, 67

Cole Abbey Presbyterian Church 323

Cornwall 54, 123, 165

Coventry 58

Crawley 96, 115-16, 118, 124, 132

Cyprus 104

D

Deutsche Bahn 437

Devon 108, 123

Dicker, the 22, 90 n. 20

Dieppe 297

Dorking 112

Dornbirn 458

Dorset 309, 373-4

Dover 202, 262, 372

Droxford 44

Duncan Road Assembly 76, 99

Duncan Road Gospel Hall 94

Dunstable 376

Dyke Road 17

E

Ebenezer Chapel 98

Edburton 101, 470

Egerton 355

Eglise Evangélique Internationale de Genève 431

Eiger 261

England xiv, 8, 44, 127, 130, 134, 139, 156, 170, 175, 179, 189, 192, 196, 208, 212, 217, 219, 228, 231, 240, 251, 253-5, 262, 292, 296-7, 305, 318-19, 321, 347, 350, 356, 362, 391, 419, 424-5, 433, 455, 458, 470, 477

English Channel 424

European Missionary Fellowship 209, 212

Eurorail 253, 255

Evangelical Press 162, 187

Exmouth 108

F

Fareham 28, 30-1, 36, 55, 57, 59, 61, 224

Feldberg 298-9

Feltham 47, 71

Finanzamt 414

Finstergrund 334

Five Ways 14

Fleet End 27

Foredown Isolation Hospital 18

Fort William 176

Fountains Abbey 150

Fraserburgh 345

Freiburg 324, 326-7, 340-1, 363, 390

Freie Evangelische-Theologische Akademie 192, 196, 210

Freudenstadt 140

Full Gospel Business Men's Fellowship 104, 338

G

Galeed Chapel 2, 6, 9, 15, 17, 23, 103

Gasthaus Engel 388-9, 395-7, 403, 419, 423, 440, 459

Geneva 140, 431

Germany xiv, 12, 136, 139-40, 191, 196-8, 201, 203, 207, 211, 215, 224, 230, 244, 247, 260, 265, 267, 271, 275, 283-4, 286-7, 289, 291-2, 295-6, 299-301,

304, 306-7, 309, 313 n. 49, 314, 317-19, 328, 334, 346, 355, 361, 364, 366-7, 370, 373, 376, 378, 382, 397, 402-3, 412, 416-17, 424, 429, 437, 442, 455, 463, 468-70

Geschwend 331, 416

Glarus 128, 189, 191, 201

Gloucester Road 14

God xiii-xvii, 3-4, 6-8, 16-20, 24, 32, 35, 39-42, 46, 52-4, 62-4, 68, 70, 73, 80-1, 85-91, 96-8, 102-4, 111, 119-20, 124-5, 131-45, 149-50, 152, 154, 160, 163-4, 166, 169, 171, 177-9, 184, 186-8, 192, 195-6, 200-1, 208, 211, 215, 217, 222-3, 225-6, 228-9, 232, 234-5, 238-41, 247, 251, 257, 259, 262-3, 265, 267-9, 276-8, 282-4, 287, 291, 294, 301, 304-6, 314-15, 317-18, 321, 327-8, 331, 336-8, 341-2, 344-5, 347-9, 353, 356-8, 360, 368-71, 376, 378, 380-2, 384, 387, 389-91, 393, 397, 400-4, 408, 411, 413-15, 420, 422, 427, 431, 433, 436, 438, 440, 442-3, 445-53, 456-8, 461, 465-8, 471, 473-9, 482-3, 485-6

Golders Green 467

Grand Ballon 350

Grassington 182

Greystones 155-6

Grossmünster 267, 430

Guildford 22, 70, 72

H

Habsburg Empire 334

Hamble 23, 27-8

Hampshire 27, 29, 44, 61, 97, 106, 272

Harrogate 156, 163, 193

Haus Barnabas xiv, 144, 231, 298, 315, 325, 331, 342, 344, 346-50, 352-3, 355-7, 360, 362, 364-5, 367, 369, 371, 374-83, 387, 393,

395-7, 400-3, 405-8, 410-11, 413-21, 424-30, 433-8, 440-56, 458-70, 472, 474, 476-8, 481-3
Heathrow 47, 262
Hebridean Islands 345
Henfield 109
Henfield Chapel 109
Hertford Road 2, 7-8, 14, 20
Highdown Road 1, 101
Hog's Back 70, 72
Holborn 87
Holland 299
Hollingbury 2, 12
Holy Spirit xiii, 6, 46, 62, 81, 89, 232, 269, 273, 276, 327, 354, 382, 402, 474, 483, 486
Hong Kong 244, 450
hook 27, 29
Horley 81, 83, 85, 87-8, 90-1, 94, 96-8, 103, 108, 111, 118, 121, 123-4, 126-8, 131-2, 137-8, 140, 152, 155, 165, 182-4, 191, 195, 247, 301, 312, 346
Horley Chapel 91, 97, 346
Hove 1, 18, 101

I

Ifield 127
India 3, 6, 245-6, 263, 466-7, 470
India Link Ministries 467
Inter-School Christian Fellowship 54
Island of Tiree 345
Isle of Lewis 382
Isle of Wight 27, 309

J

Janz Team 228
Jennyfields Evangelical Church 193
Jesus xiii, xv, 6, 16, 39-40, 42, 52-3, 60-2, 76, 80, 88, 90, 103, 110, 118-21, 126, 128-9, 165, 170, 187-8, 191, 194, 225, 228, 230-1, 233, 238, 246, 268-9, 273, 278, 280, 289, 304, 306, 310,

317, 327, 331, 333-4, 347, 354, 361-2, 365, 369, 385-6, 403-6, 413, 417, 422, 426-7, 435-6, 438, 446, 450, 454-5, 465, 468-9, 471-2, 474-5, 480, 483, 486
Jireh Chapel 17
Johannes Kirche 268
Jungfrau 261
Jura Mountains 228, 245, 479, 482

K

Kaiserstuhl 431
Kangaroo Ground 105
Karlsruhe 456
Kazakhstan 397
Kent 86, 109, 355
Keswick 86-7, 91, 347
Kielce 412
Kiev 280
Kilchzimmer 140, 228, 245, 479
King's School of Languages 395
Kirchzarten 324
Kirkby Malzeard 169
Kirkby Road 168-9, 179-80, 182, 185
Kirkbymoorside 165-7
Knaresborough 193
Krakow 412

L

L'Abri 136, 140, 212-13
Lake Constance 140, 431, 458
Lake District 86, 140, 347
Lake Thun 261
Lake Titisee 303, 344
Lake Walensee 140
Lake Zurich 140
Lancashire 366
Land's End 54-5
Langenbruck 245
Leicestershire 113, 152
Lemgo 197, 203
Lewes 17
Liestal 226
Lincolnshire 50, 113

Littlehampton 64-5, 67, 96-7, 100
Locks Heath 272
Locks Heath Junior School 272
London 1, 47, 55, 62, 64, 70-1, 80, 87,
    96, 111, 124, 129, 153, 227, 323,
    344, 360, 366, 371, 373-4, 377,
    381, 428, 448, 466-7
London Bible College 91
London Bridge 87
Lörrach 296-7, 327
Lower Swanwick 23, 27-9, 56, 60, 68,
    71, 73
Lower Swanwick Strict Baptist
    Chapel 94
Lyon 378

M

Mainau 431
Malta 47-50, 57
Mambach 192
Manchester University 80
Mayfield Chapel 102
Mediterranean Sea 47, 467
Melbourne 105
Meon Estuary 44
Messianic Testimony 470
Migros 254
Minehead 1
Mönch 261
Morgartenring 208, 214, 216-17, 233,
    243, 251
Moscow 280
Mount Schilthorn 131
Mulhouse 209, 365
Munstertal 324
Mürren 131

N

National Sunday School Union 85, 87
New Forest 46
Newcastle 80, 347
Newhaven 297
Normandy 21
North Africa 4, 13

North Boarhunt 69
North Sea 299
North Street 2, 114
Northern Island 454
Norway 321
Notschrei 341
Nutfield 85

O

Old Steine 14
Open-Air Mission 447
Operation Mobilisation 470
Oslands 28
Oslands Lane 29, 53
Oslo 321
Ostend 202
Oxfordshire 80, 272, 385

P

Park Gate 106
Patcham 101
Pateley Bridge 182
Pennabilli 253, 255, 259
Penrhyndeudraeth 447
Penzance 55
Perching Manor Farm 101
Peterborough 113
Pickering 159, 166
Pilkington 366
Pitter Patter Club 170
Poland 318, 400, 405-8, 412-13
Portsmouth 23, 373-4
Price's Grammar School 30-1, 79
Providence Chapel 17, 81, 90, 96,
    125-6, 132

Q

Queens Road 98, 103, 121-3, 126-7,
    152-3

R

Rapperswil 140
Redhill 94

Rehoboth Chapel 111
Reigate 87
Reiterhof 334-6, 338-40, 347, 380, 382
Rhine Plain 365, 431
Riehen Dorf Kirche 477
Rimini 253, 255-8
Ripon 150, 152-3, 155-6, 159, 161-2, 165-6, 169-70, 174, 176, 179-82, 186-7, 189, 192-7, 201, 203, 207-8, 216, 253, 286, 296, 477
Ripon Girls' High School 180
Riquewehr 350
River Hamble 23, 27
River Itchen 70
River Limmit 430
River Rhine 250, 409
River Wiese 292, 331
Roche 228, 269
Rolls Royce 275, 443
Roman Catholic Church 48, 267, 333, 362

S

Salfords 117
Salim 30
Salvation Army 212, 214-15, 225
Samstagern 127
Sandown 309
Sandoz 228
Sarisbury Hill 73
Scandinavia 256
Schlechtnau 291, 293, 296-9, 301, 304, 315, 317-18, 320, 324, 328, 333-4, 336, 338, 382, 463
Schönau 291, 317-18, 352, 357, 360, 362, 377, 418, 428-9, 439
Schopfheim 418
Scotland 87, 175-6, 299, 345, 431, 436, 461
Scripture Gift Mission 122
Scripture Union 268
Sheffield 86
Shepperton 104
Shoreham 29

Shropshire 44, 80
Sinai 471
Sittingbourne 355
Six-Day War 108, 471
Skell River 156
Slavic Gospel Mission 280
Slovakia 413
Sochi 280
Solent 27
South Africa 3
Southampton 23, 27, 33, 39, 46, 70, 77, 373, 382
Southampton Port 27
Southampton Road 23
Southampton Water 27, 46
Southlands Hospital 29
Sovereign Grace Union 94
Spain 201, 212, 217
Sportsreach 428
St Helens 366
St Peters Church 14
St Petersburg 456
St Wilfrid 179
Stamford 113-14
Stanmore Chapel 377-8
Staufen 324
Strasbourg 409-10
Streatham 113
Suffolk 114
Surrey 21, 132, 156, 165, 183-4, 297
Sussex 3, 22, 48, 52, 64, 90, 97, 470
Sutton Bank 166-7
Swanwick Lane 28
Swanwick Shore Chapel 23, 29, 38, 54
Swaythling 70
Sweden 470
Switzerland xiv, 126-9, 131-3, 136, 140, 189, 191-2, 194-7, 201, 207-13, 215, 218, 224-7, 230-1, 236, 238, 240-1, 245-6, 250, 257, 260, 262, 266-7, 271, 277, 280, 283-4, 286, 291-2, 299-300, 303, 305, 328, 336, 470, 477, 482

T

Tabernacle Chapel 17
Titisee 292, 303, 320, 337-8, 344
Todtnau 291, 294, 301, 304, 306-7, 312-13, 316-18, 321, 323-4, 326-7, 329, 331, 334, 337, 341, 349, 352, 354, 360, 367, 381, 388, 390, 396, 399, 401, 410, 460
Todtnauberg 320, 327, 363, 411, 457
Transworld Radio 126
Trinitarian Bible Society 49-50, 87, 91, 96-7, 108, 127, 132, 137, 142, 149-52
Trinity Street 31
Tunbridge Wells 111

U

University of Essex 378
University of Leeds 163
Utzenfeld 332, 334-5, 340, 346, 352, 355-8, 364-5, 378, 380-1, 385, 388, 390, 396, 411, 424-5, 428, 437-8, 443, 456, 478
Utzenfeld Schwarzwald 381

V

Varndean Girls' Grammar School 7
Vogesenstrasse 250
Vosges 350

W

Waldeck Hotel 319
Wales 313, 373-4, 441, 444, 447-8, 454, 461
Warsash 27, 29
Watford Gap 153
West Street 17, 31
Westminster Abbey 383
Westminster Chapel 344, 381
Weymouth 373
Whitby 166, 184
Wieden 302, 314
Wieden Road 334
Wiese Valley 297, 299, 388, 419, 437
Wiesental Valley 191
Wildhaus 430
Wiltshire 309
Wivelsfield Chapel 52
World Health Organisation 245
Writtle College 48
Wycliffe Hall 86
Wycliffe Lodge 153, 155-6, 168

Y

York 159
Yorkshire 9, 16, 147, 149-50, 152-3, 156, 159-67, 170-1, 175, 182, 184-5, 192, 202-3, 214-15, 250, 260, 296, 428, 477
Yorkshire Dales 182
Young Sowers League 58, 122

Z

Zell 292, 297, 456
Zillertal Mountains 273
Zion Evangelical Church 161, 186, 188, 193-4
Zürich 239, 267, 274, 277, 328, 350, 430
Zürich University 266-7

Printed in Great Britain
by Amazon